"SPYCATCHER IS NOT A
CAUSE CÉLÈBRE!

The uncensored, remarkably candid, and enormously revealing memoirs of a high-ranking officer in the real spy business—a powerful and important book that even Britain's Official Secrets Act couldn't silence.

Spycatcher

Spycatcher

The Candid Autobiography
of a Senior Intelligence Officer

Peter Wright with Paul Greengrass

A DELL BOOK

To my wife, Lois

Published by
Dell Publishing
a division of
The Bantam Doubleday Dell Publishing Group, Inc.
666 Fifth Avenue
New York, New York 10103

ISBN: 0-440-20132-2

Printed in the United States of America

August 1988

10 9 8 7 6 5 4 3 2 1

KRI

Author's Acknowledgments ────

I have had no access to classified information since I retired from MI5 in January 1976. This book is based entirely on my personal recollections, and I have been careful to avoid disclosing anything which, in my judgment, would adversely affect national security.

It is impossible to thank personally all the many people who have helped in the fight to have this book published. But I would like to give special acknowledgment to the following:

Malcolm Turnbull, my Australian lawyer, who took my case on when it seemed unlikely *Spycatcher* would ever see the light of day. Thanks to his tireless energy and legal skills, and the assistance of his wife, Lucy, the tide finally began to flow in my direction.

Heinemann Publishers Australia Pty., who fought with great courage for the right to publish this book, and in particular Nick and Sam Hudson, Sandy Grant, and Paul Hamlyn.

David Hooper, Heinemann's London solicitor, who gave valuable advice and assistance throughout the case.

Allan Kellock, of Viking in New York, who took a brave decision to be the first to publish *Spycatcher*, and whose sound judgment has been vindicated by events.

The *Observer, Guardian, Independent,* and *Sunday Times*

newspapers in London, who campaigned long and hard against the British Government's suppression of this book.

Lois and Tom Wallace, of Wallace and Shiel Agency in New York, who have given this project patience and encouragement throughout.

Paul Greengrass, my coauthor, who supported this project from the very beginning, and has shared with me in its trials and tribulations, and ultimate victory.

And lastly, of course, I would like to thank my family. My wife, Lois, and my children, Tessa, Jenny, and Bevis, have been my inspiration and strength throughout the past three and a half years. Without their special support and encouragement, this book could never have been written.

—Peter Wright
1988

Preface

JOHN LE CARRÉ ONCE WROTE THAT THE BRITISH SECRET SER-
vices have an image but no face. It is an image which has been
carefully cultivated since they were founded in the first decade of
the twentieth century. The CIA may have greater resources, the
KGB greater machinations, Mossad the greater ruthlessness, but
MI5 and MI6 were the first players in Kipling's Great Game;
they are its master craftsmen. They invented the principles of
tradecraft, broke the first codes, ran the best agents, bred the best
spymasters, and taught the rest everything they know. Above all,
they keep the secrets. In the intelligence world MI5 and MI6 are
still *primes inter pares*.

Britain has always carefully protected the reputation of its Secret Services. They are seen as embodying her most admirable
national qualities—subtlety of mind, pragmatism, and an ironic
detachment from the naïvetés which disfigure other nations. The
more that Britain's prestige in the real world has declined in
recent decades, the greater the importance which has been attached to them. It is almost as if clandestine expertise compen-
sates for the loss of Empire and all the increasing irrelevance of
much of British life today. The spy world remains the last arena
where wellborn Englishmen can still exercise that effortless superiority which for centuries they were born to believe was theirs by
right.

The British Secret Services have also fulfilled another vital function. They have been the guardians of the state's unconscious mind. Their files contain all that is most shameful in the national memory—assassination plots, lawbreaking, conspiracies against elected governments, and the full extent of Soviet penetration. For years MI5 and MI6 kept these memories safely hidden from view. They were the custodians of an enormous storehouse of scandal.

Britain was not alone in amassing an intolerable burden of intelligence-related scandals in the postwar years. The CIA had its anti-Castro plots, illegal surveillance programs, and foreign destabilizations, to mention but a few. The Canadian and Australian Services had their own variations, involving illegal wiretapping, burglary, and blacklisting. By the mid-1970s the strain of keeping the secrets out of view became intolerable. Like patients in therapy, each country needed to dispose of the accumulated baggage of the past in order to be able to embrace the future. They needed a ritual; a catharsis.

The CIA released its burden in the mid-1970s through a long series of Congressional and Senate Committee inquiries, in particular that headed by Senator Frank Church. Both the Canadian and Australian intelligence communities underwent similar scrutiny by senior judicial figures, Justices MacDonald and Hope respectively. In each case, following the sensational public revelations, new rules and accountabilities were formulated to encourage public confidence and take the services forward to the 1990s.

Only Britain, among the principal Western intelligence allies, stood alone in refusing to face up to the past. Ever since Burgess and Maclean defected in 1951, the British Government's rare public statements about the activities of the intelligence services have been characterized either by dishonesty, inaccuracy, or inadequacy. First there was Prime Minister Macmillan's infamous clearance of Kim Philby in 1955, then the fifteen-year cover-up of Anthony Blunt's treachery and subsequent secret pardon. More recently there have been official denials of any plot or impropriety by MI5 officers against the Labor Government of 1974.

But despite British resistance to any measure of inquiry or accountability, the burden of the past has finally proved too great. In the end the secrets had to come out, and the catharsis has come not through the official or judicial inquiries favored by our allies in the mid-1970s but through publication of this book.

Peter Wright is the only man who could have undertaken such a task. His twenty-five-year career inside the highest echelons of British intelligence gave him a unique insight into all the mistakes, venal acts, and cover-ups of a generation of British intelligence gathering—from the widespread illegalities of the 1950s and the crazed witch-hunts of the 1960s to the sinister conspiracies of the 1970s.

Peter Wright is a veteran of a hard school—that generation of intelligence officers on both sides of the Atlantic who began their secret service in the trenches of the Cold War and ended it in the mid-1970s, just as the secrets started to spill out. He has never been an old-school-tie man. Part boffin, part molehunter, he is an outsider, and proud of it.

He has been an enemy of the British Establishment ever since he began his lonely crusade to hunt down those wellborn Englishmen who turned traitor in the 1930s. The experience scarred him for life. He got little support from MI5. Few of the titled and eminent people he interviewed cared to recall the details of a prewar world which long ago had disappeared. Fewer still cared to remember their friendships with Philby, Burgess, Maclean, and Blunt, or admit the secret suspicions they had kept to themselves. A veil had been drawn over those years by an entire generation, and it gave Wright a fierce determination to tear it away.

Today Peter Wright remains true to the precepts of the Cold War. Where others of his contemporaries have sought an accommodation with the post-detente world, he has always been a man-at-arms, restlessly uneasy with peace. He is no Philip Agee, although the British Government have gone to inordinate lengths to present him as such. He does not believe in naming names and blowing operations. He is an emotional patriot who believes passionately in secret services and the role they play. He remembers warmly much of his career inside MI5. But he has an unshakable conviction that mistakes were made, truths covered up, trails not pursued, and that some account needed to be written of these turbulent years.

Peter Wright's memoirs finally provide a face for the British Intelligence Services, and in doing so shatter their image. There is ample testimony in these pages to the brilliance, dedication, and subtlety of much of British Intelligence. There is also bungling, illegality, amateurism, and conspiracy. The same vices, in fact, which afflict any modern intelligence service—plus a few more which are peculiarly British, such as class hatred and a penchant for the Establishment cover-up.

Spycatcher is the final morsel in our long postwar feast of decline. It has destroyed our last national illusion, and made the mangy old Lion choke. She has responded with hysterical outrage, launching lawsuits throughout the world in an effort to suppress the book. The courts of Australia, New Zealand, Hong Kong, Canada, and Britain have witnessed the most sustained and bitter litigation in living memory, as millions of pounds of public money have been squandered in a futile attempt to halt the inevitable.

The epic struggle began in September 1985 when Peter Wright received a letter at his home in Tasmania, Australia, from lawyers acting on behalf of the British Government informing him that they were instigating proceedings to halt his proposed book. Peter Wright and his publishers, Heinemann Publishers Australia Pty., courageously opted to fight, retaining one of Australia's brightest young lawyers, Malcolm Turnbull. After exhaustive pretrial hearings, the case finally came to full trial in the

Supreme Court of New South Wales in Sydney in November 1986.

The Crown's principal witness was Mrs. Thatcher's most senior security adviser, Cabinet Secretary Sir Robert Armstrong (now Lord Armstrong), a man renowned for his bureaucratic skills and commitment to ancient doctrines of official secrecy. His affidavits read better than any publisher's publicity brochure. *Spycatcher*, claimed Armstrong, was an intolerable breach of confidence. He stressed Wright's seniority in British Intelligence, his extraordinarily long service in posts of the highest sensitivity, and his continuous access to intelligence, much of which remains highly secret. If Armstrong was to be believed, the fabric of British public life would collapse if *Spycatcher* were published.

Wright's lawyer, Malcolm Turnbull, shared with his client a deep aversion to the hypocrisies of the British Establishment. His brilliant and often savage courtroom cross-examination of Sir Robert Armstrong was a classic confrontation between the young colonial and the old imperialist; between the New World and the Old. Rarely have the philosophies and contradictions which underpin the activities of a secret service in a democracy been so ruthlessly exposed. By the end of the trial the Government's case had been reduced to an object of ridicule.

Turnbull first addressed the scandals which lie at the heart of this book—the widespread illegalities, assassination plots, and conspiracies instigated by the British Secret Services, as well as the long history of Soviet penetrations of the British upper classes. Rather than disclose official documents relating to these events, the British Government conceded for the purposes of the litigation that Wright's allegations in *Spycatcher* were true. In that case, argued Turnbull, there was a clear public interest in such iniquities being laid open to view. The British Government had no answer.

Next Turnbull attacked the Crown's contention that their Secret Services had to be seen to be leakproof. He produced an exhaustive list of publications which proved that disclosures of confidential information had long been permitted, even encouraged, if it suited the Services and boosted their image. For instance, memoirs by former intelligence officers had been published before, but only if they lauded the achievements of the Services. Books by journalists containing enormous quantities of hitherto secret information, many relating to events described in *Spycatcher,* had also been officially condoned, even when the Government knew that the information emanated from intelligence officers.

This area of the trial was the most damaging to the Government. Sir Robert Armstrong repeatedly sought to deny the extent of official knowledge of such publications. Time and again Turnbull's evidence forced him to withdraw. By the end of the trial he emerged as a discredited witness, apologizing to the judge for misleading the court in these areas, and even, in one phrase which will haunt him forever, admitting that he had been "economical with the truth."

A sensible system was needed, argued Turnbull, whereby retired officers could write their memoirs, and submit them to the Government for vetting. Wright had already volunteered his willingness to make cuts in his manuscript if the British Government would outline the particular passages which concerned them. But the Government refused to discuss Wright's offer. Turnbull pointed out that the CIA already operated a manuscript review system. CIA officers were able to publish memoirs, and relay their experiences and knowledge to a wider public, with no noticeable detriment to the security of the free world. Why should Britain stand alone? Once again, the British Government had no answer.

After weighing the evidence, the Supreme Court of New South Wales handed down a stinging judgment in Wright's favor. But still the Government would not concede defeat. They appealed the case, and the war intensified. By spring 1987 details from the as yet unpublished *Spycatcher* manuscript began to seep into the British press, and the focus of the legal battle switched to London. Punitive injunctions were obtained prohibiting any British newspaper from referring in even the briefest form to the major allegations in Wright's book.

The habit of suppression began to spread far beyond *Spycatcher* to include virtually any publication about the workings of British Intelligence. British magazine and television offices were raided by the police, journalists' doors were hammered down, and books, articles, radio and TV programs were unceremoniously banned.

The *Spycatcher* affair was now far more than a publishing cause célèbre. It was a major constitutional crisis about the conduct and oversight of our intelligence community, the relations between Government and press, and Government and Judiciary, and the limits of freedom of expression.

Spycatcher was eventually published in the USA in July 1987, closely followed by publication in Canada, Australia, New Zealand, and Europe. Today more than a million copies have been sold worldwide, but still people in Britain are unable to buy it, or read about it in their newspapers. It is an absurd situation, yet the Prime Minister, Mrs. Thatcher, has pledged herself to continue with the fight. Further court appeals across the world are scheduled. Like the little Dutch boy, she is still trying to plug the dike with her fingers, even as she is submerged under the torrent of books pouring from the presses.

The Prime Minister has remained impervious to the mounting costs of the battle. She has repeatedly refused to sanction any independent inquiry into the allegations of illegality and domestic subversion made against the British Secret Services in *Spycatcher*, despite widespread support for such an inquiry among senior British politicians of all political persuasions. Her obduracy has succeeded only in fueling doubts about their political impartiality and lack of accountability, and ensured the tarnishing of their reputation for a generation.

The position of the Judiciary in Britain has similarly been gravely damaged. It is totally out of step with its Australian and American counterparts. In the *Spycatcher* case the Australian courts fiercely defended the public interest in freedom of expression. And in America, the British Government did not even bring proceedings, realizing that it would be unable to overcome the freedoms enshrined in the First Amendment.

But the British courts have shown themselves remarkably uninterested in attaching importance to the freedom of the press in matters of national security. They have become little more than tools of the executive doling out increasingly craven judgments in support of the Government. One British newspaper even took the unprecedented step of printing the Law Lords photographs upside down under a blazing headline reading "YOU FOOLS!" after one bizarre court ruling sought to prohibit the press from reporting Parliamentary debates about *Spycatcher*. Public respect for their independence has been seriously diminished. It will take a long time to recover.

The *Spycatcher* affair, like the Pentagon Papers case, is another watershed battle in the long-running war over the public's right to know what is done in their name in the field of national security. Whatever the final outcome, nothing in Britain will ever quite be the same again. *Spycatcher* has been published, and although it is not officially available in Britain, thousands of copies continue to pour into the country. Peter Wright and his publishers have successfully defied the perversions of secrecy which do so much to disfigure modern Britain. They have defied Mrs. Thatcher and won, and in the process made her seem foolish. They have forced Britain to confront her final illusion, and the accountability of the Secret Services is now firmly on the political agenda. They have ensured reform of Britain's antique and ramshackle approach to secrecy, not under this Government, but certainly under the next. That is no inconsiderable achievement.

But in the end, of course, *Spycatcher* is just a book; an old man's recollections after a lifetime in secret intelligence. They are war stories from long ago, told by the fire, a drink in hand. Like all the best war stories, there are lessons for today. They tell of the days when espionage was still Kipling's Great Game, before the bureaucrats, the satellites, and the computers took over and squeezed the drama and excitement out of it all. These were the years when heroes strode the trenches of the Cold War. We shall not see their like again.

—Paul Greengrass
London, January 1988

Prologue ─────────────

FOR YEARS I HAD WONDERED WHAT THE LAST DAY WOULD BE LIKE. In January 1976 after two decades in the top echelons of the British Security Service, MI5, it was time to rejoin the real world.

I emerged for the final time from Euston Road tube station. The winter sun shone brightly as I made my way down Gower Street toward Trafalgar Square. Fifty yards on I turned into the unmarked entrance to an anonymous office block. Tucked between an art college and a hospital stood the unlikely headquarters of British Counterespionage.

I showed my pass to the policeman standing discreetly in the reception alcove and took one of the specially programmed lifts which carry senior officers to the sixth-floor inner sanctum. I walked silently down the corridor to my room next to the Director-General's suite.

The offices were quiet. Far below I could hear the rumble of tube trains carrying commuters to the West End. I unlocked my door. In front of me stood the essential tools of the intelligence officer's trade—a desk, two telephones, one scrambled for outside calls, and to one side a large green metal safe with an oversized combination lock on the front. I hung up my coat and began mechanically to arrange my affairs. Having seen too many retired officers at cocktail parties loitering for scraps of news and gossip, I wanted to make a clean break. I was determined to make a new life for myself breeding horses out in Australia.

I turned the dials on the locks and swung open the heavy safe door. In front was a mass of Registry files stamped Top Secret, and behind them a neat stack of small combination boxes. Files: over the years I had drawn thousands. Now these were the last. Routine agent reports circulated routinely to me, the latest reports of the Computer Working Party, the latest analyses of Provisional IRA strength. Files always need answers. I had none to give. The Russian Diplomat's file had been sent to me by a younger officer. Did I recognize him? Not really. It was a double-agent case which had been running off and on for years. Did I have any ideas? Not really. When you join the Service each case looks different. When you leave they all seem the same. I carefully initialed off the files and arranged for my secretary to take them to the Registry.

After lunch I set to work on the combination boxes, pulling them out from the back of the safe one by one. The first contained technical details of microphones and radio receivers—remnants of my time in the 1950s as MI5's first scientific officer. I arranged for the contents to be sent over to the Technical Department. An hour later the head of the Department came over to thank me. He was very much the modern government scientist: neat, cautious, and constantly in search of money.

"They were just odd things I kept," I said. "I don't suppose you'll have much use for them. It's all satellites now, isn't it?"

"Oh no," he replied. "I'll enjoy reading them." He looked a little embarrassed. He and I had never really got on. We came from different worlds. I was a glue, sticks, and rubber-band improviser from the war; he was a defense contractor. We shook hands and I went back to sorting out my safe.

The remaining boxes held papers gathered after I joined the Counterespionage Department in 1964, when the search for spies in British Intelligence was at its most intense. The handwritten notes and typed aides-mémoire were packed with the universal currency of spying—lists of suspects and details of accusations, betrayals, and verdicts. Here, in the endless paper chase which began so clearly but ended in mystery, lay the threads of my career.

Eventually my secretary came in and handed me two blue books. "Your diaries," she said, and together we shredded them into the burn bag beside my desk until it was time for the final ritual.

I walked along to the Establishments Office. The duty officer handed me a file containing a list of my current secret indoctrinations. I began to sign off the small chits. Access to Signals Intelligence and Satellite Intelligence went first. Then I worked through the mass of case indoctrinations I held. The acquisition of secrets is such a personal thing; the loss of them is painfully bureaucratic. Each stroke of the pen shut the door a little farther. Within half an hour the secret world which had sustained me for years was closed off forever.

Toward dark I took a taxi over to MI5's old headquarters at Leconfield House in Mayfair. The organization was in the process of moving to new offices at the top of Curzon Street, but the staff bar, the Pig and Eye Club, where my farewell party was due to be held, still remained in Leconfield House.

I went into the old building. Here, in the teak-inlaid corridors and corniced offices, Philby, Burgess, Maclean, and Blunt were hunted down. And here too we had fought MI5's most secret war over suspicions of an undiscovered mole at the heart of the Service. Our suspect was the former Director-General of MI5, Sir Roger Hollis, but we had never been able to prove it. Hollis's friends had bitterly resented the accusation and for ten long years both sides had feuded like medieval theologians, driven by instinct, passion, and prejudice.

One by one in the 1970s the protagonists had retired, until finally the move to new offices signaled the end of the war. But walking the corridors of Leconfield House I could still feel the physical sense of treachery, of pursuit, and the scent of the kill.

My party was a quiet affair. People said nice things. The Director-General, Sir Michael Hanley, made a pretty speech, and I received the customary cards with their handwritten farewell messages. Lord Clanmorris, the great MI5 agent runner, wrote that my departure was "a sad, sad, irreplaceable loss." He meant to the office. But the real loss was mine.

That night I slept in the flat on the top floor of the Gower Street offices, woken occasionally by the noise of trains arriving at Euston Station. Early the next morning I dressed, picked up my briefcase, empty for the first time, and walked down to the front door. I said goodbye to the policeman and stepped outside onto the street. My career was over. A sad, sad, irreplaceable loss.

1 ────────────────────────────────

IT ALL BEGAN IN 1949, ON THE KIND OF SPRING DAY THAT REMINDS you of winter. The rain drummed against the tin roof of the prefabricated laboratory at Great Baddow in Essex, where I was working as a Navy scientist attached to the Marconi Company. An oscilloscope throbbed in front of me like a headache. Scattered across the trestle table was a mass of scribbled calculations. It was not easy designing a radar system able to pick out a submarine periscope from amid the endless rolling wave clutter; I had been trying for years. The telephone rang. It was my father, Maurice Wright, the Marconi Engineer in Chief.

"Freddie Brundrett wants to see us," he said.

That was nothing new. Brundrett had been Chief of the Royal Naval Scientific Service and was now Chief Scientist of the Ministry of Defense; he had been taking a personal interest of late in the progress of the project. A decision was needed soon over whether to fund production of a prototype system. It would be expensive. Postwar defense research was an endless battle against financial attrition, and I prepared myself for another ill-tempered skirmish.

I welcomed the chance of talking to Brundrett direct. He was an old family friend; both my father and I had worked for him in Admiralty Research during the war. Perhaps, I thought, there might be the chance of a new job.

The following day we drove down to London in a steady drizzle and parked the car close to Brundrett's office in Storey's Gate. Whitehall looked gray and tired; the colonnades and statues seemed ill suited to a rapidly changing world. Clement Attlee was still promising "teeth and spectacles," but the winter had been hard and people grew restless under rationing. The euphoria of victory in 1945 had long since given way to sullen resentment.

We introduced ourselves to the neat secretary in Brundrett's outer office. The annex hummed in that subdued Whitehall way. We were not the first to arrive. I greeted a few familiar faces: scientists from the various Services' laboratories. It seemed a large turnout for a routine meeting, I thought. Two men I had never met detached themselves from the huddle.

"You must be the Wrights," said the shorter of the two abruptly. He spoke with a clipped military accent. "My name is Colonel Malcolm Cumming from the War Office, and this is my colleague Hugh Winterborn." Another stranger came over. "And this is John Henry, one of our friends from the Foreign Office." Cumming employed the curious code Whitehall uses to distinguish its secret servants. Whatever the meeting was about, I thought, it was unlikely to concern antisubmarine warfare; not with a contingent from MI5 and MI16 present. Brundrett appeared at the door of his office and invited us in.

His office, like his reputation, was vast. Giant sash windows and high ceilings completely dwarfed his desk. He showed us to the conference table, which had been carefully lined with ink blotters and decanters. Brundrett was a small, energetic man, one of that select band, along with Lindemann, Tizard, and Cockcroft, responsible for gearing Britain for the technical and scientific demands of fighting World War II. As Assistant Director of Scientific Research for the Admiralty, and later Deputy Director of the Royal Naval Scientific Service, he had been largely responsible for recruiting scientists into government service during the war. He was not especially gifted as a scientist, but he understood the vital role scientists could play. His policy was to promote youth wherever possible and because the Service chiefs trusted him he was able to get the resources necessary to enable them to perform at their best.

As a weary and diminished Britain girded herself to fight a new war in the late 1940s—the Cold War—Brundrett was the obvious choice to advise on how best to galvanize the scientific community once again. He was appointed Deputy Scientific Adviser to the Minister of Defense and succeeded Sir John Cockcroft as Scientific Adviser and Chairman of the Defense Research Policy Committee in 1954.

"Gentlemen," began Brundrett when we were seated. "It is quite clear to all of us, I think, that we are now in the midst of war and have been since events in Berlin last year."

Brundrett made it clear that the Russian blockade of Berlin and the Western airlift which followed had made a profound impact on defense thinking.

"This war is going to be fought with spies, not soldiers, at least in the short term," he went on, "and I have been discussing where we stand with Sir Percy Sillitoe, the Director-General of the Security Service. To be frank," he concluded, "the situation is not good."

Brundrett crisply described the problem. It had become virtually impossible to run agents successfully behind the Iron Curtain, and there was a serious lack of intelligence about the intentions of the Soviet Union and her allies. Technical and scientific initiatives were needed to fill the gap.

"I have discussed the matter in outline with some of you here, Colonel Cumming from the Security Service and Peter Dixon representing MI6, and I have formed this committee to assess the options and initiate work at once. I have also suggested to Sir Percy that he obtain the services of a young scientist to help on the research side. I intend to submit the name of Peter Wright, whom some of you may know. He is currently attached to the

Services Electronics Research Laboratory and he will go over on a part-time basis until we find out how much work needs doing."

Brundrett looked across at me. "You'll do that for us, won't you, Peter?"

Before I could reply he turned to my father. "We'll obviously need help from Marconi, G.M., so I have co-opted you onto this committee as well." (Father was always known in the Navy by the name that Marconi was known by in the old days.)

It was typical Brundrett, issuing invitations as if they were orders and bending the Whitehall machine thoroughly out of shape to get his way.

For the rest of the afternoon we discussed ideas. The MI5 and MI6 contingents were conspicuously silent and I assumed it was the natural reticence of the secret servant in the presence of outsiders. Each scientist gave an extempore synopsis of any research in his laboratory which might possibly have an intelligence application. Obviously a full-scale technical review of intelligence services requirements would take time but it was clear that they urgently needed new techniques of eavesdropping which did not require entry to premises. Soviet security was so tight that the possibility of gaining entry, other than through party walls or when an embassy was being rebuilt, was remote. By teatime we had twenty suggestions of possible areas of fruitful research. Brundrett instructed me to draw up a paper assessing them, and the meeting broke up.

As I was leaving, a man from the Post Office Technical Department, John Taylor, who had talked at some length during the meeting about post office work on listening devices, introduced himself. "We'll be working together on this," he said, as we exchanged telephone numbers. "I'll be in touch next week."

On the drive back to Great Baddow, Father and I discussed the meeting excitedly. It had been so gloriously unpredictable, in the way that Whitehall often was during the war and had so seldom been since. I was thrilled at the opportunity to escape from anti-submarine work; he because it continued the thread of secret intelligence which had run through the family for four and a half decades.

2

MY FATHER JOINED THE MARCONI COMPANY FROM UNIVERSITY IN 1912, and began work as an engineer on an improved method of detecting radio signals. Together with Captain H. J. Round, he succeeded in developing a vacuum receiver which made the interception of long-range communications possible for the first time.

Two days before World War I began, he was working with these receivers in the old Marconi Laboratory at Hall Street, Chelmsford, when he realized he was picking up German naval signals. He took the first batch to the Marconi works manager, Andrew Gray, who was a personal friend of Captain Reggie Hall, and head of the Naval Intelligence Department.

Hall was the dominant figure in British Intelligence during World War I and was responsible for attacking German ciphers from the famous Admiralty Room 40. He arranged for my father to travel up to Liverpool Street Station on the footplate of a specially chartered locomotive. After studying the material he insisted Marconi release my father to build intercept and direction-finding stations for the Navy.

The central problem facing Naval Intelligence at the outbreak of World War I was how to detect the German High Seas Fleet putting to sea in time to enable the British Fleet, based at Scapa Flow, to intercept them. Naval Intelligence knew that when the German Fleet was quiescent she lay at the eastern end of the Kiel Canal. Hall believed it might be possible to detect the German

Commander-in-Chief's wireless communications on board his flagship as they passed through the Kiel Canal into the North Sea.

My father set to work to design sufficiently sensitive equipment and eventually developed "aperiodic" direction-finding. This enabled the bearing of the wanted signal to be accurately identified among the mass of other interfering signals. It took several years to become operational but eventually became an important weapon in the war against the U-boats. Even today all direction-finding equipment is "aperiodic."

In 1915, before the system was fully operational, my father suggested to Hall that the best solution was to locate a direction finder in Christiania (now Oslo). Norway at this time was neutral, but the British Embassy could not be used for fear of alerting the Germans, so Hall asked my father if he was prepared to go and run the station clandestinely for MI6. Within days he was on his way to Norway, posing as a commercial traveler trading in agricultural medicines. He set up in a small hotel in a side street in Christiania and rented an attic room high enough to rig direction-finding wireless without being conspicuous.

The MI6 station in the Embassy supplied him with communications and spare parts, but it was dangerous work. His radio equipment was bound to give him away eventually. He was not part of the diplomatic staff and would be denied if discovered. At best he faced internment for the rest of the war; at worst he risked the attentions of German Intelligence.

The operation ran successfully for six months, giving the Navy invaluable early warning of German Fleet intentions. Then one morning he came down to breakfast at his usual table. He looked casually across the street to see a new poster being pasted onto the wall opposite. It was his photograph with an offer of a reward for information leading to his arrest.

He had worked out his escape route with MI6 before the operation began. He quickly finished his breakfast, returned to his room, carefully packed his wireless equipment in its case and pushed it under the bed. He gathered up his travel documents, passport, and Naval identity card, leaving a substantial quantity of cash in the hope that it might encourage the hotelier to forget about him.

Rather than taking the road toward the Swedish coast which the Norwegian authorities would assume to be his most likely escape route, he set off to the southwest. Ten miles down the coast he sat down on a rock by the roadside. Sometime later, a British Naval lieutenant walked up to him and asked him who he was. Father identified himself and he was taken to a launch and ferried out to a waiting British destroyer.

Years later, when I was coming up for retirement, I tried to find the details of this operation in the MI6 files. I arranged with Sir Maurice Oldfield, the then Chief of MI6, to spend the day in their Registry looking for the papers. But I could find nothing; the MI6 weeders had routinely destroyed all the records years before.

I was born in 1916 at my grandmother's house in Chesterfield, where my mother had gone to stay while my father was in Norway for MI6. There was a Zeppelin raid on nearby Sheffield that night, and I arrived very prematurely. There were no hospital beds available because of the pressure of the war, but my mother kept me alive with an improvised incubator of glass chemical jars and hot-water bottles.

After World War I my father rejoined the Marconi Company. He became a protégé of Marconi himself and was made Head of Research. We moved to a large house by the sea near Frinton. But this lasted only a few months, when we moved to a house on the outskirts of Chelmsford. The house often resembled a disused wireless factory. Radios in various states of disrepair and tin boxes filled with circuitry were hidden in every corner. My father was an intense, emotional, rather quick-tempered man—more of an artist than an engineer. As early as I can remember he used to take me out into the garden or onto the open fields above the Essex beaches to teach me the mysteries of wireless. He spent hours explaining valves and crystals and showed me how to delicately turn the dials of a set so that the random static suddenly became a clear signal. He taught me how to make my own experiments and I can still remember his pride when I demonstrated my crude skills to visiting guests like Sir Arthur Eddington and J. J. Thomson.

MI6 had close connections with the Marconi Company after World War I, and my father retained his contact with them. Marconi had a large marine division responsible for fitting and manning wireless in ships. It provided perfect cover for MI6, who would arrange with my father to have one of their officers placed as a wireless operator on a ship visiting an area in which they had an interest.

Admiral Hall was a visitor to the house; he and my father would disappear into the greenhouse together for hours at a time to discuss in private some new development. My father also knew Captain Mansfield Cumming, the first Chief of MI6. He admired Cumming greatly, for both his courage and his technical ability. He knew Captain Vernon Kell, the founder of MI5, much less well, but did not like him. As with Oxford and Cambridge, people are usually disposed either to MI5 or MI6, and my father very definitely leaned in favor of MI6.

The Marconi Company during the 1920s was one of the most exciting places in the world for a scientist to work. Marconi, known to everyone by his initials, "G.M.," was a superb picker of men, and had the courage to invest in his visions. His greatest success was to create the first shortwave radio beam system, and he can justly claim to have laid the foundations of modern communications. As with so many British achievements, it was done against the opposition of the British Government and the top scientists of the day.

Before World War I Britain decided that a long-wave radio

system should be built to replace the cable system as the principal means of communication with the Empire. The decision was held in abeyance during the war. But Marconi believed it was possible to project short wavelength transmissions over vast distances using beams. The use of shortwave beams promised a greater volume of traffic at much higher speeds. Despite the advances in wireless made during the war, Marconi's vision was derided as "amateur science" by a Royal Commission in 1922. One member even concluded that radio was "a finished art."

Marconi issued a challenge. He offered to build, free of charge, any link across the world—provided the government would suspend long-wave development until the beam system had passed its trials, and provided they would adopt it if the trials were successful. The government agreed and specified the toughest contract they could devise. They asked for a link from Grimsby to Sydney, Australia, and demanded that it operate 250 words a minute over a twelve-hour period during the trials without using more than twenty kilowatts of power. Finally they demanded that the circuit be operational within twelve months.

These were awesome specifications. Radio was still in its infancy and little was known about generating power at stable frequencies. The project would have been impossible without the commitment of the Marconi technical team, consisting of my father, Captain H. J. Round, and C. S. Franklin. Marconi had a special talent for finding brilliant scientists who were largely self-taught. He found Franklin, for instance, trimming arc lamps in an Ipswich factory for a few shillings a week. Within a few years he rose to become the outstanding technical man in the company.

The proposed Grimsby-to-Sydney link astonished the rest of the radio communications industry. My father often described in later years walking down Broadway with David Sarnoff, the then head of RCA, when the project was at its height.

"Has Marconi gone mad?" asked Sarnoff. "This project will finish him. It'll never work."

Father replied: "G.M. and Franklin think it will."

"Well, you can kick my ass all the way down Broadway if it does," said Sarnoff.

Three months later the circuit was operational, on contract time. It worked twelve hours a day for seven days at 250 words a minute and was, in my view, one of the great technical achievements of this century. My father's only regret was that he never took the opportunity to kick Sarnoff's ass all the way down Broadway!

My youth was spent living through this great excitement. I suffered constantly through ill-health. I developed rickets and wore leg irons until practically into my teens. But there were compensations. Nearly every day when my father was at home he collected me from school and drove me to his laboratory. I would spend hours watching him and his assistants as the great race from Grimsby to Sydney unfolded. It taught me a lesson which stayed with me for life—that on the big issues the experts are very rarely right.

The 1930s opened hopefully for the Wright family. We scarcely noticed the growing worldwide financial crisis. I had joined Bishop's Stortford College, a small but hardily independent school, where I began to shine academically and finally threw off the ill-health which had dogged me since birth. I returned home for the summer holidays of 1931 having passed my school certificate with credits in all subjects. The following term I was due to join the University Group, with every expectation of a good scholarship to Oxford or Cambridge.

A week later my world disintegrated. One evening my father came home and broke the news that he and Franklin had both been sacked. It was days before he could even try to explain, and years before I understood what had happened.

In the late 1920s Marconi had merged with the Cable Companies in the belief that only by cooperation with them could wireless gain the investment necessary to ensure its emergence as the principal method of worldwide communications. But as the slump developed, wireless posed more and more of a threat to the cable interests. They were dominant in the new company and slashing cuts were made in wireless research and the installations of new systems. Marconi, old and sick, had retired to Italy, but not even an intervention from him could secure a change of heart in the new management. Franklin, my father, and many others were sacked. For the next decade long-distance wireless communication stagnated and we as a family passed into years of great hardship.

Within a few months my father slipped into the abyss of alcoholism. He could no longer afford to keep both his sons at school, and as I was older and already had my school certificate I was the one to leave. The trauma of those events brought back my ill-health and I was afflicted with a chronic stammer which rendered me at times virtually speechless. In the course of that short summer holiday I changed from a schoolboy with a secure future to a man with no future at all.

The decision to remove me from school and its effect on my health consumed my father with guilt. He drove himself to further drinking excesses. My mother coped as best she could, but bereft of status and income she gradually became isolated until the only visitors were the nurses called to restrain my father after a dangerously prolonged bout with the Scotch bottle.

Years later, when I began to search out for MI5 the well-born Englishmen who had become addicted to Communism in the 1930s, this period of my life came to fascinate me. They had enjoyed to the full the privileged background and education denied to me, while my family had suffered at the capricious hand of capitalism. I experienced at first hand the effects of slump and depression, yet it was they who turned to espionage. I became the hunter, and they the hunted.

In one sense the explanation was simple. It was 1932. I had no qualifications. I was fifteen, I needed a job, and I had little time for political philosophy. I advertised in the personal columns of *The Times* for any work. The first reply was from a woman named Margaret Leigh, who ran a small farm called "Achnadarroch" at Plockton near Wester Ross, Scotland. I became her farmhand. There was no pay, just board and lodgings. But amid the rolling hills and endless skies of Scotland, I gradually recovered from what had gone before, and in time discovered the greatest love of my life—agriculture.

Margaret Leigh was an idealist. She wanted to run her farm as a training ground for boys from London slums so that they could obtain employment as farm managers. In the event, the idea never took off, and she decided instead to write a novel about life on Achnadarroch; she wrote while I tended the farm. And at night, when I had finished the chores, she made me read aloud what she had written until slowly my stutter was mastered. The book was eventually published and became a great success under the title *Highland Homespun*.

In spring 1935 we were evicted from Achnadarroch by a landlord greedy for more rent than we could afford to pay. We moved to another, cheaper farm in Cornwall and our life went on much as before. My ambition at this time was to become an agricultural scientist researching into food production techniques. But with my truncated formal education I could not hope to qualify for a scholarship. There were no grants in the 1930s. Eventually, with a little help from Margaret, some astute pig dealing of my own, and a useful family connection with the Master of St. Peter's College, Oxford, I was able to raise enough money to get a place at the School of Rural Economy. A year after I reached Oxford I married my wife, Lois. It was 1938. War was in the air. Like most young people we felt we might not have too long together.

By the time I went up to Oxford my father had begun to repair the damage of the previous six years of alcoholism. At my mother's instigation he had begun to work again at the Marconi Company as a consultant. And partly, I think, he was jolted by the realization that war was once more imminent. Anxious to help as he had in 1915, he approached Sir Frederick Brundrett in the Naval Scientific Service. Brundrett told him frankly that his reputation for alcoholism made a senior position impossible. Instead Brundrett offered him a post as an ordinary scientific officer for a trial period. I always admired my father tremendously for this. He sacrificed half what he was earning from the Marconi Company as a consultant to come and work at an experimental bench with scientists who were twenty years younger than he was. He made no issue of having once been the Marconi head of research. In a sense I think he was anxious to atone for the past; but he also genuinely believed that war was coming and that everyone had a duty to contribute.

His long experience scanning the ether ensured that his career soon flourished again. He was given charge of technical developments of the Y intercepts—the tactical intercepts of German Communications—and later he became Chief Scientist at the Admiralty Signals Establishment. Once again he was back in the Great Game, and he rediscovered his youth. By 1943 he was responsible for drawing up the signal plans for D-Day. It was a massive task. But after every working day he sat into the small hours with his wireless, listening to the chatter of Morse, logging and analyzing it ready for the next day. I often think he was at his happiest hunched over those sets, headphones clamped around his head, trying to make sense of the mysterious electronic universe.

At the outbreak of war the School of Rural Economy closed and my tutor, Scott Watson, became Chief Scientist at the Ministry of Agriculture, taking most of the staff with him to begin the vital task of preparing the country's food supplies. I was now the only member of the family not in some way involved in the war effort. My brother had joined the Service Electronics Research

Laboratory and my sister was an intercept operator for the Wrens. (She later worked closely with R. V. Jones on SIGINT, and married Robert Sutton, the head of SERL.) I wrote to Brundrett in the hope that there might be a space for me somewhere in the Admiralty. To my surprise I received a telegram inviting me to his office.

Brundrett had known me for years. He was a keen farmer who successfully bred Frisian cattle and was much interested in my experiences at Achnadarroch. He asked me what I thought I could do in the Admiralty and I explained that years spent watching my father at work had given me as good a grounding in electronics as I could have got at university. Within ten minutes he had arranged for me to start at the Admiralty Research Laboratory the following week.

My section at the Admiralty Research Laboratory (ARL) was run superbly by Stephen Butterworth, who for some unknown reason was always called Sam. He was a tall, gaunt man with a curly mop of dark hair. He smoked a pipe continuously, worked like a madman, and gathered around him a team of extraordinarily talented young scientists, including Massey, Gunn, Wigglesworth, Bates, and Crick. I felt terribly insecure when I arrived at ARL because of my lack of qualifications. Every night I sat up at the kitchen table in our small flat in Hampton Wick learning advanced physics from textbooks as German bombs dropped all around. But Butterworth was a constant source of encouragement. His one failing was his greatest strength: he did the job silently, leaving self-publicity to others. At the end of the war the reward for his genius and his quiet industry was a paltry OBE.

The Admiralty Research Laboratory's contribution to winning the war has been much undervalued. One of the most pressing problems facing Britain at the outbreak of war was the threat of magnetic mines. ARL began work on developing degaussing systems to neutralize our ships' magnetic fields and thus protect them. Without a really effective system our ability to fight on in 1940 would have been seriously in question.

At Dunkirk, for instance, thousands of mines littered the shallow waters off the coast. Hitler was convinced that these would prevent any mass evacuation of British forces. Butterworth knew that the German mines worked North Pole downward only, and suggested we magnetize our ships South Pole downward so that the ships repelled the mines. The Admiralty embarked on a massive program of reversing the magnetism of all the ships going to Dunkirk. The result was that not a single ship was lost to mines.

In the turmoil of war, there was little choice but to give young people their head. Soon after Dunkirk I and another young ARL scientist, Ray Gossage, were given the job of degaussing the battleship *Prince of Wales.* She lay in dry dock in Rosyth and for her next voyage was scheduled to carry Winston Churchill to the Atlantic Conference with Roosevelt. She had been built in Belfast in a yard which had left her magnetic field running around her rather than from end to end. The original degaussing had been a failure and she was considered highly unsafe in her present form.

Gossage and I worked out an improvised system of flashing out the athwartships magnetization by winding a giant coil lengthwise around the ship. We then energized this by connecting it up to a submarine battery. The whole operation took days to arrange and involved the whole crew of the ship. As we watched from the dry dock in Rosyth, hundreds of men worked in unison to our commands, though we were both barely in our mid-twenties.

Science in wartime is often a case of improving with the materials to hand, solving a problem as best you can at the time, rather than planning ten or fifteen years ahead, when it may be too late. The war shaped my later approach to technical intelligence. It taught me the value of improvisation and showed me, too, just how effective operations can be when the men of action listen to young men with a belief in practical, inventive science. Sadly, by the end of the war this attitude had all but disappeared; the dead hand of committees began to squeeze the life out of England.

From 1942 onward I worked on the first anti-midget-submarine detection systems. They were used successfully to protect the harbors during the torch landings in North Africa and later in Northwest Europe. This work got me involved in the operation to sink the prize German battleship *Tirpitz*. She lay in Altenfjord and posed an ever-present danger to British shipping. An operation to skin her, using midget submarines, was planned. We knew that the Germans were protecting Altenfjord with submarine detectors consisting of rows of coils on the seabed which picked up the magnetic flux of a passing craft. These were similar to those I had developed at ARL, so I was asked to come up with ideas for degaussing our X-Craft midget submarines to enable them to pass into the fjord undetected.

The technical problems of degaussing a submarine are far more complex than those of a ship, but eventually I found that an electromagnet placed along the length of the submarine and energized with the right amount of current would neutralize the loops of the submarine detectors on the seabed. I also calculated that if the X-Craft went in during a magnetic storm, this would increase the chances of nondetection by a factor of between 10 and 100. I traveled up to the Magnetic Observatory at Eskdalemuir and found that they had a good chance of predicting a storm of sufficient size, so I put my findings up to the Navy.

In 1944 the degaussed British X-Craft went in under cover of a magnetic storm. With great bravery, the crews managed to place charges against *Tirpitz* and cripple her. Three VCs were won that day. But the bravery would have counted for nothing without the technical backup of ARL.

By the end of the war the course of my life had changed irrevocably. Although agriculture remained my first love, I was clearly destined not to return to it. I sat instead for the postwar Scientific Civil Service competition chaired by C. P. Snow. It was designed to sort out the best scientists among the hundred recruited during the wartime expansion. I passed out joint top with 290 marks out of 300. Butterworth congratulated me warmly. All those nights sitting up with the textbooks had finally paid off, though the credit was largely his.

My father returned to the Marconi Company as Engineer in Chief in 1946, and I began work as a Principal Scientific Officer at the Services Electronics Research Laboratory that same year. For the next four years we worked closely alongside each other, the trials of the 1930s an unspoken bond between us, until that telephone call from Sir Frederick Brundrett in 1949 brought MI5 into my life.

3

A FEW DAYS AFTER THAT FIRST MEETING IN BRUNDRETT'S OFFICE in 1949, I received a telephone call from John Taylor inviting me down to London. He suggested St. James's Park and we met on the bridge in front of Buckingham Palace. It struck me as an odd way to conduct the business of national security, strolling among the pelicans and the ducks, pausing occasionally to ponder our reflections in the pool.

Taylor was a small man with a pencil mustache and a gray, sharpish face. He had been one of Montgomery's communications officers during the North African campaign, and although now a Post Office technician, he retained his abrupt military bearing. He ran the technical research, such as it was, for MI5 and MI6 from his laboratory inside the Special Investigations Unit of the Post Office at Dollis Hill. Taylor made certain I knew he was in charge. He told me bluntly that, apart from one brief visit to MI5 headquarters at Leconfield House to meet Colonel Cumming, I would have to deal through him as an intermediary. Taylor discouraged discussion about "the office"; he merely explained that I would be given the title of "external scientific adviser" and that I would be unpaid for my duties. For several years we continued to meet in St. James's Park about once a month to talk over the written reports on technical matters which I filed to C. W. Wright, the secretary of Brundrett's committee.

(Wright later became Deputy Secretary at the Ministry of Defense.)

Taylor and I divided up the technical work. The Post Office pressed ahead with research into infrared detection. I began using the resources of the Services Electronics Research Laboratory to develop new microphones and look into ways of getting sound reflections from office furniture. I was already familiar with the technical principles of resonance from my antisubmarine work. When sound waves impact with a taut surface such as a window or a filing cabinet, thousands of harmonics are created. The knack is to detect the point at which there is minimum distortion so that the sound waves can be picked up as intelligible speech.

One day in 1951 I received a telephone call from Taylor. He sounded distinctly agitated.

"We've been beaten to it," he said breathlessly. "Can we meet this afternoon?"

I met him later that day on a park bench opposite the Foreign Office. He described how the British Air Attaché in our Embassy in Moscow had been listening to the WHF receiver in his office which he used to monitor Russian military aircraft traffic. Suddenly he heard the British Air Attaché coming over his receiver loud and clear. Realizing the Attaché was being bugged in some way, he promptly reported the matter. Taylor and I discussed what type of microphone might be involved and he arranged for a Diplomatic Wireless Service engineer named Don Bailey to investigate. I briefed Bailey before he left for Moscow on how best to detect the device. For the first time I began to realize just how bereft British Intelligence was of technical expertise. They did not even possess the correct instruments, and I had to lend Bailey my own. A thorough search was made of the Embassy but nothing was ever found. The Russians had clearly been warned and turned the device off.

From questioning Bailey on his return it was clear to me that this was not a normal radio microphone, as there were strong radio signals which were plain carriers present when the device was operating. I speculated that the Russians, like us, were experimenting with some kind of resonance device. Within six months I was proved right. Taylor summoned me down to St. James's Park for another urgent meeting.

He told me that the U.S. State Department sweepers had been routinely "sanitizing" the American Ambassador's office in Moscow in preparation for a visit by the U.S. Secretary of State. They used a standard tunable signal generator to generate what is known as the "howl round effect," similar to the noise made when a radio station talks to someone on the telephone while his home radio or television is switched on. The "howl round" detected a small device lodged in the Great Seal of the United States on the wall behind the Ambassador's desk.

The howl frequency was 1800 MH, and the Americans had assumed that the operating frequency for the device must be the same. But tests showed that the device was unstable and insensitive when operating at this frequency. In desperation the Americans turned to the British for help in solving the riddle of how "the Thing," as it was called, worked.

Brundrett arranged for me to have a new, secure laboratory in a field at Great Baddow, and the Thing was solemnly brought up by Taylor and two Americans. The device was wrapped in cotton wool inside a small wooden box that looked as if it had once held chess pieces. It was about eight inches long, with an aerial on top which fed into a cavity. Inside the cavity was a metal mushroom with a flat top which could be adjusted to give it a variable capacity. Behind the mushroom was a thin gossamer diaphragm, to receive the speech, which appeared to have been pierced. The Americans sheepishly explained that one of their scientists had accidentally put his finger through it.

The crisis could not have come at a worse time for me. The antisubmarine-detection system was approaching its crucial trials and demanded long hours of attention. But every night and each weekend I made my way across the fields at the back of the Marconi building to my deserted Nissen hut. I worked flat out for ten weeks to solve the mystery.

First I had to repair the diaphragm. The Thing bore the hallmarks of a piece of equipment which the Russians had rushed into service, presumably to ensure it was installed before the Secretary of State's visit. They clearly had some kind of microscopic jig to install the diaphragm, because each time I used tweezers the thin film tore. Eventually, through trial and error, I managed to lay the diaphragm on first and clamp it on afterward. It wasn't perfect, but it worked.

Next I measured the length of the aerial to try to gauge the way it resonated. It did appear that 1800 MH was the correct frequency. But when I set the device up and made noises at it with an audio-signal generator, it was—just as the Americans had described—impossible to tune effectively. But after four weekends I realized that we had all been thinking about the Thing upside down. We had all assumed that the metal plate needed to be opened right out to increase resonance, when in fact the closer the plate was to the mushroom the greater the sensitivity. I tightened the plate right up and tuned the radiating signal down to 800 megacycles. The Thing began to emit a high-pitched tone. I rang my father up in a state of great excitement.

"I've got the Thing working!"

"I know," he said, "and the howl is breaking my eardrums!"

I arranged to demonstrate the Thing to Taylor, and he traveled up with Colonel Cumming, Hugh Winterborn and the two American sweepers. My father came along too, bringing another self-taught Marconi scientist named R. J. Kemp, who was now their Head of Research. I had installed the device against the far wall of the hut and rigged up another monitor in an adjoining room so that the rounds of the audio generator could be heard as if operationally.

I turned the dials to 800 and began to explain the mystery. The

Americans looked aghast at the simplicity of it all. Cumming and Winterborn were smug. This was just after the calamity of the Burgess and Maclean affair. The defection to the Soviet Union of these two well-born Foreign Office diplomats in 1951 caused outrage in the USA, and any small way in which British superiority could be demonstrated was, I soon realized, of crucial importance to them. Kemp was very flattering, rightly judging that it would only be a matter of time before Marconi got a contract to develop one themselves.

"How soon can we use one?" asked Cumming.

Kemp and I explained that it would probably take at least a year to produce equipment which would work reliably.

"I should think we can provide the premises, Malcolm," said Kemp to Cumming, "and probably one man to work under Peter. That might get you the prototype, but after that you'll have to get funding . . ."

"Well, it's quite impossible for us to pay, as you know," replied Cumming. "The Treasury will never agree to expand the secret vote."

Kemp raised his eyebrows. This was obviously an argument Cumming had deployed many times before in order to get facilities for nothing.

"But surely," I ventured, "if the government are serious about developing things technically for MI5 and MI6, they will have to allocate money on an open vote."

"They're most reluctant to do that," replied Cumming, shaking his head. "As you know, we don't really exist."

He looked at me as if a sudden thought had occurred to him.

"Now, perhaps if you were to approach the Admiralty on our behalf to ask for assistance on their open vote . . ."

This was my initiation into the bizarre method of handling Intelligence Services finance. It was a problem which was to plague me until well into the 1960s. Instead of having resources adequate for their technical requirements, the Intelligence Ser-

vices were forced to spend most of the postwar period begging
from the increasingly reluctant Armed Services. In my view, it
was this more than any other factor which contributed to the
amateurism of British Intelligence in the immediate postwar era.

But, as bidden, I set out to persuade the Admiralty to carry the
development costs of the new microphone. I made an urgent
appointment to see Brundrett's successor as Chief of the Naval
Scientific Service, Sir William Cook. I knew Cook quite well. He
was a wiry, red-haired man with piercing blue eyes and a
penchant for grandiose schemes. He was a brilliant organizer and
positively bubbled with ideas. I had first dealt with him after the
war when he asked me to work under him on a prototype Blue
Streak project, which was eventually cancelled when Sir Ben
Lockspeiser, then Chief Scientist at the Ministry of Supply, had a
crisis of conscience. Ironically, Cook himself came to share a
suspicion about nuclear weapons, though more for practical and
political reasons than moral ones. He felt that Britain was being
hasty in the production of the A-Bomb, and feared that as modern rocketry developed, the Navy would inevitably lose out. He
realized too, I suspect, that our obsession with the bomb was
faintly ludicrous in the face of growing American and Russian
superiority. This, incidentally, was a view which was quite widely
held by scientists working at a lower level in the Services in the
1950s.

I explained to Cook that the new microphone might have as
yet unforeseeable intelligence advantages, from which the Navy
would obviously benefit if they agreed to fund the project. He
smiled at this transparent justification but by the end of the meeting agreed to provide six Navy scientists from his staff and to
finance a purpose-built laboratory at Marconi to house the work.

Within eighteen months we were ready to demonstrate the
first prototype, which was given the code name SATYR. Kemp and
I presented ourselves at the front door of MI5 headquarters at
Leconfield House. Hugh Winterborn met us and took us up to a

spartan office on the fifth floor and introduced a tall, hunched man wearing a pin-striped suit and a lopsided smile.

"My name is Roger Hollis," he said, standing up from behind his desk and shaking my hand stiffly. "I am afraid the Director-General cannot be with us today for this demonstration, so I am standing in as his deputy."

Hollis did not encourage small talk. His empty desk betrayed a man who believed in the swift dispatch of business. I showed him the equipment without delay. It comprised a suitcase filled with radio equipment for operating SATYR, and two aerials disguised as ordinary umbrellas which folded out to make a receiver and transmitter dish. We set SATYR up in an MI5 flat on South Audley Street with the umbrellas in Hollis' office. The test worked perfectly. We heard everything from test speech to the turn of the key in the door.

"Wonderful, Peter," Hollis kept on saying, as we listened to the test. "It's black magic."

Cumming tittered in the background.

I realized then that MI5 officers, cocooned throughout the war in their hermetic buildings, had rarely experienced the thrill of a technical advance. After the test was over, Hollis stood behind his desk and made a formal little speech about what a fine day this was for the Service and how this was just what Brundrett had in mind when he formed his working party. It was all rather condescending, as if the servants had found the lost diamond tiara in the rose garden.

SATYR did indeed prove to be a great success. The Americans promptly ordered twelve sets and rather cheekily copied the drawings and made twenty more. Throughout the 1950s, until it was superseded by new equipment, SATYR was used by the British, Americans, Canadians, and Australians as one of the best methods of obtaining covert coverage. But more important to me, the development of SATYR established my credentials as a scientist with MI5. From then on I was consulted on a regular basis about an increasing number of their technical problems.

I still dealt exclusively with Cumming but I began to learn a little about the structure of his Department—A Branch. He controlled four sections: A1 provided resources for MI5, ranging from microphones to lockpicks. A2 was the technical department, which contained personnel like Hugh Winterborn who used the resources of A1. A3 was police liaison with the Special Branch, and A4 was the growing empire of Watchers, responsible for tailing foreign diplomats and others around the streets of London. Cumming had one fundamental flaw when it came to technical matters. He felt A Branch should run science, rather than the other way around. Consequently the Service as a whole was denied long-overdue modernization. As long as we were discussing specific technical requirements, our relationship was fruitful. But sooner or later we would move into an area in which I could not advise MI5 unless he or Winterborn took me fully into his confidence. For instance, Winterborn often asked if I had any ideas on telephone interception. I explained that it was impossible to work on the problem unless I knew what current techniques were employed.

"Well, of course, now we are coming onto an area which is highly classified and I rather feel we should steer away from it," Cumming would say, slapping the table nervously, much to Winterborn's irritation.

The same thing happened with the Watchers. The main problem facing MI5 during the 1950s was how to detect and follow the increasingly large number of Russians through the streets of London without giving themselves away.

"Have you any ideas, Peter?" asked Cumming, as if I might have a solution in my top pocket. I suggested that at the very least I would need to see at first hand the scale of the watching operation. Cumming said he would see what he could arrange, but I heard nothing more.

But, despite the difficulties, it was clear that MI5 found me useful. By 1954 I was spending two full days a week at Leconfield House. After one lengthy session, Cumming invited me to lunch at his club. We walked together across St. James's Park and made our way down Pall Mall to the In and Out Club, Cumming swinging the umbrella he habitually carried.

As we sat down at our table I realized that, even though I had been dealing with Cumming for five years, this was the first time we had ever socialized. He was a short man, not overly endowed with intellectual skills but intensely loyal to MI5. Like the policemen in John Buchan novels, he seemed as likely to be chasing the hero as the villain. He had been a Rifle Brigade Officer and belonged to the long military tradition inside MI5 which stretched back to the founder, Vernon Kell. He was related to the first Chief of MI6, Captain Mansfield Cumming, a fact which he made sure I knew almost as soon as I had met him. He had also been responsible for recruiting the present Director-General of MI5, Sir Dick Goldsmith White. They had taken a party of boys on a camping holiday together in the 1930s. White was not happy as a schoolteacher and Cumming persuaded him to apply to MI5. White proved a brilliant, intuitive intelligence officer and soon far outstripped his mentor, but the debt he owed Cumming served the latter well in the 1950s.

Cumming was wealthy in his own right. He owned a large estate in Sussex. In the country he played the squire, while in town he became the spy. It appealed to the boy scout in him. In fact most of his career had been spent doing MI5's books and other routine administration and he had coexisted uneasily with the gifted university élite who were drafted into Intelligence during the war. But Cumming did have one astonishing talent. He maintained a legendary number of contacts. These were not just clubland cronies, of which he had many. He maintained them in all kinds of bizarre places. If the office wanted a one-legged washerwoman who spoke Chinese, Cumming could provide her.

When the A Branch directorship became vacant, Cumming was the obvious man to fill it.

Cumming ordered quails' eggs and asked a little about my life history. He listened in an uninterested way over lunch until finally he ordered two brandies and turned to the purpose of his hospitality.

"I wanted to ask you, Peter, about how you felt things were going in the Service, technically speaking?"

I had half anticipated his approach and decided it was time to speak my mind.

"You won't get anywhere," I told him flatly, "until you appoint a problem-solving scientist and bring him fully into the picture."

I paused while brandy was served.

"You've got to let him have access to case officers, and he has to help plan and analyze operations as they happen."

Cumming cupped his glass and gently rolled its contents.

"Yes," he agreed, "we had rather come to that conclusion ourselves, but it's very difficult to find the right person. Jones* has been making a play for the job, but if we let him in, he'll be wanting to run the place next day."

I agreed.

For a while I had been indicating to Winterborn that I would be interested in joining the Service full-time if a suitable vacancy arose.

"I suppose Hugh has told you that I am interested in joining?" I asked.

"Well, that's just the problem, Peter," he replied. "We have a no-poaching agreement with Whitehall. We simply can't recruit you from there, even if you volunteer."

Cumming drained his glass with a flick of the wrist.

---

* R. V. Jones worked closely with Churchill on scientific intelligence during the war. His contributions were brilliant but he was widely distrusted in Whitehall for his independence. Like so many others, he was never allowed to make the impact in peacetime that he had made in war.

"Of course," he went on, "if you were to leave the Navy, things might be different . . ."

It was typical Cumming; he wanted me to make the first move. I raised the problem of my Admiralty pension. I would lose all fourteen years of it if I left, and unlike Cumming I had no private income to fall back on. Cumming tapped the side of his brandy glass gently and assumed an expression of surprise that I should even raise the subject.

"I am sure you're well aware that this would be a tremendous opportunity for you, Peter," he said.

He paused and returned to one of his favorite themes.

"We're not Civil Service, and you have to be prepared to trust us. There is always the secret vote. I don't think we could make any written undertakings, but I am sure when the time comes we will be able to arrange something. We don't like to see our chaps suffer, you know."

After lunch we emerged from the rich leather and brandy of the In and Out Club to the watery brightness of Piccadilly.

"Do let me know if you decide to leave the Admiralty, won't you, Peter," said Cumming, "and I'll take some soundings among the Directors."

We shook hands and he strode off toward Leconfield House, his umbrella tucked under his arm.

Cumming's approach was fortuitous. The antisubmarine project was coming to an end. The Admiralty were anxious to move me to new work in Portsmouth which I was not keen to do. The Marconi Company, meanwhile, had a contract to develop the Blue Steak project in conjunction with English Electric. Eric Eastwood, deputy head of the Marconi laboratory, offered me the job of engineering the Blue Steak guidance system. Within a month I had resigned from the Admiralty and joined the Marconi Company as a Senior Principal Scientist.

I found missile research utterly demoralizing. Partly it was because I was hoping I would soon be joining MI5. But I was not alone in realizing that the missile system was unlikely ever to be built. It was a folly, a monument to British self-delusion. In any case this kind of science was ultimately negative. Why spend a life developing a weapon you hope and pray will never be used?

I telephoned Cumming and told him I had left the Admiralty and waited for his next move. Finally, after six months, I received another invitation to lunch. Hospitality was noticeably less generous than the last time and Cumming came straight to the point.

"I have discussed your proposal with the Board and we would like to have you. But we will be in difficulties with Whitehall if we take you on as a scientist. We have never had one before. It might complicate matters. What we suggest is that you come and join us as an ordinary officer, and we'll see what you make of it."

I made it clear to Cumming that I was not very happy with his proposal. The only difference, so far as I could see, was that he would be paying me at the Principal Scientist (Ordinary Officer) level, rather than at my current Senior Scientist level—a difference of five hundred pounds a year. There was also an issue of principle which my father had raised when I discussed the matter with him.

"Don't go unless they appoint you as a scientist," he told me. "If you compromise on that, you'll never be able to operate as a scientist. You'll end up being a routine case officer before you know it."

Cumming was surprised by my refusal but made no further attempt to persuade me. He soon left, claiming a pressing appointment at Leconfield House.

A month later I was in my laboratory at Great Baddow when I received a summons to Kemp's office. Cumming and Winterborn were sitting there, Winterborn grinning broadly.

"Well, Peter," said Kemp, "it looks as if I am finally losing you. Malcolm wants to take you on as MI5's first scientist."

Winterborn later told me that Cumming had gone to see Kemp to ask what he would have to pay to get me, to which

Kemp, familiar with the extraordinary lengths to which Cumming would go to save a few pounds of government money, had replied: "The same rate I would join for—a fair wage!"

"Of course, there will be a Board," Cumming told me, "but it's just a formality."

I shook hands with everyone and went back to my lab to prepare for a new life in the shadows.

4 ————————————————

FOUR DAYS LATER I WENT TO LECONFIELD HOUSE FOR MY SELEC-
tion Board. The frosted-glass partition in the alcove slid back and
a pair of eyes scrutinized me carefully. Although I was a familiar
face, I still had no pass. I waited patiently while the policeman
telephoned Cumming's office to arrange for my escort.

"In to see the DG today, then, sir?" he said as he pushed the
lift bell. The iron gates slid back with a heavy crash. It was an old-
fashioned lift, operated by a lever on a brass box. It clanked and
wheezed up the building. I counted the floors crawling past until
we got to the fifth, where the MI5 senior management had their
offices.

A little way down the corridor we turned into a large rectangu-
lar room which housed the DG's secretariat. It looked just like
any other Whitehall office—secretaries who had seen better days,
tweeds, and clacking typewriters. Only the combination safes opposite the window gave the place away. In the middle of the far
wall of the room was the door to the Director-General's office.
The length of the outer office was deliberately designed to foil
any intruder. It gave the DG time to operate the automatic lock
on his door before anyone could burst through. When the green
light above his door flashed, a secretary accompanied me across
the vast expanse and showed me in.

The DG's office was bright and airy. Antique walnut furniture
and leather-backed chairs made it feel more like Bond Street than

Whitehall. Portraits of the three previous Director-Generals stared austerely across the room from one wall. On the other side the full board of MI5 Directors sat behind the polished conference table. I recognized Cumming and Hollis, but the rest were unknown to me.

The Director-General, Sir Dick Goldsmith White, invited me to sit down. I had met him before on one of the many visits to Cumming's office, but I could not pretend to know him well. Ironically, he had also been at Bishop's Stortford College, where he had held the record for the mile, but it was well before my time. He was tall with lean, healthy features and a sharp eye. There was something of David Niven about him, the same perfect English manners, easy charm, and immaculate dress sense. Indeed, compared with his Board, he was positively raffish.

When we were seated he opened the interview on a formal note.

"I hear you wish to join us, Mr. Wright. Perhaps you could explain your reasons."

I began by explaining some of the things I had already done for the Service. I stressed, as I had done earlier to Cumming, that it was impossible for me to do more unless I was brought inside, and fully trusted.

"I think I speak for all my Directors," he replied, "when I assure you that we would not contemplate bringing in a scientist without providing him with the access necessary to do the job. You will be fully indoctrinated."

Cumming nodded.

"However," White went on, "I think I should make it clear that the Security Service is not like other Whitehall departments with which you may be familiar. If you join us, you will never be eligible for promotion."

He explained that entry to the Service was generally at an older age than to the Civil Service, and followed a set career pattern involving general officer training in a wide variety of MI5 branches. Few of these ordinary officers made the next step to the limited number of Senior Officer posts (later Assistant Director), and fewer still had any realistic chance of aspiring to one of the six Directorships. By entering at the Senior Officer's grade to do a highly specialized job, I effectively precluded any chance of a Directorship. I told the Board frankly that, since I was by nature a lone furrower rather than one of life's bosses, this did not worry me at all.

We talked briefly about integration with Whitehall, which was something I felt needed urgent attention in the technical field, and after twenty minutes the questions began to dry up. Finally Dick White summed up. "My view, Mr. Wright, is that I am not sure we need an animal like you in the Security Service." He paused to deliver his punch line: "But if you are prepared to give it a try, so are we."

The stiffness melted away. The other Board members got up from behind the table and we chatted for a few minutes. As I was leaving, Dick White beckoned me over to his desk at the far end of the room.

"Peter, I am going to start you off in A2 with Hugh Winterborn, and obviously Malcolm will be responsible for tasking but I have told him I anticipate that you will be spending most of your time on D Branch matters—the Soviet problem."

He drummed his fingers lightly on his desk diary and gazed out of the window in the direction of the Russian Embassy complex in Kensington.

"We're not winning that battle yet by any means." He snapped the diary shut and wished me luck.

After lunch I made my way back along the fifth floor for the routine interview with the Personnel Director, John Marriott. During the war Marriott had served as Secretary to the Double Cross Committee, the body responsible for MI5's outstanding wartime success—the recruitment of dozens of double agents inside Nazi intelligence. After the war he served with Security Intelligence Middle East (SIME) before returning to Leconfield House. He was a trusted bureaucrat.

"Just wanted to have a chat—a few personal details, that sort of thing," he said, giving me a distinctive Masonic handshake. I realized then why my father, who was also a Mason, had obliquely raised joining the brotherhood when I first discussed with him working for MI5 full-time.

"Need to make sure you're not a Communist, you understand."

He said it as if such a thing were impossible in MI5. In the weeks before Cumming's final approach I was aware that a retired policeman attached to the DG's secretariat had made a routine inquiry about me at the Marconi Company. But apart from this interview I was not subject to any other vetting. Indeed, although this was the period when MI5 were laying down strict vetting programs throughout Whitehall, it was not until the mid-1960s that any systematic vetting was brought into MI5 at all.

Marriott's desk was empty, and I assumed the interview was being taped for inclusion in my Record of Service. Marriott took the session seriously enough, but asked only a few questions.

"Expect you were pretty left-wing when you were young?"

"Mildly. I taught in the Workers' Educational Association in the thirties."

"Fairly Communist, was it?"

"Not in Cornwall," I replied.

"Voted Labor in 1945, did you?"

"I thought most people in the services did."

"Pretty middle-of-the-road now, though?"

I told him I abhorred Nazism and Communism. He seemed pleased at the lengthy speech I made. We moved onto my personal life. He danced around the subject until finally he asked:

"Ever been queer, by any chance?"

"Never in my life."

He studied me closely.

"Have you ever been approached by anyone to do clandestine work?"

"Only by you."

He tried to laugh, but it was clearly a line he had heard a thousand times before. He unlocked his desk drawer and gave me a form to fill in with details of next of kin. I was vetted. No wonder it was so easy for Philby, Burgess, Maclean, and Blunt.

Before formally joining A2 as the Scientific Officer, I underwent two days' training together with a young officer joining MI5 from university. The training program was the responsibility of a tough, no-nonsense officer named John Cuckney. We got on well. Cuckney could be downright rude, but I soon realized that he was just tired of knocking into shape young MI5 recruits of generally poor caliber. He was altogether different from the average MI5 officer. He refused to submit to the monotony of the dark pinstripe, preferring bolder styles. Cuckney was his own man and had broad horizons beyond the office. It was no surprise to me when he left MI5 to pursue a successful career in business, first with Victoria investments, and later with the Crown Land Agents and as Chairman of the Port of London Authority. Today, Sir John Cuckney is Chairman of Westland Helicopters.

Cuckney began our training with a routine lecture on the legal status of MI5.

"It hasn't got one," he told us bluntly. "The Security Service cannot have the normal status of a Whitehall Department because its work very often involves transgressing propriety or the law."

Cuckney described various situations, such as entering premises without a warrant, or invading an individual's privacy, where the dilemma might arise. He made it clear that MI5 operated on the basis of the 11th Commandment— "Thou shalt not get caught" —and that in the event of apprehension there was very little that the office could do to protect its staff. He described the way liaison with the police was handled. They were prepared to help

MI5 if something went wrong, particularly if the right person was approached. But there were very definite tensions between the two organizations.

"Special Branch would like to be us, and we don't want to be them."

Cuckney handed us the current MI5 internal directory and explained how the Service was organized. There were six Directorates: A Branch handled resources; B Branch was the Personnel Department; C Branch controlled protective security and vetting throughout all government installations; D Branch was Counterespionage; E Branch ran British Intelligence in the still lengthy list of colonies and was responsible for the counterinsurgency campaigns in Malaya and Kenya; and finally F Branch was the domestic surveillance empire, which principally meant keeping tabs on the Communist Party of Great Britain, and especially its links in the trade union movement.

Cuckney talked a little about the sister Service, MI6, or SIS (Secret Intelligence Service), as it was more popularly known in Whitehall. He gave us the standard MI6 directory and discussed the very few departments there with which MI6 maintained regular liaison. In practice this amounted to MI6's Counterintelligence Section, and a small Research Section dealing with Communist Affairs, although this latter was wound up not long after I joined MI5. Cuckney was studiously noncommittal in his comments, and it was only later, when I began to cultivate my own liaison with MI6's technical people, that I realized the depth of antipathy between the two Services.

At the end of two days we were photographed and issued with our MI5 passes. Then Cuckney introduced a retired Special Branch policeman from C Branch, who gave us a lecture on document security. We were told on no account to remove files from the office, to always ensure our desk was cleared of all papers and our doors locked before going out, even if only for ten minutes. I was also issued with my combination safe number and told that a duplicate number was kept in the Director-General's safe, so that the management could obtain any file at any time of the day or night from an officer's safe. It was all sensible stuff, but I could not help contrasting it with the inadequacy of the vetting.

After the first week Cuckney showed me into an office which was empty apart from a tape recorder on the desk. He took a series of large tape reels from a cupboard.

"Here," he said, "you might as well get it from the horse's mouth!"

The subject of the tape was printed on the spool. "A Short History of the British Security Service," by Guy Liddell, Deputy Director-General 1946–1951. Liddell was a towering figure in the story of MI5. He joined in 1927, from the Special Branch, where he almost single-handedly ran a Soviet counterespionage program. He controlled MI5 counterespionage throughout the war with determination and élan, and was the outstanding candidate for the Director-General's chair in 1946. But Attlee appointed a policeman, Sir Percy Sillitoe, instead, almost certainly as a snub to MI5, which he suspected of engineering the Zinoviev letter in 1929. Liddell soldiered on under Sillitoe, barely able to contain his bitterness, only to fall foul of the Burgess/Maclean scandal in 1951. He had been friendly with Burgess for many years, and when Burgess went, so too did whatever chances Liddell still had for the top job. He retired soon after, heartbroken, to the Atomic Energy Commission.

I carefully threaded the tape and placed the headphones on. A soft, cultivated voice began to describe part of the secret history of Britain. MI5 was formed under Captain Vernon Kell in 1909, the War Office finally realizing that the impending European conflict required at least a modicum of counterintelligence. MI5 soon proved its usefulness by rounding up almost all German spies operating in Britain soon after the outbreak of war. Liddell spoke warmly of Kell, who he felt had built a prestigious organization from inauspicious beginnings through the force of his personality. MI5 budgets were strictly limited in the years after World War I, and MI6 furiously lobbied to swallow up its competitor. But Kell fought cannily to retain control of MI5 and gradually extended its influence.

The zenith of its post–World War I prestige came with the successful ARCOS raid in 1927. The Soviet Trade Delegation, based at their offices at 49 Moorgate along with the All Russia Cooperative Society Limited (ARCOS,) was raided by police acting under the instructions of MI5, and a vast quantity of espionage activity was uncovered. The ARCOS raid justified the widespread belief inside MI5 that the newly established Soviet State was the principal enemy, and that all possible resources should be deployed to fight her. This view was further confirmed by a succession of other spy cases in the 1930s, culminating in a major Soviet attempt, in 1938, to penetrate the Woolwich Arsenal using a veteran Communist engineer employed there, named Percy Glading. MI5's brilliant agent runner Maxwell Knight succeeded in planting a female agent who betrayed the plot.

By 1939 Kell had lost his touch. He was old. Liddell offered generous excuses for MI5's failure to prepare for World War II. When Churchill became Prime Minister, determined to shake Whitehall until it submitted, it was only a matter of time before Kell went. But although Liddell lamented the loss of Kell, he heartily welcomed the incoming Director-General, Sir David Petrie. Petrie oversaw the recruitment of a vast influx of gifted intellectuals, and under his supervision (and Liddell's, though this went unstated) the famed Double Cross System emerged. Every German spy landing in Britain was either captured or turned to feed disinformation back to the German High Command. The operation was an outstanding success and was a major factor in deceiving the Germans over the location of the D-Day landings. Liddell had a simple verdict on MI5 during the war. He called it "the finest liaison of unlike minds in the history of intelligence."

But Liddell's account ended soon after the war. And in truth his lecture made poor history. Case after case, incident after incident was accurately recorded, but the theme of continuous MI5 success was misleading. He knew full well the inadequacies of the postwar period, the roots of which, in fact, lay in the 1930s. There was no mention of Burgess and Maclean, or what they meant, and no mention either of the vast program of modernization which both he and Dick White knew in the late 1940s was long overdue.

In many ways Liddell was a tragic figure. Gifted, universally popular in the Service, he could justly claim to have been a principal architect of our wartime intelligence mastery. Yet he had been undone by his unwise friendships. As I listened to the tape it was as if he were talking to himself in a darkened room, searching history for the justification of a thwarted career.

I also played a lecture by Dick White on the Russian Intelligence Service. It had obviously been recorded at one of the seminars held for incoming junior officers, because I could hear the audience laughing at his jokes. Dick White's delivery was much more in the style of the Oxbridge don. He had a wonderful light touch, peppering his talk with puns, epigrams, and allusions to Russian literature. Dick White was well qualified in Soviet affairs, having been Director of the old counterespionage B Division before becoming Director-General.

He talked animatedly about the Russian obsession with secrecy, and how the modern KGB had its roots in the Tsar's Secret Police. He was perceptive in his analysis of the historical importance of the KGB to the Bolshevik Party. The Russian Intelligence Service was the guarantor of Party control in a vast and often hostile country. He spoke, too, about why the British and Russian Intelligence Services were inevitably the main adversaries in the game of spies. Secrecy and intelligence went far back in both their histories, and both services, he believed, shared a caution and patience which reflected their national characters. He contrasted this, much to the amusement of his audience, with the zealous and often overhasty activities of "our American cousins."

But Dick White, for all the elegance of his delivery, was essentially an orthodox man. He believed in the fashionable idea of "containing" the Soviet Union, and that MI5 had a vital role to play in neutralizing Soviet assets in the UK. He talked a good deal about what motivated a Communist, and referred to documents found in the ARCOS raid which showed the seriousness with which the Russian Intelligence Service approached the overthrow of the British Government. He set great store on the new vetting initiatives currently under way in Whitehall as the best means of defecting Russian Intelligence Service penetration of government.

He believed that MI5 was in the midst of great reforms, which in a sense, under his guidance, it was. The clearest impression he gave was of an intense pride in the Service. This emotion remained strong with him throughout his career, even after he had left MI5 to join MI6. He was above all a team player, and he believed very much in preserving the morale of the the organizations he ran. This made him a popular and humane man to work for, even if he always remained a slightly distant, ascetic figure.

Toward the end of my training I began to tour the building, often escorted by Cuckney or Winterborn. The whole place was ludicrously overcrowded, with officers crammed in four to a room. I had the luxury of my own office—more like a broom cupboard —next to High Winterborn on the fifth floor. The space problem was a legacy of the long-standing antipathy between MI5 and MI6. At the end of the war, plans had been drawn up to create a joint Headquarters of Intelligence to house both Services. A site for new premises was even acquired in the Horseferry Road. But for years a working party of both Services bickered about the precise division of office space, and MI5 muttered darkly about being unable to trust MI6 because of Kim Philby. The situation remained unresolved until the 1960s when MI6 were finally banished across the Thames to their own building, Century House.

In a sense, the indecision over office space was indicative of the lack of clear thinking in Whitehall about the relative roles of MI5 and MI6. It was not until well into the 1970s that MI5 finally persuaded the Treasury to fund a move to permanent, purpose-built headquarters at Curzon House. Until then the constant overspill problem was dealt with by a succession of short-term leases on buildings. Firstly there was Cork Street, which in the 1950s housed the booming empire of C Branch. Then in the 1960s Counterespionage operated from an office building in Marlborough Street, and we all had to pick our way through the peep shows, flower stalls, and rotting vegetables of Soho Market to get to our Top Secret files. It may have been appropriate, but it was hardly practical.

MI5 in the 1950s seemed to be covered with a thick film of dust dating from the wartime years. The whole organization was rather like Dickens' Miss Havisham. Wooed by the intellectual élite during the war, she had been jilted by them in 1945. They had gone off to new pursuits in the outside world, leaving MI5 trapped in her darkened rooms, alone with memories of what might have been, and only rarely coming into contact with the rest of Whitehall.

The atmosphere reminded me of a minor public school. The Directors were treated with that mixture of reverence and sycophancy reserved by schoolboys for their schoolmasters, and section heads were their prefects. But the DG and DDG were the only people addressed as "Sir," and first names were normally used. Within the atmosphere of MI5 flowered exotic and extravagant personalities, men and women so drawn to the Great Game of intelligence that they rose above the pettiness of it all, and made a career there endlessly fascinating.

On the face of it, life was a mixture of the quaint and the archaic. Every year the Office virtually closed to attend the Lord's Test Match, where MI5 had an unofficial patch in the Lord's Tavern. And every morning senior officers, almost without exception, spent the first half hour of the day on *The Times* crossword. The scrambled telephones, which normally hummed with the most highly classified secrets in the Western world, relayed a series of bizarre, coded questions from office to office.

"My left rump is giving me trouble," meaning "I can't make head or tail of seven down in the bottom left-hand corner," or "My right breast is vacant," meaning "What the hell is twelve across in the middle?" Courtney Young, who ran the Soviet Counterespionage Section (D1) in the 1950s, was the undisputed Security Service crossword king. He always claimed that it was too easy to do the crossword with a pencil. He claimed to do it in his head instead. For a year I watched him do this, until finally I could resist the temptation no longer. I challenged him, whereupon he immediately wrote in each answer without hesitation. Every night for a week I had to stand drinks for a gleeful Courtney in the local pub.

The nerve center of MI5 was the Registry. It spread across the whole ground floor of Leconfield House. The Registry had been moved to Wormwood Scrubs Prison during World War II to ensure the files would be safe if their London home were bombed. It was an unwise move. Within the year the prison was bombed and many files were destroyed or damaged by fire. Those that could be saved were stored in moisture-resistant polythene bags. In the 1960s, when we began to study the history of recruitments in the 1930s, I often examined prewar files. It was a difficult process, prizing apart the charred pages with tweezers and wooden spatulas.

After the disaster at Wormwood Scrubs MI5 put a lot of thought into designing an effective Registry. Brigadier Harker, who, as Sir David Petrie's wartime Deputy, was the ideal administrative foil, recruited an expert in business systems, Harold Potter, to reorganize the Registry. Potter was an excellent choice. He had a neat, methodical mind and the will to impose order even in the chaos of wartime.

In 1955 Potter was approaching retirement, but he took great delight in showing me around. The Registry was based in a central hall, which housed the main file index and the files themselves. The rooms leading off from the central concourse held the other specialist card indexes. Duplicate copies of all files and indexes were routinely made on microfilm, and stored in a specially protected MI5 warehouse in Cheltenham to prevent the catastrophe of Wormwood Scrubs occurring again. Potter's office, tucked in one corner of the Registry, was a paragon of neatness.

"Make sure you return your files promptly, won't you, Peter? I don't want to have to start chasing you like I do some of these buggers!"

He could have been a kindly, small-town librarian. Sadly for Potter, I became one of the worst abusers of the Registry, routinely holding scores of files at a time, though never, I suspect, as bad as Millicent Bagot, the legendary old spinster in F Branch who kept tabs on the International Communist Party for decades. I have always assumed Millicent to have been the model for John le Carré's ubiquitous Connie. She was slightly touched, but with an extraordinary memory for facts and files. Potter and his successors in the Registry despaired of Millicent. "I only hope we get the files back when she retires," he would mutter to himself after a particularly heavy file request from F Branch.

The Registry always fascinated me. Just being there filled me with anticipation, an irresistible feeling that inside the mass of dry paper were warm trails waiting to be followed. Potter explained to me the correct system for signing on and off a file to show that it had been received and dealt with. He had designed the filing system so that each file read chronologically, with papers and attachments on the right, and the index and minutes placed on the left for quick access.

The whole system depended on accurate and disciplined classification. When an officer wished to file something, it had to be approved by one of Potter's staff. Very often file requests were rejected as being too generalized. When an officer wished to draw a file he filled in a request form. These trace requests were always recorded, and if a trace was requested on an individual more than once, a file automatically opened on him. There were three basic categories in the Registry. The first category was Personal Files, or PFs, which were buff-colored files arranged in alphabetical order. There were about two million PFs when I joined the Service in 1955. That figure remained fairly static and began to rise dramatically only in the late 1960s and early 1970s with the onset of student and industrial militancy. Then there were subject files, or organizational files, such as for the Communist Party of Great Britain. Subject files very often ran into several volumes and were elaborately cross-referenced with the PFs. The final main category was the duck-egg-blue List File. This generally comprised material gathered during a particular case which could not easily be placed within either of the two previous categories. There were also Y-Boxes. These were a means of separating particularly sensitive files from general access. For instance, all suspected spies were Y-Boxed, as were most defectors. An officer could obtain the material from a Y-Box only by obtaining indoctrination into its contents from the controlling officer or sometimes from the Director-General himself.

"The integrity of the file is vital," Potter told me, and warned me that under no circumstances could papers be removed from a file without the written consent of a senior officer. The sanctity of files were something which, quite rightly, was drummed into every officer from the very beginning of his service.

Files were located by using the card indexes. Potter had devised a system of mechanically searching these indexes. Each card was classified with a series of punched holes to identify the category of files to which it belonged. To search a category of files, for instance to find a Russian intelligence officer using several aliases, an officer drew a master card corresponding to that category. Long needles were placed through the holes in the master card to locate any other cards which fitted the same constellation. These could then be searched by hand. It was old-fashioned, but it worked, and it meant that MI5 resisted the change to computerization long after it should have happened.

The concourse of the Registry was always busy with trolleys transporting files from the Registry shelves to special lifts. The trolleys ran on tracks so that files could be shifted at great speed up to the case officers working on the floors above—F Branch on the first floor, E Branch on the second, D on the third and fourth, and A Branch on the fifth. The Registry employed enormous numbers of girls to maintain efficient delivery of files within the building, as well as the massive task of sorting, checking, and filing the incoming material. In Kell's day the Registry Queens, as they were known, were recruited either from the aristocracy or from the families of MI5 officers. Kell had a simple belief that this was the best vetting of all. The debutantes were often very pretty, as well as wealthy, which accounts for the large number of office marriages, to the point where it became something of a joke that the average career expectancy of a Registry Queen was nine months—the time it took her to get pregnant.

By the early 1970s the staffing of the Registry had become a major problem for MI5. There were more than three hundred girls employed and with the surge of file collection at that time the pressure for more recruits was never-ending. Openly advertising was considered impossible. Yet it was becoming very difficult to recruit this number of girls, let alone vet them properly. In at least one case, the Communist Party managed to infiltrate a girl into the Registry, but she was soon discovered and quietly sacked. This problem, rather than dissatisfaction with the increasingly antiquated filing system itself, finally pushed MI5, belatedly, into accepting a computerized Registry.

Underneath the Registry were the Dungeons. They were actually a collection of storerooms and workshops run by Leslie Jagger, who worked under Hugh Winterborn in A2. Jagger was one of Cumming's famed contacts. He was a huge, broad-shouldered former Sergeant Major who had served with Cumming in the Rifle Brigade. Jagger always wore a black undertaker's suit.

Jagger was the MI5 odd-job technical man, and must have felt slightly apprehensive when I joined, but he never showed it and we soon became good friends. Jagger had an extraordinary array of skills, of which the most impressive was his lockpicking. Early on in training I attended one of the regular classes he ran for MI5 and MI6 in his lockpicking workshop. The cellar room was dominated by a vast array of keys, literally thousands of them, numbered and hung in rows on each wall. Jagger explained that as MI5 acquired or made secret imprints of keys of offices, hotels, or private houses, each one was carefully indexed and numbered. Over the years they had developed access in this way to premises all over Britain.

"You never know when you might need a key again," explained Jagger as I stared in astonishment at his collection.

"The first rule if you are entering premises is only pick the lock as the last resort," said Jagger, beginning his lecture. "It's virtually impossible to pick a lock without scratching it—and that'll almost certainly give the game away to the trained intelligence officer. He'll know the premises have been entered. What you have to do is get hold of the key—either by measuring the lock or taking an imprint of the key."

Jagger demonstrated how to attack various locks. Burmah locks, used for diamond safes, were by far the most difficult. The pins move horizontally through the lock and it is impossible to pick. The Chubb, on the other hand, although billed as being unpickable, was fair game for Jagger.

"This is the one you'll have to deal with most often."

He picked up a demonstration Yale mechanism mounted on a board and explained that the Yale consisted of a series of pins sitting in various positions inside the barrel of the lock. The bites in the Yale key acted on the pins to push them up and allow the key to be turned in the barrel. Jagger produced a small piece of wire with a hook on one end. He inserted it into the keyhole and began to stroke the inside of the lock in a steady, rhythmical action.

"You just stroke the first pin until"—Jagger's wrist tensed and suddenly relaxed— "it goes a notch, and then you know you've got one up into line."

His big hands moved like a concert violinist's with a bow, tensing as each pin pushed up in turn.

"You keep the pressure on until you've got all the pins up . . ." He turned the piece of wire and the Yale sprang open. "Then you're inside . . . Course, what you do inside is your business."

We all laughed. Leslie was always most mysterious about the source of his expert knowledge on lockpicking, but for years I carried a piece of wire and stroking tool that he made for me.

"Make sure you carry your police pass," he told me when he first gave it to me, pointing out that I was, technically, breaking the law by going about equipped for burglary.

"Couldn't be thought of as common or garden burglars, could we?"

He laughed heartily and strode back to the Dungeons.

5

missed the air suddenly around a wisp. I repositioned. Now the
results were consistent. I drew many mysterious diagrams of electromagnetic spaces as I gradually came to be the import and
complexes came out.

A FEW DAYS AFTER THE LOCKPICKING CLASS I WENT ON MY FIRST
operation.

"The Third Man business is brewing up again," said Hugh
Winterborn. "MI6 are interrogating one of their officers—chap
named Philby. They want us to provide the microphone."

I had met Kim Philby briefly on my first visit to Leconfield
House in 1949. I was in Cumming's office discussing the work for
Brundrett when Philby popped his head around the door. He
immediately apologized for disturbing us.

"No, come in, Kim," said Cumming in his usual gushing way.
"There's someone you ought to meet."

Cumming explained that I had just been appointed the External Scientific Adviser. Philby shook my hand warmly. He had a
lined face, but still looked youthful.

"Ah, yes," he said, "that's Brundrett's committee. The Americans are very keen on that, I gather."

I took to Philby immediately. He had charm and style, and we
both shared the same affliction—a chronic stutter. He had just
been appointed MI6 Head of Station in Washington, and was
saying goodbye to his friends in MI5 and getting various briefings
from them before his departure. Philby had developed close links
with MI5 during the war, one of the few MI6 officers to take the
trouble. At the time the visit seemed typical of Philby's industriousness. Only later did the real reason become clear. Philby

quizzed me on my thinking about science. I explained that the Intelligence Services had to start treating the Russians as a scientist would treat the subject—as a phenomenon to be studied by means of experiments.

"The more you experiment, the more you learn, even if things go wrong," I said.

"But what about resources?" asked Philby.

I argued that the war had shown scientists could help solve intelligence problems without necessarily needing a huge amount of new apparatus. Some was needed, certainly, but more important was to use the materials already available in modified ways.

"Take Operational Research," I said, referring to the first anti-submarine-research program in the Navy during the war. "That made a tremendous difference, but all we scientists did was to use the gear the Navy had more efficiently."

Philby seemed skeptical, but said that he would bear my thoughts in mind when he reviewed American thinking on the subject on his arrival in Washington.

"I'll look you up when I get back," he said. "See how you've got on." He smiled graciously and was gone.

Two years later, Burgess and Maclean defected. It was a while before Cumming mentioned the subject, but by 1954 I had gathered enough snippets from him and Winterborn to realize that Philby was considered the prime suspect for the Third Man who had tipped off the two defectors. In 1955 he was sacked by a reluctant MI6, even though he admitted nothing. On September 23, 1955, three weeks after I formally joined MI5, the long-awaited White Paper on the Burgess and Maclean affair was finally released. The press savaged it. Philby's name was well known in Fleet Street by this time, and it was obviously only a matter of time before it was debated publicly.

In October, MI5 and MI6 were informed that the question of the Third Man was likely to be raised in the House of Commons when it reconvened after the recess, and that the Foreign Secretary would have to make a statement about Philby's situation. MI6 was ordered to write a review of the case, and called in Philby for another interrogation. They, in turn, asked MI5's A2 section to provide recording facilities for the interrogation.

Winterborn and I took a taxi to the MI6 safe house near Sloane Square where Philby was due to meet his interrogators. The room MI6 had chosen was sparsely furnished—just a patterned sofa and chairs surrounding a small table. Along one wall was an ancient sideboard with a telephone on top.

As it was important to get as high a quality of recording as possible, we decided to use a high-quality BBC microphone. Speech from a telephone microphone is not very good unless it is high level. We lifted a floorboard alongside the fireplace on the side on which Philby would sit and inserted the microphone beneath it. We arranged an amplifier to feed the microphone signal to a telephone pair with which the Post Office had arranged to feed the signal back to Leconfield House.

The Transcription Center was hidden behind an unmarked door at the other end of the corridor from the MI5 staff canteen and only selected officers were allowed access. Next to the door were a bell and a metal grille. Hugh Winterborn identified himself and the automatic lock clattered open. Directly opposite the entry door was a door giving entrance to a large square room in which all the recording was done by Post Office employees. When the material was recorded, the Post Office could hand it over to the MI5 transcribers, but it was illegal to let MI5 monitor the live Post Office lines (although on occasion they were monitored, particularly by Winterborn or me, if there was something causing difficulties or very important). The telephone intercepts were recorded on dictaphone cylinders and the microphone circuits were recorded on acetate gramophone disks. This room was MI5's Tower of Babel. The recordings were handed over to women who transcribed them in small rooms running along a central corridor.

The Department was run by Evelyn Grist, a formidable woman who had been with MI5 almost from the beginning. She had a fanatic devotion to Vernon Kell, and still talked darkly of the damage Churchill had done to the Service by sacking him in 1940. In her eyes, the path of Intelligence had been downhill ever since.

Hugh Winterborn arranged for the link to be relayed into a closed room at the far end. We sat down and waited for the interrogation to start. In fact, to call it an interrogation would be a travesty. It was an in-house MI6 interview. Philby entered and was greeted in a friendly way by three former colleagues who knew him well. They took him gently over familiar ground. First his Communist past, then his MI6 career and his friendship with Guy Burgess. Philby stuttered and stammered, and protested his innocence. But listening to the disembodied voices, the lies seemed so clear. Whenever Philby floundered, one or another of his questioners guided him to an acceptable answer.

"Well, I suppose such and such could be an explanation."

Philby would gratefully agree and the interview would move on. When the pattern became clear, Winterborn fetched Cumming, who strode into the office with a face like thunder. He listened for a few moments, slapping his thigh. "The buggers are going to clear him!" he muttered. Cumming promptly sent a minute to Graham Mitchell, the Head of MI5 Counterespionage, giving an uncharacteristically blunt assessment of the MI6 whitewash. But it did no good. Days later, Macmillan got up in the House of Commons and cleared him. I realized for the first time that I had joined the Looking-Glass world, where simple but unpalatable truths were wished away. It was a pattern which was to be repeated time and time again over the next twenty years.

The Philby interview gave me my first experience of the MI5 surveillance empire. The seventh floor was, in fact, only one part of a network of facilities. The most important outstation was the headquarters of the Post Office Special Investigations Unit near

St. Paul's. MI5 had a suite of rooms on the first floor run by Major Denman, an old-fashioned military buffer with a fine sense of humor. Denman handled the physical interception of mail and installation of telephone taps on the authority of Post Office warrants. He also housed and ran the laboratory for MI5 technical processes into ways of detecting and sending secret writing. Each major sorting office and exchange in the country had a Special Investigations Unit Room, under the control of Denman, to place taps and intercept mail. Later we moved the laboratories up to the Post Office Laboratory at Martlesham, Suffolk. Then, if a letter which had been opened in St. Paul's needed further attention, it was sent by motorcycle courier up to Suffolk.

Denman's main office was lined with tables running the length of the room. Each table carried mail addressed to different destinations: London letters on one side, Europe on another, and behind the Iron Curtain on a third. Around twenty Post Office technicians worked at these tables opening pieces of mail. They wore rubber gloves so as not to leave fingerprints, and each man had a strong lamp and a steaming kettle beside him. The traditional slit-bamboo technique was sometimes used. It was ancient, but still one of the most effective. The split bamboo is inserted into the corner of the envelope, which is held up against a strong light. By turning the bamboo inside the envelope, the letter can be rolled up around the slit and gently pulled out.

Where a letter had an ordinary typed address it was sometimes torn open and a new envelope typed in its place. But to the end of my career we were never able to covertly open a letter which had been sealed at each edge with self-adhesive tape. In those cases, MI5 took a decision as to whether to open the letter and destroy it, or send it on in an obviously opened state. Pedal-operated microfilming cameras copied the opened mail and prints were then routinely sent by the case officer in charge of the interception to the Registry for filing.

Denman's proudest memento was a framed letter which hung

on the far wall. It was addressed to a prominent Communist Party member whose mail was regularly intercepted. When the letter was opened the Post Office technicians were amused to discover that it was addressed to MI5 and contained a typewritten message, which read: "To MI5, if you steam this open you are dirty buggers." Denman classified it as "obscene post," which meant that legally he had no duty to send it on to the cover address.

In fact, Denman was very particular about warrants. He was prepared to install a tap or intercept an address without a warrant only on the strict understanding that one was obtained as soon as possible. MI5 were, however, allowed to request a form of letter check without a warrant. We could record everything on an envelope, such as its origin and destination and date it was sent, as long as we did not actually open it. Denman, like everyone in the Post Office who knew of the activity, was terrified in case the Post Office role in telephone and mail intercepts was discovered. They were not so worried about overseas mail, because that could be held up for days at a time without arousing suspicion. But they were always anxious to get domestic mail on its way to the receiver as soon as possible.

Responsibility for warrants lay with the Deputy Director-General of MI5. If an officer wanted a tap or an interception, he had to write out a short case for the DDG, who then presented any problem. Once a month the Home Secretary vetted all applications. Like the Post Office, the Home Office was always highly sensitive on the issue of interceptions, and they were always strictly controlled.

As well as St. Paul's, there was also Dollis Hill, the rather ugly Victorian building in North London where the Post Office had its research headquarters in the 1950s. John Taylor ran his small experimental laboratory for MI5 and MI6 in the basement behind a door marked "Post Office Special Investigations Unit Research." The rooms were dark and overcrowded, and thoroughly unsuitable for the work that was being attempted inside.

When I joined MI5, Taylor's laboratory was overrun with work for the Berlin Tunnel Operation. A joint MI6/CIA team had tunneled under the Russian sector of Berlin in February 1955, and placed taps on the central communications of the Soviet Military Command. The actual electrical taps were done by Post Office personnel. Both the CIA and MI6 were reeling under the sheer volume of material being gathered from the Tunnel. So much raw intelligence was flowing out from the East that it was literally swamping the resources available to transcribe and analyze it. MI6 had a special transcription center set up in Earl's Court, but they were still transcribing material seven years later when they discovered that George Blake had betrayed the Tunnel to the Russians from the outset. There were technical problems too, which Taylor was desperately trying to resolve, the principal one being the ingress of moisture into the circuits.

Taylor's laboratory was also busy working on a new modification to SF (Special Facilities), called CABMAN. It was designed to activate a telephone without even entering the premises by radiating the telephone with a powerful radio beam. It worked, but only over short distances.

They were also in the early stages of developing a device called a MOP. A MOP made a cable do two jobs at once—transmit captured sound and receive power. It was in its early stages, but it promised to revolutionize MI6 activity by removing the extra leads which were always likely to betray a covert microphoning operation. I spent a lot of time in my first years in MI5 ensuring the correct specifications for MOP, and it was eventually successfully manufactured at the MI6 factory at Boreham Wood.

Soon after the Philby interview I began to look into ways of improving and modernizing the seventh floor. The method of processing a tap followed a set pattern. A case officer responsible for a tap or microphone provided the Transcription Department with a written brief detailing the sort of intelligence he thought might be obtained from the interception. The transcription staff then scanned the conversation for passages which corresponded to the brief. When I first joined, the taps were normally transferred onto acetate, rather than tape. The acetates were scanned by "dubbing" into the disc at various points to sample the conversation. If anything of relevance was found, the transcribers placed a chalk mark on the appropriate place and worked from the chalk marks. It was an inefficient and time-consuming operation but more efficient than standard tape-recording methods.

Most of these transcribers had been recruited in Kell's day from the émigré communities who fled to Britain at the end of World War I. They had turned the seventh floor into a tiny piece of Tsarist Russia. Most of them were members of the old Russian aristocracy, White Russians who talked with certainty of returning to the lands which had been expropriated after the Revolution. To them the KGB was not the KGB, it was the old Bolshevik Cheka. Most were fiercely religious, and some even installed icons in their rooms. They were famed throughout the office for their tempers. They considered themselves artists and behaved like prima donnas. Hardened case officers seeking clarification of a transcription approached the seventh floor with trepidation in case their request caused offense. The difficult atmosphere was inevitable. For years these women had listened, day after day, hour after hour to the indecipherable mutterings and labyrinthine conspiracies of Russian diplomats. Spending a lifetime looking for fragments of intelligence among the thousands of hours of worthless conversation (known in the trade as "cabbages and kings") would be enough to turn any mind.

The first thing I did was to institute hearing tests on the women, many of whom were becoming too old for the job. I encouraged those with failing hearing to handle material with a high sound quality, such as the telephone intercepts. I gave the corrupted microphone transcription to younger officers, of whom undoubtedly the best was Anne Orr-Ewing, who later joined me as a junior officer in the Counterespionage Department. Microphone transcription is difficult because you usually have only one microphone source for a multichannel conversation. I decided to design a piece of equipment to ease this problem. I went out to an electronics exhibition at Olympia and bought a tape machine which provided two heads. The second head gave a constant number of milliseconds (or more) delay on the sound as it went through, making it much fuller-bodied. In effect it simulated stereo sound, and made even the worst tapes much easier to understand. I installed the equipment on the seventh floor, and it made me a friend for life in Mrs. Grist.

It was my first small victory for science. But beneath the seventh floor the great MI5 antique showroom slumbered on, undisturbed.

The Department which required most urgent attention, and yet resisted modernization with the greatest determination, was A4. Since the war the Watchers had been outnumbered and outmaneuvered by the increasing numbers of Soviet and Soviet satellite diplomats on the streets of London. My first priority was to make a full review of the way the Watchers operated.

I made arrangements to visit one of the MI5 observation posts in an MI5 house opposite one of the main gates of the Russian Embassy in Kensington Park Gardens. The observation post was in an upstairs bedroom. Two Watchers sat on either side of the window. A camera and telephoto lens on a tripod stood permanently trained down into the street below. Both men were in shirt-sleeves, binoculars hanging around their necks. They looked tired. It was the end of their shift; the ashtrays were full to overflowing, and the table standing between them was scattered with coffee cups.

As each Russian diplomat came out of the gates of Kensington Park Gardens one or the other of the men scrutinized him through binoculars. As soon as he had been accurately identified, the observation post radioed his name back to Watcher headquarters in the form of an enciphered five-figure number. All the numbers of people leaving Kensington Park Gardens were called out on the radio. Each car or Watcher was tagged with certain numbers to follow. When one of his numbers came up he would follow the person involved without replying to the broadcast. The person being followed did not know if he was a target or not. The radio crackled intermittently as one of the mobile Watcher units parked in the streets nearby was ordered to pick up the diplomat as he made his way out of sight of the observation post toward the West End.

The Watchers who manned these static posts had done the job for years. They developed extraordinary memories for faces, instantly recognizing KGB officers who had been out of Britain for years. To assist them in identification the post had three bound volumes containing photographs and identities of every single Russian intelligence officer known to have visited the UK. Those currently resident in the Embassy were flagged in plastic holders for easy reference. If an unknown face was noted entering or leaving the premises, it was photographed and handed over to MI5's Research Section, and the endless process of identification would begin from scratch. It was numbing work, requiring patience and dedication. But none was more vital. If the Registry is MI5's central nervous system, the Watchers are its fingertips. They must be constantly outstretched, feeling out the contours of the enemy's formations.

The bound volumes of Russian intelligence officer identifications were the product of decades of careful intelligence gathering from every possible source—visa photos, defectors, double agents, or whatever. The faces stared mordantly from the pages. They were mostly KGB or NKVD strong-arm men, interspersed with the occasional cultured, European-looking resident or uniformed military attaché. It soon struck me that the observation posts were relying mostly on photographs available from the Russians' diplomatic passports. These were always sent to MI5 but were often of poor quality, or deliberately out of date, and made identification difficult to determine.

I suggested that the Watchers expand their selection of action stills. These are often much easier to recognize than mug shots. This was graphically illustrated in the Klaus Fuchs case. When Fuchs had confessed in 1949 to passing details about atomic weapons, he began to cooperate. MI5 tried to obtain details of his co-conspirators and showed him a passport photograph of Harry Greenglass, a fellow atom spy. Fuchs genuinely failed to recognize him until he was provided with a series of action stills.

For many years MI5 had realized that if Watchers operated from Leconfield House they could be followed from the building and identified by Russian countersurveillance teams. They were housed in an unmarked four-story Georgian house in an elegant terrace in Regent's Park. The central control room was dominated by a vast street map of London on one wall which was used to monitor the progress of operations. In the middle of the room was the radio console which maintained communications with all observation posts and mobile Watcher teams.

On one floor Jim Skardon, the Head of the Watchers, had his office. Skardon was a dapper, pipe-smoking former policeman. He had originally been a wartime MI5 interrogator, and in the immediate postwar period had been the chief interrogator in a number of important cases, particularly that of Klaus Fuchs. Skardon had a high opinion of his own abilities, but he was an immensely popular man to work for. There was something of the manner of a trade union shop steward about him. He felt that the Watchers did arduous and difficult work, and needed protection from exploitation by hungry case officers back at Leconfield House. In a sense this was true. There were around a hundred Watchers when I joined the Service, but the demand for their services was unquenchable in every part of MI5's activity. But I soon came to feel that Skardon was not facing up to the modern reality of watching on the streets of London. It was quite clear that the Russians, in particular, operated very extensive countersurveillance to prevent their agents from being followed. Having watched the system for a few weeks I doubted that Watchers, using their current techniques, had any realistic chance of following anyone without speedy detection.

When I first raised the question with Skardon of extensively remodeling the Watchers, he dismissed it out of hand. MI5 sections were like fiefdoms, and Skardon took it as an affront to his competence and authority. Eventually he agreed to allow Hugh Winterborn and me to mount an operation to test the effectiveness of current Watcher techniques. We split a team into two groups. The first group was given a photograph of an MI5 officer who was unknown to them and told to follow him. The second group was told the general area in which the first group was operating. They were instructed to locate them and then identify the person they were following. We did this exercise three times, and each time the second group made the identification correctly. We filmed the third experiment and showed it at Watcher headquarters to the whole Department. It did at least remove any remaining doubts that Watcher operations, as currently organized, were perilously vulnerable to countersurveillance.

We suggested to Skardon that as a first step he should employ a number of women. A great deal of watching involves sitting for hours in pubs, cafés, and parks, waiting or monitoring meetings. A man and a woman would be far less conspicuous than a single man or a pair of men. Skardon opposed the plan strongly. He feared it might introduce extramarital temptations which might adversely affect the morale of his team.

"The wives won't like it," he said grimly.

Hugh Winterborn scoffed.

"So what if they kiss and cuddle. It's better for the cover!"

Skardon was not amused. The other reform we wanted implemented was in the way Watchers were debriefed. It was never done immediately they came in from a job. Sometimes it was overnight, sometimes even at the end of the week. I pointed out to Skardon that it had been proved again and again in wartime that debriefing had to be done immediately to be accurate. If there is a delay the memory stops recollecting what happened and begins to rationalize how it happened.

"My boys have done eight hours slogging the streets. They don't want to come back and spend hours answering questions when they can write up a report themselves," he stormed. In the end he did agree to bring them back from each shift fifteen minutes early, but it was a constant struggle.

The mobile Watchers presented different problems. I went out for the day with them to get an idea of the work. MI5 cars were inconspicuous models, but they were fitted with highly tuned engines in the MI5 garages in Battersea. Every three months the cars were resprayed to disguise their identities, and each car carried a selection of number plates, which were were changed at intervals during the week.

It was boyish fun chasing Russian diplomatic vehicles through the streets of London, up and down one-way streets and through red traffic lights, secure in the knowledge that each driver carried of Police Pass to avoid tickets. The driver of my car told with great glee the story of how he had been following a Russian car down the Mall toward Buckingham Palace on a winter day. The Russian had slammed on his brakes to go around the roundabout, and the cars had skidded into each other. Both sides got out and exchanged particulars with poker faces. The knack of mobile following is to pick the parallel streets wherever possible. But in the end the success of the operation depends on the radio control at headquarters. They have to predict the likely path of the Russian car, so that reserve units can be called in to pick up the chase.

The first problem with mobile watching was quite simple. There were three men in each car, and since so much of the time was spent parked on street corners, or outside premises, the cars stood out like sore thumbs. Once again, Winterborn and I made a field study. We went to an area where we knew the Watchers were operating. Within half an hour we had logged every car. One was particularly easy. The number plates had recently been changed. But the driver had forgotten to change them both over! I suggested to Skardon that he cut down the number of men in the cars, but in true British Leyland style he gave me a lecture on how it was essential to have three men.

"There's one to drive, one to read the map, and the third to operate the radio," he said with conviction, seemingly unaware of the absurdity of it all.

But there was one area which decidedly was not a joke, and which gave me more worry than all the others put together. Communications are any intelligence organization's weakest link. The Watchers relayed hundreds of messages daily to and from the observation posts, the cars, and headquarters. The first thing which made them vulnerable was that they were never acknowledged. The Russians could easily identify Watcher communications by simply searching the wavebands for unacknowledged call signs. MI6 were just as bad abroad. For a long time the best way of identifying MI6 staff in the Embassy was to check which diplomats used outside lines which were not routed through the main switchboard. Later, MI5 brought in a complicated system of enciphering Watcher communications. I pointed out that this made no difference, since their signals would now stand out even more against the Police, Fire and Ambulance Service communications, all of which were en clair (uncoded). They did not seem to understand that the Russians were gathering most of the intelligence from the traffic itself, rather than from the contents of the messages. Traffic analysis would tell them when and where a following operation was being conducted, and by cross-checking that with their own records they would learn all they needed to know.

I lobbied hard for a major effort to be mounted to try to find out if the Russians were systematically monitoring Watcher communications. Theoretically it was a feasible thing to do, because any receiver will give off a certain radiation which can be detected at short distances. I raised my plan through the correct channels with GCHQ, which had the technical apparatus and manpower necessary for such an experiment. I waited for months before I got what was described as a "considered" answer. GCHQ's verdict was that it was not technically feasible to conduct such experiments. It was another two years before GCHQ and MI5 realized how wrong that judgment was.

In the meantime I remained a worried man. If Watcher communications were vulnerable, and Watcher tradecraft as poor as we had shown it to be, then MI5 had to assume that a substantial part of its counterespionage effort had been useless over many years. At least some operations in which Watchers had been used had to have been detected by the Russians. But which, and how many?

6 —————————————

IN THE TRENCHES OF THE COLD WAR, A2 WAS MI5'S FRONT LINE,
Hugh Winterborn and I its storm troopers. Hugh Winterborn
was a fine comrade in arms. He had served with the Army in
China and Japan and in Ceylon and Burma before joining MI5,
and spoke Chinese and Japanese fluently. Winterborn was a Field
Marshal manqué. His operations were always beautifully planned
right down to the last detail, and although often complex, were
invariably executed with military precision. But he was not a dry
man. He approached each operation with the purpose of gathering intelligence, but also to have fun. And we did have fun. For
five years we bugged and burgled our way across London at the
State's behest, while pompous bowler-hatted civil servants in
Whitehall pretended to look the other way.

Winterborn and I were a perfect match, both sharing a fervent
belief that modernization was badly needed at almost every level
of the Service, and especially in the technical field. I tended to
concentrate on ideas. He acted as the foil, winnowing out the
sensible from the impractical in my suggestions and planning how
to make them operational reality.

When I first teamed with Winterborn he was bubbling over
with news of the latest A2 job he had completed, called Operation PARTY PIECE. It had been a typical Winterborn operation—
thoroughness and outrageous good fortune linked harmoniously
together. One of the F4 agent runners learned, from a source

inside the Communist Party of Great Britain, that the entire Party secret membership files were stored in the flat of a wealthy Party member in Mayfair. A2 were called in to plan an operation to burgle the flat and copy the files.

The flat was put under intensive visual, telephone, and letter surveillance, and in due course MI5 had a stroke of unexpected luck. The woman of the house rang her husband at work to say that she was going out for an hour. She told him she would leave the key under the mat. Within twenty minutes of the call's being monitored in Leconfield House, we were around at the flat taking a plasticine imprint of the key.

The burglary was carefully arranged for a time when the occupants were away for a weekend in the Lake District. Winterborn sent a team of Watchers to monitor the occupants in case they decided to return home early. Banks of pedal-operated microfilming machines were set up in Leconfield House ready to copy the files. A team from A2 entered the flat and picked the locks of the filing cabinets where the membership files were kept. The contents of each drawer of each cabinet were photographed with a Polaroid camera. Each file was carefully removed and indexed in the flat so that it could be replaced in the identical spot. Then they were removed in bundles and driven over to Leconfield House for copying in sequential order. In all, 55,000 files were copied that weekend, and the result was a priceless haul of information about the Communist Party.

PARTY PIECE gave MI5 total access to the Party organization. Every file contained a statement, handwritten by the recruit, explaining why he or she wished to join the Party, accompanied by full personal details, including detailed descriptions of the circumstances of recruitment, work done for the Party, and contacts in the Party organization. More important than this, the PARTY PIECE material also contained the files of covert members of the CPGB, people who preferred, or whom the Party preferred, to conceal their identities. Most of these covert members were not

of the same generation as the classical secret Communists of the
1930s, many of whom had been later recruited for espionage.
These were people in the Labor Party, the trade union movement
or the Civil Service, or some other branch of government work,
who had gone underground largely as a result of the new vetting
procedures brought in by the Attlee Government.

In the years after World War II, largely as a result of our
alliance with the Soviet Union in the war, the CPGB retained a
significant body of support, most importantly in the trade union
movement. They were increasingly active in industrial disputes,
much to the consternation of Prime Minister Attlee in his later
years. In the late 1940s, MI5 began to devote resources in an
effort to monitor and neutralize CPGB activity in the trade union
movement. By 1955, the time of PARTY PIECE, the CPGB was
thoroughly penetrated at almost every level by technical surveillance or informants. Obtaining the PARTY PIECE material, the
very heart of the CPGB's administration, was the final proof of
MI5's postwar mastery. Ironically, within a year the Soviet Union
invaded Hungary, and the Party began its slow decline in popular-
ity.

Once MI5 was in possession of the PARTY PIECE material, the
CPGB was never again in a position to seriously threaten the
safety of the realm. From then on, MI5 was able to locate every
single active Party member, particularly the covert ones, and
monitor their activities, preventing them from obtaining access to
classified material where the risk arose. The PARTY PIECE material
was Y-Boxed, and remained of enormous assistance right up until
the early 1970s, especially when the CPGB later began to protest
that it had renounced secret membership and was now merely an
open party.

I first operated against the CPGB in the late 1950s, when
Hugh Winterborn and I installed yet another microphone into its
King Street headquarters. The CPGB knew that its building was
under constant technical surveillance, and regularly switched the

location of important meetings. An agent inside King Street told his F4 controller that Executive Committee discussions had been moved to a small conference room at the far end of the building. There were no windows in the room and we knew from the agent that there was no telephone either, so SF could not solve the problem of providing coverage. Later, in the 1960s, the reason for the lack of a telephone became clear. One of the first things Anthony Blunt had betrayed to the Russians was the existence of SF, immediately after it was first installed in King Street, and they had alerted the Party and instructed them to remove all telephones from sensitive areas. But the Party did not really believe it. They took precautions only for very sensitive matters.

Winterborn and I drove down to King Street in my car and sat outside studying the external walls, trying to decide the best way to attack the target room. Low down on the left-hand side of the street-facing wall was an old coal chute which had been out of use for many years. It seemed to present the best possibility. We checked with the agent where this chute went and were told that it led straight into the conference room. I suggested to Winterborn that we make a false door identical to the one already in the chute, clipping it over the top of the old door with a radio microphone between the two feeding into the keyhole.

Hugh immediately began to make the arrangements. First he designed a new door which could lock against the chute with spring catches. The door obviously had to be painted the same color as the existing one, which was a heavily weather-beaten brown. We contacted the Building Research Station in Garston and sent them sample flecks of the paint which Hugh removed with a screwdriver one night while casually walking past. They identified the paint for us and acquired some of a similar vintage. Using a blowtorch and a sink of water we were able to simulate a weathering process. I handled the installation of the radio microphone on our door. I used a small plastic audio tube to run from the keyhole in the chute to the microphone, filling the rest of the space with batteries so that the microphone could run without being serviced for up to six months. The receiver was hidden in the telephone footway box at the end of King Street which luckily was just within range of the microphone, and telephone lines relayed the signal back to the seventh floor of Leconfield House.

The most risky part of the operation was fitting the false door on the pavement of King Street. It had to be done in full view of the CPGB building, and they were constantly alert to anything suspicious. Hugh Winterborn devised a typically complex plan. He decided to make the installation late on a Saturday night, as theater revelers thronged the streets in Covent Garden. He arranged for all available A2 and F4 officers and their wives to converge on King Street from different directions at a set time. We were all choreographed carefully by Winterborn to arrive in two groups pretending to be much the worse for drink. We met on the pavement and exchanged greetings. Behind the huddle Winterborn dropped down to his knees and began to hand drill four small holes in the wall of the chute, ready to receive the spring catches of our door, using his pocket handkerchief to catch the telltale brick dust. Within a minute our noisy socializing began to wear a little thin, but Winterborn had nerves of steel. He patiently finished the drilling, and slipped the false door out from under his coat and clipped it into place. .The operation, known as TIEPIN, worked perfectly as planned and for some months MI5 had full coverage of every important CPGB meeting. But in the end the microphone was detected. A CPGB official happened to settle on our frequency when tuning his radio and a "howl round" alerted him to the presence of a device. The entire building was turned upside down in the search for the bug. Fortunately Hugh Winterborn was living in the flat on the top floor of Leconfield House at the time while his wife was away visiting relatives in Norway. He was alerted as soon as the microphone was detected and went around straightaway, unclipped the false door, and brought it back to the office like a trophy of war.

The most extensive microphoning operation Winterborn and I ever undertook was in Lancaster House, the ornate building which hosted the Colonial Conferences of the 1950s and 1960s. As soon as Macmillan became Prime Minister the pace of change in Colonial Affairs became more marked. MI5, which was responsible for security and intelligence-gathering in all Crown Territory, including the Empire, came under increasing pressure to provide intelligence assessments during negotiations toward the various independence settlements. Lancaster House was almost impossible to cover effectively in a piecemeal way. We could never be sure which rooms were going to be used, and this seriously impaired our intelligence-gathering. Winterborn and I proposed that MI5 install a comprehensive microphone system throughout the building which could be used whenever and wherever it was required. The Colonial Office agreed enthusiastically to our request, and Lancaster House was closed for "renovations" for a fortnight while an A2 team moved in. Hugh and I had already studied the room plans with great care and drawn up a circuit diagram specifying the locations of each microphone. We supervised the installation, and throughout the rest of the 1960s and the 1970s the system was used whenever high-level diplomatic negotiations took place in London.

But bugging the CPGB headquarters and covering Third World delegations were, in the end, interruptions of the main task, which was to confront the Soviet Union and her allies. The first A2 operation I undertook against the Russians was Operation CHOIR. It actually began some months before I joined MI5, when Hugh Winterborn mounted an operation to bug the Russian Consulate on the Bayswater Road. The opportunity arose when the building next door was refurbished in preparation for new occupants. MI5 went in under cover as decorators and Winterborn fitted a new device called the probe microphone, which had been developed by John Taylor in the Dollis Hill Laboratory.

The probe microphone was a large, high-sensitivity microphone, which was used to gain covert access through a party wall. The device was lodged inside the wall about eighteen inches from the target side. The eighteen inches between the probe microphone and the target room were drilled out by hand at a quarter-inch diameter in steps of half an inch. Half an inch from the target side the quarter-inch-diameter hole ended and a small pinhole was drilled, again by hand, using a No. 60-size bit, so that the intrusion into the target side was almost invisible to the naked eye. The eighteen-inch bore hole was then lined with a smooth perspex tube which was acoustically matched into the microphone. The microphone fed out into the street and back along telephone wires to Leconfield House, where amplifiers boosted the captured sound into intelligible speech.

Six months after Winterborn installed the CHOIR microphone it suddenly went dead. MI5 had, at the time, an agent who worked as an occasional decorator and odd-job man for the Russians. His name was Nutkin, which earned him the inevitable nickname of "Squirrel." Nutkin told us that the target room had been repainted. Although it seemed most likely that the pinhole had been covered with paint, we were still puzzled. Before the installation was made, Winterborn had obtained detailed measurements of the target wall from Nutkin. Using these he had planned the microphone pinhole to emerge behind a plaster leaf of the elaborate cornicework fourteen feet above the floor. It seemed unlikely that anyone would paint so carefully as to actually seal the hole. Still, Winterborn and I decided to drill it out again.

The new operation involved considerable planning. The renovation work in the building next door to the Consulate had finished. It was now a busy office with a constant stream of visitors, some of whom we knew to be Russians checking on security. We had to work at night and in total silence. We needed scaffolding to work fourteen feet up as well as plaster and paint to repair any damage. Winterborn arranged for a prefabricated scaffolding system and quick-drying decorating materials, specially developed for MI5 by the Building Research Station, to be delivered to the office in small packages so as not to alert the ever-vigilant Consulate.

A week later Jagger and I took a taxi to the top of Bayswater Road. It was winter and the streets were dark and crowded with returning commuters. We walked briskly down toward the Consulate and let ourselves into the building next door using one of Jagger's famous keys. We unpacked our attaché cases, which contained our tools and a small radio receiver. The observation post opposite the Consulate was under instructions to monitor the building for any signs of movement. We monitored the broadcasts on our receiver without acknowledgment, so that we could cease work if anyone came into the target room.

Every microphone MI5 installs is recorded in the A Branch Index, which logs technical specifications, a history of its operation, and, most important of all, its precise location. While Jagger erected the scaffolding in total silence, I studied the wall plan, which we had brought with us from the A Branch Index, and made the triangular measurements. We began scraping away the plaster. It was tense work. Each piece of plaster had to be removed by hand before it fell to the floor, and could then be placed in a bag for removal. After an hour we unearthed the microphone, carefully sealed inside the wall in a layer of plasticine. I disconnected the cables and slid out the perspex acoustic tube which led into the target room.

The No. 60 drill bit had a special stop on it ensuring the bit turned so slowly that a flake of plaster or paint could not be pushed out into the target room. I inserted the drill bit and held the body steady while Jagger delicately turned the handle. After two turns there was still resistance. Whatever was blocking the hole, it was obviously not a thin layer of paint. In the light of passing car headlights we exchanged puzzled glances. The drill turned again. And again. Still resistance. Then suddenly the bit ran free and almost immediately encountered another obstacle. I gently pulled the drill back to our side of the wall and Jagger packed the bit into a small box for examination in Leconfield House. Listening down the hole with an acoustic tube, I could hear the ticking of a clock in the target room, so without doubt the drill had entered the target room as originally designed, behind the rear side of a plaster leaf in the cornice.

We swiftly packed the microphone back into the wall, reconnected the cables, and replastered the hole. We had three hours to kill, waiting for the plaster to set before we could repaint the damage. We sat smoking, our receiver crackling intermittently. Even at the dead of night both sides were still dancing the Cold War waltz, as Watcher cars chased Russian diplomats through the darkened streets of London. But the Consulate remained silent.

The next day on the seventh floor Winterborn and I listened to the CHOIR microphone. It was muffled, but clearly working. The only problem was that nobody was saying anything in the target room. All I could hear was the steady clacking of a solitary typewriter. We went down to the basement to examine the No. 60 drill bit under a microscope. It was covered to a depth of three-eighths of an inch with plaster dust. Whoever the Russian decorator was, he had been mighty conscientious.

"That's no bloody redecoration," said Winterborn, squinting down the microscope. "You can't trowel plaster three-eighths of an inch down a pinhole. That's been down with a bloody syringe!"

A month or so later, "Squirrel" Nutkin was able to catch a sight of the target room. It had been completely remodeled with a sound-proofed partition across the party wall. Behind the partition a single secretary worked with a typewriter. The Russians obviously knew, as we did, that party walls were vulnerable to attack. But, as far as we could tell, they did not know about the probe microphone. And yet it seemed probable that they had detected the pinhole and stopped it.

In July 1955 I tackled the Soviets once again, this time in Canada. MI5 received a request for technical assistance in an operation the Royal Canadian Mounted Police (RCMP) were planning to install microphones in the Russian Embassy in Ottawa. The old three-story Embassy building overlooking the Rideau River had recently burned down. The RCMP planned to install eavesdropping equipment during the rebuilding work, but needed access to the latest equipment, so they contacted MI5.

I was met at the airport by Terry Guernsey, the head of the RCMP's Counterespionage Department, B Branch. With him was his assistant, a Welshman named James Bennett. Guernsey was a lanky Canadian whose outwardly unflappable manner was constantly betrayed by the nervous, explosive energy underneath. Guernsey was trained in Britain by both MI5 and MI6 and returned to Canada in the early 1950s convinced that the RCMP was unsuited, as a uniformed police force, to the delicate work of counterespionage. Guernsey began to recruit civilian intelligence officers and single-handedly built up B Branch into one of the most modern and aggressive counterespionage units in the West. Many of the ideas which later played a major role in British and American thinking, such as computerized logging of the movements of Russian diplomats in the West, began as Guernsey initiatives. But he constantly ran up against the oppressive restrictions of the Mountie tradition, which believed that the uniformed RCMP officer was inherently superior to his civilian counterpart. This was a struggle which ran deeply, not just through Canadian Intelligence, but also in the FBI. Guernsey believed that the British were correct in drawing a distinction between criminal detective work and the entirely different skills of intelligence-gathering, and he fought many battles to ensure that B Branch remained independent of the mainstream of the RCMP. But the effort virtually cost him his career. The Mountie senior officers never forgave him, and he was eventually banished to the UK, where he acted as RCMP liaison with MI5 and MI6, before ill-health finally drove him into retirement.

But in 1956, when I made my first trip to Canada to help plan Operation DEW WORM, Guernsey was still very much in charge. Over dinner that first night he described where the operation stood. The RCMP had successfully recruited the contractor who was rebuilding the Russian Embassy, and had installed RCMP officers under cover as workmen on the site. With the help of Igor Gouzenko, a Russian who had worked inside the old Embassy as a cipher clerk until he defected to the Canadians in 1945, Guernsey had been able to pinpoint the area in the northeast corner of the building where the KGB and GRU (Soviet Military Intelligence) secret sections, and the cipher rooms, were located.

After studying the plans I decided that a SATYR operation, using a cavity microphone activated from outside by microwaves, was not technically feasible. The distance from the device to safe ground was too great to be assured of success. It had to be a wired operation. Wired operations have one major advantage. If they are skillfully installed, they are almost impossible to detect. The best plan to attach was to conceal the microphones inside the aluminum sash windows on the target side of the building. Guernsey obtained a sample frame from the contractor. They were friction windows with no sash weight, perfect for concealing a device. There was an air path into the sash where the two pieces locked together, ensuring a good sound quality. The metal window frames would effectively dampen the electromagnetic field emitted by the microphones, making them impervious to sweeper detection.

But the main problem was how to conceal the cables leading to the microphones. The walls of the new Embassy building were planned to be nearly two feet thick, with a fourteen-inch concrete block inner lead, a two-inch air gap in the middle, and then four-inch-thick stone facing on the outside of the wall. I checked with MI6 for details of Russian electronic sweeper operations. They told me that the Russians never swept the outsides of their buildings, only the insides. The Russians apparently considered it demeaning to be seen to be sweeping their premises. I told Guernsey that the best plan was to lead the cables up through the air gaps, where they would be virtually assured of non-detection through fourteen inches of concrete, especially as MI5 had developed a new thin cable which gave off far less electromagnetic emission.

Once the building work got under way we had to find a way of concealing the cables from the Russian security teams who regularly visited the site to check on the Canadian contractors. We buried large coils beneath each of the eight-foot concrete footings, and cut them into the bitumen coverings. Every night, as each course of masonry was installed, RCMP workmen went onto the site and lifted a length of cable from the coil into the air gap. There were eight cables. Each was labeled at random from one to twenty to mislead the Russians in the event they were ever discovered. It was a nice touch; the sort of joke the Russians would appreciate after they had finished tearing down the Embassy searching for the phantom cables.

The most difficult part of the whole operation was connecting the wires to the microphones. The windows in the northeast section of the building had been successfully fitted, supervised by an RCMP officer to ensure the frames went into the right places. The cables had been painstakingly raised inside the air gaps over months of construction work. But connecting the two together was impossible to conceal. It could be done only by an engineer working outside, four floors up on the scaffolding. The job was given to one of Guernsey's technical men, a young engineer who handled the operation brilliantly. He was a big man, but he scaled the building in pitch dark in a temperature approaching minus forty degrees centigrade, carrying his soldering tools in a shoulder bag. Taking each of the eight microphones in turn, he carefully joined the cables and ensured the connections were solid.

As soon as the connections were made, RCMP technicians began to dig a twenty-yard tunnel from an RCMP safe house next door to the Embassy, through to the coils buried under the footings. The coils were led back ten feet underground to the safe house and the tunnel backfilled with three feet of concrete. The eight cables connected to head amplifiers concealed in the garage of the safe house, with power fed to them over output leads from RCMP headquarters. When the microphones were tested, each one worked perfectly.

But then, just as this almost flawless operation was nearing completion, disaster struck. A workman was installing a fuel tank on the outside wall near the northeast corner of the new Embassy, unaware that just at that point all the cables from all the windows above came together to go underground to our safe house. As he drove in metal hasps to support the ventilation pipe, he pushed one straight through the bundle of cables buried inside, completely destroying the connections to all the microphones.

There was no choice but to reenter the building. But this time the operation was even more risky. The building was more or less complete, and the Russians on the verge of occupation. There was little chance of the Russians believing the undercover RCMP team were just innocent workmen if they were discovered. It was another bitterly cold night when they went back in. They managed to extract six of the eight cables from behind the hasp, rejointed them, abandoning the other two, and built them back into the wall with the hasp. Although two microphones were lost, at least one remained operational in each of the target rooms, so the major disaster was averted.

As soon as the Russians reoccupied their Embassy, we heard sounds from some of our microphones. GRU officers discussed earnestly where they should put their furniture. Then, forty-eight hours later, they suddenly vacated their offices, the Ambassador left for Moscow, and a team of Russian workmen moved in. It was soon clear from the materials the Russians were taking into the Embassy that they were constructing a new KGB and GRU sanctum elsewhere in the building, probably supplied by an independent power generator.

Shortly after this, the microphones, which were being constantly monitored back at RCMP headquarters, began to pick up the telltale sounds of a sweeper team in operation. RCMP had tentatively identified their arrival in the building some days before, but it wasn't until they began work in the northeast corner, tapping at the walls for signs of hollowness, and running metal detectors across the ceilings, that we were sure. For twenty days they swept the rooms we had microphoned, as if they knew they were bugged. But they never found either the cables or the microphones. By Russian Embassy standards worldwide, the new building was small, but despite what must have been cramped conditions, the northeast corner remained virtually unused apart from routine consular work, even after the departure of the sweepers. Eight years later the microphone sweepers arrived in Ottawa. They went straight to the rooms where the microphones were and within an hour had found the microphone cables and thus the microphones. There were forty-two rooms in the Embassy. The sweepers searched only in six rooms where the microphones were. They must have known where to look!

Like Operation CHOIR, something about DEW WORM troubled me. Partly, of course, it was disappointment. The operation had been an outstanding technical success, but the months of patient preparations had yielded no intelligence whatever. Of course, at the outset of the operation the biggest gamble had been to assume, as Gouzenko had, that the Russians would rebuild their secret section in the same place as they had it in the old Embassy. But based on an analysis of the power supply to the building, it was a reasonable gamble. The fact that they had decided to resituate the secret section and screen it off was not in itself unusual. Both the British and the Americans had begun to realize, as almost certainly had the Russians, that the best way to protect an Embassy secret section from microphone attack was to construct it deep inside, preferably with its own power supply. But the certainty with which the Russian sweepers attacked the northeast corner, as if they were looking for something they knew to be there, introduced the worm of doubt into my mind.

Within a year the same thing happened, again in Canada. The Polish Government were given permission to open a consulate in Montreal. They bought an old house and began renovations. In January 1957 I flew over to Montreal to assist the RCMP install a microphone. The RCMP knew the identity of the UB (Polish Intelligence) officer and the location of his room, but the building was being completely gutted, so a wired operation was out of the question. Only a SATYR cavity microphone would do. The premises were being rewired using steel conduits for the cables, and as with the DEW WORM window frames I reckoned that the SATYR devices would be virtually impossible to detect if they were placed close to the conduits. Within a fortnight of installing the system the Poles suddenly ordered the contractor to remove the wall containing our SATYR devices and replace it with another. The RCMP did manage to retrieve one device, but the other was lost to the Poles. Later the RCMP learned from a source inside the Polish Embassy that they had been tipped off to the likely presence of microphones by the Russians. They had been one step ahead of us again.

It was not just in Canada that things like this occurred. There was also Operation *MOLE* in Australia. It began with a visit to London by Sir Charles Spry, the head of Australia's overseas intelligence-gathering organization, ASIO, in 1959. I received a telephone call saying that he would like to see me. Spry had once been a good-looking man, with hooded eyes and a full mustache, but responsibility and a liking for the good things in life had left him florid in appearance. Spry was appointed head of ASIO on its formation in 1949. He had previously been Director of Military Intelligence, but along with a group of like-minded officials, dubbed the "gnomes of Melbourne," he lobbied hard for the creation of a proper security intelligence-gathering agency similar to MI5. Spry ran the service with an iron fist for nineteen years, and became one of the towering figures of postwar intelligence. Only toward the end of his career, when he began to lose touch with his staff, did his grip on the organization falter.

Spry liked visiting London. He had originally served in the Indian Army on the Khyber Pass in the 1930s. The common background and shared sense of what constituted an officer and a gentleman ensured him many friends in the clubbable world of British Intelligence. But Spry was far from being an old buffer. He came straight to the point as soon as our meeting began. He told me he had recently been over in Canada and Terry Guernsey had recommended he talk to me about a microphone operation ASIO was planning against the Russians. He explained that since the well-publicized defection of the Petrovs, a husband and wife who worked together inside the cipher section of the Russian Embassy in Canberra, the Russians had broken off diplomatic relations and placed their Embassy under the control of the Swiss. But recently they had been making overtures to return and ASIO wanted to mount an operation against the Embassy before they occupied the premises. After studying the plans, I advised Spry to mount a SATYR operation, and demonstrated the device to him. The best place to install SATYR was in the wooden sash window frames, and I sent my assistant out to Australia to supervise the details. The device was successfully installed, and as a further precaution, I instructed ASIO not to activate the device for a year, in case the Russians monitored the building for microwaves in the first months of reoccupation. As with DEW WORM, Operation MOLE was a technical success, but not a single scrap of intelligence was gleaned. Every sound in the KGB resident's room, every shuffle of his papers, every scratch of his pen, was audible. But he never said a word. Operation MOLE was another failure.

The demands on MI5's slender resources were, in the 1950s, impossible to satisfy. Consequently, the pressure of work on individual officers, particularly those in A2 who had of necessity become involved in such a wide range of operations, was at times practically intolerable. Operations merged one into another. Plans, maps, briefings, technical reports crossed my desk in a paper whirl. It was often difficult at any fixed point to be sure which operations had ended and which were still deep in the midst of gestation. Intelligence-gathering, even at its best, is a thoroughly confused business. But there is always an empty space in the mind of every professional intelligence officer worth his salt reserved for scraps and fragments which for one reason or another raise unanswered questions. Operations CHOIR, DEW WORM, and MOLE were all stashed away in that compartment, submerged under the welter of current operations, but never quite forgotten, until years later they suddenly assumed a new significance.

The profession of intelligence is a solitary one. There is camaraderie, of course, but in the end you are alone with your secrets. You live and work at a feverish pitch of excitement, dependent always on the help of your colleagues. But you always move on, whether to a new branch or department, or to a new operation. And when you move on, you inherit new secrets which subtly divorce you from those you have worked with before. Contacts, especially with the outside world, are casual, since the largest part of yourself cannot be shared. For this reason, intelligence services are great users of people. It is built into the very nature of the profession, and everyone who joins knows it. But early in my career I encountered a man whose experience at the hands of British Intelligence suddenly stripped the veneer of national importance away from the whole business. It arose out of the work I had been doing for Brundrett's committee on resonance. I had spent a lot of time researching ways in which innocuous objects, like ashtrays or ornaments, could be modified to respond to sound waves when radiated with microwaves of a certain frequency. If a system could be perfected, it promised enormous advantages. The object itself would carry no transmitter or receiver, so detection would be virtually impossible. By 1956 we had successfully developed prototypes, and decided to attempt an operation against the Russian Embassy in London.

One of MI5's agents at that time was the MP Henry Kirby, who had frequent dealings with the Russian diplomatic community. The plan was simple. MI5 would design an ornament modified to reflect sound, and Kirby would give it as a gift to the Russian Ambassador. The first thing that we needed to know was the kind of present the Ambassador might be likely to accept and place prominently on his desk or in his office. Malcolm Cumming suggested that I visit an old MI5 agent runner named Klop Ustinov, the father of the actor Peter Ustinov.

Klop Ustinov was German by descent, but he had strong connections in the Russian diplomatic community and was a frequent visitor to the Embassy. Ustinov had the unique distinction of having held commissions in the Russian, German, and British Armies. He had dabbled in intelligence throughout the interwar period. He spoke a vast array of languages, and his German/Russian background made him a useful source of information. When Hitler came to power, Ustinov began to work strenuously against the Nazis. He approached Robert Vansittart, a prominently anti-Nazi Foreign Office diplomat, offering to work for British Intelligence. He claimed to be in contact with Baron Wolfgang zu Putlitz, then a First Secretary at the German Embassy in London, who he said was secretly working against the Nazis. Ustinov was recruited by MI5, and began to obtain high-grade intelligence from zu Putlitz about the true state of German rearmament. It was priceless intelligence, possibly the most important human-source intelligence Britain received in the prewar period. After meeting zu Putlitz, Ustinov and he used to dine with Vansittart and Churchill, then in the wilderness, to brief them on the intelligence they had gained. Zu Putlitz became something of a second son to the urbane English diplomat. Even after the outbreak of war Ustinov continued meeting zu Putlitz, by now working in Holland as an Air Attaché. Finally in 1940 zu Putlitz learned that the Gestapo were closing in and he decided to defect. Once more Ustinov traveled into Holland and, at great personal risk, led zu Putlitz to safety.

I took a taxi over to Ustinov's flat in Kensington, expecting to meet a hero of the secret world living in honorable retirement. In fact, Ustinov and his wife were sitting in a dingy flat surrounded by piles of ancient, leather-bound books. He was making ends meet by selling off his fast-diminishing library.

Despite the hardship, Ustinov was thrilled by my visit. He remained a player of the Great Game down to his fingertips. Two small glasses and a bottle of vodka appeared, and he began to pore over the plans I had brought with me from the office. He was a round old man with a guttural, polyglot accent, and a sharp eye for the real interests of the Soviet diplomats in Kensington Park Gardens.

"The real danger, my friend, is that they will sell the gift, rather than display it, if it is too valuable," he intoned in a knowing voice. "These are Bolsheviks—men of orthodox tastes. A silver effigy of Lenin, or model of the Kremlin. These perhaps will be more sacred to them."

A bust of Lenin was unsuitable, I explained, because the smooth contours of Vladimir Ilyich's skull were too rounded to be sure of reflecting sound waves. But a model Kremlin offered possibilities. It would be easy to conceal the right type of concave indentations in the complex architecture of the symbol of Mother Russia. Klop Ustinov saw the whole operation as a piece of rich theater and offered to pay a visit to the Ambassador to gather more direct evidence of his tastes.

As the vodka took hold we began to talk of old times. He was an old man, but his memory was still fresh. Tears began to wet his cheeks as he told me the story of what he and zu Putlitz had done for the country. Finally his reserve broke.

"I do these things, Peter, and they leave me here. My wife and I . . . penniless."

"But what about your pension?" I asked.

"Pension? I have no pension," he flashed back bitterly. "When you work for them you never think about the future, about old age. You do it for love. And when it comes time to die, they abandon you."

I sat silent. It seemed scarcely credible to me that such a man could be left in such circumstances, forced almost to beg. I wanted to ask him why Churchill or Vansittart had forgotten him, but I felt it would only wound him more. Ustinov drank and composed himself.

"But it was fun," he said finally. He poured more vodka with an unsteady hand. There was silence for a moment, and then he spoke again.

"My boy. He is an actor." He pointed to a picture of young Peter on the mantelpiece. "Do you have children, Peter?" I told him I had three, two girls and a young boy.

"Tell him not to join, then," he said quietly. "I would not want my boy to join this game of ours. The gentlemen run the business, and gentlemen have short memories . . ."

Almost as soon as it arrived, his bitterness melted away. He asked about the office, about Guy Liddell, Dick White, and Malcolm Cumming, all of whom had been closely involved with him during the wartime years. Finally, as late-afternoon darkness closed in on the room, I left. We shook hands and he returned alone to the vodka and his piles of books.

I was too drunk that night to do anything other than go home. But the next morning I tackled Cumming on the subject. He looked embarrassed.

"But I'm sure we sorted his pension out years ago," he barked in a voice louder than usual. "Good God, poor Klop. I'll see Dick straightaway."

Further questioning was pointless. Who precisely had been to blame for forgetting Klop Ustinov was lost in the chase around the mulberry bush of responsibility, an occupation much favored by bureaucrats when oversights are discovered. Ustinov did get his pension, although I never saw him again after that meeting. Not long afterward he died. But at least his widow had the benefit of it. The silver Kremlin operation soon petered out, overruled by the foreign Office. In truth my heart went out of it that afternoon in Kensington. But I learned a lesson I never forgot: that MI5 expects its officers to remain loyal unto the grave, without necessarily offering loyalty in return.

But in the main, the 1950s were years of fun, and A Branch a place of infectious laughter. As Hugh Winterborn always said: "MI5 is a great life, if you can stand the excitement!" Like the time when we were fitting listening devices in a safe house next door to the Hungarian Embassy. I climbed onto the roof to install an aerial and was seen by a neighbor, who reported seeing a burglar on the prowl. Within ten minutes the police were knocking at the door, accompanied by the neighbor, and pandemonium reigned. Here we were, surrounded by the latest listening technology, receivers and cables spread across the floor. Winterborn desperately lifted the floorboards and began to shovel tens of thousands of pounds' worth of equipment underneath. The knocking got louder. Then burly shoulders began to force the front door. They were clearly convinced by the noise that a burglary was in progress. Finally, everything was relatively shipshape, and I opened the door sheepishly and explained that I was doing some authorized late-night renovations for the owner. I gave the policeman a number to ring to confirm the fact. It was the local Special Branch number.

Even funnier was the time we did a similar job against the

Polish Embassy in Portland Street. The house next door was temporarily empty, and A2 obtained access to install a series of microphones. Hugh Winterborn and I led a team of twelve officers from A Branch. Silence was imperative because we knew that the target premises were permanently manned near the party wall. I made a tremendous fuss insisting that everyone remove his shoes to avoid making noise on the bare floorboards. We worked nonstop for four hours in the freezing cold. All the floorboards on the first floor had been raised and I was patiently threading the cables along the void between the joists. After a time one of the leads became tangled on a split joist. Unable to clear the obstruction by hand, I began to ease myself down until one foot was resting on a masonry nail sticking out from one side of a joist. Just as I was inching toward the tangled cable, the nail gave way, and I plunged through the ceiling below. A large section of ceiling crashed fourteen feet to the floor below, reverberating around Portland Place like a wartime bomb. The noise and dust subsided, leaving me wedged tightly up to my waist in the hole in the ceiling. For a moment there was total silence.

"Good thing we removed our shoes," quipped Winterborn dryly as laughter began to echo around the empty building.

Luckily the neighbors must have been asleep, because no policemen arrived. Leslie Jagger quickly repaired the lath work, replastering and repainting the damage before morning with his quick-drying materials.

"Close shave, that one, Peter," he said as he applied the final lick of paint. "If you'd come through the ornamental rose we'd have been absolutely buggered!"

But accidents like these were rare occurrences. In the main, MI5 technical operations became, under Hugh and me, highly professional, in sharp contrast to MI6 activities in the same field. MI6, in the mid-1950s, never settled for a disaster if calamity could be found instead. The best example I ever heard concerned one of their training operations. They placed a junior officer in an

MI6 flat, and detailed another team of recruits to find and interrogate him. MI5 were always routinely informed about these operations in case anything went wrong.

One afternoon A2 got a phone call from MI6 pleading for help. The MI6 search party had apparently miscounted the floors of the apartment block where their target was holed up. They picked the lock of the flat one floor above, and proceeded to go to work on the man inside. He, of course, protested his innocence, but believing this to be part of the ruse, the search party consulted the MI6 textbook marked "persuasion," and went to work as only enthusiastic amateurs can. By the time they had finished, the man was stripped naked and singing like a bird. He was, in reality, a jewel thief, who had recently pulled off a diamond robbery. He produced the baubles still in his possession, obviously believing that his captors were visitors from a vengeful underworld.

Hugh Winterborn split his sides laughing as the unfortunate MI6 officer begged for advice on what to do with the jewel thief, the diamonds, and a wrecked flat. In the end the thief was given two hours to make the Continent and Leslie Jagger went over to the flat and repaired the damage.

After I had been in A2 for two or three years, MI6 began to call on me to help them plan their technical operations. I never much enjoyed working with MI6. They invariably planned operations which, frankly, stood little chance of technical success. They were always looking for a successor to the Berlin Tunnel—something on the epic scale which would have the Americans thirsting to share in the product. But they never found it, and in the process failed to build a sensible bedrock of smaller successes. There was, too, a senseless bravado about the way they behaved which I felt often risked the security of the operations. In Bonn, for instance, we were planning a DEW WORM–style operation on the Russian Embassy compound.

Local MI6 station officers wandered onto the site and even, on one occasion, engaged the KGB security guards in casual conversation. It made for good dining-out stories, but contributed little to the weekly ministerial intelligence digests. The foolhardiness was invariably punctuated by flights of absurd pomposity. In Bonn I made the perfectly sensible suggestion that we should use German cable so that if the operation were discovered MI6 could disown it and blame it on the local intelligence service.

"Good Lord, Peter! We can't do that," gushed the MI6 station chief with his nose in the air. "It wouldn't be ethical."

Ethics, so far as I could ascertain, were displayed by MI6 purely for Whitehall or MI5 consumption. In fact MI6, under its chief, Sir John Sinclair, had become a virtual liability. It still refused to face up to the appalling consequences of Philby's being a Soviet spy. It was operating in the modern world with 1930s attitudes and 1930s personnel and equipment. It was little surprise to me when they stumbled, in April 1956, into their greatest blunder of all, the Crabbe affair.

The Soviet leaders Khrushchev and Bulganin paid a visit to Britain on the battleship *Ordzhonikidze*, docking at Portsmouth. The visit was designed to improve Anglo-Soviet relations at a sensitive time. MI5 decided to operate against Khrushchev in his rooms at Claridge's Hotel. Normally Claridge's has permanent Special Facilities installed on the hotel telephone system, because so many visitors stay there who are of interest to MI5. But we knew the Russians were sending a team of sweepers in to check Khrushchev's suite before he arrived, so we decided it was the right time to use for the first time the specially modified SF which John Taylor had developed in the Dollis Hill Laboratory. The new SF did not require a washer to be fitted, so it was virtually undetectable. The telephone could be activated over short distances using shortwave high-frequency megacycles. We set the SF activation up in an office of the Grosvenor Estates near Claridge's. It worked perfectly. Throughout Khrushchev's visit his room was permanently covered. In fact, the intelligence gath-

ered was worthless. Khrushchev was far too canny a bird to discuss anything of value in a hotel room. I remember sitting up on
the seventh floor with a transcriber translating loosely for me. We
listened to Khrushchev for hours at a time, hoping for pearls to
drop. But there were no clues to the last days of Stalin, or to the
fate of the KGB henchman Beria. Instead, there were long mono-
logues from Khrushchev addressed to his valet on the subject of
his attire. He was an extraordinarily vain man. He stood in front
of the mirror preening himself for hours at a time, and fussing
with his hair parting. I recall thinking that in Eden, Khrushchev
had found the perfect match. Both were thoroughly unscrupulous
men, whose only interest lay in cutting a dash on the world stage.

But while MI5 were discreetly bugging Khrushchev, MI6
launched a botched operation against the *Ordzhonikidze*. The
operation was run by the MI6 London Station, commanded by
Nicholas Elliott, the son of the former headmaster of Eton. MI6
wanted to measure the propeller of the Russian battleship, because there was confusion in the Admiralty as to why she was able
to travel so much faster than had originally been estimated by
Naval Intelligence. Elliott arranged for a frogman, the unfortunate Commander "Buster" Crabbe, to take on the assignment.

In fact, this was not the first time MI6 had attempted this
operation. A year before, they tried to investigate the hull of the
Ordzhonikidze while she was in port in the Soviet Union. They
used one of the X-Craft midget submarines which MI6 kept
down in Stokes Bay. They had dry compartments to enable a
diver to get in and out and were small enough to pass undetected
into inshore waters. A Naval frogman had attempted to enter the
harbor, but security was too tight and the mission was aborted.

The second attempt in Portsmouth ended in disaster. Crabbe
was overweight and overage. He disappeared, although a headless
body which was later washed up was tentatively identified as his.
John Henry, MI6 London Station's Technical Officer, had informed me that MI6 were planning the Crabbe operation, and I

told Cumming. He was doubtful about it from the start. It was a typical piece of MI6 adventurism, ill-conceived and badly executed. But we all kept our fingers crossed. Two days later a panic-stricken John Henry arrived in Cumming's office telling us that Crabbe had disappeared.

"I told Nicholas not to use Buster; he was heading for a heart attack as it was," he kept saying.

We were highly skeptical of the heart attack theory, but there was no time for speculation. The secret MI6 parlor game was at risk of becoming embarrassingly public. Crabbe and his MI6 accomplice had signed into a local hotel under their own names.

"There'll be a fearful row if this comes out," snapped Cumming. "We'll all be for the pavilion!"

Cumming buzzed through to Dick White's office and asked to see him immediately. We all trooped upstairs. Dick was sitting at his desk. There was no hint of a welcoming smile. His charm had all but deserted him, and the years of schoolmaster training came to the fore.

"The Russians have just asked the Admiralty about the frogman, and they've had to deny any knowledge. I'm afraid it looks to me rather as if the lid will come off before too long," he said tersely.

"John, how on earth did you get yourself into this mess?" he asked with sudden exasperation.

Henry was chastened, but explained that the Navy had been pressing them for months for details of the *Ordzhonikidze*'s propeller.

"You know what Eden is like," he said bitterly, "one minute he says you can do something, the next minute not. We thought it was an acceptable risk to take."

White looked unconvinced. He smoothed his temples. He shuffled his papers. The clock ticked gently in the corner. Telltale signs of panic oozed from every side of the room.

"We must do everything we can to help you, of course," he

said, finally breaking the painful silence. "I will go and see the PM this evening, and see if I can head the thing off. In the meantime, Malcolm will put A2 at your disposal."

A thankful John Henry retreated from the room. Cumming telephoned the CID in Portsmouth and arranged for the hotel register to be sanitized. Winterborn and Henry rushed down to Portsmouth to clear up any loose ends. But it was not enough to avert a scandal. That night Khrushchev made a public complaint about the frogman, and a humiliated Eden was forced to make a statement in the House of Commons.

The intelligence community in London is like a small village in the Home Counties. Most people in the senior echelons know each other at least well enough to drink with in their clubs. For some weeks after the Crabbe affair, the village hummed in anticipation at the inevitable reckoning which everyone knew to be coming. As one of the few people inside MI5 who knew about the Crabbe affair before it began, I kept my head down on John Henry's advice.

"There's blood all over the floor," he confided to me shortly afterward. "We've got Edward Bridges in here tearing the place apart."

Shortly after this, Cumming strode into my office one morning looking genuinely upset.

"Dick's leaving," he muttered. "They want him to take over MI6."

The decision to appoint Dick White as Chief of MI6 was, I believe, one of the most important mistakes made in postwar British Intelligence history. There were few signs of it in the mid-1950s, but MI5, under his control, was taking the first faltering steps along the path of modernization. He knew the necessity for change, and yet had the reverence for tradition which would have enabled him to accomplish his objectives without disruption He was, above all, a counterintelligence officer, almost certainly the greatest of the twentieth century, perfectly trained for the Director-General's chair. He knew the people, he knew the problems, and he had a vision of the sort of effective counterespionage organization he wanted to create. Instead, just as his work was beginning, he was moved on a politician's whim to an organization he knew little about, and which was profoundly hostile to his arrival. He was never to be as successful there as he had been in MI5.

But the loss was not just MI5's. The principal problem in postwar British Intelligence was the lack of clear thinking about the relative role of the various Intelligence Services. In the post-imperial era Britain required, above all, an efficient domestic Intelligence organization. MI6, particularly after the emergence of GCHQ, was quite simply of less importance. But moving Dick White to MI6 bolstered its position, stunted the emergence of a rationalized Intelligence community, and condemned the Service he left to ten years of neglect. Had he stayed, MI5 would have emerged from the traumas of the 1960s and 1970s far better equipped to tackle the challenges of the 1980s.

The departure was conducted with indecent haste. A collection was swiftly arranged. The takings were enormous, and he was presented with an Old English Silver set at a party held in the MI5 canteen. It was an emotional occasion. Those who knew Dick well, and at that time I was not among them, claimed that he agonized over whether to move across to MI6, perhaps realizing that he was leaving his life's work undone. Dick was nearly crying when he made his speech. He talked of the prewar days, and the bonds of friendship which he had formed then. He thanked Cumming for encouraging him to join the Office, and he talked with pride of the triumphs of the war years. He wished us well and made his final bequest.

"I saw the Prime Minister this afternoon, and he assured me that he had the well-being of our Service very much at heart. I am pleased to announce that he has appointed my Deputy, Roger Hollis, as my successor as proof of his faith in this organization. I am sure that you will agree with me that the Service could not be in safer hands."

The tall, slightly stooping figure in the pinstripe suit came forward to shake Dick White's hand. The era of elegance and modernization had ended.

7

ROGER HOLLIS WAS NEVER A POPULAR FIGURE IN THE OFFICE. He was a dour, uninspiring man with an off-putting authoritarian manner. I must confess I never liked him. But even those who were well disposed doubted his suitability for the top job. Hollis, like Cumming, had forged a close friendship with Dick White in the prewar days. For all his brilliance, Dick always had a tendency to surround himself with less able men. I often felt it was latent insecurity, perhaps wanting the contrast to throw his talents into sharper relief. But while Hollis was brighter by a good margin than Cumming, particularly in the bureaucratic arts, I doubt whether even Dick saw him as a man of vision and intellect.

Hollis believed that MI5 should remain a small security support organization, collecting files, maintaining efficient vetting and protective security, without straying too far into areas like counterespionage, where active measures needed to be taken to get results, and where choices had to be confronted and mistakes could be made. I never heard Hollis express views on the broad policies he wanted MI5 to pursue, or ever consider adapting MI5 to meet the increasing tempo of the intelligence war. He was not a man to think in that kind of way. He had just one simple aim, which he doggedly pursued throughout his career. He wanted to ingratiate the Service, and himself, with Whitehall. And that meant ensuring there were no mistakes, even at the cost of having no successes.

Hollis grew up in Somerset, where his father had been the Bishop of Taunton. After public school (Clifton) and Oxford, he traveled extensively in China before joining MI5 in the late 1930s. During the war he specialized in Communist affairs, as Assistant Director of F Branch. Under Sillitoe, Hollis was promoted to Director of C Branch, which gave him responsibility for all forms of vetting and protective security, such as document classification and the installation of security systems on all government buildings. Hollis' service in C Branch accounted for the importance he accorded this work when he later became Director-General.

When Dick White succeeded Sillitoe as DG in 1953, he appointed Hollis as his Deputy. On the face of it, it was a sensible appointment. While Dick did the thinking and the planning, Hollis would provide the solid administrative skills which Dick often lacked. Hollis, during the time I knew him as Deputy, never struck me as an ambitious man. He had already risen beyond his expectations, and seemed happy to serve out the rest of his career as Dick White's hatchet man and confidant. The only notable item of information commonly known about this excessively secretive man was his long-standing affair with his secretary, an ambitious girl who, when Dick White suddenly left for MI6, moved into the Director-General's office with a good deal more enthusiasm than Roger Hollis. Hollis, I suspect, always knew his limitations, and, once appointed, sought to cover them by relying on the rigid exercise of authority. The inevitable result was a quick sapping of whatever goodwill people held for him in the early days of his command.

Hollis took over at a time of unprecedented collapse in relations between the various British Intelligence Services. There had always been tensions between MI5 and MI6, dating back to the earliest years. But they had emerged from World War II as partners for the first time in a coordinated intelligence bureaucracy, along with the newly formed GCHQ, which was responsible for all forms of communications and signals intelligence. (For an account of this see *Secret Service* by Christopher Andrew.) But within ten years this close and effective relationship had almost entirely disintegrated. MI6 were deeply hostile to MI5 as a result of what they saw as unjustified attempts by MI5 to meddle in the Philby affair. Moreover, the entire organization viewed Eden's appointment of Dick White in place of Sinclair as a mortal insult.

The most serious lack of liaison was undoubtedly that between MI5 and GCHQ. During the war MI5 worked extremely closely with its own signals intelligence organization, the Radio Security Service (RSS) on the Double Cross System. The RSS intercepted and broke the ciphers used by the German Intelligence Service, the Abwehr, enabling MI5 to arrest incoming German spies as they landed in Britain. RSS was run by MI6 for MI5. B Branch then supervised the screening of these agents. Those who were prepared to cooperate with the British were turned and began feeding false radio reports back to the Germans. Those who refused were executed. But the success of any disinformation operation depends on being able to monitor how far your enemy accepts the disinformation you are feeding him. Through the RSS wireless interceptions and the break into German Armed Forces ciphers, ENIGMA, the Twenty Committee running the Double Cross operation knew precisely how much influence their deception plays were having on German military policy.

In the postwar period MI5, stripped of their wartime intellectual élite, showed scant interest in maintaining the signals intelligence connection. They had, in any case, lost formal control of RSS early on in the war to MI6. But the most powerful impediment was GCHQ, who jealously guarded their monopoly over all forms of signals and communications intelligence. By the time I joined MI5 full-time in 1955, liaison at the working level with GCHQ had dwindled to a meeting once every six months between a single MI5 officer and a higher clerical officer from GCHQ. In February 1956 I attended one of these meetings for the first time. The experience was shattering. Neither individual seemed to appreciate that in the Cold War, as in World War II, GCHQ had a vital role to play in assisting MI5 in its main task of counterespionage. Nor did they seem to realize that, as MI5 technology advanced, there might be ways in which MI5 could help GCHQ. I began with a list of suggestions, one of which was checking whether the Russians were listening to Watcher radios. but Bill Collins, the GCHQ representative, seemed utterly thrown by this positive approach to committee work.

"I shall have to take a bit of guidance on that one," he would say, or "I really don't think we've got the time to spare for that sort of thing."

I complained to Cumming, but he too seemed uninterested.

"It's their turf. Best leave it to them."

The MI5 officer in charge of liaison with GCHQ was Freddie Beith, an energetic agent runner working for D Branch. His father was Welsh and his mother Spanish, which gave him a fervent love of rugby and a volatile Latin temperament. He was a fluent German speaker and during the war he had been involved in the Double Cross System, running double agents in Portugal and Spain. Beith's liaison with GCHQ stemmed from Operation HALT, which he controlled. HALT began in the early 1950s when GCHQ asked MI5 if they could help obtain intelligence about diplomatic ciphers being used in London. Beith ran HALT by asking any agent D Branch recruited inside an embassy to try to obtain access to the cipher room. GCHQ hoped that one of Beith's agents might be able to steal some of the waste cipher tape, which they could then use to attack the cipher.

Beith threw himself enthusiastically into the task, but it was virtually impossible. Cipher rooms in most embassies, especially Soviet Bloc ones, were by far the most restricted areas in the compounds, and the chances of infiltrating an agent into them was remote. Nevertheless, Beith did achieve one outstanding success in Operation HALT, when he recruited an agent who worked inside the Czech Embassy who had access to the keys to the main cipher safe. Working to Leslie Jagger's commands, the agent took a plasticine imprint of the key. It was a high-grade Chubb, but by using high-quality plasticine and a micrometer to measure the indentations with exceptional accuracy, Jagger was able to make a copy which fitted the safe. The agent successfully opened the safe and copied the incoming code pads before they were used to encipher the Czech diplomatic cipher. For six months GCHQ read the traffic. Then suddenly the codes were changed, and the agent, inexplicably, was sacked.

Since then Beith had had no success. When I joined, I could see that there were ways MI5 could help the HALT program using technical devices rather than agents. But Beith was, by his own admission, not a technical man, and found it difficult to follow my arguments. But since he was the only officer allowed to liaise with GCHQ, I had to strike out on my own if my ideas were to get a decent hearing. In the end I took Freddie out for a drink one night and asked him if he would be offended if I made an appointment to go down to GCHQ headquarters at Cheltenham and see things for myself.

"Not at all, old man," said Freddie cheerfully, "you go right ahead. All this radio lark is a bit over my head. The human vices are more my territory."

I made an appointment to see an old friend of mine from the Navy, Freddie Butler, who worked on GCHQ senior management. I explained to Butler that I felt the whole system of MI5/GCHQ liaison needed a complete rethink. Butler arranged for me to bypass Bill Collins, and meet the top GCHQ cryptanalysts, Hugh Alexander and Hugh Denham.

Alexander ran GCHQ's H Division, which handled cryptanalysts, ably assisted by the quiet, studious Denham, who eventually succeeded him in the 1960s. Alexander joined Bletchley Park, GCHQ's prewar forerunner, at the outbreak of the war and, along with Alan Turing and Gordon Welchman, was primarily responsible for breaking the Enigma codes. After the war Turing went to Manchester University to design computers and tragically died by his own hand after being hounded over his homosexuality. Welchman went to work on advanced computers in the USA. Alexander, alone of the three, stayed to pursue a peacetime career in GCHQ. He was a brilliant international chess player, as well as codebreaker. Despite the intellectual demands of both work and hobby, Alexander remained on the outside a calm, reassuring tweed-clad figure. Yet I am sure that the mental contortions in the end told on him. He spent all his life quietly in the country, he never smoked or drank, and then suddenly died of cancer at a comparatively early age.

I told Alexander and Denham that I had been indoctrinated into Operation HALT, and felt MI5 could contribute much more to GCHQ's work. I explained that tremendous advances had been made in MI5 technology since the Brundrett Committee was formed in 1949, especially in the field of new microphones. It might be possible, I suggested, to obtain HALT intelligence through technical means, rather than using agents, a method which at the present moment seemed destined for continual failure.

"I'm not sure I know myself precisely how we can help until I have had a chance to experiment," I continued, "but I am sure that with the new high-sensitivity microphones we have, it must be possible to get something out of a cipher machine. They have to be reset every morning by the cipher clerk. Suppose we could pick up the sound of the new settings being made. Wouldn't that help?"

The two cryptanalysts were supportive as I made my somewhat nervous presentation. They were clearly curious to see for themselves the first example of an unknown species in the Intelligence menagerie—an MI5 scientist.

"Any help is gratefully received in this department," said Alexander. "After all, compared to your organization, we are the new boys. We haven't even finished building yet."

He gestured to the window. In the distance a team of building workers was installing another line of Nissen huts behind the main GCHQ complex.

"Our problem is that our theories are running beyond our computer capacity," he went on.

"So many ciphers today we could crack—we know how to crack them. We just don't have sufficiently powerful computers to do the job. We'll get them soon, of course, but in the meantime, any help may give us a shortcut."

I asked Alexander what the prime target was at the moment. He looked a little uneasy at my direct question.

"Well, of course, we have many targets, they're constantly updated. JIC demands, that sort of thing."

"Yes," I persisted, "but if you had to single one out as the most important today, which would you choose?"

Alexander shifted in his seat and exchanged glances with Denham.

"I should say it was the Gyppies," said Alexander finally. "The Foreign Office have been pushing us for months to get something on the cipher. We've got little bits, but it's only now and again, and never current stuff."

It was spring 1956. Tension between Britain and Egypt was fast mounting, as Nasser began the moves which led to the Suez Crisis later that year.

"What machine do they use?"

"It's a Hagelin," replied Denham, referring to a cipher machine manufactured by the Swiss firm Crypto AG and much favored in the 1950s by Third World countries.

I arranged to borrow one of GCHQ's sample Hagelins, and took it back up to London in the boot of my car. I set the machine up with Leslie Jagger in an MI5 safe house in Regent's Park and began experiments to see if my theory was practical.

This Hagelin was a keyboard machine, with tape containing the enciphered message leading out from one side. The principle of the machine was simple. Seven rotating wheels, powered by switched currents, automatically substituted mechanically produced random figures for whatever was typed into the machine. Every morning the cipher clerk operating a Hagelin inside an embassy reset the wheels before beginning transmissions. If any of our microphones could detect the sounds of these new settings being made, I felt sure that GCHQ would be able to use them to determine what is known as the "core position" of the machine, and from there be in a position to attack the cipher. Alexander and Denham explained to me that if we could get the settings of three, possibly four, wheels of the machine, they would have broken the cipher.

I installed a series of high-sensitivity microphones at various distances from the Hagelin, as well as a probe microphone in the wall behind it. Each microphone was connected in turn to an oscilloscope, so that the sounds it recorded were translated into visual readings. Leslie Jagger rigged up a film camera to record the oscilloscope screen. I opened the lid of the Hagelin and carefully reset the wheels, making a note of the old and new settings. The machine began to clatter as it enciphered a stream of dummy traffic. I sent the results down to Denham in Cheltenham for his comments.

As soon as we got the films developed, I could see that the oscilloscope readings were firm enough to provide some clue to the Hagelin machine settings. They also produced evidence of the setting of at least three wheels out of seven. I decided to make further experiments with SATYR equipment, which gave a far less sensitive sound. We did detect movements on the wheels, but it was highly corrupt. I sent the findings down to Cheltenham by courier. The next day Denham telephoned on the scrambled line.

"They're marvelous, Peter," he said. I could tell he was excited.

The distortion from the scramble made him sound positively lunatic.

"The acoustic microphones are best. We can get two, maybe even three wheels out using those readings. The radio one isn't so good, but I think, given time, we might be able to make something of it."

The line fractured under a haze of static.

"When can we go into action with it?" he shouted down the line.

"As soon as you've got the ministerial clearance," I replied.

The next day GCHQ sent Ray Frawley from the planning staff up to London. Frawley was an astute, practical man, bridging the gap between the intellectual brilliance of Alexander and Denham and the administrative demands of a huge sprawling organization like GCHQ. Frawley was a radical atheist who believed that one day mankind would be coupled directly to computers. Dangerous irrationality would be banished forever. It was rather a childlike ideal for a man to hold in the grim years of the Cold War, but he and I became close colleagues even though I remained at heart an irrationalist, believing in the sudden burst of inspiration or intuition to solve a problem.

As soon as Winterborn, Frawley, and I sat down to plan the operation against the Egyptians we realized that the best way was the simplest way. I checked with the Post Office Investigations Unit and obtained a complete list of all telephone installations in the Embassy. There appeared to be one either inside or very close to the cipher complex, so we decided to install Special Facilities on the telephone and use the microphone to capture the sounds of the cipher machine. The Post Office faulted the phone system and we waited for the Egyptians to call in the Post Office. I arranged to go in myself, disguised as an engineer, with the man who would install the SF device on the telephone receiver. I wanted the chance to look over the room in case any waste cipher material was lying around.

The next morning I met the Post Office team over at St. Paul's and we drove over to the Embassy in their van. The security was tight at the Embassy door and we were escorted from room to room. The cipher room was in an annex, the Hagelin clattering away inside. Three cipher clerks were busy operating the telex machines and processing the diplomatic cables. I looked carefully for any signs of spare tape waste, but the section seemed well organized and tidy. One of the clerks came out and engaged our escort in animated conversation. After a while he went back in and turned the machines off. When he reappeared he came over to me and gesticulated toward the telephone. He could speak no English, but through sign language I understood that he wanted me to move the telephone closer to his seat near the machine. Scarcely able to believe our luck, I began to extend the cable, slowly turning my back on him so that the engineer could slip the small washer into the receiver to modify it for SF. I placed the telephone back on top of his desk, not more than two feet from the Hagelin machine. The clerk tapped it, and grinned at me broadly. I grinned back, but somehow I felt we were not quite sharing the same joke.

I hurried back from the Egyptian Embassy to the seventh floor to monitor the sounds from the receiver. It seemed at first to be an electronic haze, but after some fine tuning the clatter of the Hagelin was clearly audible. MI5 arranged a special link down to GCHQ, and every morning, as the clerk reset the machine, GCHQ's H Division calculated the new settings and read the cipher straight off, a process known as "leading the machine." The new technique of breaking ciphers by detecting intelligence about the machines through technical surveillance became known by the code word ENGULF. It was a vital breakthrough. The combined MI5/GCHQ operation enabled us to read the Egyptian cipher in the London Embassy throughout the Suez Crisis. The Egyptians used four different key ciphers worldwide, and by mounting operations against their embassies abroad using the same ENGULF technique, we were able to break into most of the other channels. The operation against the Egyptian cipher was a tremendous success for MI5. It came at a time when MI6 had conspicuously failed in their efforts to provide intelligence. Virtually their entire network in Egypt was rounded up and arrested on Nasser's instructions at an early stage in the crisis, and their only contribution was a bungled attempt to assassinate Nasser.

For Hollis, who had stepped into the Director-General's chair just as the Suez Crisis reached boiling point, the triumph could not have been better timed. It gave him a solid achievement in those crucial first few months. In the light of later events, I always thought it ironic that it was I who had given it to him.

The single most important intelligence which we derived from the cipher break was a continuous account of Egyptian/Soviet discussions in Moscow, details of which were relayed into the Egyptian Embassy in London direct from the Egyptian Ambassador in Moscow. The information from this channel convinced the Joint Intelligence Committee (JIC) that the Soviet Union were indeed serious in their threat to become involved in the Suez Crisis on the Egyptian side. One message was particularly influential. It detailed a meeting between the Soviet Foreign Minister and the Egyptian Ambassador in which the Russians outlined their intentions to mobilize aircraft in preparation for a confrontation with Britain. The panic provoked by this cable, which was handed straight to the JIC, did as much as anything to prompt Eden into withdrawal. Similarly, since all GCHQ product was shared with its American counterpart, the National Security Agency (NSA), the intelligence, I am sure, did play an important part in shaping American pressure on Britain to end the crisis.

Soon after the SF was installed inside the Egyptian Embassy we nearly lost the whole operation. The Russians, anxious to bestow client status on Egypt as the Suez Crisis deepened, sent a team of Russian sweepers to sanitize their London Embassy of any bugs or microphones. It was the sort of friendly gesture the Russians loved to bestow, enabling them to pick up useful intelligence for themselves at the same time. Our static observation post overlooking the entrance of the Egyptian Embassy detected the Russian sweepers as soon as they entered the building. I was called up to the seventh floor to monitor their progress in the cipher section. I listened helplessly as they entered the cipher room. They started with the fuse box and then began electronically sweeping the walls and ceilings with large instruments which looked like metal detectors. The microphone thumped ominously as a Russian hand picked up the telephone and began to unscrew the bottom. There was a muffled pause, and then the sound of the telephone being reassembled. Hugh Winterborn breathed a sigh of relief.

At the time we knew that the Russians had discovered the SF and would remove it if they found it, but they didn't! If the Russians knew about SF, which they did, and were so wary of it, for instance in the Russian Embassy, why had they overlooked it in the Egyptian Embassy? It would suit them not to alert us to the fact that they knew about SF, so that we would continue to use it. They could, after all, have sent intelligence via their own cipher circuit, Moscow-London, and handed the messenger over to the Egyptians in London. This would have been unbreakable. But I believe that there was another reason. The Russians wanted us to read the signals of their resolve in the Suez Crisis correctly. They did not want us to assume they were bluffing. The best way of ensuring we took their posture seriously would be if we obtained intelligence about it from an unimpeachable source, for instance from a secret cable. It was my first insight into the complexities of Soviet disinformation.

After the Suez Crisis had collapsed, I began to pester GCHQ again with suggestions of future cooperation. But they seemed to want relations to drift back to the languid state they were in before. And GCHQ, while happy to take the results of ENGULF, were unwilling to step up their help, in return, for MI5. In short, they did not mind MI5 working for them, so long as the arrangement was not reciprocal.

I felt that GCHQ had a major role to play in helping MI5 confront the Soviet espionage networks in the UK by tackling Soviet spy communications. The Russian Intelligence Service has always favored running really sensitive operations "illegally," using agents who operate entirely independently of the "legal" Embassy Intelligence Officers, communicating with Moscow Center by using their own radio transmitters. I felt sure that if we devoted effort to tracing and logging these transmissions we might get a break which could lead us right into the heart of the Soviet Intelligence apparatus. I wanted GCHQ to provide MI5 with the service that we had received from RSS during the war, of continuous monitoring of illegal radio broadcasts to and from the UK. It seemed to me to be straightforward common sense. But GCHQ were devoting a paltry one and a half radio positions to taking this traffic. It was a pathetic effort, and no amount of persuasion could make them devote more.

Shortly after the first ENGULF Operation against the Egyptian cipher I went to Canada to plan Operation DEW WORM. Toward the end of the trip Terry Guernsey, the head of RCMP Counterespionage, asked me to study an RCMP case which had recently ended in mysterious circumstances. During this review I ran across a detail which convinced me beyond any doubt that GCHQ had to be forced to change their mind. Guernsey showed me into a private room. Sitting on the table were three volumes of files marked KEYSTONE. The KEYSTONE case began in 1952, when a Russian entered Canada under a false name, intent on developing cover as an illegal agent for the KGB. In fact, his eventual destination was the USA, but the KGB often send their illegals into Canada first to establish for themselves a secure "legend," or false identity, before going across the border. But soon after the illegal, code-named Gideon by the RCMP, arrived in

Canada he fell in love with a woman. It was strictly against KGB rules, and it wasn't long before Gideon developed doubts about his mission.

Eventually Gideon was ordered by Moscow Center to make plans for his emigration to the USA. He managed to persuade them that it was too risky, and the emigration plan was aborted. Instead he was appointed the KGB illegal resident in Canada, responsible for running other illegal agents throughout Canada. The new responsibilities were arduous. Gideon, who was in any case a lazy man, had to spend long hours receiving messages on his radio, and to make endless journeys throughout Canada to collect intelligence. Gideon began to fall behind on his schedule, and was bullied by his controllers. Finally he decided to confess everything to his lover and together they decided to approach the RCMP.

Terry Guernsey, with his instinctive feel for the importance of the case, immediately decided to run Gideon on as a double agent, rather than accept him as a defector. The decision seemed well justified when Gideon was given control of an illegal agent working for the Russians on the Canadian Avro Arrow Aircraft program. For a year the RCMP monitored Gideon as if he were a laboratory specimen. The workings of Soviet illegals were virtually unknown in the West. Guernsey carefully logged the tradecraft the Russians used for Gideon, the way he was instructed to gather intelligence, the dead letter drops he used; most important of all, the RCMP monitored all his coded radio communications.

Everything went well until the summer of 1955, when suddenly Gideon was recalled to Russia by his controller for extensive debriefing. After initial hesitation, the double agent decided to make the journey. He never returned. The RCMP waited for months and years for a sign that Gideon had survived. But they heard nothing. After a while, transmissions from Moscow to Canada began again on Gideon's cipher, suggesting that a replacement agent had arrived, but months of fruitless searching by the

RCMP failed to uncover him. The case, which had promised so much in its early stages, was finally closed down by a weary Guernsey. He was convinced that something had gone wrong in the case, but it was impossible to put a finger on what it was, still less investigate it. Bennett, his assistant, was convinced that Gideon had fallen under Russian control and that the case was being run on to deceive the RCMP.

Reading the files it was clear to me the case bore all the hallmarks of Russian interference from an early stage, but beyond that there was little I could suggest. Then I came across a detail in the case which struck a chord. Although Gideon was an illegal agent, the Russians still required him to make very occasional meetings with a legal diplomat from the Russian Embassy, almost certainly the Illegal Support Officer. The probable reason for these meetings was that the KGB believed Gideon to be such a difficult and unreliable agent that only face-to-face meetings would ensure he was kept on the right track. During one of these meetings, which was covered by the RCMP, a furious row broke out between Gideon and his controller. Gideon had been missing his broadcasts from Moscow and failing to respond. Gideon claimed that he had been unable to receive the messages on his radio set because the atmospheric conditions were too bad. His KGB controller was totally unimpressed. He handed Gideon a detailed list of the transmissions he had missed, complete with their times and duration, and made it clear he knew Gideon was lying. Although the Russian never specifically mentioned the fact, it was obvious to me that he must have been monitoring the broadcasts sent to Gideon inside the Embassy.

I read the report of this meeting again and again to ensure that I had understood it correctly. As I turned the crisp pages of the file I began to realize that if the KGB Illegal Support Officer in Canada monitored transmissions from Moscow, it was at least possible that his counterpart in the London Embassy would be doing the same thing. If GCHQ could be persuaded to operate flat out against the Embassy we might be able to identify the transmissions, even perhaps tentatively identify the Illegal Support Officer by correlating his movements against those of the transmissions. Once we had done that we would be in a position to put him under total surveillance in an effort to catch him meeting his agents.

As soon as I got back to London I raised the whole question with GCHQ. They listened patiently as I pleaded for more effort. But I was operating on my own. There was no great enthusiasm for the venture inside MI5 either, and although GCHQ did agree to provide a few more positions to monitor broadcasts, it was nothing like enough. I suggested GCHQ mount a major effort to locate receivers inside the Russian Embassy, just as I had earlier done over the Watcher radios. But once again my request was deemed impractical and the subject was soon lost in the dense undergrowth of the intelligence bureaucracy.

The situation remained at stalemate until 1958, when a new case emerged which totally changed the relationship between MI5 and GCHQ. In the process it pitched Hollis into his first internal crisis and introduced him to a subject which was to dog him throughout his career.

I was sitting in my office poring over the plans for a microphone installation when I received a summons to Hollis' office. He was sitting in the armchair at one end of the conference table, holding several loose files. He looked gray and drawn. He motioned me to the chair opposite.

"I would like you to help me with a problem," he said, handing me a file. I read the contents swiftly. They were source reports from an agent named Frantisek Tisler, who evidently worked as a cipher clerk in the Czech Embassy in Washington. Tisler was being run by the FBI, and they had handed on to MI5 items of his intelligence which related to British security. Tisler claimed he had gone back to Czechoslovakia in the summer of 1957 and met by chance an old friend, Colonel Pribyl, who at the time was also on leave from his posting to London as the Military Attaché. They had got drunk and Pribyl told Tisler that he was running an important spy in Britain, a man named Linney, who was designing simulators for use in a guided-missile project for the RAF. It had not taken long for MI5 to locate the spy. Attached to the Tisler source report was a copy of Linney's Personal File entry in the MI5 Registry. He was a senior engineer working in the Miles Aircraft Development Laboratory at Shoreham in Sussex, where he had total access to the operational and performance details of the missiles.

"I don't see the problem, sir. Why don't we place him under surveillance, and arrest him when he next makes a meet with Pribyl?"

"This is the problem," said Hollis grimly, handing me an additional sheet of paper.

It was a letter to Hollis from J. Edgar Hoover, the Director of the FBI, typed on Hoover's personal italicized typewriter. The letter outlined another, much more serious allegation made by Tisler. He claimed that Pribyl had also told him that he knew the Russians had a spy inside MI5 in London. Pribyl had discovered this when he was debriefing an important agent in a car traveling through the streets of London. He became aware that he was being followed by a vehicle, which he presumed to be an MI5 Watcher car, and took evasive action to throw the car off. Anxious to ensure that the identity of his agent had not been blown, he decided to contact his Russian opposite number, Colonel Rogov, for help. Rogov told him that it would take a day or two to check, but eventually he was able to reassure Pribyl that although a Watcher car had followed him, it had given up the chase, as they believed he was just giving a driving lesson to a colleague. Rogov also told him that he should be aware of the fact that the MI5 Watcher service had recently changed tactics, and instead of openly tailing diplomats as soon as they left their embassies, they were picking them up on the bridges across the Thames, where countersurveillance was more difficult.

When I read the note, I knew immediately that what Pribyl had learned was genuine. The change in Watcher operations had indeed taken place, largely at my instigation as part of the attempted modernization program. The RCMP had been experimenting with this idea with some success. It was called Operation COVERPOINT. No wonder Hoover insisted that his letter be delivered by hand via his deputy Al Belmont, who refused to meet Hollis inside Leconfield House. The letter was handed over at a secret meeting in an MI5 safe house, and Belmont flew straight back to Washington incognito.

"You can see our problem, Peter," said Hollis. "If we make a move against Linney we may blow Tisler, and the FBI are anxious to retain him in place for as long as possible. And if we try to investigate the case by other means, we'll be blown by the Russian source inside the office. Whatever happens, we must get to the bottom of this penetration."

Hollis told me that for the past three months extensive investigations had been made in the Watcher and Watcher support services by Malcolm Cumming and Courtney Young, the head of Russian Counterespionage. It was felt that the leak must emanate from there, but nothing had been found. Finally, Hugh Winterborn had prevailed on Cumming to persuade Hollis to indoctrinate me.

"Have you got any ideas, Peter?"

"Only to string up those buggers down at Cheltenham, sir!"

"I'm sorry. I don't think I follow . . ."

I explained to Hollis that I had long held the theory that the Russians might be obtaining intelligence through intercepting and analyzing our Watcher communications.

"My father and I did something similar in 1940 on the Sussex Downs. We tracked signals, and managed to plot the course of the British Fleet as it went down the Channel. I'm sure that's how Rogov got the information. It would be relatively easy for them to do it, sir. Just cross-referencing direction-finding of our signals with the records of where their own people go would tell them a lot. Basically, they must always know when we're following them."

I told him that I had repeatedly pushed GCHQ to conduct thorough tests to check if receivers were operating inside the Embassy which correlated with our own communications.

"I'm afraid, sir, it was never high on their list of priorities."

Hollis groaned.

"But can you do it, Peter?"

"Yes, I think so. What we've got to do is try to trace emissions from the receiver."

The principle was simple. Every radio set contains a local oscillator to "beat down" the incoming signal into a fixed frequency which can be much more easily filtered. The local oscillator always radiates sound waves as it operates, and it is these emissions which reveal the presence of a receiver.

"You realize, of course, that this is SIGINT, sir. Strictly speaking we're not allowed to do that work. GCHQ will take my guts for garters when they find out . . ."

Hollis hunched forward thoughtfully, cupping his hands across his face. There was a painful silence.

"They would need to be told about the Tisler allegation, of course, if we brought them in," he said finally. It was the kind of Whitehall demarcation dispute Hollis understood only too well.

"I could always have a go," I ventured. "If you can square my back upstairs with Cheltenham when they find out, at least we'll know one way or the other about Tisler's source within a few months. If we go to GCHQ, it'll take a year or more to arrange."

Hollis began to collect the files together into a pile.

"I think that is the best course of action," said Hollis. "Keep me informed, won't you."

He looked at me squarely.

"Of course, Peter, you realize what a terrible thing this would be for the Service, don't you? If it's true, I mean. Quite apart from the effect in Washington. A lot of good work will have been wasted."

"Including my own," I thought bitterly, angry at myself for not pushing GCHQ harder over the Watcher radios.

As soon as I got back to my office I contacted Courtney Young and asked him to send over any intelligence reports he had detailing the types of electronic equipment the Russians had either bought in London or imported into the UK since the war. Working through the files of reports I was able to pull together a reasonably accurate picture of the range and types of receiver the Russians were using inside the Embassy. I calculated that the probable range of emissions from their local oscillators was around two hundred yards. That ruled out operating from our static observation posts. But A Branch had been busy for some time developing a radio transparent mobile van with plastic walls. I pressed Winterborn to finish the project as soon as possible. Within a fortnight the van was rigged with an internal power supply and two receivers, one to detect the emissions from the Russian local oscillator and the other to confirm the relationship to the A4 frequency.

One spring day in March 1958, my assistant Tony Sale and I took the van out for the first time. We obtained permission to drive it up Kensington Park Gardens in front of the Embassy as if we were making a delivery to a house nearby. Sale and I sat inside with fingers crossed, earphones clamped over our heads, watching for the faintest flicker out of the amplifier. We made two passes. Nothing happened. The static hummed. We drove across to the Consulate on Bayswater Road and made a pass along the front of the building. As we neared No. 5, the Russian premises, we began to pick up the faint flutterings of a signal. As I tuned the receiver we heard a whistle as it encountered the frequency of the local oscillator. We slowed in front of the front door and the signal gained rapidly in strength, tailing off as we made our way up toward Marble Arch. There was certainly a receiver operating inside the Embassy. But was it tuned to the Watcher frequency?

For the next few days we made a series of passes at various different times of the day and night to try to gain some idea of what times the receiver inside the Embassy was in use, and whether there was a correlation with Watcher radios. It looked as if it were going to be a long, laborious, imperfect task. Then, by coincidence, as we were making a pass in front of the Consulate, a Watcher car drove past the other way, transmitting on the Watcher frequency back to Watcher headquarters. Inside the van our receiver, which was tuned to the local oscillator inside the Consulate, squawked loudly.

"What the hell do you suppose that is?" I asked Tony Sale.

He looked up with a quizzical look on his face. Then the truth suddenly dawned on us both. The Watcher car had overloaded the input circuit going into the Embassy local oscillator. We had picked up the squawk of pain as its frequency distorted under the overload. In other words, it was proof that the receiver inside the Embassy was tuned to the Watcher frequency.

The implications of this new discovery, code-named RAFTER, were enormous. Not only could we prove beyond any doubt that the Russians were listening to our Watcher frequencies; we could also use the same technique to check the frequencies being listened to on any receiver we could detect inside the Embassy. All we needed was to radiate at the Embassy and listen for the local oscillator overload. The ideas I had nursed since reading the KEYSTONE files were finally in a position to be put into practice. Using RAFTER we could detect which broadcasts from Moscow to illegal agents in the field were being monitored inside the Embassy. RAFTER, potentially, offered us a shattering breakthrough into the hitherto secret world of Soviet illegal communications.

But while RAFTER proved our Watcher communications were a major source of intelligence for the Russians, there was still the question of the missile spy, Linney. Obviously, the investigation of Linney had to be done in such a way that our Watcher radios would not give away the operation. I decided that since radio silence was unrealistic, the best solution was to drastically change the frequencies of the vehicles assigned to the operation. I went to see the Ministry of Defense and asked to pirate one of their military frequencies, seventy megacycles away from the current Watcher frequency, so that the Linney vehicle transmissions would melt into the mass of other military traffic on nearby wavebands. But first I had to install new crystals in the Watcher radio sets so that they could operate on the new frequency. Every communications radio contains a crystal which controls the frequency at which it can receive or transmit. Rather than risk handling this through MI5 channels, I paid a private visit to my old colleague R. J. Kemp, the Marconi Chief of Research, and asked him if he would produce the new crystals for me in the Great Baddow Laboratory. I gave him a sample crystal so he could build one of the correct shape, and stressed that the new frequency should be held only by him and his immediate assistant. As an additional security precaution, we decided to mark the new crystals with an entirely different frequency from the actual one used. Within three weeks Kemp had produced enough crystals for a dozen transmitter and receiver units, and they were installed by the MI5 engineers who normally handled Watcher radios, so as not to raise suspicions.

The details of this operation, code-named LOVEBIRD, were severely restricted inside MI5. Only Winterborn and I knew the correct frequency and none of the new radios were used within range of the Soviet Embassy. The consulate receiver was continuously monitored using RAFTER, so that we could record how the Russians behaved during the operation against Linney. D Branch had already extensively analyzed the movements of Linney and his controller, Pribyl. By comparing the two, they discovered that their regular meet was on the South Downs near Brighton. We arranged with Special Branch to arrest Linney and Pribyl in the act of passing over secret material at their next rendezvous.

Linney was followed to the meeting place by Watchers equipped with the new frequency. He waited for two hours and then went back home. Pribyl, meanwhile, remained in London. Subsequently, Linney was interrogated, and unexpectedly confessed. He was sentenced to fourteen years imprisonment.

On the face of it, the case had been concluded successfully. But one detail troubled Winterborn, me, and the D Branch officers in charge of the case. Why had Pribyl missed his meeting? There were many reasons which might explain his failure to show up. He had not missed any other meets. But if he had learned of the planned arrest, it could not have been from the Watcher radios. It could only have been as a result of a tip-off from a human source.

I decided to conduct another experiment to resolve the question of whether or not there was a two-legged source operating for the Russians in conjunction with the intelligence they were obtaining from our Watcher radios. I arranged to change all Watcher radio crystals simultaneously while monitoring, by means of RAFTER, the Russian receiver, to see precisely what they did. It was impossible to make a change on this scale without recording the details inside Leconfield House, but I was confident that none of the Watchers would learn of the plan in advance.

We began RAFTER on the Russian receiver on a Monday morning, and chased Russian diplomats normally on our usual frequency. On the Tuesday and Wednesday we closed down all Watcher operations entirely while we switched the crystals. The Watcher force was told that the frequency was being moved up two megacycles, when in fact it was being moved down two instead. We opened up again on Thursday, chasing diplomats normally on our new frequency. We watched the RAFTER readings carefully for any signs that the Russians were searching for our new frequency in the area where we had indicated to the Watchers that it was being relocated. They did appear to check their equipment, as if it was faulty, but remained on the old frequency until the end of the week.

When we opened up again on Monday morning, everything had changed. A Russian receiver was already listening on the new frequency, but from inside the Embassy in Kensington Park Gardens, rather than from the Consulate. We were faced with another riddle. This new receiver had either searched for the new Watcher frequency the previous week, undetected by us as we concentrated on the Consulate, or the Russians had been tipped off to the new frequency during the weekend. It is unlikely that we would have missed the Russians lining up another receiver on the new frequency the previous week.

I discussed the whole investigation at length with Courtney Young, the head of Russian Counterespionage, and we decided to try one more experiment. If there was a human leak, we all assumed that it had to be among the Watcher or peripheral support services. So we decided to feed what is known in the business as a "barium meal," in other words, offer a bait of sufficiently important intelligence that the two-legged source, if he existed, would have to relay it back to the Russians.

Courtney Young had a double-agent case running. The agent, code-named Morrow, was in contact with the Russian Naval Attaché, Lieutenant Commander Lulakov. We decided on a straightforward plan. We briefed the Watchers about the Morrow case as if he were a genuine spy. They were told that the following day Special branch had been instructed to arrest Morrow in the process of handing over secret documents to Lulakov at a meeting in Hampstead. Full Watcher surveillance of both Morrow and Lulakov was required. If there was a traitor inside the Watcher service, we assumed he would alert the Russians, who would either fail to turn up for the meeting or try to warn Morrow in some way.

In fact, Lulakov turned up for the meeting right on schedule, got into Morrow's car in a quiet street near Hampstead Heath, and swiftly exchanged packages with him. Both men were promptly arrested. Lulakov established his diplomatic credentials and was released, and left the country soon afterward. The charges against Morrow were quietly dropped.

At first sight it seemed as if the Lulakov/Morrow affair proved there was no human penetration. But as with every previous experiment, there were worrying inconsistencies. Lulakov was known from previous surveillance to be infinitely patient in his preparations for meetings. On previous occasions he had taken hours to wend his way around London, by taxi, by bus, in and out of tubes and shops, before finally making his rendezvous with Morrow. On this occasion, he simply left his office, hailed a taxi, and went straight to the meeting. The handover even took place with the car's interior light on. To anyone with a close knowledge of the Russian Intelligence Service, these were inexplicable deviations from their normal tradecraft.

At the end of 1958 I composed a long report on the whole investigation into the Tisler allegations and sent it to Hollis. I went through the items Tisler had learned from his garrulous friend Colonel Pribyl and gave Hollis my assessment of how the Russians might have learned of them.

I was in no doubt from RAFTER, the technique of which I explained in the report at some length, that the monitoring of our Watcher communications was a major source of intelligence for the Russians about MI5, and had been so for a number of years. It definitely explained the Pribyl "driving test" story, and almost certainly accounted for the Russian knowledge of Operation COVERPOINT, although our traffic analysts doubted that the Russians would have been able to deduce that we were following Russians from the Thames bridges so quickly from monitoring our transmissions alone. But the failure of Pribyl to meet Linney, the speed with which the Russians detected the new Watcher radio frequency when we had it changed, and the Lulakov/Morrow affair were all open to varying interpretations. The balance of probability was that there was not a two-legged source in addition to the intelligence derived from monitoring our Watcher communications, but the possibility could not be ruled out.

A day or two after I submitted my report. Hollis summoned me to his office. He was hunched over a file, scratching at it with a fountain pen, when I entered the room. He did not look up. I stood there like an errant schoolboy while he continued to write. The room had not changed much since Dick White vacated it. There was an additional portrait on the wall reserved for venerable Directors-General. A single photograph of Hollis' son stood on his desk alongside the three telephones which connected him to the Cabinet Office, the Ministry of Defense, and MI6. But other than that there was no stamp of personality.

"Thank you for your report, Peter," said Hollis without looking up. He sounded a different man from when he had handed me the Tisler file earlier in the year. The crisis was clearly over. He was back in charge. He went on writing.

"I've written to Hoover outlining a broad explanation for Tisler's material about the MI5 spy," he went on, "but I think it would be a good idea if you went over and briefed their technical staff on the background to the case, RAFTER, that sort of thing. Make it a useful trip, won't you. Get around and make some friends."

He looked up and smiled suddenly.

"It's good to know we've been one step ahead of them this time. Well done."

He went back to his file, signaling that our brief encounter had ended. I turned to leave the room.

"Oh, and Peter . . ." he said as I reached the door, "stick to the technical findings, won't you. I don't think we should give Hoover the impression that anything is . . . unresolved."

"Of course not, sir. I quite understand."

I did not know it then, but the first stone had been cast.

8

THE CAPITOL BUILDING WAS A GIANT FRESCO OF PINK BLOSSOM, blue sky, and white marble, capped by a shining dome. I always loved visiting Washington, especially in the spring. London was so drab; MI5 so class-ridden and penny-pinching. Like many of the younger, postwar recruits to secret intelligence, I felt America was the great hope, the hub of the Western intelligence wheel. I welcomed her ascendancy with open arms.

Ironically, relations between British and American Intelligence in the late 1950s were at their lowest postwar ebb. Collaboration between MI6 and the CIA had virtually collapsed after the Suez Crisis, and they found themselves increasingly in conflict, not just in the Middle East but in the Far East and Africa as well. Many of the old guard in MI6 found it hard to accept that their wartime control of the Anglo-American intelligence relationship had long since given way to junior status.

Relations between MI5 and the CIA were fraught for different reasons. The CIA was a new organization, flexing its muscles on the world stage for the first time. Its aim was to collect intelligence, and although it was not supposed to operate in London without notifying MI5, both Hollis and Dick White believed the CIA flouted this understanding.

Behind all the difficulties lay the simmering distrust created by the defections of Burgess and Maclean, and the public clearance of Kim Philby. MI6 could never be seen in the same light again, particularly as so many senior officers had been close friends of Philby, whereas MI5's failure to apprehend any of the three made it seem, to American eyes, almost criminally incompetent. Only GCHQ, which had a formal charter of cooperation with its American counterpart, the National Security Agency (NSA), under the terms of the 1948 UKUSA agreement, remained relatively immune to the turbulent currents which battered the previously intimate wartime Anglo-American intelligence relationship.

When Hollis became Director-General he tried manfully to improve relations with the FBI. Hoover was famously anti-British, stemming from the war, when British Security Coordination (BSC) was set up in New York under Sir William Stephenson, the so-called Man Called Intrepid. BSC operated against the Germans in the United States, but Hoover vehemently opposed the idea of any organization, let alone one which was foreign controlled, having rights to collect intelligence on American soil. For years he refused to associate with Stephenson's staff. The Burgess and Maclean affair reinforced Hoover's prejudices, and for a while MI6 officers were not even allowed on FBI premises, and MI5 were prohibited access to any FBI intelligence source reports.

In 1956 Hollis visited Hoover in an attempt to improve relations, and persuade him to place MI5 on the distribution list again. Oddly enough, Hollis and Hoover got on rather well. They were both sensitive to any encroachments on their respective empires, yet Hollis had an essential weakness of character which enabled him to play the earnest supplicant to Hoover's blustering bully. Hoover, like many self-made Americans, had a strong streak of snobbery, and his gargantuan conceit was stroked by the sight of an English upper-class spymaster with his cap outstretched.

I became an important peace offering. Hollis claimed my appointment as MI5's first scientist was proof of his intention to modernize the Service and step up the fight against Soviet espionage. Following Hollis' visit, Hoover invited me to visit FBI headquarters to see the range of their technical equipment. I was very keen to make the trip, as I believed from my first day inside MI5 that the key to long-term success lay in restoring relations with the Americans, so that we could gain access to their technical resources. But my views were not popular. Delusions of Empire still ran strongly inside Leconfield House. Cumming, for instance, although Head of MI5's technical branch, never visited the United States, and saw no reason to do so.

My first impression of the FBI was the sheer scale of the technical resources at their disposal, far beyond anything MI5 could ever imagine. But for all their riches, I could not help feeling that they made poor use of them. They relied almost entirely on commercially available equipment, rather than developing their own. Their radios were standard Motorola equipment used in police cars and taxis, although they had an impressive microwave network which connected the various FBI stations across the USA. The one really interesting part of FBI technical work was the use they made of fingerprints in espionage investigations. There were no fingerprint records in the MI5 Registry, and I felt it was one area where the FBI's quasi-police identity gave it an advantage.

Dick Millen was the FBI officer who ran their technical research. Millen was a lawyer rather than a scientist by training, which limited his effectiveness, but he put on a splendid show. I was taken down to the firing range in the basement of FBI headquarters, and given a lesson in pistol-firing techniques. Millen proudly informed me that even "the old man himself," Hoover, regularly practiced his prowess. I was taken down to the FBI training depot on the Maryland coast, where an old American Indian taught FBI agents advanced gunslinging. He demonstrated his skills, shooting targets in mirrors, and firing over his shoulder at a Ping-Pong ball perched on the top of a water fountain. It was rugged, all-American stuff, and the FBI's roots in the lawlessness of 1930s America was never far from the surface. But

I somehow doubted that it had much to do with modern counter-espionage.

I did not relish the prospect of briefing the FBI on the Tisler affair. There was more than a hint, in the way Hoover had handled the case, that he hoped we would fail to resolve the suspicions about a spy inside MI5, so that he could use it as a pretext for recommending to the President that the intelligence exchange with Britain be terminated. I hoped that the previous visits Hollis and I had made would do something to smooth my path.

I was accompanied by Harry Stone, the MI5 liaison officer in Washington. Harry was as genial a soul as you could ever meet. He had once been an Irish international rugby player, and shared with Hollis a love of the golf course and an almost professional handicap. Everyone liked Harry, primarily because he saw his job as basically a social one, but he was unsuited in temperament and intellect for the modern age of satellite and computer intelligence which was dawning in Washington in the late 1950s.

Harry hated meeting Hoover, and took a simple approach when a confrontation could not be avoided.

"Take a tip from me, Peter, old chap, let him do the talking, don't interrupt for God's sakes, and remember to say 'Thank you very much, Mr. Hoover' when he's finished . . . I've booked us a nice table for lunch. We'll need it."

We swept through the archway at the front of the magnificent, triumphalist FBI mausoleum. We were met by Al Belmont, the head of FBI domestic intelligence, and his deputy, Bill Sullivan, who handled the Communist desk. (Sullivan was found dead in the mid-1970s while shooting duck in New England. He is thought to have been murdered.) Belmont was a tough, old-fashioned "G-Man," as FBI men were once known, who had been with the Bureau from its earliest times. Sullivan was the brains to Belmont's brawn (but Belmont was no fool); both believed in the virtues of the stiletto rather than the Magnum. Belmont had many enemies, but I always got along with him. Like me, he had suffered a difficult childhood. His father was shot in a street brawl, and his mother worked day and night to save enough to put him through law school. Hard work and unswerving loyalty to "the old man" brought him to the top of the FBI.

But for all the outward toughness, and the seniority of their positions, both men were cowed by Hoover. Such unswerving loyalty was, I felt, positively unnatural. Of course, they admired Hoover for his achievements in the early years, when he turned a corrupt and incompetent organization into an efficient and feared crime-fighting force. But everyone knew Hoover suffered from God disease, and it seemed odd to me that they never acknowledged the fact, even privately.

I discussed the Tisler affair and the technical implications of RAFTER with both men for most of the day, until it was time to meet Hoover. We trooped down a maze of corridors, past an endless procession of Identikit young FBI officers, well scrubbed, very fit, well suited, closely cropped, and vacant-looking. The FBI offices always reminded me of sanitary clinics. Antiseptic white tiles shone everywhere. Workmen were always busy, constantly repainting, cleaning, and polishing. The obsession with hygiene reeked of an unclean mind.

Hoover's room was the last of four interconnecting offices. Belmont knocked, and entered the room. Hoover stood behind his desk, dressed in a piercing blue suit. He was taller and slimmer than he appeared in photographs, with wrinkled flesh which hung off his face in small drapes. He greeted me with a firm and joyless handshake.

Belmont began to describe the reason for my visit, but Hoover cut him off sharply.

"I've read the report, Al. I want to hear Mr. Wright tell me about it."

Hoover fixed me with coal-black eyes, and I began to outline the discovery of RAFTER. Almost at once, he interrupted me.

"I gather your Service is now satisfied about the intelligence provided by our Czech source . . . ?"

I began to answer, but he swept me aside.

"Your security organizations enjoy many facilities here in Washington, Mr. Wright."

There was more than a hint of a threat in his voice.

"I have to advise the President of the United States when those facilities raise questions about our national security. I have to take a close personal interest in a case like this, particularly in view of the recent problems the United Kingdom has suffered in this area. I need to know I am on firm ground. Do I make myself clear?"

"Of course, sir, I understand perfectly . . ."

Harry Stone busily studied his shoelaces. Al Belmont and Bill Sullivan sat to one side of Hoover's desk, half hidden in shadow. I was on my own.

"I think you will find in my report . . ."

"My staff have digested your report, Mr. Wright. I am interested in the lessons you have learned."

Before I could answer, Hoover launched into a passionate diatribe about Western inadequacy in the face of the Communist onslaught. I agreed with many of the sentiments; it was just the manner of the telling that was objectionable. Inevitably the subject of Burgess and Maclean came up, Hoover sounding each syllable of their names with almost prurient venom.

"Now in the Bureau here, Mr. Wright, that sort of thing could not happen. My officers are thoroughly screened. There are lessons to be learned. Do I make myself clear?"

I nodded.

"Of course, Mr. Hoover," chimed Harry Stone.

Hoover fixed me with a sudden stare.

"Total vigilance, Mr. Wright. Total vigilance. The lights always burn here in Bureau headquarters."

He stood up abruptly, signaling the end of the meeting.

The day after my ordeal with Hoover, I lunched with James Angleton, the CIA Chief of Counterintelligence. We had met once before on my first trip to Washington in 1957, and I was struck then by his intensity. He had a razor-sharp mind and a determination to win the Cold War, not just to enjoy the fighting of it. Every nuance and complexity of his profession fascinated him, and he had a prodigious appetite for intrigue. I liked him, and he gave enough hints to encourage me into thinking we could do business together.

Angleton's star was fast rising in Washington in the late 1950s, particularly after he obtained the secret text of Khrushchev's denunciation of Stalin from his contacts in Israel. He was one of the original wartime OSS recruits, and was trained in the arts of counterespionage by Kim Philby at the old MI6 office in Ryder Street. The young Yale intellectual struck up an instant friendship with his pipe-smoking English tutor, and the relationship deepened when Philby was posted to Washington as Station Chief in 1949. Ironically it was Philby who first detected the obsession with conspiracy in the fledgling CIA Chief of Counterintelligence. Angleton quickly acquired a reputation among British Intelligence officers for his frequent attempts to manipulate to his own advantage the mutual hostility of MI5 and MI6.

I taxied over to Georgetown. I could see why so many Washington government officials lived there, with its elegant red brick houses, tree-lined streets, bookshops, and cafés. When I arrived at Harvey's, Angleton was already sitting at his table, a gaunt and consumptive figure, dressed in a gray suit, clutching a large Jack Daniel's in one hand and a cigarette in the other.

"How was Hoover?" he asked, as I joined him, with a voice like gravel being tossed onto a path.

"You're very well informed today, Jim," I responded.

His cadaverous features creased back into a smile, in stark contrast to his funereal clothing. I knew he was fishing. The CIA knew nothing about Tisler, or his allegation, and we had agreed to brief the FBI on RAFTER on the understanding that knowledge of it was strictly controlled.

"Just routine, you know, making friends with the Bureau. It's the vogue in London at the moment."

"It's a waste of time," he said. "You've been trying to get in with him since as far back as I can remember. He always tells us he can't stand the Brits."

I bristled slightly, although I knew that was his intention.

"Well, I can't say the Agency has been much friendlier."

"You've used up a lot of credit in Washington in the last ten years," said Angleton, pouring himself another drink.

"People like Hoover," he went on, "they look at Burgess and Maclean, and they look at the state of MI5, and they say 'What is the point?' "

He called the waiter over, and we ordered.

"You're off the mark, Jim," I said finally. "Things are changing. Ten years ago they would never have appointed me as a scientist. But I'm there now, and new people are coming in all the time."

"I went to an English public school," he said with heavy sarcasm. "I know the score with you guys."

"It's no good complaining about Burgess and Maclean all the time. That's all in the past. The world's a smaller place. We've got to start working together again."

I surprised myself with my sudden passion. Angleton remained motionless, wreathed in a halo of swirling tobacco smoke.

"You won't get any help from Hoover," he grunted, but made no offers of his own.

It was a long lunch. Angleton gave little away, but pumped me with questions with every drink. What about Philby? I told him straight that I thought he was a spy. Suez was still a raw nerve, even in 1959, but Angleton wanted to know every detail. He even asked me if I could get the MI5 file on Armand Hammer, the head of Occidental Petroleum, who inevitably came to the attention of Western Intelligence in view of his extensive business links in the Soviet Union. But I thought this was just a shade indelicate.

"We're friends, Jim, but not quite that close, yet!"

Around five I saw Angleton back to his car. It was a smart Mercedes. For all the gauntness of his persona, I soon learned, he cultivated expensive tastes with his share of the family National Cash Register Company fortune. Much to Angleton's annoyance, he discovered he had locked his keys inside, but I produced Leslie Jagger's lockpicking wire from my pocket and within half a minute had the door open.

"Not bad, Peter, not bad!" said Angleton, smiling broadly. He knew I had savored the moment.

"By the way," I said, "I am serious. If you won't help me in Washington, I'll find someone else who will."

"I'll see what I can do," he muttered, slipping behind the steering wheel. Without a sideways glance, he was gone.

In fact, despite the skepticism in Washington, important changes were taking place on the technical side of British Intelligence in the late 1950s. MI5 devoted a major effort to expanding its new techniques, RAFTER and ENGULF.

As a first step we placed the Soviet Embassy under continuous RAFTER surveillance. Hollis persuaded a reluctant Treasury to purchase, over and above the MI5 secret allocation, a house for MI5 in the middle of the cluster of Soviet diplomatic buildings. We installed RAFTER receivers in the loft and relayed the signals we detected inside the Embassy along cables laid inside a specially constructed tunnel which MI5 dug between the new house and one which we already used for visual surveillance in the next street. We installed a former wartime MI5 officer, Cyril Mills, the famous circus owner, in the house as a tenant. Mills operated his circus business from the house for many years, and every time we needed to deliver staff or equipment to the house, or remove debris from the tunnel, we used a garishly painted Mills Circus van. It was perfect cover, and the Russians never suspected a thing.

We were careful to use straight receivers for the RAFTER operations, each operating on a single megacycle frequency, so there were no local oscillators on our side, in case the Russians had themselves developed a form of RAFTER. The secret of the Mills house remained intact through the 1960s, until one night the alarm systems detected two Soviet diplomats climbing onto the roof. They broke a skylight, but before they could enter the roof space, the housekeeper frightened them off. Cyril Mills made a formal protest to the Soviet Embassy, but we assumed that the Russians had somehow or other detected our presence in the house.

Once the house was ready, I was able to put into operation the kind of experiment I had envisaged while reading the KEYSTONE files in Canada. The Embassy was systematically searched for signs that receivers inside were monitoring signals beamed out from Moscow to agents in Britain. These were high-frequency (HF) signals, whereas the Watcher radio transmissions were VHF. The Russians used large radio frequency amplifiers with the HF receivers, which made RAFTER much more difficult. But GCHQ developed more sophisticated equipment, and within six months we had successfully monitored four signals from Moscow which were being routinely monitored by the Soviets inside the Embassy.

The first signal we found was code-named GRUFF. We picked it up one Tuesday night at ten-thirty. The Morse signal came in loud and clear, and our receivers immediately detected the whine of a local oscillator as the Russians tuned to the same frequency. GCHQ analyzed GRUFF; it came from the Moscow area and followed a twice-weekly schedule. The cryptanalysts were quite certain the Morse contained genuine traffic. The Radiations Operations Committee decided to make a major effort to track the GRUFF signal down.

I approached Courtney Young, then the D1 (head of Russian Counterespionage) and asked him if he had any intelligence which might help us locate an illegal we believed to be currently operating in the UK and receiving radio transmissions from Moscow. He was astonished by my approach. He explained that D Branch had recently run a double-agent case which had convinced him that an illegal was operating in the London area. The double agent was a young male nurse who had once been in the CPGB. Some years later, he was approached and asked to work clandestinely for the Russians. The nurse was reluctant at first, but eventually his contact convinced him that he was not being asked to spy. All he had to do was post some letters and store the occasional suitcase. After a while the nurse became frightened and approached the police, and the case was routinely referred to MI5 by Special Branch.

Courtney Young doubled the agent back against the Russians, and for a short while they appeared to continue to accept him as genuine. The nurse lived in the Midlands, but he was asked to lease a flat in the Clapham area of South London in his own name. Then his controller instructed him to activate and service a number of dead letter boxes on Clapham Common, near the new flat. Courtney Young was sure that he was being trained up by the Russians as an illegal support agent—someone who assists the actual illegal agent by preparing his communications and accommodation before he moves into the area. But suddenly, all contact with the agent was cut, and he was given no further instructions. Either the entire operation had aborted or the illegal was already securely established in the area through other means.

It was a long shot, but it had to be at least a possibility that Courtney Young's illegal was the same person who was receiving the GRUFF signal from Moscow. The Radiations Operations Committee searched the Clapham area intensively for any further clues. We drove our radio-transparent RAFTER van over to Clapham, and made a base in the walled forecourt of the old air raid shelter which ran under the south side of Clapham Common. We took power from inside the shelter, and rigged up an aerial which I estimated would give us a range of about half a mile.

I sat with Tony Sale in the cold, poorly ventilated van, watching, waiting, listening. The GRUFF broadcast was due at 10 A.M., so we tuned our first receiver to GRUFF, and searched the nearby frequencies with our other receiver to see if we could detect any oscillator. In the second week, we got a "hit," a strange, owl-like hoot, modulated with the Morse from Moscow. Someone was listening to the GRUFF broadcast within half a mile of us. Tony Sale looked across at me, momentarily, the scent of prey in his nostrils. The tape recorders began to roll with a subdued click. We switched to battery power supply, and drove slowly down Clapham High Street toward the tube station, weaving our way through the traffic. The pubs were full. Daffodils were just appearing in the neat front gardens of the suburban houses along our route, those inside oblivious of the chase passing in front of their doors.

Tony Sale was monitoring the local oscillator signal, using its strength as a guide to its location. We knew GRUFF stayed up in the air for twenty minutes. We had seventeen left. As we reached the tube station the signal became fainter, so we doubled back toward Wandsworth, but again the signal dropped away. We went south, toward Balham, but this time the signal disappeared before we even left the Common.

There were six minutes to go. Barely a word had been spoken inside the van. We only had one direction left. GRUFF had to be sitting up to the north, somewhere in the crowded maze of Battersea back streets. Our special van lumbered into Latchmere Road. Frustration welled up inside me. I wanted to career around the corners, shout out for help through a loud hailer, set up roadblocks. All we could do was stare at the flickering dials, willing them to move up, and not down. But by the time we crossed

Wandsworth Road the signal was already trailing away, and shortly after that, Moscow signed off. GRUFF was gone. Tony Sale thumped the side of the van. I tore my headphones off, feeling drained and angry. How many more months might we sit in Clapham before we got as close again?

I lit my thirteenth cigarette of the day and tried to make sense of the previous twenty minutes. We had traveled in every direction. But the fact that the local oscillator signal got weaker each time we moved, proved beyond any doubt that we had genuinely detected another receiver besides our own. But it was located neither to the north nor south, not to east or west. Slowly the awful truth dawned on me. GRUFF must have been right on top of us, listening within yards of the air raid shelter. We drove back to our base, and searched the area. Behind a high wall at the back of us was a large wasteland car park. GRUFF must have been parked there in a car, or perhaps a van like ours.

Back at Leconfield House I printed out the tape recordings of the local oscillator on a sonargram. The sound waves modulated with a small mains ripple. But the wave form was not at mains frequency. It was similar to that produced by battery power packs used in cars and vans to produce alternating current. The coincidence was almost too painful to contemplate.

For the next six months the Radiations Operations Committee flooded Clapham with every spare man at our disposal. We listened in hundreds of locations. Officers scrutinized every street, searching for signs of a telltale aerial. Discreet inquiries were made of radio equipment suppliers. But all to no avail. And every Tuesday and Thursday night the GRUFF signal came through the ether from Moscow, mocking us as we searched.

As well as mobile RAFTER, we began, through ROC, to arrange airborne RAFTER. An RAF transport plane equipped with receivers similar to those in the van made regular sweeps across London. We thought that with the extra height we would be able to get a general idea of where receivers were operating in London.

Then, having located a signal to a specific area, we could flood it with mobile RAFTER vans.

We spent our first flight over the Soviet Embassy to check our equipment was working, and picked up their receivers immediately. We got a series of radio hits in the Finsbury Park area, and we flooded the locality, as we had in Clapham. But, like GRUFF, the agent remained undetected, comfortably camouflaged in the dense undergrowth of London's suburbs.

The RAFTER plane flights were a kind of agony. I spent night after night up in the indigo sky, listening to the signals coming in from Moscow, insulated from the deafening sound of the plane's propellers by headphones. Down below, somewhere amid the endless blinking lights of London, a spy was up in an attic, or out in a car, listening too. I knew it. I could hear him. But I had no way of knowing where he was, who he was, whether he worked alone or as part of a ring, and, most important of all, what Moscow was telling him. I was caught between knowledge and the unknown, in that special purgatory inhabited by counterespionage officers.

But although the RAFTER side did not immediately bear fruit, the ENGULF side, using technical means to break ciphers, soon proved enormously successful. Things really took off with a meeting in Cheltenham chaired by the GCHQ Assistant Director of Research, Josh Cooper, in 1957. Cooper realized the need for close coordination between all three Services if the new breakthrough was going to lead to further cipher-breaking success. He brought together for the first time the various interested parties— Hugh Alexander and Hugh Denham from GCHQ's H Division (Cryptanalysis); John Storer, the head of GCHQ's Scientific section responsible for Counter Clan in M Division; and Ray Frawley, me, and my opposite number in MI6, Pat O'Hanlon.

Apart from the Russians, the Egyptians still remained GCHQ's first priority. They used Hagelin machines in all their embassies, split into four groups, each group containing different cipher wheel settings. Providing we could get a break into any one machine, every machine in that group would be vulnerable. If we could obtain samples of any one machine, every machine in that group would be vulnerable. MI6 and GCHQ drew up a list of the Egyptian embassies worldwide, along with details of which machine group they belonged to. The committee then evaluated which embassy in each group presented the best possibility for a successful ENGULF operation, and I briefed the MI6 teams on how to plan the operations. Within a year we had broken into every Egyptian cipher group.

Although ENGULF made all classes of Hagelin machines vulnerable, these tended to be the preserve of Third World countries. Cooper hoped, by calling his meeting, to find ways of applying the ENGULF principles to more advanced cipher machines, which GCHQ lacked the computer power to attack. My approach was simple; we had to put operations into practice even if, on paper, they looked unlikely to yield results.

"We've got to approach the problem scientifically," I said. "We don't know how far we can push these new breakthroughs, so we have to experiment. Even if things go wrong, we'll still learn things we didn't know before."

I had the germ of an idea. Any cipher machine, no matter how sophisticated, has to encipher the clear text of the message into a stream of random letters. In the 1950s, most advanced ciphers were produced by typing the clear text into a teleprinter, which connected into a separate cipher machine, and the enciphered text clattered out on the other side. The security of the whole system depended on thorough screening. If the cipher machine was not electromagnetically screened from the input machine carrying the clear text, echoes of the uncoded message might be carried along the output cables along with the enciphered message. With the right kind of amplifiers it was theoretically possible to separate the "ghosting" text out and read it off.

Of course, we had no way of knowing which countries screened their cipher rooms thoroughly, and which did not, and any operation along the lines I suggested would take up to two years to reach fruition. There was little point expending vast effort trying to break the Russian cipher, when we knew it was almost certain to be well protected. It was a question of picking targets which were important, and against which we stood some chance of success.

The French cipher stood out from all the rest as the most suitable target for further ENGULF experiments. Both MI6 and GCHQ were under pressure from the Foreign Office to provide intelligence about French intentions with regard to the pending British application to the European Economic Community. Moreover, GCHQ had studied the French system in London. They used two ciphers—a low-grade one which sent traffic along a telex line to the Quai d'Orsay, and a high-grade cipher for Ambassadorial communications which was generated independently of the cipher machine for additional security. Hugh Alexander's view was that the high-grade cipher was unbreakable, but that the low-grade one might be vulnerable to the type of attack I had outlined. Cooper gave his approval, and Operation STOCKADE began.

The first task in this joint MI5/GCHQ operation was to make a detailed technical reconnaissance of the layout of the French Embassy and, in particular, locate the area of the cipher room. I arranged to have the rating drawings sent over from the local council, and contacted the Post Office Research Unit. John Taylor had retired by this time, and had been replaced by H. T. Mitchell. Mitchell was paralyzed down one side as a result of a stroke, but although his speech was poor, his mind remained crystal clear. Mitchell gave me full diagrams of all telex and telephone cables going into and out of the Embassy, and by comparing these with the rating drawings we were able to establish the likely location of the cipher room.

We asked the Post Office to fault the telephones, and went in to make a visual inspection of the cipher room area. Unlike the Egyptians, the French security staff watched our every move, but we got the information we required. There was no telephone in the cipher room. It was tucked away down a corridor. The cipher and telex machines were in adjoining rooms, separated only by a plasterboard partition.

Using the Post Office charts, we traced the output cables back to the street, and into the footway box at the end of Albert Gate entrance to Hyde Park. I arranged with Mitchell to place a reasonably broad band radio frequency tap on the cable inside the footway box, and the captured signal was relayed into a special operations room we had taken in the Hyde Park Hotel. The hotel telephone system was faulted to give us cover while the cables were laid up through the hotel to the fourth-floor room we had commandeered. Special blocking condensers were placed on the circuit to ensure it was one-directional, and nothing could leak back into the Embassy to give away the operation. GCHQ routinely intercept radio and telex traffic coming in and out of every London embassy, from their premises in Palmer Street. We arranged for a line containing the French Embassy traffic to be fed from Palmer Street to our operations room in the Hyde Park Hotel. Using that line as a guide, we could check whether the signal we were getting on our radio frequency tap was the correct one.

The first morning we found the low-grade cipher and matched it with the Palmer Street traffic. The tap was connected to our own teleprinter, and the intercepted French cipher began to clatter out in front of us. It was clear straightaway that more than one signal was traveling down the cable we were tapping. It was just a matter of sitting down with a pencil and marking off the en clair text from the coded message, and the cipher could be read straight off.

I began to pick out a translation and found traces of another signal on the teleprinter. I checked on the sonargram to make sure I was not mistaken, and called over the GCHQ technicians.

The steady peaks and troughs of the signal blipped across the screen silently. The line from the low-grade cipher was strong, and its ghost was easily identifiable. But at each pinnacle there was a murmur as another signal crossed.

"Good God," the GCHQ man murmured, "that's the high-grade cipher as well! We must be picking it up through the partition wall."

I hastily contacted Palmer Street and got them to relay the high-grade cipher down the line so that we could compare the signals. The GCHQ technicians reset the amplifiers so that the traffic was sufficiently strong to print out, and using the Palmer Street feed as a guide, I marked off the en clair text. Within ten minutes I had a rough translation of a cable from the French Ambassador in London to President De Gaulle's private office.

For nearly three years, between 1960 and 1963, MI5 and GCHQ read the French high-grade cipher coming in and out of the French Embassy in London. Every move made by the French during our abortive attempt to enter the Common Market was monitored. The intelligence was avidly devoured by the Foreign Office, and verbatim copies of De Gaulle's cables were regularly passed to the Foreign Secretary in his red box.

In fact, STOCKADE was a graphic illustration of the limitations of intelligence. De Gaulle was determined to thwart our application, and no amount of high-grade intelligence could change that fact. We did pass on to the Americans details of French deliberation over their independent nuclear "Force de Frappe." It helped encourage American suspicions about De Gaulle, but the advantage we gained as a result was slight.

Nevertheless, STOCKADE was considered a major triumph inside the Foreign Office. I was sent for by the Permanent Secretary, who congratulated me on the ingenuity of the operation.

"Priceless material," he said, beaming, "simply priceless," leaving me in no doubt that "reading the Frog's traffic" was a worthy successor to Agincourt, the burning of Calais, and other ancient blows against the perfidious French.

9

THROUGHOUT THE LATE 1950s AND EARLY 1960s, BRITISH INTELLI-
gence built on the success of the ENGULF (Egyptian) and STOCK-
ADE (French) operations. GCHQ produced a mammoth list of all
their targets, divided into domestic and overseas priorities. MI5
gathered intelligence about each domestic embassy, including information about the location of the cipher room, and details of all
input and output cables, as well as an assessment of the feasibility
of ENGULF or STOCKADE operations against that particular target.
MI6 did the same thing overseas. They made detailed technical
reconnaissance of GCHQ's targets, although without the invaluable assistance of the Post Office they were forced to rely much
more on traditional agent running.

After STOCKADE, plans were laid to attack most European ciphers, starting with the Germans. But after much effort, we
aborted the operation, because their machines were too well
screened. But we successfully placed a probe microphone behind
the cipher machine in the Greek Embassy in London. This was a
particularly valuable target, since the Greeks were giving considerable support to Colonel Grivas, the Cypriot guerrilla leader,
during the Cyprus Emergency. We operated in the same way
against the Indonesian Embassy at the time of the Indonesian/
Malaysian confrontation, and read the cipher continuously
through the conflict.

For MI6, undoubtedly the sweetest ROC operation was against

the Russian cruiser *Ordzhonikidze*. Despite the "Buster" Crabbe fiasco in Portsmouth, MI6 remained determined to hunt the ship down. In 1959 she was due to dock in Stockholm, and MI6 learned that the Swedish Signals Intelligence Service were planning to operate against her. The local MI6 Station Chief suggested to the Swedes that Britain might be prepared to offer advanced technical assistance. Although nominally neutral, the Swedish SIGINT organization retained informal secret liaison with GCHQ, and they gratefully accepted the offer.

I went to Stockholm to plan an ENGULF operation against the *Ordzhonikidze* cipher machine in 1959. I scuttled along the dockyard in the dead of night, disguised as a Swedish engineer, accompanied by two burly local SIGINT technicians. We also had two GCHQ people with us. We ducked into a warehouse opposite the *Ordzhonikidze*, and made our way upstairs to the operations room, where the ENGULF equipment had been delivered. We were cooped up in that small room for five days. It was high summer, and the temperature outside was in the nineties. The warehouse had a corrugated-tin roof, and inside we sweltered, finding solace in the crates of extra-strong lager stacked in the refrigerator. Although we detected some cipher noises, we were never able to break the cipher, but MI6 and GCHQ judged the whole operation a success.

"Just like the Mounties," beamed Pat O'Hanlon, the MI6 representative at the next ROC meeting. "We always get our man!"

The scale of RAFTER and ENGULF operations dramatically escalated, as the results of the technical reconnaissances flowed in, and operations based on them proliferated. The Radiations Operations Committee (ROC), comprising the technical staffs of MI5, MI6, and GCHQ, was formed in 1960 to coordinate the workload. ROC met once a fortnight, either in Cheltenham or at Leconfield House. I was the first Chairman, although Ray Frawley, a crisp, self-disciplined GCHQ staff officer, took upon himself the task of controlling the flow of business, and he came, before long, to dominate ROC. He was an administrative genius, with none of the hidebound instincts of some of his peers in Cheltenham. He controlled the paperwork, provided the technical resources and the GCHQ operators to man each operation, as well as organizing getting the all-important ministerial clearances.

ROC was one of the most important committees in postwar British Intelligence. For ten years, until the new generation of computers came in at the end of the 1960s, ROC was crucial to much of the success of GCHQ's cryptanalytical effort. But of even greater importance was the way it began to break down the barriers which had previously separated MI5, MI6, and GCHQ at working level. As in the war, British Intelligence once again began to function as a coordinated unit, and as a result was much more successful.

On the research side, too, there were some important improvements in the late 1950s. When I joined MI5, the principal forum for scientific research was the Colemore Committee. Once a year MI6 invited a dozen top scientists from outside the secret world into a safe conference room in Carlton House Terrace. In return for a lavish lunch, MI6 expected these eminent persons to act as private scientific consultants to the Secret Services, providing guidance, ideas, and contacts. As soon as I attended my first Colemore Committee, I could see it was a waste of time. The morning discussion was desultory and unstructured and after a few pints, gins, and lashings of the best claret, few members of the Committee were in a fit state to turn their attention to complex scientific matters. After the day's labors, Peter Dixon took us all out on the town for more feeding and watering. I will always treasure the look on Dick White's face as, toward midnight, we ended up in a less than salubrious club in Soho, featuring what might politely be described as "an exotic cabaret." He smiled wanly at the red-faced gents around the table, but I could see that, like me, he felt it was not the answer to the deep-seated scientific problems facing MI5.

The Colemore committee had some use as a sounding board, but I realized from the start that MI5 needed a comprehensive in-house research program, properly staffed and properly funded. It seemed to me absurd that the Treasury should expend vast sums on weapons research at the stroke of a pen, and yet balk at the petty sums required by the Secret Services for modernization.

Shortly after I joined MI5 in 1955, I approached Sir Frederick Brundrett again, and asked him for help in obtaining the necessary resources. He was sympathetic, and suggested that my application would stand a better chance if I first made a thorough study of the current state of KGB scientific and technical advances and wrote a paper outlining the areas in which MI5 and MI6 were deficient.

I approached my opposite number in MI6, the H Tech 1, but it was soon obvious that they had very little intelligence on the subject. I decided to make a thorough study of the debriefings of all the German scientists, who, at the end of the war, had been forcibly taken back to the Soviet Union and made to work for a number of years in Soviet government laboratories as the price of freedom. These scientists were know as the Dragon Returnees, and their debriefings had provided much useful intelligence about the state of Soviet rocket, jet engine, and nuclear research, since this was the area which the Russians had been most anxious to develop.

I went over to the Defense Scientific Intelligence Unit (DSI), and asked General Strong if I could study the papers. I was shown into a room in Northumberland Avenue which contained all the dragon material, stacked up in dozens and dozens of dusty volumes. Incredibly, neither MI5 nor MI6 had bothered to process any of this material for its own use.

It took months for me to sort through the Dragon papers, but it was soon obvious that considerable numbers of the Dragon scientists had been detailed to work on technical intelligence research in laboratories on the outskirts of Moscow controlled by the KGB. I drew up a list of specific Dragon scientists I wanted to interview again. The original debriefings were mostly conducted by ordinary British or American military staff, who did not have scientific training or knowledge of the intelligence-collection field, and I was sure that I could obtain more information from them.

I traveled to Germany in 1957, and was met by MI5's senior German representative, Peter Domeisen, who had arranged facilities for the interviews at British Military Intelligence Headquarters in Hanover and München Gladbach. Most intelligence officers loved Germany in the 1950s. It was the front line, and the action was free and easy. But Domeisen was depressed by the growing tension in Berlin, and was convinced that it would not be long before the Russians made another attempt to swallow up the Western sector.

The interviews were difficult and depressing. Many of the scientists were desperate to ingratiate themselves with Britain and America. I stuck very closely to technical questioning, since the opinions they voiced were so obviously shaped to what they felt I wanted to hear. They had undeniably suffered during their incarceration in Moscow, and many of their friends had died. But it was impossible not to remember on whose side they had been working during the war.

One of the first scientists I interviewed was the man who had developed "the Thing," which Americans found in 1950 inside the Great Seal behind the American Ambassador's desk in their Moscow Embassy. It was gratifying to hear him confirm that the device worked exactly as I had predicted that Sunday afternoon in my Marconi Nissen hut. But as I questioned him, I felt again the dismay which ran through MI5 in 1950, when we realized the KGB was already deploying something which was barely at the research stage in Britain.

I submitted my paper on the Dragon scientists to MI6 in early 1958 for their approval. Brundrett advised me strongly to do this, because the application for resources would carry far greater weight if it came from both Services. When it was countersigned, it was placed before the Defense Research Policy Committee (DRPC), of which Brundrett was Chairman. The paper caused widespread consternation in the DRPC. Never before had KGB advances over the West been so clearly documented. I could prove that the KGB had obtained areas of major technical superiority through the efforts of the Dragon scientists, especially in the field of electronics and surveillance devices, including the use of infrared systems, which had put them in a commanding position since the late 1940s.

Largely through Brundrett's foresight, technical research was already under way through his own ad hoc committee, of which I had been a member since 1949. But we needed to formalize and expand this program of research with more staff and resources. I submitted a further joint MI5/MI6 paper, which came to be known as the Technics Document (which is what the KGB called it!), describing what progress needed to be made, and placing much greater emphasis on advanced electronics. As a result of the Dragon paper and the Technics Document, technical research for the intelligence services as a whole, but particularly for MI5, was given a much higher priority within Defense Research Policy. Unfortunately, the DRPC still vetoed the idea of specific resource allocations for the intelligence services, hoping to fill the gap by fitting our requirements into existing Defense Research programs. I still had to go cap in hand, but at least the climate was changing.

In 1958, as the Technics Document was being considered, Hollis introduced me to a man who did more than most to secure the modernization of MI5, Victor Rothschild. Rothschild worked inside MI5 during the war (he won the George Medal for opening bombs), and maintained close friendships with many of the senior officers, but especially with Dick White. At the time I met him, Rothschild was Head of Research for the Shell Oil Corporation, controlling more than thirty laboratories worldwide. Hollis told him of my appointment as an MI5 scientist, and Rothschild expressed an interest in meeting me. He invited me to supper at his elegant London flat in St. James's Place.

I doubt I have ever met a man who impressed me as much as Victor Rothschild. He is a brilliant scientist, a Fellow of the Royal Society, with expertise in botany and zoology, and a fascination for the structure of spermatozoa. But he had been much, much more than a scientist. His contacts, in politics, in intelligence, in banking, in the Civil Service, and abroad are legendary. There are few threads in the seamless robe of the British Establishment which have not passed at some time or other through the eye of the Rothschild needle.

Rothschild was fascinated by my plans for the scientific modernization of MI5, and offered me many suggestions of his own. I soon realized that he possessed an enormous appetite for the gossip and intrigue of the secret world, and we were soon swapping stories about some of the more bizarre colleagues he remembered from the war. We talked until late into the night, and I came away feeling for the first time that, with his backing, great achievements were possible.

Rothschild offered to put some of his Shell laboratories at MI5's disposal, and began work on a variety of technical developments, including a special grease which would protect equipment if it was buried underground for long periods. The grease was developed, and both **MI5 and MI6** used it extensively. Rothschild also suggested that I approach Sir William Cook, then the Deputy Head of the Atomic Weapons Research Establishment (AWRE), for resources. I knew Cook well, but Rothschild was a close friend, and his well-timed lobbying made my visit much easier.

Cook listened attentively as I outlined my requirements. The essence of my approach to counterespionage was to develop technical ways of attacking Soviet spy communications. Communications are the only vulnerable point in an agent's cover, because he has to send and receive messages to and from his controller. I explained to Cook that RAFTER already provided us with the most valuable weapon of all—an entrée into Russian radio communications—but that we urgently needed new techniques to attack their physical methods of communications as well, such as secret writing, microdots, and dead letter drops. Progress on these would vastly improve our chances of counterespionage success.

"Let's solve some of these right away," said Cook, picking up his telephone. He spoke to one of his senior scientists, Dr. Frank Morgan.

"Frank, I'm sending down someone to work with you on a new project. He'll explain when he arrives. You'll enjoy it—he's a man after your own heart."

With typical Cook generosity, he provided a team of two principal scientific officers, as well as junior staff and resources for the sole use of MI5. In all I had thirty people at AWRE, and for two years AWRE carried the entire cost, after which time the Defense Research Policy Committee agreed to continue the funding. Frank Morgan was the most valuable gift of all. He attacked the problems with zest and flair, and within those two years MI5 obtained results far beyond anything dreamed of in the USA.

The techniques of secret writing are the same the world over. First the spy writes his cover letter. Then he writes the secret message on top, using a special sheet of carbon paper treated with colorless chemical. Tiny particles of the chemical are transferred to the letter, which can then be developed by the recipient. Most developing agents make the chemical traces grow, so that the message becomes legible, and unless the correct agent is known, the message remains undetectable. But Morgan created a universal developing agent, using radioactivity, which transformed the possibilities of detection.

Microdots are another method of surreptitious communication between an agent in the field and his controller. Photographs are reduced down to microscopic size, so that they are practically invisible to the naked eye. Microdots are generally concealed under stamps, on top of punctuation marks in typewritten letters, or under the lips of envelopes. Morgan produced a process for detecting microdots using neutron activation.

A third method of spy communication, and one of the most common, is the dead letter drop. An agent leaves a package, for instance of exposed film, in an arranged place, and his controller collects it at a later stage, so that the two are never seen to meet. The KGB frequently gave their agents hollow containers which were specially treated, so that they could tell if the container had been surreptitiously opened. Morgan developed a soft X-ray technique which enabled us to inspect the interiors of suspect containers without tampering with them or fogging the unexposed film inside.

The last of Morgan's four programs was the development of a number of special X-ray methods for use against advanced combination safes. These were proving more than a match, even for Leslie Jagger, but the use of Morgan's X-ray device enabled the combination to be read off from outside, and gave MI5 potential access to every safe in Britain.

Despite the improvements on the technical and research side, MI5's counterespionage record remained lamentable in the 1950s. After Dick White became Director-General in 1953, he recognized the great deficiencies in this area. Most of the talented wartime Double Cross case officers had either left, retired, or moved, like Dick White, into senior management positions. Their replacements tended to be second-rate former colonial policemen with little or no experience of counterespionage, who found it hard to make the adjustment from the wartime superiority over the German Abwehr to the new war against a more skilled and more numerous Russian Intelligence Service. He formed a new counterespionage department, D Branch, and appointed me largely to provide them with scientific and technical advice. But improvements were slow to come. For some long time the D Branch staff resented my access to their secrets. They wallowed in their own technical ignorance. I remember one case officer saying, as I explained some technicality in terms of the Ohm's law:

"That's all right, Peter, old chap, I don't need to know about Ohm's law. I read Greats."

"Good God," I exploded, "every schoolboy learns about Ohm's law!"

The head of D Branch, Graham Mitchell, was a clever man, but he was weak. His policy was to cravenly copy the wartime Double Cross techniques, recruiting as many double agents as possible, and operating extensive networks of agents in the large Russian, Polish, and Czechoslovakian émigré communities. Every time MI5 were notified of or discovered a Russian approach to a student, businessman, or scientist, the recipient was encouraged to accept the approach, so that MI5 could monitor the case. He was convinced that eventually one of these double agents would be accepted by the Russians and taken into the heart of the illegal network.

The double-agent cases were a time-consuming charade. A favorite KGB trick was to give the double agent a parcel of money or hollow object (which at that stage we could inspect), and ask him to place it in a dead letter drop. D Branch was consumed every time this happened. Teams of Watchers were sent to stake out the drop for days on end, believing that the illegal would himself come to clear it. Often no one came to collect the packages at all or, if it was money, the KGB officer who originally handed it to the double agent would himself clear the drop. When I raised doubts about the double-agent policy, I was told solemnly that these were KGB training procedures, used to check if the agent was trustworthy. Patience would yield results.

The truth was that the Russians used double-agent cases to play with MI5, identify our case officers, disperse our effort, and decoy us from their real operations. The standard of MI5 tradecraft was appalling. KGB monitoring of our Watcher radios certainly gave away our presence on a large number of the double-agent cases. But the D Branch case officers were just as bad, rarely employing anything other than the most rudimentary counter-surveillance before meeting their agents. An entire department in the Foreign Office provided MI5 with "chicken feed," secret material given to double agents to pass on to the Russians as proof of their bona fides. The chicken feed consisted of wholly unbelievable faked secret documents about weapons we did not have, and policies we had no intention of pursuing. I raised the whole question of the chicken feed with D Branch, and pointed out that the material was bound to be spotted as suspect, and that only real secrets would convince the Russians. That, I was told, was quite out of the question.

The other main area of D Branch activity was in the émigré communities. The agent-running sections of D Branch ran extensive networks, and used agents in London to recruit others inside their host countries. This was a particularly attractive option for MI5. Emigrés were easy to recruit, and enabled MI5 to compete directly with MI6 in the production of Iron Curtain intelligence, much to their irritation. But in reality, by the early 1950s, these émigré rings were utterly penetrated by the KGB, or their allied Eastern European services, and as with the double-agent cases, served only to soak up our effort, and identify our agent runners.

MI5 were living in the past, copying the techniques of Double Cross, in an intelligence world which had changed enormously since the war. They lacked not only case officers with the requisite skills but, much more important, the codebreaking advantages MI5 had enjoyed over the Germans.

Throughout the 1950s, MI5 avoided confronting the most obvious counterespionage problem facing Britain at the time—the results of the 1930s Soviet infiltrations of the British Establishment. The extent of the recruitment of "Stalin's Englishmen" became apparent with the convictions of Alan Nunn May and Klaus Fuchs for nuclear espionage in the late 1940s, closely followed by the defection of Burgess and Maclean in 1951. It was obvious to anyone with access to the papers that the Russian Intelligence Services had capitalized on the widespread intellectual disillusionment among well-born British intellectuals of the 1930s, and succeeded in recruiting important agents, some of whom, at least, remained loyal to the Soviet cause after the war.

The defections of Burgess and Maclean traumatized MI5. Philby and Blunt also fell under suspicion, but faced with their adamant denials, the cases ran quickly into sand. The only remaining way forward was to launch a major, intensive program of research and investigation among the network of people who had been friendly with the two diplomats at Oxford and Cambridge. Such a policy entailed enormous difficulties. Most of those friendly with Burgess and Maclean were now rising to positions of considerable eminence, not just in the Intelligence Services but in the Civil Service as well. There was potential political embarrassment if such inquiries leaked at a time when all concerned were doing everything to suppress any information about the defections. Moreover, there was always the ghastly possibility that vigorous investigations might provoke further departures to Moscow, with incalculable consequences. No one was prepared to grasp the nettle and from 1954 onward all work virtually ceased, MI5 apparently believing that the new vetting procedures then being implemented were enough to protect the national security. It was like locking the chicken house door with the fox inside.

One man stood out against this policy of neglect. He was Arthur Martin, a former Army signals officer who joined MI5 soon after the war. Martin quickly proved himself a brilliant and intuitive case officer, handling in quick succession the Fuchs and Maclean investigations, ably assisted by Evelyn McBarnet, a young woman research officer, whose contribution to these cases has never been adequately acknowledged. Martin had one huge advantage in his approach to counterespionage work: he never attended a public school. Once it was known that a serious leakage of secrets had occurred at the British Embassy in Washington, the conventional view was to search for the culprit among the clerks, cleaners, and secretaries. But Martin realized at an early stage that the culprit was a senior diplomat. He doggedly pursued the investigation, and was only foiled when Maclean defected.

After the defections, Martin pressed the management of MI5 to sanction urgent inquiries into the whole complex network of Communist infiltrations of Cambridge in the 1930s. But his requests for permission to interview the numerous members of the Philby, Burgess, and Maclean social circles were mostly refused. For two years he struggled against this woeful policy, until finally he went to see the Director-General, Dick White, and told him that he intended to resign and take a job with the new Australian Security Intelligence Organization, ASIO.

White, who had a high regard for Martin's abilities, persuaded him to go to Malaya instead, as MI5's Security Liaison Officer, until the climate in D Branch was better. It was, at the time, a vital job, and Martin played a leading role in the successful counterinsurgency campaign in Malaya, but the consequences for counterespionage were disastrous. For most of the decade MI5's most talented, if temperamental, officer was missing.

When Hollis became Director-General in 1956, a new head of D Branch, Martin Furnival Jones, was appointed. Furnival Jones was a lawyer by training, who joined MI5 during the war. On the surface he seemed an orthodox, taciturn man, lacking flair and vigor. But Furnival Jones was easy to underestimate. He had an officer's gift for leadership, and a logical, ordered mind which was surprisingly open to new ideas. But most of all, he possessed a streak of determination, if not ruthlessness, which made him a superb head of counterespionage. He realized that the main problem facing MI5 was the sheer scale of Soviet Bloc intelligence activity in Britain. D1, for instance, had the task of monitoring and working against around 300 Russian intelligence officers. Its total staff was eleven, of whom four were secretaries. We were swamped, never knowing whether we were chasing spies or shadows.

One of his first decisions was to bring Arthur Martin back from the wilderness of Leconfield House, first as D2, in charge of Czech and Polish affairs, and then, in 1959, as D1, responsible for Soviet Counterespionage. Furnival Jones had great admiration for Arthur Martin's skills, and the strength of character to get the best out of him, despite his sometimes truculent manner. Arthur Martin moved quickly to restore D1's emphasis on active counterespionage investigation, and he instinctively grasped the importance of new techniques like RAFTER, having worked in signals intelligence during the war. For the first time, I found someone with seniority who listened sympathetically and acted on my ideas for change. We quickly became close friends. We formed a Resources Index in A Branch, recording anyone and anything which could be of use to MI5. Forms were sent around the office, asking for entries, and over a period of months we built up an index so that a case officer who required, for instance, a nurse, or a plumber, or access to a particular company's files, or a lock-up garage, could consult the index, rather than having to spend time obtaining the resource from scratch.

We made radical changes in the order-of-battle approach, bringing in Movements Analysis, an idea which Terry Guernsey, the RCMP head of counterespionage, first began. This involved logging all known movements of Soviet Embassy personnel to build up an overall picture of their activities. Through this, it was possible to gain important intelligence about the identities of likely KGB officers.

But the most radical changes were made in the Operations section, which was dominated by a brilliant agent runner and investigator, Michael McCaul. Martin and McCaul put the section on a war footing. Even though our forces were so much smaller than the Russians', we went on the offensive, changing our tactics, and aiming to disrupt the KGB, who were accustomed to the utter predictability of our approach. Some of the schemes were madcap, like the operation to pickpocket all known KGB officers on the streets of London, in the hope that scraps of intelligence might be gleaned. It didn't work, but it made the Russians feel they were under attack for the first time in years. Other changes were much more significant. The Soviet émigré networks, undoubtedly the most penetrated of all, were rolled up. The double-agent cases were run much more aggressively. Case officers accompanied double agents to meetings with their KGB controller, and warned the KGB man that if he was caught recruiting British nationals again, he would be reported to the Foreign Office and expelled. McCaul and his men began to make brazen attempts to recruit KGB men. We never succeeded, but the change of tactic was enough, we hoped, to sow the seeds of doubt in Kensington Park Gardens.

McCaul implemented these new tactics brilliantly. On one occasion, a technician who worked in a Royal Ordnance Factory, making a new Bofors shell, told MI5 that he had been approached by a KGB officer and asked to provide a sample of the new shell. McCaul arranged for a dummy shell to be made up and filled with sand so that it felt as if it were full of explosive. As soon as the double agent handed over the shell in a South London park, McCaul pounced from the bushes. He told the Russian that he was in serious trouble, and flagrantly in possession of a piece of Top Secret British military equipment. He would certainly be declared persona non grata. KGB officers feared expulsion. For one thing they lost the perks of overseas service, but more important, it represented a failure, and any failure automatically made them suspect in the eyes of their own counterintelligence officers. The KGB man began to shake uncontrollably, as McCaul con-

jured up visions of a burly London policeman carting the hapless
Russian off to some secret dungeon for a spot of torture.

"Don't shake the shell, for Christ's sake," he shouted, "you'll
trigger the fuse!"

The Russian dropped the shell to the ground and sprinted out
of the park as if pursued by the furies. The next day he was on the
plane home.

In fact, the Foreign Office was notoriously reluctant to give
support. Numerous times we sent forward recommendations to
expel Russians we caught recruiting or running agents, but the
Foreign Office Northern Department, responsible for Anglo-Soviet relations, more often than not vetoed our case. Occasionally I
attended these Northern Department meetings to give technical
briefings on what the particular Russian diplomat had been doing.
They always followed a set pattern. The MI6 contingent would
object to expulsion, fearing a reprisal in Moscow. Then the Foreign Office would weigh in with a sermon about the importance
of not disrupting pending arms control negotiations, or jeopardizing an imminent trade deal. Courtney Young turned to me on
one occasion as we emerged from the ornate committee room and
muttered:

"I've never seen such a hotbed of cold feet!"

The lack of Foreign Office support meant we had to rely on less
orthodox methods of warning off the Soviets. Around this time
we received a spate of reports from Watchers detailing approaches to them by Russians. One Watcher described how a
KGB officer came up to him in a pub and handed him an envelope containing a large quantity of money, and tried to talk him
into providing information about his MI5 work.

Michael McCaul decided that direct action was needed. He
telephoned the Chief KGB Resident in his office in the Soviet
Embassy, and asked for an appointment, using his cover name
Macauley, which was well known to the Russians. He strode into
the Embassy as bold as brass, and warned the Russians against

any further approaches to the Watchers, making dire threats of diplomatic interventions which, in reality, were unlikely ever to have been sanctioned. McCaul was highly amused by his trip into the lion's den. The Resident made him lavishly welcome and they took afternoon tea together under a giant aspidistra. The Russian doubted that any of his staff could be so indelicate as to engage in espionage on foreign soil, but agreed to look into the matter in case one of the staff had, perhaps, been a little overzealous.

"Perhaps the British Security authorities have made a mistake," he suggested. "The business has become so crowded these days. So many countries, so many embassies, so many diplomats. Sometimes it is difficult to be sure who is working for whom . . ."

There were no more approaches to the Watchers.

In the summer of 1959, just as things began to improve in D Branch, the Tisler case came alive again, clouding our minds with doubt and confusion. It began when the young male nurse, whose recruitment led to the chase for the GRUFF signal in Clapham, was suddenly reactivated. His Russian controller handed him a suitcase, and asked him to store it at home. Inside the suitcase was an old World War II radio set, which made us immediately suspect the whole thing was another game designed to lure us out of London. But we had no definite proof that the Russians knew we had turned the nurse, so we decided to follow it up. D1 placed continuous Watcher coverage on the nurse's house in the Midlands, and all Watcher activity closed down in London. I arranged for Watcher headquarters to continue to transmit notification of Russians and Czechoslovakians leaving Kensington Park Gardens, so they would think we were still following them.

Thirty-six hours after the Watchers left London, the Russian receiver monitoring their communications closed down. As soon as Tony Sale told me, I was highly suspicious, remembering the inconclusiveness of the previous tests after the Tisler affair. Six weeks later we returned to London convinced the suitcase was bogus, and I mounted a special RAFTER operation to check when the Russians reactivated their receiver.

No Russians were followed on the first Monday morning, and we opened up at 2:30 in the afternoon on a Czech diplomat. Within half an hour the Russian receiver was reactivated on the Watcher frequency. I took the RAFTER printouts to Furnival Jones and Hollis. Here, for the first time, was a firm indication that a human source existed inside MI5. Hollis and Furnival Jones were visibly shocked by the information. The recent Russian approaches to Watchers, which we thought had been terminated following McCaul's visit to the Embassy, confirmed Hollis in his view that, if a leak existed, it must be in the Watcher service. More barium-meal tests were done to try to locate the source, but nothing was found. As 1959 drew to a close there was a growing feeling among the few officers who knew about Tisler's allegation that the issue ought to be resolved once and for all, even if it meant more extensive investigations. In December I was called in by Hollis, who told me that he intended closing down the Watcher inquiries.

"I am sure our original Tisler conclusions were correct," he told me, "and I think we should let the matter lie."

He was courteous, but firm. I thought the time had come to bring the worries into the open.

"I do think, sir, we would be advised to widen our inquiries. The leak may be higher up in the Service."

Hollis made no obvious reaction.

"It's a very delicate issue, Peter," he replied smoothly. "It would have a terrible effect on morale in the service."

"Not necessarily, sir. I think you would find out that most officers would welcome something being done. After all, if we have a penetration, particularly one at a relatively high level, most people have been wasting their time."

"It's simply not practical," he replied, his tone hardening.

I pointed out that there was already an investigations section of

D1, which could quite easily accommodate the work. Hollis finally bridled.

"I am not prepared to debate the issue," he snapped, "and I simply cannot accept any course of action which would lead to the establishment of a privileged Gestapo in the office."

He scrawled "No further action" on the file and initialed it off, signaling our meeting was over. The cancer was left to grow.

10

"SNIPER SAYS THE RUSSIANS HAVE GOT TWO VERY IMPORTANT SPIES in Britain: one in British Intelligence, the other somewhere in the Navy."

It was April 1959, and a CIA officer, Harry Roman, was briefing a group of MI5 and MI6 officers, in the fourth-floor conference room of MI6's Broadway headquarters, about a high-grade defector. Sniper was an anonymous source who earlier in the year began sending letters to the CIA, written in German, detailing information about Polish and Soviet intelligence operations.

"He's almost certainly in the UB [the Polish Intelligence Service]," said Roman. "His German's odd, and the Polish stuff is Grade 1 from the inside."

Sniper (who was given the MI5 code name LAVINIA) christened his spies Lambda 1 and Lambda 2. There was little to go on with Lambda 2, beyond the fact that he served in Warsaw in 1952 and was blackmailed into espionage after the UB discovered his activities in the black market. Lambda 1, however, looked more hopeful. Sniper gave enough details in one of his letters to enable us to identify three MI6 documents he had seen.

The first was the "Watch List" for Poland, detailing Polish nationals the Warsaw MI6 station considered possible or desirable targets for recruitment approaches. The second document was the Polish section of the MI6 "R6," an annual report circulated to MI6 stations, summarizing, country by country and region by region, the straight intelligence received by MI6. The third document was a part of the "RB," the annual MI6 report circulated to stations abroad, detailing the latest MI6 scientific and technical research and operations.

Berlin and Warsaw were the most probable MI6 stations where the leak of this vital intelligence had taken place, and we drew up a list of the ten people at these stations who had access to all three documents. The records of all ten were investigated, and all were exonerated, including one named George Blake, a rising young MI6 officer who had played a key role in the Berlin Tunnel. Blake, MI5 and MI6 concluded, could not possibly be a spy. The best explanation for the leak, in the absence of any credible human candidate, was a burglary of an MI6 station safe in Brussels, which had taken place two years before. Unfortunately, there was no accurate record of the contents of the safe before the burglary. There was evidence that one, and possibly two, of the documents seen by Sniper had been in the safe, but no certainty that all three had been there. In spring 1960, when all ten MI6 officers had been cleared, MI5 and MI6 officially told the Americans that the burglary was the source of Sniper's Lambda 1.

In March 1960, Sniper suddenly sent further information about Lambda 2. His name was something like Huiton, and Sniper thought he had been taken over and run illegally by the Russians when he returned to London to work in Naval Intelligence. Only one man fitted Sniper's description: Harry Houghton, who was working in the Underwater Weapons Establishment at Portland, Dorset, and had served in Warsaw in 1952 before joining Naval Intelligence. When Houghton was checked in the MI5 Registry, D Branch found, to their consternation, that he was already listed. Some years before, Houghton's wife had approached the security officer at Portland and told him that her husband had deserted her for a girl who worked at the base. She had claimed that Houghton was meeting with foreigners, went regularly to London to meet a foreigner whom she could not identify, and had large amounts of money stored in a tin in the garden shed.

The security officer forwarded the report to the Admiralty Security Division, advising that it was probably a malicious accusation by a deserted wife. The Admiralty passed it on to MI5's C Branch, where it landed on the desk of a young officer named Duncum Wagh. He looked up Houghton in the Registry, found no entry, and concluded that the original security officer's assessment had been right. He decided to dismiss the allegation. He minuted the file to his C Branch section head, who sent a suitable reply to Portland, and the matter was put to rest.

Hollis and Furnival Jones (who was head of C Branch at the appropriate time) were desperately embarrassed by the revelation that Houghton was the likely spy. But there was little time for recrimination, as the case swiftly gathered momentum. The investigation was handled by the Polish section, D2, and they soon discovered that Houghton visited London once a month with his girlfriend, Ethel Gee. The Watchers were detailed to cover Houghton's July visit, and they saw him meet a man in the Waterloo Road, hand over a carrier bag, and receive an envelope in return. All attention immediately focused on the man Houghton had met. He was followed back to his car, a white Studebaker, and visually identified by the Watchers as a Polish intelligence officer stationed in London. But checks on the car registration number showed it to belong to a Canadian named Gordon Arnold Lonsdale, who ran a business leasing jukebox machines. The Watchers were sent around to the Polish Embassy to recheck on the Polish officer, and returned sheepishly, saying they had made a mistake.

Lonsdale was put under intensive surveillance. He had an office in Wardour Street, and a flat in the White House, near Regent's Park. Both were bugged, and visual observation posts established nearby. To all intents and purposes, he lived the life of a London playboy, traveling abroad frequently and pursuing a succession of glamorous girls attracted by his easy money and good looks.

Houghton and Gee next visited London at the beginning of August, and again met Lonsdale, this time in a café near the Old Vic theater. The Watchers monitored them closely, even slipping into a table next to them. Lonsdale told Houghton and Gee that there would be no meeting in September, as he was visiting the USA on business, but that he was confident he would return in time to meet them on the first Sunday in October. If he did not appear, someone else they knew would come in his place.

On August 27 Lonsdale was followed from his flat on the sixth floor of the White House to the Midland Bank in Great Portland Street, where he deposited a suitcase and a brown paper parcel. Shortly after, he disappeared. The DG approached the Chairman of the Midland Bank, and obtained permission to open Lonsdale's safety deposit box. On the evening of Monday, September 5, the suitcase and package were removed from the bank and taken over to the MI5 laboratory at St. Paul's. The contents were spread out on a trestle table and carefully examined by Hugh Winterborn and me. After years of trying, we had stumbled across the real thing—the complete toolbag of the professional spy. There was a Minox and a Praktina, specialist miniature cameras for document copying. The Minox contained an exposed film, which we developed and recopied before replacing in the camera. The photographs seemed innocuous enough: snaps of Lonsdale and a smiling woman taken in a city which, after considerable analysis, we concluded was probably Prague. There was also a book on how to learn typewriting, which I knew at once must be connected with secret writing. By shining a narrow beam of horizontal light along the edges of each page, I picked out the minute indentations, where Lonsdale had used the pages as a carbon for his invisible secret messages. The typewriting book was sent down to Dr. Frank Morgan at AWRE, and became invaluable in boosting his research program into new methods of detecting secret writing.

The most interesting object was a Ronson cigarette lighter set in a wooden bowl. We X-rayed the lighter using Morgan's method, which showed the base to be hollow, containing several small items. They were removed with a rubber suction cup and tweezers, and were found to be two sets of miniature one-time code pads, one of which was clearly in current use. There was also a list of map references on a folded piece of paper, based on the London map book used by our Watchers.

Ever since RAFTER began, I had studied everything I could find about Soviet clandestine radio communications, and as soon as I saw Lonsdale's cipher pads, I could identify them as Soviet issue. This was no Polish intelligence officer—this was a full-blown KGB operation. With Lonsdale in radio communication with Moscow, we knew that if we could copy his pads and trace his signals, we would be able to decrypt them as they came in. Unfortunately, there were in Lonsdale's suitcase no signal plans giving a schedule of when and at what frequency to listen to his broadcasts among the thousands of messages which were pouring out every week from Moscow. RAFTER gave us the vital breakthrough. We decided to set up in the flat next door to Lonsdale in the White House, and by using active RAFTER, we would be able to tell when and at what frequency he was listening to his receiver.

Copying the code pads without arousing Lonsdale's suspicions was much more difficult. Without access to each sheet of the pads we would be unable to decipher his traffic. I knew from the Radiations Operations Committee that the Swiss intelligence service had recently found an abandoned KGB one-time pad, so I arranged for MI6 to ask the Swiss if they would be prepared to allow us to borrow it. They agreed, and I drove out to London Airport to meet the RAF plane which flew it over specially for us. The Swiss pad was very similar to Lonsdale's; each edge was covered with a thin film of glue to hold the pages together. We took it apart, and analyzed the glue. It was non-Western, but the Post Office technicians were confident they could make some up.

We went into the bank again on the evening of Saturday, September 17, removed the suitcase, and took it to St. Paul's. The pads were delicately taken apart and each page individually photographed. Then the originals were placed in a specially made jig, which held them tightly together so we could recoat the edges with our newly made-up glue solution. In the early hours of Sunday morning, we took the suitcase back to the bank, and waited for Lonsdale to return.

A few days later, I received a call from Tony Sale. He sounded distinctly agitated.

"There's something you ought to see. Some of the LIONSBEARD recording . . ."

LIONSBEARD was the code name given to the continuous RAFTER operation on the Russian Embassy. I took a taxi to Kensington Park Gardens, and ducked into our safe house on the next street. Tony Sale met me in the hall, and handed over a sheet of the LIONSBEARD needle printout.

"Any idea what that is?" he asked, pointing to two sudden bursts of receiver activity inside the Embassy in September.

"What dates are these?"

"Seems to be September 6, which was a Tuesday, and the other one is last Sunday—that's the 18th," he replied.

"Good God," I gasped, "they're the dates of the bank operations!"

Watchers had been used lightly during both operations to remove Lonsdale's suitcase from the bank. With a mixture of panic and despair, I took the printouts back to Leconfield House, and tabulated the exact times the Russian receiver was operating against A4's records of Watcher operations. The LIONSBEARD readings matched the A4 records perfectly. The Russians must have guessed we were onto Lonsdale.

I called for all the LIONSBEARD records, going back two and a half years, and laboriously checked through them all to see if there were other examples where the Russians had used their receivers in the middle of a Saturday or a Monday night. There was not a single occasion, other than these two, where the Russians listened between the hours of midnight to 5 A.M.

I took the material to Furnival Jones, and we went straight up to Hollis' office. He took the news calmly, and agreed the evidence of a leak looked strong. He instructed Furnival Jones to begin another urgent investigation into the Watcher service, and in view of the fact that Lonsdale was almost certainly a KGB illegal, transferred control of the case from D2 (Czechs and Poles) to Arthur Martin in D1 (Soviet Counterespionage).

On the face of it, Lonsdale's departure abroad provided the best test as to whether our suspicions were well founded. We all agreed that if he stayed away, it would prove he knew we were onto him. If he came back, it would indicate we were in the clear. Lonsdale had told Houghton he would try to get back for their meeting on October 1. Tension began to rise inside Leconfield House, as Furnival Jones' Watcher investigations once more drew a blank. Houghton traveled to London, but no one turned up to meet him. Even Furnival Jones seemed visibly shaken as the days ticked by without any sign of Lonsdale. Then, on October 17, our observation post opposite Lonsdale's office in Wardour Street identified him entering the building. The doubt and suspicion, which had been growing in intensity, melted away as we threw our energies into the hunt.

Lonsdale soon picked up his old life, running his jukebox business, meeting Houghton, and dating a great variety of attractive girls. He was not due to repossess his flat in the White House until early November, but where he was staying was a mystery. Every night he left his offices in Wardour Street and headed westward. Arthur and I laid down strict controls on the Watcher operations after Lonsdale's return. We were determined there would be no more mistakes. Overt watching was prohibited, and strict radio silence was imposed on all operations. Jim Skardon exploded at this apparent intrusion into his empire. He was not indoctrinated for RAFTER, and could not understand why radios were prohibited. He complained to Furnival Jones but was told firmly that there were good reasons for the new policy.

Arthur and I realized it would be impossible to follow a trained and experienced intelligence officer like Lonsdale for any distance without alerting him to the fact, so we devised a new semistatic technique. Every night a team of Watchers picked him up and followed for a short distance, before peeling off. The next day Lonsdale was picked up by a new set of Watchers where the previous team had given up the chase, and followed another short distance, and so on, at successively increasing distance from his Wardour Street office. The whole operation took two weeks, and we even employed wives and volunteers from the office to supplement the Watcher staff so we never used the same faces twice. Eventually we tracked Lonsdale to 45 Cranleigh Gardens, Ruislip, in West London. Lonsdale was evidently staying with the occupants of the small house, Peter and Helen Kroger, a New Zealand couple who ran a small bookshop specializing in Americana antique books. We set up a static observation post in the house opposite, and waited, confident that none of the occupants knew of our presence.

In mid-November Lonsdale moved back into his flat in the White House, collecting his suitcase from the Midland Bank shortly beforehand. We immediately arranged for a GCHQ technician, Arthur Spencer, to move into the flat next door to begin our RAFTER operations. For the next three months Spencer scarcely set foot outside the tiny flat. We installed a noncontact tap on the mains supply feeding Lonsdale's receiver which was connected to a silent buzzer. The buzzer was worn as an earpiece by Spencer, so that even if Lonsdale used his radio set during the night, the buzzer would alert him. Whenever the buzzer sounded, Spencer tuned the RAFTER receivers, found the frequency Lonsdale was listening to, and alerted GCHQ Palmer Street. Palmer Street then relayed the signal down to GCHQ in Cheltenham. There, using our copy of Lonsdale's one-time pad, a GCHQ cryptanalyst named Bill Collins decrypted the message, and relayed it back up to London to Arthur and me in Leconfield House via an enciphered telex link.

The first time Lonsdale received a message, Bill Collins was unable to decipher it. There was no indicator group in the traffic. An indicator group is a group en clair, in other words a group from the one-time pad with no coded additive. The recipient uses this to position the message on the pad at the right place, so it can be deciphered. (After Lonsdale was arrested we discovered that the indicator group was in fact enciphered, using his real date of birth.)

Arthur and I began to wonder if, perhaps, Lonsdale realized his pads were compromised, and was using a new set brought back with him from abroad. The only thing we could do was burgle his flat and check inside the lighter again, to see if the pads had been used. Winterborn and I went in on a day when Lonsdale went to Suffolk for his jukebox business. It was a small flat, rather depressingly spartan, with barely space for more than a bed. We opened the lighter; the pads were still there, and new pages had been torn away, so they were obviously still in use. When I looked carefully I realized that Lonsdale had used more lines than were needed to encipher the message he had received from Moscow. When the message was stepped down the pad by the number of excess lines, the message read satisfactorily.

For the next two months we successfully monitored Lonsdale's biweekly messages from Moscow. Most of them concerned "the Shah," the KGB cryptonym for Houghton. Lonsdale was given specific instructions on how to handle him, which questions to ask, and what documents he should attempt to procure from Portland. But other messages were personal, containing family news about his wife and children back in Russia. They wanted him home after five years' undercover service.

On Monday, January 2, Hollis chaired a full review of the case. Arthur argued strongly that we should allow the case to run on. He felt instinctively that Lonsdale was too valuable an illegal to be running simply the one spy, Houghton. We still knew very little about the Krogers, and their house at 45 Cranleigh Gardens, beyond that fact that shortly after Lonsdale went to stay, high-grade Chubbs and window locks were fitted to the house, including the access to the roof. For all we knew, Lonsdale might be only one part of a much larger network. Furnival Jones and I supported Arthur, and Hollis agreed to approach the Admiralty (whose secrets Houghton was betraying) to ask permission to leave Houghton unmolested for a further three months. The Admiralty agreed, and Arthur decided to minimize any further risk by running the case on without any form of physical surveillance, relying simply on our interception of Lonsdale's radio traffic to lead us to further spies.

Two days later our plan was rudely shattered. A sealed message was delivered to Hollis by Cleve Cram, the CIA officer assigned to the American Embassy in London for liaison with MI5. The message warned MI5 that Sniper had informed the CIA that he intended defecting to the United States on the following day, January 5. Once again, we convened in Hollis' office. There was really only one course of action: Houghton, Lonsdale, and presumably also the Krogers would all be blown by the defection. We had to arrest them before they were withdrawn. Fortunately, Houghton was due for his January meeting with Lonsdale on the Saturday, January 7, and we also knew that Lonsdale was due to receive his radio message early that morning, so we would know if Moscow sent him a warning.

Arranging the arrests was a prodigious feat of logistics, and for the next three days I barely slept. Charles Elwell, Houghton's case officer, was sent to Portland, ready to search Houghton's

premises as soon as he was given word the arrests were successfully accomplished. Bill Collins came up from Cheltenham and
based himself in Palmer Street, ready to decrypt Lonsdale's message the instant it came through. The Special Branch were put on
standby outside Lonsdale's flat, ready to make an immediate arrest if the Moscow message sent him scurrying for cover.

On the Friday night Arthur and I gathered in the third-floor
operations room in Leconfield House, ready for the all-night vigil.
It was a small office, painted a ghastly Civil Service brown. It
could have been a prison cell. A metal-framed bed ran along one
wall. A small table stood in the middle. Cables trailed across the
floor in thick, tangled bunches. Telephones linked us to Special
Branch headquarters, to GCHQ, and to the DG, and a small
speaker relayed to us every sound inside Lonsdale's flat in the
White House.

Arthur sat hunched over the table, chain-smoking. Hugh
Winterborn was tense and excited, and said very little. Furnival
Jones was there too, with his shoes off, reclining on the bed in his
braces. Although he was the Director of D Branch, he felt a
strong loyalty to the troops, and was determined to see it through
with us. He even went to the pub in Shepherd's Market and
brought us back sandwiches. We drank Scotch through the small
hours, as the ashtrays filled up.

We listened as Lonsdale returned late from a carefree evening
on the town. He was with a girl. I discreetly muted the volume as
the sound of their passionate lovemaking filtered through to us.
When it was all quiet in the flat, I asked Arthur how long he
thought Lonsdale would serve in prison.

"Fifteen at least," he replied.

Hugh Winterborn looked troubled. He was a religious man,
and found no joy in the thought of a man's life ruined. I poured
myself another drink.

"I can't help thinking of his wife and kids . . ." I said lamely.
They knew what I meant. They had seen the intercepts of Lons-

dale's messages, as I had: the talk of home, and family hardships, and birthdays, and children who missed their father. Lonsdale, for all his professionalism, was a very human spy. Like many men away on business, he was homesick, and sought solace in the company of other women.

"It's not as if he's a traitor . . . not like Houghton. He's just doing his job like us."

"That's enough!" Furnival Jones flashed angrily from the bed. "He went into this with his eyes wide open. He could have come as a diplomat. He knew what the risks were. He deserves everything he gets!"

I stayed silent. But the thought was there inside us all. We had seen almost too much of Lonsdale over the past two months.

Toward morning Lonsdale woke the girl up, and persuaded her to leave. He said he had urgent business to attend to, which in a way was true. When she left we heard him pull out his radio set, and prepare his pads to receive the message from Moscow. The radio crackled for a few minutes, and Lonsdale's pencil scratched out the decrypt. We could tell there was no warning from the way he sauntered into the bathroom, singing jauntily to himself in Russian. A few minutes later the green telephone rang, and Bill Collins gave us the text of the message over a scrambled line. It was a routine report: more talk of the family, more news from home. There was no warning or alarm.

Special Branch were told to prepare to make the arrest as Lonsdale received his package from Houghton that afternoon. At five the Special Branch line rang.

"Last Act is finished!" said a voice. Last Act was Lonsdale's code name. His prison performance was about to begin.

Hugh Winterborn went straight over to the White House to search Lonsdale's flat, while Arthur and I waited for news of the Krogers' arrest. At seven, tired but elated, we drove out to Ruislip in my car. By the time we reached Cranleigh Gardens, the place was in chaos. Police were everywhere, searching the house almost at random. I tried to take control, but it was useless. Arthur vainly protested as a detective took out a plastic bag containing chemicals.

"Sorry, sir, I am afraid it's evidence," said the policeman. "It's a criminal matter now, and if you boys want to see it, you'll have to go through the channels . . ."

The police operation was led by Detective Superintendent George Smith of the Special Branch, a man renowned inside MI5 for his powers of self-promotion. Before the arrests, we stressed to Smith that we needed a forty-eight-hour blackout on any news about the arrests, so that we could monitor the next radio broadcast coming in from Moscow. But within hours word spread around Fleet Street that a major espionage ring had been smashed, and Smith began briefing selected reporters on the role he claimed to have played in the operation. The Moscow broadcast carried no traffic.

Despite the hamfisted search instituted by the police, it was obvious the house was packed full of espionage equipment. Two sets of different cipher pads were hidden in a cigarette lighter similar to the one used by Lonsdale. There were signal plans for three separate types of transmissions from Moscow, secret-writing material, and facilities to make microdots. Mrs. Kroger had even tried to destroy the contents of her handbag, containing details of meetings with spies, by flushing them down the toilet, but a vigilant woman PC stopped her. The most interesting find of all was a signal plan for special high-speed transmissions from Moscow. Hidden in a cookery jar we found a bottle of magnetic iron oxide used to print out the Morse from the high-speed message onto a tape, so that it could be read without being transferred onto a sophisticated tape recorder and slowed down. It was a new technique, and explained why we had failed to detect any transmissions to the Kroger house in the months before the arrests.

Toward the end of the evening the police began to vacate, leaving us to search among the debris, under the watchful eyes of a couple of young constables. We searched the house for nine days. On the last day we located the transmitter. It was hidden in a cavity under the kitchen floor, along with cameras and other radio equipment. Everything was carefully concealed in moisture-resistant sealed packages, and the whole system had obviously been designed to be stored for a considerable length of time.

On the following Wednesday, Hollis called everyone together in his office, and congratulated them on the triumph. The new D Branch team under Martin Furnival Jones and Arthur Martin had faced its stiffest test, and completely outplayed the Russians for the first time since Maxwell Knight smashed the Woolwich Arsenal Ring in 1938. The key to the Lonsdale success, as with the ENGULF and STOCKADE achievements, lay in the new techniques which I had worked to develop with GCHQ and AWRE. RAFTER and the X-raying and copying of the code pads enabled MI5 to run the case from a position of strength. I was intensely proud of the capture of the ring; for the first time I had played a major role in a counterespionage case, and shown the MI5 management what was possible. As a result, it was acknowledged that the workload passing through the Radiations Operations Committee was simply too great, and it was separated into two distinct units. Clan handled all clandestine operations against cipher targets here and abroad, while Counterclan controlled all the counterespionage side of ROC, such as RAFTER.

Hollis asked me to produce a detailed report, showing the role played in the Lonsdale case by the new techniques, with a view to encouraging similar approaches to counterespionage in the future. I began by paying a visit to the Old Bailey, where Lonsdale, the Krogers, Houghton, and Gee were on trial. The latter pair looked pasty-faced, flicking glances around the wood-paneled courtroom from the dock.

Lonsdale and the Krogers appeared completely unmoved by the proceedings. The Krogers occasionally whispered to each other, or passed notes; Lonsdale said nothing until the end, when he gave a short speech claiming the Krogers knew nothing about his activities. The Krogers were soon identified by the Americans as Morris and Lona Cohen, wanted by the FBI in connection with the Rosenberg nuclear espionage case. This was more than a little embarrassing for me; months before the arrests I saw Al Belmont of the FBI in Washington and briefed him on the progress of the case. He wondered then if the Krogers might turn out to be the Cohens. But I had not taken his offhand suggestion seriously, and failed to make a check. Lonsdale's identity proved much more of a mystery, and it was a year before we positively identified him as Konan Trofimovich Molodi, the son of a well-known Soviet scientist, and an experienced KGB officer who assumed the identity of Gordon Lonsdale, a long-deceased Finnish Canadian, in 1955.

I began my analysis of the Lonsdale case by asking GCHQ to provide me with files of any known Soviet espionage case, like the Lonsdale case, which had involved clandestine radio broadcasts. They produced leaflets, around a hundred in all, listing first the details of the agent under consideration—when he started and finished, what his targets were, which service he worked for, and so forth; they then produced a detailed summary of the agent's signal plans, and finally lists of the traffic that he received from the Soviet Union, including the numbers of messages, their group counts, details of the cipher systems used, and dates when they were changed.

I organized this mass of material into KGB and GRU categories, and secondly into types of agent—singletons, sleepers, illegal spies actively running one or more sources, and so forth. I found, to my astonishment, that changes in the radio traffic mirrored the different types of agent. For instance, by looking at the operational radio procedures, such as the types of call signs used, it was possible to tell whether the spy was of KGB or GRU origin. Similarly, by analyzing the group counts and the lengths of the messages, it was possible to tell what type of spy was receiving the traffic. For instance, the singleton sleeper received very little traffic, the GRU singleton not much more, while the KGB singleton received a quite considerable volume. The KGB illegal resident, the most important spy of all, always took the greatest amount of traffic—generally between five hundred and a thousand groups a month.

I soon began to realize that the Lonsdale case was utterly different from any other single case among the hundreds I had studied. No other case had so many different forms of communications, some duplicated, and some even triplicated. Yet there was apparently only one spy—Houghton—serviced by the whole Lonsdale/Kroger apparatus. He was an important spy, it was true, with access to vital details about British and American submarine-detection systems. But why involve the Krogers? Why not just use Lonsdale?

Even at face value, it seemed unlikely that other spies would not have been involved in the ring. The Krogers were located in Ruislip, close to American Air Force installations, while Lonsdale, we discovered, had earlier studied at the School of Oriental Studies, on a course commonly used by British military officers and MI6 trainees.

Lonsdale was certainly the illegal resident in Britain, and I carefully tabulated the communications he received from Moscow after he returned to Britain in October. He averaged 300–350 groups per month. Yet in each of the other illegal cases I studied, the resident received 500–1000 groups a month, and generally closer to the higher figure. Where was Lonsdale's missing traffic? Lonsdale had a three-character call sign which included a figure 1 if the broadcast carried traffic, and omitted the figure 1 if it was a dummy stream. I asked GCHQ whether they could find any messages similar in length to those we knew Lonsdale received after October, for the period preceding his departure in August. After considerable search GCHQ found what is called a "continuity," which went back six years, to roughly the time when Lonsdale entered Britain.

The average group count of this continuity was in the correct range of 500–1000 groups per month, and it ceased suddenly in August 1960, at the same time Lonsdale returned to Moscow. Of course, without the pads, we could not read any of the messages, but if, as seemed likely, this was Lonsdale's original traffic, the question remained: why did it suddenly diminish when he came back?

I turned my attention to the Krogers' communications. These were the most baffling of all. Most of them were for their use, yet they appeared not to be running any spies at all—merely acting as support for Lonsdale. But some of the communications were clearly being stored by the Krogers for Lonsdale. The pads, for instance, hidden like Lonsdale's in a cigarette lighter, were almost certainly his. I calculated up the group counts on the pads. The total was equivalent to the groups missing from Lonsdale's traffic after his return in October. The Russians, it seemed, had split Lonsdale's traffic when he came back, leaving the Shah (Houghton) on the channel we could read, and placing his other communications, perhaps containing his other spies, onto a secure channel with the Krogers, and using their high-speed transmitter, which we could not detect, to send any messages he needed.

This apparent alteration in radio procedures suggested that Lonsdale knew, in some way or other, that the messages he was receiving from Moscow in the White House, using the pads in the cigarette lighter, were compromised. But why, if he feared that, not just use new pads? And why, if the Russians feared he was compromised, was he sent back at all?

I began to analyze the sequence of events over the weekend of the arrests. I had arranged a continuous coverage of the Russian Embassy diplomatic transmitters from the Friday before the arrests until midday Monday. The last Embassy transmission took place at 11 A.M. on the Saturday morning, well before the arrests, and the next was not until 9 A.M. on the Monday morning. So, although a major espionage ring had been smashed, the Russians apparently made no contact at all with Moscow. This beggared belief, unless, of course, the Russians already knew we were about to lift them.

I checked what we knew about the movements of known Soviet intelligence officers in London over that weekend. On the Sunday night, when news of the arrests first broke on the television bulletins, an illegal KGB resident, Korovin, and Karpekov, the KGB legal deputy resident, had dinner together. Our probe microphones picked up every part of their conversation. We heard them listen to the news. They made no comment, and no move to contact the Embassy.

I then looked at the beginnings of the case, and made a shattering discovery which convinced me that the case must have been blown to the Russians. In its early stages, the case was handled by D2 when it was suspected that Lonsdale was Polish. Checking the records, I discovered that D2 were not indoctrinated into RAFTER. They had no knowledge of the fact that the Russians were listening to our Watcher radios, and therefore, prior to the case's being handed over to Arthur, they used Watchers on each of the seventeen occasions they followed Lonsdale in July and August.

Ever since the beginning of LIONSBEARD, all Watcher communications were recorded by MI5 and retained, so I organized a test. I gave Evelyn McBarnet, who worked with Arthur as a research officer, the tape of the Watcher communications during the day that D2 followed Lonsdale to the bank for the first time. I also gave her a London street map book, similar to that used by the Watchers, and asked her to mark out the route she thought the Watchers were following, based solely in listening to their radio communications. Evelyn McBarnet was not experienced in traffic analysis, and had no previous access to the case, but within three and a half hours, she reconstructed the movements flawlessly. If she could do it, the Russians, who had been analyzing our Watcher communications for years, were certainly capable of it too. They must have known from the beginning that we were onto Lonsdale.

By the time I was writing my report, Sniper was safely in a CIA safe house near Washington, where he identified himself as an officer in the Polish Intelligence Service named Michael Goleniewski. One fragment of his story seemed devastating in the context of the thread of ambiguity which ran through the Lonsdale case. He told the CIA that in the last week of July a senior officer in the UB told him the Russians knew there was a "pig" (a spy) in the organization. Goleniewski said that initially he was deputed to assist in the search for the spy, but eventually, by Christmas, realized that he himself was falling under suspicion, so he defected.

"The last week in July." I read the CIA account of Sniper's debriefing. It stared out at me from the page. It seemed so innocuous a phrase. I checked back. Lonsdale was first seen by MI5 meeting Houghton on July 2. He was positively identified on the 11th. We began following him on the 17th. Allow a week for the news to filter through to the Russians. A day to get across to the UB. That takes you to the last week in July!

The Lonsdale report was the most painful document I have ever written. My triumph turned to ashes before my eyes. I remember going off sailing in the Blackwater estuary, near my home in Essex, the weekend before submitting it in May 1961. The clouds scudded across the flat landscape, the wind filling my lungs and cleansing my mind of stress and turmoil. But no matter how I turned the boat, no matter how I adjusted the rigging, I came down to the same conclusion. They knew we were onto Lonsdale from the beginning; they had withdrawn him, and then sent him back. But why?

There was only one explanation which covered all the inconsistencies of the case: a leak. If the Russians possessed a source inside MI5, he would alert them to the existence of Sniper, which would explain why pressure mounted on Goleniewski from the last week in July, although of course, like us, the Russians could only guess at Sniper's real identity. That would explain why the Russians knew about our bank operations. Once they realized Lonsdale was blown, the Russians recalled him to Moscow, but once I alerted the management to the LIONSBEARD information, and Furnival Jones began his inquiries, the source would contact the Russians in a panic. The Russians were then faced with a simple choice. Lonsdale, or the MI5 source? The only way of forestalling the hunt inside MI5 was to send Lonsdale back, hoping that he could extract some last intelligence from Houghton before we rounded the ring up. But before sending him back the Russians took the precaution of switching his other spies to alternative secure communications via the Krogers. If this was the case, the Russians had severely misjudged the sophistication of the new D Branch team they were facing. Despite their advantages, we managed to outplay them and capture the Krogers, a significant additional part of the Soviet team. As for the source, it could only be one of a dozen people at the top of MI5. This was no Watcher, or peripheral source. The Russians would never sacrifice anyone as valuable as Lonsdale for a low-level source. The evidence of continuous interference throughout the Lonsdale case pointed much higher up—to the very summit of the organization.

I submitted my report to Furnival Jones in May 1961. He passed my report on to the Deputy Director-General, Graham Mitchell, with a short accompanying minute which read: "It should be borne in mind while reading this analysis, that the Lonsdale case was a personal triumph for Peter Wright."

For months I heard nothing. I sat in on dozens of meetings with Mitchell and Hollis on other matters, and often hung back, expecting that they would call me in to discuss what, at the very least, was a disturbing hypothesis. But there was nothing. No minute, no letter, no threats, no casual conversation. It was as if my report did not exist. Then, in October, I was finally called into Hollis' office late one afternoon. He was sitting at his desk, with Mitchell to one side.

"Graham will handle this discussion, Peter," said Hollis in a distant manner. He fingered my report with evident distaste. I turned to face Mitchell. He was sweating slightly, and avoided looking me in the eye.

"I have read your Lonsdale analysis," he began, "and I am bound to say that a lot of it passes over my head. In my experience espionage has always been a simple business . . ."

I bridled at this.

"I will gladly explain any of the anomalies I have detailed in the report, sir, if that will help. It is often difficult to put technical matters into lay language."

Mitchell went on as if I had made no interruption.

"The simple fact is, we have arrested and convicted three professional Russian illegals—these are the first Russian nationals to be brought before the courts here for generations. We arrest two immensely dangerous spies inside the country's most secret underwater research establishment. By any measure that is success. What on earth is the advantage to the Russians of allowing us to do that?"

I began to plod through the sections of my report, pointing up the ambiguities, and trying hard not to draw any conclusions. But Mitchell attacked every point. How did I know? How could I be sure? The bank could have been a coincidence. The Russians might not have known we were following Lonsdale, even if they did listen to our Watcher radios.

"They're not ten feet tall, you know, Peter!"

I went through the change in radio operations. But Mitchell brushed it aside, saying he was not a statistician.

"You say there were more spies, you speculate that the Russians deliberately sent Lonsdale back. But you've no proof, Peter, that it went like that."

"But you've got no proof, sir, that it went as you think it did. We are both hypothesizing."

"Ah yes," cut in Hollis, "but we have them in prison."

"But for how long, sir? We have faced this problem persistently since Tisler, and every time we leave it, it reemerges . . ."

"The Deputy and I have discussed this whole matter very carefully, and I think you know my feelings on that point."

"So, am I to understand there will be no further investigations?"

"That is correct, and I would be grateful if you could keep this matter entirely confidential. The Service has been tremendously boosted, as you have been too, Peter, by this case, and I should not like to see progress set back by more damaging speculation."

Hollis smiled at me oddly, and began to sharpen a pencil. I stood up abruptly, and left the room.

11

DESPITE THE SECRET DOUBTS EXPRESSED INSIDE MI5 ABOUT THE provenance of the Lonsdale case, it was hailed as an outstanding triumph in American intelligence circles. Never before had an illegal network been monitored while it ran, and there was great interest in Washington in the work of the Radiations Operations Committee, which had coordinated the new range of techniques.

The U.S. National Security Agency (NSA) had already learned about ROC's work from GCHQ, and was envious of the close relationships being forged between GCHQ and her sister clandestine services, MI5 and MI6. However bad the problems had been in Britain, they were infinitely worse in Washington. Hoover vehemently opposed the establishment of the CIA after the war, and maintained open hostility to it throughout the 1950s. The CIA, its senior ranks mostly comprising Ivy League graduates, treated the G-men with arrogant disdain. The only policy which united the two organizations was their shared determination to thwart the NSA wherever possible. They both claimed NSA was an insecure organization, an accusation given substance in 1959, when two NSA cryptanalysts defected to the Soviet Union, betraying vital secrets.

Louis Tordella was the deputy head of NSA, and effectively ran the organization for nearly twenty years. (The head of NSA is a rotating Armed Services appointment.) He knew full well that the real reason for FBI and CIA hostility was resentment at

NSA's control of SIGINT. He knew also that both organizations were busy challenging his monopoly. The CIA had begun its own ultra-secret SIGINT operations, STAFF D, and the FBI were also active in the same field. In May 1960, just as the Lonsdale case was getting under way, Al Belmont visited London, and I took him down to Cheltenham to demonstrate the ENGULF operation against the Egyptian cipher, and the STOCKADE operation against the French cipher, which was in its early stages. Belmont was much impressed, and immediately sent over Dick Millen, who spent a fortnight with me learning the technical details of STOCK-ADE. Shortly after, the FBI conducted a similar successful operation against the French Embassy cipher machine in Washington.

Tordella wanted desperately to develop a Radiations Operations Committee of his own with NSA in control, and in October 1961 he invited Hugh Alexander, Hugh Denham, Ray Frawley, and me to Washington, along with Christopher Phillpotts, the MI6 Station Chief, for a special conference to discuss the British cipher breakthroughs. He also invited the CIA and FBI in the hope that by listening to our descriptions of the work of ROC, they would appreciate the benefits of closer cooperation.

I realized from the start that this conference was a priceless opportunity for Britain's Secret Services to redeem themselves in the eyes of the entire American intelligence establishment. The CIA was, by 1961, the dominant intelligence voice in Washington, and although powerful figures there viewed the Anglo-American intelligence alliance as a sentimental luxury in an increasingly unsentimental Cold War, I was confident that if we could demonstrate to them at working level the technical advances made since 1956, we would convince them we were worth cultivating.

Hugh Alexander knew, as I did, that we were taking a gamble. There were no guarantees that the Americans would tell us anything in return at the conference; indeed, it was likely they would not. There were obviously security considerations, too. But the potential gains were enormous. At the very least, we could remove the shadow cast over Anglo-American intelligence relations since the Philby/Burgess/Maclean affair. More important than that, Hugh Alexander had plans for developing the cipher-breaking side of ROC, and I for developing the counterespionage side, which would be possible only with the resources and backing of the Americans. As with the development of the atomic bomb in World War II, we needed to persuade the Americans to fund our ideas into reality. In the long run we would gain the benefits, as the intelligence would flow back to us through the GCHQ/NSA exchange agreement.

The conference was held in specially swept rooms inside NSA headquarters at Fort Meade, Maryland—a vast glasshouse surrounded by electric wire fences, and topped with the tangled arthritic stems of hundreds of aerials and receiver dishes, linking it to the hundreds of NSA listening posts dotted around the world. Louis Tordella and his top cryptanalyst, Art Levinson, attended for NSA. The FBI sent Dick Millen and Lish Whitman; the CIA was represented by Jim Angleton and a bull-like man named Bill Harvey, who had recently returned to Washington to run Staff D, after running the Berlin Tunnel operation.

Harvey was already a living legend in the CIA for his hard drinking and his cowboy manners. He began his career handling Soviet counterespionage for the FBI, until Hoover sacked him for drunkenness. He promptly took his invaluable FBI knowledge and put it to work for the fledgling CIA, becoming along with Angleton one of the most influential American operators in the secret war against the KGB. Through most of the 1950s he served in Berlin, running agents, digging tunnels, and taking the battle to the Soviets wherever possible. For him, the Cold War was as real as if it had been hand-to-hand combat. But for all his crude aggression, Harvey was smart, with the nose for a spy. It was he who first fingered Philby in the USA after the defection of Burgess and Maclean. Harvey had amazing recall for the details of defections and cases decades before, and it was he, before anyone else, who put together the contradictory strands of the MI6 man's career. While others paused for doubt, Harvey pursued Philby with implacable vengeance, and the incident left him with a streak of vindictive anti-British sentiment.

The five-day conference began inauspiciously. Tordella was anxious for a free exchange of ideas, and discussed one or two laboratory experiments NSA was conducting into possible ways of breaking embassy ciphers in Washington, remarking pointedly that in view of the FBI charter, they were unable to go beyond the experimental stage. The CIA and FBI boys were uneasily silent, neither wanting to discuss technical developments in front of the other, or the NSA, or in the CIA's case, in front of us. Angleton took copious notes, while Harvey slumped in his chair with ill-concealed hostility, occasionally snoring loudly, particularly after lunch.

"The Company [the CIA] is here in a listening capacity only," he snapped on the first morning. "We do not discuss our secrets in open session!"

Things began to improve when I read a long paper describing the success of ENGULF against the Egyptians, and the advances we had made since then on the radio illumination of cipher noises and what could be achieved aurally, using our new range of microphones. I went on to give the details of STOCKADE, and at last discussion began to flow. Even Harvey shifted in his seat and began to listen.

On the third day Richard Helms, then CIA Director of Plans, took the chair for a discussion about ways in which these new techniques could be applied to Russian ciphers. I argued strongly that we had to predict the next generation of cipher machines the Russians would develop, and begin work immediately trying to crack them. The non-scientists present were skeptical, but I pointed out that we had done just this during the war at the Admiralty Research laboratory, when we predicted the new generation of German torpedoes and mines, and were able to counter them as soon as they came into operation. By the end of the discussion, NSA and GCHQ had committed themselves to begin work against the new Russian "Albatross"-class cipher machine.

Hugh Alexander was much more interested in the implications for cryptanalysis of the new generation of computers being developed in America. He was obsessed by the Ergonomic Theory, which held that the production of truly random numbers, even electronically as in a cipher machine, was a mathematical impossibility. Alexander believed that if sufficiently powerful computers could be developed, no code, no matter how well enciphered, would be safe, and for the next decade a vast joint research program began to investigate the whole area. (According to a 1986 report in the *Guardian* newspaper, advances in Ergonomic Theory since 1980 have revolutionized cryptanalysis in the way Alexander predicted.)

As expected, the CIA told us next to nothing about the state of their technical intelligence. They gave the impression that we were not to be trusted with their secrets, but we suspected there were probably other reasons for their reticence. Harvey's Staff D was almost certainly a department designed to bypass the terms of the UKUSA agreement, which specified the total exchange of SIGINT intelligence between NSA and GCHQ. If the Americans wanted to mount a cipher attack and did not wish to share the product with us, or if they wanted to operate against the UK, or a Commonwealth country, as we were sure they were doing, Staff D was the obvious place from which to do it.

Nevertheless, the conference was a milestone in Anglo-American intelligence relations. For the first time in a decade, all six intelligence services sat down and discussed at length how they could cooperate on a wide variety of problems. Major joint research programs were launched, particularly in the computer field, and we had taken a first step in breaking down the walls of mistrust.

Before I left London, Arthur Martin had arranged for me to brief the CIA on the technical side of the Lonsdale case and, in particular, the development of RAFTER. There was some embarrassment about this in Leconfield House because, although we had informed the FBI about RAFTER from the beginning, the CIA knew nothing. Hollis agreed that they should be indoctrinated fully as soon as the Lonsdale case was concluded, particularly since it had been their information from Sniper which led us to Lonsdale in the first place. The briefing was scheduled after the end of Tordella's conference, and it was held in one of the huge Nissen huts the CIA occupied temporarily next to the reflecting pool in the center of Washington while their Langley headquarters were under construction. I was taken through into a large conference room by Jim Angleton, and shown to a podium in front of at least two hundred CIA officers.

"Are you sure all these people are SIGINT indoctrinated?" I hissed at Angleton.

"Just tell the story, Peter, and let us handle the security," he replied. "There's a lot of people want to hear this!"

I stood up nervously and, fighting my stutter by speaking slowly and deliberately, began to describe the beginnings of the Lonsdale case. After an hour I turned to the blackboard to explain the complicated technical details of active RAFTER.

"Of course, from our point of view, RAFTER represents a major new counterespionage weapon. We are now in the position to establish without question when Soviet agents in the field are receiving clandestine broadcasts from Moscow, and moreover we can use it to detect the frequency of their transmissions . . ."

RAFTER was not well received. At first it was just a rustle; then I noticed a couple of people talking to each other in the front row with more than usual animation. I knew something was wrong when I caught sight of Harvey sitting on one side of the stage. He was leaning over in front of Angleton, gesticulating angrily in my direction.

"Are there any questions?" I asked, unsure of what was upsetting my audience.

"Yes!" yelled someone at the back. "When the hell did you say you developed this RAFTER?"

"Spring 1958."

"And what the hell date is it today . . . ?"

I stuttered, momentarily lost for words.

"I'll tell you," he shouted again, "it's 1961!"

"Hell of a way to run an alliance," yelled someone else.

I sat down sharply. People began to leave. There were no more questions.

Angleton and Harvey came up afterward. There was no disguising Harvey's rage.

"Look, Peter," said Jim, trying hard to be urbane, "this whole subject needs a lot more discussion, and I really don't feel it's appropriate to continue it in such a large forum. Bill and I would like you to have dinner with us tonight. We'll arrange somewhere secure, where we can talk."

He hustled me away before Harvey could speak.

Joe Burk, Angleton's technical man, collected me from my hotel that evening. He had little to say, and it looked to me as if those were his orders. We crossed the George Washington Bridge, passed Arlington cemetery, and drove out into the Virginia countryside.

"The new headquarters," said Burk, pointing to the right.

There was nothing but trees and gathering darkness.

After an hour's drive, we arrived at a detached timber-framed house set well back from the road. At the back was a large veranda with a table and chairs, completely enclosed with fly netting. It was a warm, humid, late-summer evening. The scent of pine and the sound of crickets floated down from the foothills of the Appalachians. Angleton came out on the veranda and greeted me coolly.

"Sorry about this afternoon," he said, but offered no explanation. We sat down at the table and were joined by the head of the CIA's West European Division. He was polite but nothing more. After a few minutes another car drew up at the front of the house with a squeal of brakes. Doors slammed, and I heard the sound of Bill Harvey's voice inside the house asking where we were. He threw back the flimsy metal mosquito door, and emerged onto the veranda clutching a bottle of Jack Daniel's. He had obviously been drinking.

"Now you limey bastard," he roared, smashing the bottle down on the table, "let's have the truth about this case!"

I knew immediately it was a setup. Normally Harry Stone would accompany me to any serious discussion of MI5 business, but he was in the hospital recovering from a heart attack.

"This is most unfair, Jim, I thought this was a dinner party," I said, turning to Angleton.

"It is, Peter," he said, pouring me a massive Scotch in a cut-glass tumbler.

"I'm not going to be browbeaten," I replied flatly.

"No, no," said Angleton quietly, "we just want to hear it again . . . from the beginning. There's a lot of things we've got to get straight."

I went over the Lonsdale story a second time, and by the time I finished Harvey could contain himself no longer.

"You untrustworthy motherfuckers!" he spat at me. "You come over here and ask for us to pay for your research, and all the time you've got a thing like RAFTER up your sleeve . . ."

"I don't see the problem . . ."

"You don't see shit!"

Harvey spun open the second bottle of Jack Daniel's.

"The problem, Peter, is our operations," said Angleton. "A hell of a lot of our agents use HF radio receivers, and if the Soviets have got RAFTER, a lot of them must be blown . . ."

"Have the Soviets got it?" asked Angleton.

"Not at first, but I'm sure they have now," I said, quoting a recent case where an MI6 Polish source inside the UB described a joint Polish-Soviet espionage investigation. Toward the end, when they were closing in on the suspect agent, the KGB brought a van up to the apartment building where the spy lived. The UB, according to the MI6 source, were never allowed to see inside the van, but he knew enough to guess that it had something to do with radio detection.

"Jesus Christ," hissed Harvey, "that's our whole Polish setup lost . . . !"

"But we sent those source reports to your Polish section," I said. "Whoever the agent was, he wasn't one of ours, so we assumed it must have been one of yours. It should at least have warned you that radio communications to Poland were vulnerable."

"We'll check it in the morning," said the head of the West European Division, looking flushed.

"Who else knows about RAFTER?" asked Harvey.

I told him we briefed the FBI and the Canadian RCMP fully as our development progressed.

"The Canadians!" exploded Harvey, thumping the table in anger. "You might as well tell the fuckin' Papuans as the Canadians!"

"I'm afraid we don't see it like that. The Canadians are trusted members of the Commonwealth."

"Well, you should tell them to get another cipher machine," he said, as Angleton, fearful that Harvey in his rage would spill out the secrets of Staff D, kicked him hard under the table.

The argument raged on and on; the intimidation was obviously carefully planned. They wanted to make me feel guilty, to say something indiscreet I might regret later, to tell them more than I should. We gave you Sniper, they said, and look what you do in return. We agree to plow millions of dollars into research for you, and how do you repay us? Harvey cursed and raged about every weakness, every mistake, every piece of carelessness that the

Americans had overlooked since the war: Philby, Burgess, Maclean, the lack of leadership, the amateurism, the retreat from Empire, the encroachment of socialism. Angleton lectured me darkly on the need to respect American superiority in the alliance if we wanted access to their sources.

"Just remember," roared Harvey, "you're a fuckin' beggar in this town!"

I rolled with the punches. Yes, we had a poor record on counterespionage, but Arthur was back now, and Lonsdale was just the beginning. No, we had no obligation to tell you about RAFTER from the beginning. It was our secret to do with as we judged fit.

"I've come over here and just given you my life's work—EN-GULF, STOCKADE, RAFTER—everything. You sat opposite me for five days at NSA and told me nothing. Where's the exchange in that? The truth is, you're just pissed off because we stole a march on you . . . !"

Harvey was all puffed out and purple like a turkeycock, sweat pouring off his temples, his jacket open to reveal a polished shoulder holster and pistol, his gross belly heaving with drink. It was now four o'clock in the morning. I had had enough for one night, and left. I told Angleton that the program for the next day was off. I took a poor view of what had happened. It was up to them to make the peace.

The next day Angleton called on me at my hotel, unannounced. He was charming, and full of apologies. He blamed the previous night's scene on Harvey.

"He drinks too much, and thinks you have to give a guy a hard time to get the truth. He believes you now. He sees you as a threat, that's all."

He invited me out for dinner. At first I was wary, but he said he understood my point of view, and hoped I understood his, and talked enthusiastically about his plans to help with resources. The tension soon disappeared. He offered to take me to see Louis Tordella to persuade him to help with the counterespionage side of ROC, and the following day sent a car to take me down to Fort Meade. Technically, I was not supposed to visit NSA without being accompanied by someone from GCHQ, so I was taken into the side entrance, and whisked up to Tordella's office on the top floor. We had lunch there, and I outlined the Lonsdale case for the third time.

At the end Tordella asked how he could help, and I explained that the main weakness was that despite the breakthrough offered by my classification of illegal broadcasts from Moscow, GCHQ had insufficient coverage of the traffic. There had been substantial improvements since Lonsdale, but we still had only between twelve and fifteen radio positions intercepting these signals, which meant we were really only sampling them. We needed at least 90 percent of the take to make real progress on the classifications. Tordella was much taken with the possibilities, and agreed to guarantee a worldwide take of 100 percent for at least two years. He was as good as his word, and soon the intelligence was flooding back to GCHQ, where it was processed by the section supporting the Counterclan Committee. A young GCHQ cryptanalyst named Peter Marychurch (now the Director of GCHQ) transformed my laborious handwritten classifications by processing the thousands of broadcasts on computer and applying "cluster analysis" to isolate similarities in the traffic, which made the classification infinitely more precise. Within a few years this work had become one of the most important tools in Western counterespionage.

On the drive back to Washington I was elated. Not only had my visit to Washington secured American backing for the ENGULF side of ROC's work, but I had their commitment to run the counterespionage side as well. I had almost forgotten the run-in with Harvey until Angleton brought the subject up again.

"Harvey wants to see you again."

I expressed astonishment.

"No, no—he wants to ask your advice. He's got a problem in Cuba, and I told him you might be able to help."

"But what about the other night?" I asked.

"Oh, don't worry about that. He just wanted to know whether you could be trusted. You passed the test."

Angleton was typically elliptical, and refused to explain further, saying that he had arranged lunch with Harvey in two days' time, and I would find out more then.

The year 1961 was the height of the CIA's obsession with Cuba. The Bay of Pigs invasion had recently failed, and Angleton and I regularly discussed the subject, since I had been heavily involved in MI5's counterinsurgency campaign against the Greek Cypriot guerrilla leader, Colonel Grivas, in the 1950s. When I visited Washington in 1959, Richard Helms and Richard Bissell, in charge of operations in Southeast Asia, asked me to lecture on my experiences to a group of senior officers concerned with counterinsurgency. Even then it was obvious the CIA had plans in Cuba, where Fidel Castro was busy establishing a Communist state. Bissell subsequently took over the running of the Bay of Pigs operation, but when it failed it was common knowledge in Washington that his days were numbered, as the Kennedys purged all those responsible for the Cuban fiasco.

When I arrived at the restaurant two days later, Harvey stood up to greet me and gave me a firm handshake. He looked well scrubbed and less bloated than usual, and made no reference to the events of two nights before. He was a hard man, who gave and expected no quarter. He told me that he was studying the Cuban problem, and wanted to hear from me about the Cyprus campaign.

"I missed your briefing in 1959," he said, without a trace of irony.

I first became involved in Cyprus shortly after I joined MI5, when the Director of E Branch (Colonial Affairs), Bill Morgan, sent me some papers on the escalating conflict. The Greek Cypriot Archbishop Makarios was leading a vigorous campaign for full independence, supported by the Greek Government, the AKEL Communist Party, and EOKA, the guerrilla army led by Colonel Grivas. Britain, anxious to retain Cyprus as a military base, was resisting, and by 1956 a full-scale military emergency was in force, with 40,000 British troops pinned down by a few hundred Grivas guerrillas.

British policy in Cyprus was an utter disaster. The Colonial Office was trying to pursue political negotiations in a deteriorating security situation, relying on the Army to keep order. Grivas needed to be located, isolated, and neutralized before political negotiations stood a chance, but although the Army launched massive searches, they failed to find him. I was convinced, studying the papers, that MI5 could do far better than the Army, and I told Magan I was confident that, given time, we could locate Grivas accurately by tracing his communications in the same way I planned our attacks against the Russians.

Magan immediately took me to see Sir Gerald Templar, who led the successful counterinsurgency campaign in Malaya, and was a great advocate of the use of intelligence to solve colonial problems. Templar was enthusiastic about my plan and agreed to lobby the Colonial Office on MI5's behalf. But the Colonial Office remained adamant; they wanted to pursue their own security policy, and had no wish to involve MI5. There was no great enthusiasm, either, inside MI5 for becoming embroiled in what was fast becoming an insoluble situation. Hollis, in particular, was opposed to becoming involved in Colonial Affairs without a clear invitation from the Ministry. His attitude was that MI5 was a domestic organization, and while he would provide a Defense Liaison Officer to advise the Army, that was all.

In 1958, Grivas stepped up his guerrilla campaign in an effort to thwart the determined efforts to achieve a political solution being made by the new Governor, Sir Hugh Foot. The Army launched another massive search for Grivas, this time in the Paphos mountains, but once again he slipped through the net. Foot continued to press for a political solution, but agreed to call in MI5 as the situation was rapidly deteriorating. From the start we were in a race: could we find Grivas before the Colonial Office stitched up a ramshackle deal?

Magan was convinced that sufficient intelligence about Grivas' location must exist in the files of the local Special Branch, and that it had just not been interpreted correctly. The problem was how to get at it. EOKA had thoroughly penetrated the local Special Branch, and studying the files would be a dangerous business once an MI5 man's identity became known. One of our officers had already been shot in the high street of Nicosia.

Magan was a remarkable man who had spent a great deal of time on the North-West Frontier and in Persia, where he lived by himself with the natives in tents, speaking their languages and cooking his meals on cow dung fires. He knew at first hand the dangers of terrorism, and rather than delegate the dangerous mission to a junior officer, he insisted that he go himself, supported by the local Cyprus liaison officer, Colonel Philip Kirby Green, a tall soldierly officer of boundless courage and rectitude who was also a distinguished painter in his spare time. I was to follow shortly afterward to plan and execute the technical side of the operation, which was given the code name SUNSHINE.

It would be too crude to say that SUNSHINE was an assassination operation. But it amounted to the same thing. The plan was simple: to locate Grivas, and bring up a massive concentration of soldiers. We knew he would never surrender, and like two of his trusted lieutenants who had recently been cornered by the Army, he would die in the shoot-out.

I arrived in Nicosia on January 17, 1959, and went to Special Branch headquarters to study Magan's analysis of the files. Grivas' campaign was clearly well organized. There were numerous examples of well-coordinated terrorist strikes and civil disturbances across the whole island. He had therefore to be in regular communication with his field officers. It was unlikely that EOKA would use either the telephone or the postal system for these, even though they had been thoroughly penetrated. Communications rested on a system of couriers, and from studying the files it was obvious these were mainly women, traveling on the public transport system. We plotted each sighting and interception, and the overall pattern showed Limassol to be the hub of the EOKA communications network. There were also clusters of sightings in the Yerasa and Polodhia villages, several miles from Limassol. The best hypothesis was that Grivas maintained headquarters in each of these villages.

The first step was to place a secure telephone tap on Makarios' palace. We were certain that Makarios, and probably EOKA at certain times, used the line secure in the knowledge that their post office spies would automatically alert them to the presence of a tap.

We decided to place a concealed tap on one of the overhead cables leading into the palace, using a radio transmitter which took power from the telephone circuit to radiate the signal out to our waiting receiver a mile or two away. John Wyke, MI6's best technical operator, and the man who actually placed the taps inside the Berlin Tunnel, with the Vopos' feet just inches above his head, came out to help me. The whole operation was fraught with danger. Wyke had to climb a telephone pole in total darkness, in full view of the road, which was constantly patrolled by Makarios' armed bodyguards and EOKA guerrillas. He bored a hole in the top of the pole to conceal the electronics, and made a concealed connection to the telephone cable. Down at the bottom I selected his tools and relayed them up to him. Every five minutes we froze as a patrol came past, expecting at any moment to hear rifle fire. Two hours later, our nerves frayed, the tap was successfully installed, and gave us the essential base coverage of Makarios.

But the real purpose of SUNSHINE was to find Grivas. I was sure he must be using radio receivers to monitor British Army communications, and was aware every time an effort was mounted to search for him. I decided on a two-pronged attack. Firstly we would search intensively for the aerial which he used with his receiver. Then, simultaneously, I planned to plant a radio receiver on him containing a radio beacon, which would lead us right to him. We knew Grivas obtained a great deal of his military supplies from the Egyptians, who were selling off British equipment they had confiscated after the Suez war at knockdown prices. MI6 recruited a Greek Cypriot arms dealer, who purchased a consignment of receivers in Egypt which I modified to include a beacon, and we set about trying to feed it into Grivas' headquarters.

The first part of Operation SUNSHINE went well. K.G., as Kirby Green was universally known in the Service, Magan, and I made a series of dawn reconnoiters of the Limassol area looking for the aerial. It was dangerous work, meandering down dusty side streets and across the sunbaked market squares, pretending to be casual visitors. Old men under wicker shades looked at us as we passed. Small boys eyed us suspiciously and disappeared down alleys. I felt the sweat dripping down my back, and the uncanny sensation of an unseen rifle permanently trained on me from somewhere behind the terra-cotta roofs and ancient flint walls.

In Yerasa I noticed a spike on the peak of the pyramid-shaped roof of a church. It appeared, at first sight, to be a lightning conductor, mounted on an insulator going through the roof. There was also a metallic strip going down into the ground, but when I scrutinized the conductor carefully through field glasses, I could see that the strip was disconnected from the spike. It was obviously modified to act as an aerial. Rather foolishly, we tried to get closer, and, from nowhere, an angry crowd of local children emerged and began to stone us. We beat a hasty retreat, and made our way over to Polodhia, where there was a similar setup. I was sure then that we had been right to pinpoint the two villages as the center of Grivas' operations.

I began to work feverishly on the radio beacons. We estimated that SUNSHINE would take six months to complete, but just as we moved into top gear, in late February 1959, the Colonial Office hurriedly settled the Cyprus problem at a Constitutional Conference at Lancaster House. The carpet was roughly pulled from under our feet, and the entire SUNSHINE plan aborted overnight. Magan was furious, particularly when Grivas emerged from the precise area we had foreseen and was flown to Greece, ready to continue to exert a baleful influence on the island. Magan felt the settlement was at best temporary, and that few of the outstanding problems had been resolved. In his view, Colonial Office short-term expediency would lead to long-term misery. He has been proved right.

Shortly before we left Cyprus, Magan and I had a strained encounter with the Governor, Sir Hugh Foot. He was pleased that at last he was extricated, and made it clear that he had always seen SUNSHINE as a last resort solution, to be implemented only in the event of the failure of diplomacy. He seemed incapable of understanding that intelligence, to be effective, has to be built into diplomacy from the start. Looking back, I am certain that, had we been allowed to implement Operation SUNSHINE when we first lobbied for it, in 1956, we could have neutralized Grivas at the outset. The Colonial Office, rather than EOKA, would then have been able to dictate the terms of the peace, and the history of that tragic but beautiful island might have taken a different course over the past thirty years.

The entire Cyprus episode left a lasting impression on British colonial policy. Britain decolonized most successfully when we defeated the military insurgency first, using intelligence rather than force of arms, before negotiating a political solution based on the political leadership of the defeated insurgency movement, and with British force of arms to maintain the installed government. This is basically what happened in Malaya and Kenya, and both these countries have survived intact.

The fundamental problem was how to remove the colonial power while ensuring that the local military forces did not fill the vacuum. How, in other words, can you create a stable local political class? The Colonial Office were well versed in complicated, academic, democratic models—a constitution here, a parliament there—very few of which stood the remotest chance of success. After the Cyprus experience I wrote a paper and submitted it to Hollis, giving my views. I said that we ought to adopt the Bolshevik model, since it was the only one to have worked successfully. Lenin understood better than anyone how to gain control of a country and, just as important, how to keep it. Lenin believed that the political class had to control the men with the guns, and the intelligence service, and by these means could ensure that neither the Army nor another political class could challenge for power.

Feliks Dzerzhinsky, the founder of the modern Russian Intelligence Service, specifically set up the CHEKA (forerunner of the KGB) with these aims in mind. He established three main directorates—the First Chief Directorate to work against those people abroad who might conspire against the government; the Second Chief Directorate to work against those inside the Soviet Union who might conspire; and the Third Chief Directorate, which penetrated the armed forces, to ensure that no military coup could be plotted.

My paper was greeted with horror by Hollis and the rest of the MI5 Directors. They told me it was "cynical," and it was never even passed to the Colonial Office, but looking back over the past quarter of a century, it is only where a version of Lenin's principles has been applied in newly created countries that a military dictatorship has been avoided.

These ideas were also hotly contested by the CIA when I lectured to them in 1959. Helms told me flatly I was advocating

Communism for the Third World. He felt that we had a decisive intelligence advantage which they lacked. We were the resident colonial power, whereas in the insurgencies which they faced in the Far East and Cuba, they were not, and therefore they felt the only policy they could pursue was a military solution. It was this thinking which ultimately led the USA into the Vietnam War.

More immediately, it led them into the Bay of Pigs, and when, two years later, Harvey listened to my Cyprus experiences, he was struck by the parallel between the two problems: both small islands with a guerrilla force led by a charismatic leader. He was particularly struck by my view that without Grivas, EOKA would have collapsed.

"What would the Brits do in Cuba?" he asked.

I was a shade anxious about being drawn into the Cuban business. Hollis and I had discussed it before I came to Washington, and he made no secret of his view that the CIA were blundering in the Caribbean. It was a subject, he felt, to steer clear of if at all possible. I was worried that if I made suggestions to Angleton and Harvey, I would soon find them being quoted around Washington by the CIA as the considered British view of things. It would not take long for word of that to filter back to Leconfield House, so I made it clear to them that I was talking off the record.

I said that we would try to develop whatever assets we had down there—alternative political leaders, that kind of thing.

"We've done all that," said Harvey impatiently, "but they're all in Florida. Since the Bay of Pigs, we've lost virtually everything we had inside . . ."

Harvey began to fish to see if I knew whether we had anything in the area, in view of the British colonial presence in the Caribbean.

"I doubt it," I told him, "the word in London is steer clear of Cuba. Six might have something, but you'd have to check with them."

"How would you handle Castro?" asked Angleton.

"We'd isolate him, turn the people against him . . ."

"Would you hit him?" interrupted Harvey.

I paused to fold my napkin. Waiters glided silently from table to table. I realized now why Harvey needed to know I could be trusted.

"We'd certainly have that capability," I replied, "but I doubt we would use it nowadays."

"Why not?"

"We're not in it anymore, Bill. We got out a couple of years ago, after Suez."

At the beginning of the Suez Crisis, MI6 developed a plan, through the London Station, to assassinate Nasser using nerve gas. Eden initially gave his approval to the operation, but later rescinded it when he got agreement from the French and Israelis to engage in joint military action. When this course failed, and he was forced to withdraw, Eden reactivated the assassination option a second time. By this time virtually all MI6 assets in Egypt had been rounded up by Nasser, and a new operation, using renegade Egyptian officers, was drawn up, but it failed lamentably, principally because the cache of weapons which had been hidden on the outskirts of Cairo was found to be defective.

"Were you involved?" Harvey asked.

"Only peripherally," I answered truthfully, "on the technical side."

I explained that I was consulted about the plan by John Henry and Peter Dixon, the two MI6 Technical Services officers from the London Station responsible for drawing it up. Dixon, Henry, and I all attended joint MI5/MI6 meetings to discuss technical research for the intelligence services at Porton Down, the government's chemical and biological Weapons Research Establishment. The whole area of chemical research was an active field in the 1950s. I was cooperating with MI6 in a joint program to investigate how far the hallucinatory drug lysergic acid diethylamide (LSD) could be used in interrogations, and extensive trials took place at Porton. I even volunteered as guinea pig on one occasion. Both MI5 and MI6 also wanted to know a lot more about the advanced poisons then being developed at Porton, though for different reasons. I wanted the antidotes, in case the Russians used a poison on a defector in Britain, while MI6 wanted to use the poisons for operations abroad.

Henry and Dixon both discussed with me the use of poisons against Nasser, and asked my advice. Nerve gas obviously presented the best possibility, since it was easily administered. They told me that the London Station had an agent in Egypt with limited access to one of Nasser's headquarters. Their plan was to place canisters of nerve gas inside the ventilation system, but I pointed out that this would require large quantities of gas, and would result in massive loss of life among Nasser's staff. It was the usual MI6 operation—hopelessly unrealistic—and it did not remotely surprise me when Henry told me later that Eden had backed away from the operation. The chances of its remaining undeniable were even slimmer than they had been with Buster Crabbe.

Harvey and Angleton questioned me closely about every part of the Suez Operation.

"We're developing a new capability in the Company to handle these kinds of problems," explained Harvey, "and we're in the market for the requisite expertise."

Whenever Harvey became serious, his voice dropped to a low monotone, and his vocabulary lapsed into the kind of strangled bureaucratic syntax beloved of Washington officials. He explained ponderously that they needed deniable personnel, and improved technical facilities—in Harvey jargon, "delivery mechanisms." They were especially interested in the SAS. Harvey knew that the SAS operated up on the Soviet border in the 1950s tracking Russian rocket signals with mobile receivers before the satellites took over, and that they were under orders not to be caught, even if this meant fighting their way out of trouble.

"They don't freelance, Bill," I told him. "You could try to pick them up retired, but you'd have to see Six about that."

Harvey looked irritated, as if I were being deliberately unhelpful.

"Have you thought of approaching Stephenson?" I asked. "A lot of the old-timers say he ran this kind of thing in New York during the war. Used some Italian, apparently, when there was no other way of sorting a German shipping spy. Probably the Mafia, for all I know . . ."

Angleton scribbled in his notebook, and looked up impassively.

"The French!" I said brightly. "Have you tried them? It's more their type of thing, you know, Algiers, and so on."

Another scribble in the notebook.

"What about technically—did you have any special equipment?" asked Harvey.

I told him that after the gas canisters plans fell through, MI6 looked at some new weapons. On one occasion I went down to Porton to see a demonstration of a cigarette packet which had been modified by the Explosives Research and Development Establishment to fire a dart tipped with poison. We solemnly put on white coats and were taken out to one of the animal compounds behind Porton by Dr. Ladell, the scientist there who handled all MI5 and MI6 work. A sheep on a lead was led into the center of the ring. One flank had been shaved to reveal the coarse pink skin. Ladell's assistant pulled out the cigarette packet and stepped forward. The sheep started, and was restrained by the lead, and I thought perhaps the device had misfired. But then the sheep's knees began to buckle, and it started rolling its eyes and frothing at the mouth. Slowly the animal sank to the ground, life draining away, as the white-coated professionals discussed the advantages of the modern new toxin around the corpse. It was the only time in my life when my two passions, for animals and for intelligence, collided, and I knew at that instant that the first was by far the greater love. I knew also, then, that assassination was no policy for peacetime.

Beyond that, there was little help I could offer Harvey and Angleton, and I began to feel I had told them more than enough. The sight of Angleton's notebook was beginning to unnerve me. They seemed so determined, so convinced that this was the way to handle Castro, and slightly put out that I could not help them more.

"Speak to John Henry, or Dixon—they'll probably know more than me," I said when we were out on the street making our farewells. I was due to fly back to Britain the next day.

"You're not holding out on us over this, are you?" asked Harvey suddenly. The shape of his pistol was visible again under his jacket. I could tell he was thinking about RAFTER.

I hailed a taxi.

"I've told you, Bill. We're out of that game. We're the junior partner in the alliance, remember? It's your responsibility now."

Harvey was not the kind of man to laugh at a joke. Come to that, neither was Angleton.

12 ──────────────────────────

1961. OUTSIDE IN THE STREETS OF LONDON, PEOPLE WERE STILL saying they had "never had it so good," while in Washington a new young President was busy creating a mythical Camelot of culture and excellence. But in the subterranean world of secret intelligence, the shape of the turbulent decade was already becoming clear. Throughout the 1950s American and British services pursued the Cold War with clarity of purpose and single-minded dedication. It was not a subtle war, and there were precious few complications. But in the early 1960s a rash of defectors began to arrive in the West from the heart of the Russian intelligence machine, each carrying tales of the penetration of Western security. Their stories were often contradictory and confusing, and their effect was to begin the slow paralysis of British and American intelligence as doubt and suspicion seeped through the system.

The first defector arrived in December 1961. I was in my office a few weeks after returning from my trip to Washington when Arthur strolled in, cigarette in one hand, clutching a copy of *The Times* in the other. He passed the paper to me neatly folded across the spine.

"Sounds interesting . . ." he said, pointing to a small paragraph which referred to a Soviet Major, named Klimov, who had presented himself to the American Embassy in Helsinki with his wife and child and asked for asylum.

It was not long before we heard on the grapevine that Klimov was, in fact, a KGB Major, and that he was singing like a bird. In March 1962, a frisson of excitement went around the D Branch offices. Arthur smoked more energetically than usual, his baby face flushed with enthusiasm as he strode up and down the corridors. I knew Klimov's information had finally arrived.

"It's the defector, isn't it?" I asked him one day.

He ushered me into his office, closed the door, and told me a little of the story. "Klimov," he said, was in reality Anatoli Golitsin, a high-ranking KGB officer who had worked inside the First Chief Directorate, responsible for operations against the UK and the USA, and the Information department in Moscow, before taking a posting in Helsinki. In fact, Golitsin had been on a previous CIA watch list during an earlier overseas tour, but he was not recognized under the cover of his new identity until he presented himself in Helsinki.

After the initial debriefing, the CIA sent to MI5 a list of ten "serials," each one itemizing an allegation Golitsin had made about a penetration of British Security. Arthur initially held the complete list. Patrick Stewart, the acting head of D3 (Research), conducted a preliminary analysis of the serials, and drew up a list of suspects to fit each one. Then individual serials were apportioned to different officers in the D1 (Investigations) section for detailed investigation, and I was asked to provide technical advice as the investigations required.

Three of the first ten serials immediately struck a chord. Golitsin said he knew of a famous "Ring of Five" spies, recruited in Britain in the 1930s. They all knew each other, he said, and all knew the others were spies. But Golitsin could identify none of them, other than the fact that one had the code name Stanley, and was connected with recent KGB operations in the Middle East. The lead perfectly fitted Kim Philby, who was currently working in Beirut for the *Observer* newspaper. He said that two of the other five were obviously Burgess and Maclean. We thought that a fourth might be Sir Anthony Blunt, the Surveyor of the Queen's Pictures, and a former wartime MI5 officer who fell under suspicion after the Burgess and Maclean defections in 1951. But the identity of the fifth was a complete mystery. As a result of Golitsin's three serials concerning the Ring of Five, the Philby and Blunt cases were exhumed, and a reassessment ordered.

The two most current and precise leads in those first ten serials were numbers 3 and 8, which referred to Naval spies, indicating, as with Houghton, the importance the Russians attached to obtaining details of the British and NATO submarine and antisubmarine capability. Serial 3 was a recruitment allegedly made in the British Naval Attaché's office in the Embassy in Moscow, under the personal supervision of General Gribanov, Head of the Second Chief Directorate, responsible for internal intelligence operations in the Soviet Union. A Russian employee of the British Embassy named Mikhailski had been involved in the operation, and the spy provided handwritten notes of the secret documents which passed across his desk. Then, in 1956, said Golitsin, the spy returned to London to work in the Naval Intelligence Department, and his KGB control passed to the Foreign Operations Department.

The second Naval spy, Serial 8, was a more senior figure, according to Golitsin. Golitsin claimed to have seen numbered copies of three NATO documents, two of which were classified Top Secret. He had seen them by accident while working on the NATO desk of the KGB Information Department, which prepared policy papers for the Politburo on NATO matters. Golitsin was in the middle of preparing a report on NATO naval strategy, when three documents came in from London. Normally all material reaching Golitsin was bowdlerized, in other words rewritten to disguise its source, but because of the urgency of his report, he was provided with the original document copies. The CIA tested Golitsin on his story. The three documents in question, detailing plans to expand the Clyde Polaris submarine base, and the reorganization of NATO naval dispositions in the Mediterranean, were shown to him, mixed up with a sheaf of other NATO documents. He immediately identified the correct three, and even explained that the Clyde document he saw had four sets of numbers and figures for its circulation list, whereas the copy we showed him had six sets. When the original circulation list was checked, it was found that such a copy had indeed existed but we were unable to find it. Patrick Stewart analyzed the circulation of the three documents, and a senior Naval Commander, now retired, appeared as the only credible candidate. The case was handed over to DI (Investigations).

Within months of Golitsin's arrival, three further sources in the heart of the Soviet intelligence machine suddenly, and apparently independently, offered their services to the West. The first two, a KGB officer and a GRU officer, both working under cover in the Soviet delegation to the UN, approached the FBI and offered to act as agents in place. They were given the code names Fedora and Top Hat. The third walk-in occurred in Geneva in June 1962. A senior KGB officer, Yuri Nossenko, contacted the CIA and offered his services.

Nossenko soon gave a priceless lead in the hunt for the British Naval spies. He claimed that the Gribanov recruitment had been obtained through homosexual blackmail, and that the agent had provided the KGB with "all NATO" secrets from a "Lord of the Navy." The combination of NATO and the Gribanov recruitment led MI5 to combine the two serials 3 and 8. There was one obvious suspect, a clerk in Lord Carrington's office, John Vassall. Vassall had originally been placed at the top of Patrick Stewart's preliminary list of four Serial 3 suspects, but when the case was handed over to the investigating officer, Ronnie Symonds, Symonds had contested Stewart's assessment. He felt that Vassall's Catholicism and apparent high moral character made him a less serious suspect. He was placed at the bottom of the list instead.

After attention focused on him strongly following Nossenko's lead, it was soon established that Vassall was a practicing homosexual, who was living way beyond his means in a luxury flat in Dolphin Square. MI5 faced the classic counterespionage problem. Unlike any other crime, espionage leaves no trace, and proof is virtually impossible unless a spy either confesses or is caught in the act. I was asked if there was any technical way we could prove Vassall was removing the documents from the Admiralty. I had been experimenting for some time with Frank Morgan on a scheme to mark classified documents using minute quantities of radioactive material. The idea was to place a Geiger counter at the entrance of the building where the suspected spy was operating so that we could detect if any marked documents were being removed. We tried this with Vassall, but it was not a success. There were too many exits in the Admiralty for us to be sure we were covering the one which Vassall used, and the Geiger counter readings were often distorted by luminous wristwatches and the like. Eventually the scheme was scrapped when fears about the risks of exposing people to radiation were raised by the management.

I looked around for another way. It was obvious from the CIA tests that Golitsin had a near-photographic memory, so I decided to make another test, to see if he could remember any details about the type of photographic copy of the NATO documents he had seen. Through this it might be possible to deduce whether he was handing over originals for them to copy and return to him. I made twenty-five photographs of the first page of the Clyde Base NATO document, each one corresponding to a method we knew the Russians had in the past recommended to their agents, or which the Russians themselves had used inside the Embassy, and sent them over to Golitsin via the CIA. As soon as Golitsin saw the photographs he picked out the one which had been taken with a Praktina, illuminated at each side by two anglepoise lamps. Armed with this knowledge, we arranged to burgle Vassall's flat when he was safely at work. Hidden in a drawer at the bottom of a bureau we found a Praktina document-copying camera, and a Minox as well. That evening he was arrested, permission for a search warrant having been obtained, and his apartment was stripped bare. In the base of a corner table a secret drawer was found which contained a number of exposed 35mm cassettes, which were developed to reveal 176 classified documents. Vassall swiftly confessed to having been homosexually compromised in Moscow in 1955, and was convicted and sentenced to eighteen years in prison.

As the intelligence from the throng of new defectors was being pieced together in London and Washington, I faced a personal crisis of my own. The Lonsdale case reawakened the whole issue of technical resources for MI5 and MI6. Although the AWRE program which I and Frank Morgan designed in 1958 had been an outstanding success, little else had changed. The attempt to satisfy Intelligence Service needs within the context of the overall defense budget had failed, especially in the advanced electronics field. We were moving rapidly into a new era of satellite and computer intelligence, and when the Radiations Operations Committee was split into Clan and Counterclan, it was obvious that the scale and range of their operations would require a far more intensive degree of technical and scientific research and development than had hitherto been possible. Everyone realized at last that the old ad hoc system which I had struggled to change since 1958 would have to be comprehensively reformed. Both MI5 and MI6 needed their own establishments, their own budgets, and their own staffs. Shortly after the Lonsdale case I approached Sir William Cook again with the approval of both Services, and asked him to make a thorough review of our requirements. We spent several days together visiting the various defense establishments which were currently servicing us, and he wrote a detailed report, one of the most important in postwar British Intelligence history.

The essence of Cook's report was that the Hanslope Communications Center, the wartime headquarters of the Radio Security Service, and since then the MI6 communications center for its overseas agent networks, should be radically expanded to become a research establishment servicing both MI5 and MI6, with special emphasis on the kinds of advanced electronics necessary in both the Clan and the Counterclan committees. Cook recommended that the new staff for Hanslope should be drawn from the Royal Naval Scientific Service. This was, to me, the most important reform of all. Since joining MI5 I had lobbied to remove the artificial barrier which separated the technical divisions of the Intelligence Services from the rest of the scientific Civil Service. This barrier was wholly damaging; it deprived the Intelligence Services of the best and the brightest young scientists, and on a personal level meant that I had to forfeit nearly twenty years of pension allocation earned in the Admiralty, in order to accept MI5's offer to work for them. I pressed Cook continually on this point during the time he was writing his report, and he recognized that my arguments were correct. As a result of his report fifty scientists were transferred to Hanslope, with their pensions intact, and with the option of transferring back if they so wished at a future date. Since I was the first scientist, I was not covered by these new arrangements, although I was not at the time unduly worried. I believed that when the time came the Service would, as they promised, make some recompense. Unfortunately, my trust was sadly misplaced.

There was one further Cook recommendation. He wanted MI5 and MI6 to set up a joint headquarters staff in separate accommodation, controlled by a Chief Scientist, to plan and oversee the new research and development program for both services. It was a bold new move, and I confess I wanted the job more than anything in the world. I felt, in truth, that I had earned it. Most of the technical modernization which had occurred since 1955 was largely at my instigation, and I had spent long years fighting for budgets and resources for both Services. But it was not to be. Victor Rothschild lobbied vigorously on my behalf but Dick White told him that the animosity inside MI6 stimulated by his own transfer from MI5 was still too great to hope to persuade his senior technical staff to serve under any appointee from MI5. In the end the situation was resolved at a meeting of the Colemore Committee. When Cook's conclusions were discussed, Hector Willis, the head of the Royal Naval Scientific Service, volunteered there and then to fill the post of Chief of the new Directorate of Science, resigning from the RNSS to do it, and Hollis and White, aware of the bureaucratic influence Willis would bring with him, gratefully accepted. I became the joint deputy head of the Directorate, along with Johnny Hawkes, my opposite number in MI6, who ran Hanslope for MI6, and developed the MI6 Rockex cipher machine.

Willis and I knew each other well. He was a pleasant North countryman, small, almost mousy, with white hair and black eyebrows. He always dressed smartly, with pepper-and-salt suits and stiff collars. I had worked under him during the war on a leader cable scheme and antisubmarine warfare. He was a good mathematician, far better than I, with first-rate technical ingenuity. But although we were both essentially engineers, Willis and I had diametrically opposed views about the way the new Directorate should be run. I saw the scientist/engineer's role in intelligence as being a source of ideas and experiments which might or might not yield results. Whatever success I had achieved since 1955 was obtained through experimentation and improvisation. I wanted the Directorate to be a powerhouse, embracing and expanding the kinds of breakthroughs which had given us the Radiations Operations Committee. Willis wanted to integrate scientific intelligence into the Ministry of Defense. He wanted the Directorate to be a passive organization: a branch of the vast inert defense-contracting industry, producing resources for its end users on request. I tried to explain to Willis that intelligence, unlike defense contracting, is not peacetime work. It is a constant war, and you face a constantly shifting target. It is no good planning decades ahead, as the Navy do when they bring a ship into service, because by the time you get two or three years down the track, you might find your project leaked to the Russians. I cited the Berlin Tunnel—tens of millions of dollars poured into a single grandiose project, and later we learned it was blown to the Russians from the beginning by the Secretary of the Planning Committee, George Blake. I agreed that we had to develop a stock of simple devices such as microphones and amplifiers, which worked and which had a fair shelf life, but I opposed the development of sophisticated devices which more often than not were designed by committees, and which would probably be redundant by the time they came to fruition, either because the Russians learned about them or because the war had moved onto different territory.

Willis never understood what I was driving at. I felt he lacked imagination, and he certainly did not share my restless passion for the possibilities of scientific intelligence. He wanted me to settle down, forget the kind of life I had lived thus far, put on a white coat and supervise the rolling contracts. I was forced to leave Leconfield House and move into the Directorate's headquarters offices at Buckingham Gate. The latter part of 1962, coming so soon after the excitements and achievements of 1961, was undoubtedly the most unhappy period in my professional life. For seven years I had enjoyed a rare freedom to roam around MI5 involving myself in all sorts of areas, always active, always working on current operations. It was like swapping the trenches for a spell in the Home Guard. As soon as I arrived in the new offices, I knew there was no future there for me. Cut off from Leconfield House I would soon perish in the airless, claustrophobic atmosphere. I decided to leave, either to another post in MI5 if the management agreed, or to GCHQ, where I had been making soundings, if they did not.

Arthur was terribly considerate at this time. He knew that I was chafing over at Buckingham Gate, and he used every excuse he could to involve me in the ongoing work with Golitsin. During spring 1962 he paid a long visit to Washington and conducted a massive debriefing of the KGB Major. He returned with a further 153 serials which merited further investigation. Some of the serials were relatively innocuous, like his allegation that a then popular musical star had been recruited by the Russians because of his access to London high society. Others were true but we were able to satisfactorily account for them, like the baronet whom Golitsin claimed had been the target for homosexual blackmail, after the KGB photographed him in action in the back of a taxi. The baronet was interviewed, admitted the incident, and satisfied us that he had refused to bend to the KGB ploy. But the vast majority of Golitsin's material was tantalizingly imprecise. It often appeared true as far as it went, but then faded into ambiguity, and part of the problem was Golitsin's clear propensity for feeding his information out in dribs and drabs. He saw it as his livelihood, and consequently those who had to deal with him never knew, when they were pursuing a particularly fruitful-looking lead, whether the defector had more to tell them.

I was asked to help with one of the strangest Golitsin serials which ran into the dust at this time, the Sokolov Grant affair. In many ways it was typical of the difficulties we faced in dealing with his debriefing material. Golitsin said that a Russian agent had been introduced into Suffolk next to an airfield which had batteries of the latest guided missiles. He was sure the agent was a sleeper, probably for sabotage in the event of an international crisis. We contacted the RAF and pinpointed Stretteshall, near Bury St. Edmonds, as the most likely airfield. We then checked the electoral roll in the area around Stretteshall to see if we could find anything interesting. After a few days we came across a Russian name, Sokolov Grant. We cross-checked with the Registry and found that he had a file. He was a Russian refugee who had arrived in Britain five years before, married an English girl, and taken up farming on rented land near the airfield.

The case was handed over to Charles Elwell for investigation. Letter and telephone checks were installed and inquiries made with the local police, which drew a blank. I was asked to make a search of his house, when Sokolov Grant and his wife went up north for a holiday, to see if there was any technical evidence which might incriminate him. I drove up to Bury St. Edmonds with John Storer, a short, gray-haired, smiling man from GCHQ's M Division who worked on Counterclan, arranging the RAFTER plane flights, and analyzing the RAFTER signals. Sokolov Grant lived in a pretty Queen Anne red-brick farmhouse which was in a state of some disrepair. From the back garden you could see the end of the runway stretching across the swaying fields of barley. The scene seemed so perfect, so idyllic, it was hard to be suspicious. But that was the thing which always struck me about espionage: it was always played out in such ordinary humdrum English scenes.

John Storer went off to search the farm buildings for signs of clandestine radio systems, while I slipped the catch and went inside the house. The house was unbelievably untidy. All along the corridors and passageways piles of junk lined the walls. Books were stacked up in mounds in the downstairs rooms. At first I thought perhaps they were moving house, until I noticed the thick layer of dust on top of everything. In the backroom study stood two desks side by side. The one on the left was a huge roll-top desk crammed so full that it could not be closed. The one on the right was a small bureau. I opened the flap, and it was completely empty. I slid the drawers out. They were empty too, with not a trace of dust. The whole thing had obviously been emptied recently. I sat for a moment in a polished Windsor chair staring at the two desks, trying to make sense of one so full and the other so empty. Had the contents of one been transferred into the other? Or had one been emptied, and if so why? Was it suspicious, or was it just what it seemed—an empty desk in a junk-infested house?

I made a start on the papers in the other desk, but they were mostly farm business. John Storer found nothing outside, and we left. To search the place properly would have taken twenty men a week. In the end Charles Elwell went up to see Sokolov Grant and asked a few questions in the village. He came back satisfied that he was in the clear. He was popular locally, and his wife was the daughter of the local squire. We assumed Golitsin had seen Sokolov Grant's name on a KGB watch list, marked down as someone they contemplated approaching but never in fact did.

Shortly afterward Sokolov Grant and his wife left the area. Our inquiries had probably leaked in the village, and he presumably wanted to make a new start. But for all the apparent meaninglessness the Sokolov Grant story has always had symbolic importance to me: an ordinary man suddenly falling under suspicion, and just as abruptly cleared again, his life utterly changed because of something a man he has never met says in a darkened room on the other side of the world. The quiet rural world of Suffolk colliding with the secret world of betrayal, where there is no such thing as coincidence, where suspicion can be fueled at the sight of an empty desk.

The most tightly held of all Golitsin's serials were those which suggested a penetration of MI5. I first learned of them from Arthur shortly after he returned from Washington. Golitsin said that he had seen the special safe in KGB headquarters where documents from British Intelligence were stored. He had seen the index to the documents stored in the safe, and he was positive that very recent material from MI5 was in there. He also claimed the KGB had acquired a document from British Intelligence which they called the "Technics" Document: a thick document listing technical equipment for British Intelligence. He was unable to study it closely, as he was only called in to see if he could translate a small passage from it. But it was obviously an important document, as there was great urgency in obtaining the translation. He said that security arrangements were different in the London Embassy. There was no special security officer (known as the "SK" officer [Soviet Kolony]). Golitsin assumed none was needed because the penetration of MI5 was so complete. Then there was the Crabbe Affair. He said the KGB got advance warning of Crabbe's mission against the cruiser *Ordzhonikidze.*

In August 1962, as MI5 were busy digesting the mass of Golitsin material, we had a major breakthrough with the three original Philby serials. Victor Rothschild met Flora Solomon, a Russian émigré Zionist, at a party at the Weizmans' house in Israel. She told him that she was very indignant about articles Philby had written in the *Observer* which were anti-Israel. She then confided that she knew Philby to have been a secret agent since the 1930s. With great difficulty, Victor managed to persuade her to meet Arthur Martin in London, to tell him her story. I was asked to microphone Victor's flat, where the interview was to take place. I decided to install temporary SF, which made Victor nervous.

"I don't trust you buggers to take the SF off!" he told me, and made me promise to personally supervise the installation and its removal. Victor was always convinced that MI5 were clandestinely tapping him to find out details of his intimate connections with the Israelis, and his furtiveness caused much good-humored hilarity in the office. But I gave Victor my word and met the Post Office technicians in the afternoon before the interview, carefully checking as they modified the telephone receiver. Later, when the interview was finished, I solemnly watched while they removed the washer again.

I monitored the interview back at Leconfield House on the seventh floor. Flora Solomon was a strange, rather untrustworthy woman, who never told the truth about her relations with people like Philby in the 1930s, although she clearly had a grudge against him. With much persuasion, she told Arthur a version of the truth. She said she had known Philby very well before the war.

She had been fond of him, and when he was working in Spain as a journalist with *The Times* he had taken her out for lunch on one of his trips back to London. During the meal he told her he was doing a very dangerous job for peace—he wanted help. Would she help him in the task? He was working for the Comintern and the Russians. It would be a great thing if she would join the cause. She refused to join the cause, but told him that he could always come to her if he was desperate.

Arthur held back from quizzing her. This was her story, and it mattered little to us whether she had, in reality, as we suspected, taken more than the passive role she described during the 1930s. Every now and then she became agitated.

"I will never give public evidence," she said in her grating voice. "There is too much risk. You see what has happened to Tomas since I spoke to Victor," she said, referring to the fact that one of Philby's friends, Tomas Harris, the art dealer, had recently died in a mysterious car accident in Spain.

"It will leak, I know it will leak," she would screech, "and then what will my family do?"

But although she professed fear of the Russians, she seemed to have ambivalent feelings toward Philby himself. She said she still cared for him, and then later rambled on about the terrible way he treated his women. Although she never admitted it, I guessed from listening to her that she and Philby must have been lovers in the 1930s. Years later she was having her revenge for the rejection she felt when he moved into a new pair of sheets.

Armed with Golitsin's and Solomon's information, both Dick White for MI6 and Roger Hollis agreed that Philby should be interrogated again out in Beirut. From August 1962 until the end of the year, Evelyn McBarnet drew up a voluminous brief in preparation for the confrontation. But at the last minute there was a change of plan. Arthur was originally scheduled to go to Beirut. He had pursued the Philby case from its beginning in 1951, and knew more about it than anyone. But he was told that

Nicholas Elliott, a close friend of Philby's, who had just returned from Beirut where he had been Station Chief, would go instead. Elliott was now convinced of Philby's guilt, and it was felt he could better play on Philby's sense of decency. The few of us inside MI5 privy to this decision were appalled. It was not simply a matter of chauvinism, though, not unnaturally, that played a part. We in MI5 had never doubted Philby's guilt from the beginning, and now at last we had the evidence we needed to corner him. Philby's friends in MI6, Elliott chief among them, had continually protested his innocence. Now, when the proof was inescapable, they wanted to keep it in-house. The choice of Elliott rankled strongly as well. He was the son of the former headmaster of Eton and had a languid upper-class manner. But the decision was made, and in January 1963 Elliott flew out to Beirut, armed with a formal offer of immunity.

He returned a week later in triumph. Philby had confessed. He had admitted spying since 1934. He was thinking of coming back to Britain. He had even written out a confession. At last the long mystery was solved.

Many people in the secret world aged the night they heard Philby had confessed. I was nearly forty-five. It is one thing to suspect the truth; it is another to hear it from a man's lips. Suddenly there was very little fun in the game anymore; a Rubicon had been crossed. It was not the same as catching Lonsdale; that was cops and robbers. To find that a man like Philby, a man you might like, or drink with, or admire, had betrayed everything; to think of the agents and operations wasted: youth and innocence passed away, and the dark ages began.

A few days later Arthur stopped me in the corridor. He seemed strangely calm, for such a tense, almost hyperactive man. It was almost as if he had seen a bad road accident.

"Kim's gone," he said quietly.

"Good God, how . . . ?"

Arthur smiled weakly. "It's just like 1951, when the boys went . . ."

Philby's defection had a traumatic effect on morale inside the senior echelons of MI5. Until then, theories about the penetration of MI5 had been nursed secretly; afterward they became openly expressed fears. It seemed so obvious that Philby, like Maclean before him in 1951, had been tipped off by someone else, a fifth man, still inside. And of course, the possibility of a fifth man chimed completely with Golitsin's evidence about a Ring of Five. Burgess, Maclean, Philby, almost certainly Blunt, and a fifth. Someone who survived 1951, who stayed on undetected, who even now was watching the crisis unfold.

Hugh Winterborn and I often talked about the subject. He was convinced that we were penetrated at a high level.

"I just can't believe we are as apparently incompetent as we appear to be," he used to say.

Operation CHOIR, where we found the Russians had blocked up the pinhole for our probe microphone, had a major effect on his thinking, and even eight years later he used to talk animatedly about it. There were other incidents, too, which made him suspicious. We installed SF on the Chinese Embassy telephones, and almost immediately the Russians went around and took it out. Then there was the Falber Affair. After the PARTY PIECE operation, MI5 went on the hunt for the CPGB files which listed the secret payments made to the Party by the Soviets. We suspected that perhaps they might be held in the flat of Reuben Falber, who had recently been made cashier of the Russian funds. Falber is a prominent CPGB member, so when he advertised for a tenant to live in the flat on the ground floor of his house, we installed an agent there. Almost immediately, as we were planning to burgle the flat above, the agent was evicted by Falber, who gave no reason for the eviction.

But as a wave of anxiety passed through Leconfield House, I was still marooned inside the Directorate of Science. I decided to make my own freelance inquiries. Over a period of months I slowly drew out files from the Registry. First I took out the files for the microphoning operations I had been involved with in the mid-1950s—Operation CHOIR in London, DEW WORM and PIG ROOT in Canada, all of which went inexplicably wrong, and MOLE in Australia. I examined the cases carefully. Each had failed, and although complicated hypotheses to explain each failure could be adduced, the possibility that each had been blown by a spy inside MI5 was also a serious one. Then there were the cases which preoccupied Winterborn. Again, alternative explanations could be found. Maybe we had been clumsy. Maybe Falber just guessed the identity of our agent, but I find it very difficult to believe. A leak was just as possible. Next I pulled out the files on each of the double-agent cases I had been involved with during the 1950s. There were more than twenty in all. Each one was worthless. Of course, our tradecraft and Watcher radios were mainly to blame, but the Tisler affair had left a nagging doubt in the back of my mind. The Lulakov-Morrow test did not exclude the possibility of a human source beyond the monitoring of our Watcher radios. Then there was Lonsdale, and lastly Philby. Again the same pattern. Not one single operation had succeeded as planned, and all had some degree of evidence of Russian interference.

There is a point in any mystery when the shape of the answer becomes suddenly clear. Over those unhappy months in Buckingham Gate, in the winter of 1962–63 as I pored through the files, back-checking and cross-checking the complex details of nearly eight years of frantic work, it all became suddenly very obvious. What until then had been a hypothesis, became an article of faith. There was a spy; the only question was who? More weeks were spent laboriously checking the dates when files were signed off and on, when access began and when it ended. And always it came down to the same five names: Hollis, Mitchell, Cumming, Winterborn at a stretch, and I myself. I knew it wasn't me; Hugh Winterborn never really fitted, and I knew it could not be him;

Cumming I dismissed from the start. He would never have had the subtlety to carry it off. Which left Hollis and Mitchell. Was it Hollis, the aloof, pedestrian autocrat with whom I enjoyed a civil but distant relationship? Or Mitchell, his deputy, a man I knew less well? There was a secretiveness about him, a kind of slyness which made him avoid eye contact. He was a clever man, clever enough to spy. I knew my choice would be based on prejudice, but in my mind I plumped for Mitchell.

Early in 1963 I realized that one of the two men knew what I was doing. When I began my private investigations, I used to place the files in my safe on top of minute pencil marks, so that I could tell if they were being moved. One morning I came in, and they had been moved. Only two men had access to my safe: the Director-General and the Deputy, who retained copies of all combinations. The shadows were gathering; treachery stalked the corridors.

After Philby's defection Arthur became curiously distant. I could see he was preoccupied, but he deftly turned aside all attempts by me to find out what he was doing. I spent several evenings with him at his flat near Euston Station, and although we discussed Golitsin in general terms, he refused to be drawn out on what further inquiries he was making. Convinced that I might be sacked at any moment, or at least removed from access in some way, I began to make excuses to visit Arthur's office after hours, bringing with me files which I had used in my freelance examination of thirty-eight cases.

"Do you think that's significant?" I would ask, drawing his attention to a small ambiguity in the handling of a double-agent case, or an unexplained termination of a microphoning case. Arthur invariably gazed silently at whatever it was I showed him, thanked me, and said nothing more. Finally one night Arthur said to me, "You know who it is, don't you, Peter?"

I said, "Well, it's either Roger or Graham."

He said that he was carrying out an investigation of Mitchell.

He told me that he thought there had been a leak which had led to Philby's defection. He too had come to the conclusion that it was either Roger or Graham but he did not know which, so after Philby defected he had gone to Dick White and put the whole problem to him. Dick was his mentor, the man who gave him his head in the late 1940s, and Arthur never forgot the debt he owed. Dick asked him to come back and see him the next day when he had had time to think about it. This Arthur did. Dick had been very sensible. He was sure Roger could not be a spy, but he felt it was possible of Mitchell. He advised Arthur to tell Hollis of his fears, and as a result Hollis instructed Arthur to begin an investigation of the Deputy Director-General. He had been doing this for a short time until he and I exchanged ideas.

"How long have you been worried about this?" he asked.

"Since Tisler . . ."

Arthur opened his desk drawer and pulled out a small bottle of Scotch. He poured us both a small measure in his coffee cups.

"Have you told Roger?"

I told him that I had raised the issue twice before, once after Tisler, and once after Lonsdale. Both times I had been stifled. He seemed surprised.

"I suppose you've guessed what I'm doing . . . ?"

"It's Mitchell, isn't it?"

"Somebody told Kim when to run," he said, hardly answering my question, "I'm sure of it. Only someone in Graham's place could have known enough to do it . . ."

He told me that after Philby defected he went to see Dick White to tell him about his suspicion that either Hollis or Mitchell was a spy. It was a natural thing for Arthur to do.

Arthur told me to see Hollis myself.

"Tell him we've talked, and that I suggested you see him. It's the only way."

I rang up to Hollis' office, and to my surprise got an almost immediate appointment. I took the lift to the fifth floor and waited for the green light to flash above his door. I was shown in by his secretary. Hollis was sitting upright at his desk under the bay window, working on a single file, a line of pencils on one side, each one carefully sharpened to a precise point. I advanced until I was standing a few feet from the other side of the desk. He did not look up. I waited for almost a minute in silence while Hollis' predecessors gazed balefully out at me from the wall. Still I waited. Still his pen scratched at the file.

"How can I help you, Peter?" he asked at length.

At first I stuttered badly. The last hour had been a strain.

"I've been talking with Arthur Martin, sir."

"Oh?" There was no trace of surprise in his voice.

"I have let my hair down about my worries . . ."

"I see . . ."

Still he worked on.

"I have done another analysis, sir, and he said I should come and show it to you."

"Take it over to the table, will you . . ."

I retreated back across the room, and sat at the huge polished conference table. Hollis joined me, and began to read in silence. Occasionally he queried a point in my analysis. But I could sense that today he was no opposition. It was almost as if he were expecting me.

"Did you know he's retiring in six months?" he asked when he had finished reading.

"Mitchell?" I asked, in genuine confusion. As far as I knew, he had at least a couple of years to go.

"He asked for it a while ago," said Hollis. "I can't change it now. I'll give you that long to prove it. You can join Martin, and I'll square it with Willis."

He handed me the file back.

"I don't have to tell you that I don't like it. You know that already. Not one word of this investigation is to leak out, understood?"

"Yes, sir!"

"You'll need to know Mitchell's background," he said, as he returned to his desk and pencils. "I'll arrange for Arthur to have his Record of Service."

"Thank you, sir."

He was already writing again as I went out.

13 ————————————————

AS SOON AS I JOINED THE MITCHELL CASE, I WAS INDOCTRINATED
into the greatest counterintelligence secret in the Western world
—the VENONA codebreak. To understand what VENONA was, and
its true significance, you have to understand a little of the complex world of cryptography. In the 1930s, modern intelligence
services like the Russian and the British adopted the one-time
code pad system of communications. It is the safest form of encipherment known, since only sender and receiver have copies of
the pad. As long as every sheet is used only once and destroyed,
the code is unbreakable. To send a message using a one-time pad,
the addresser translates each word of the message into a four-
figure group of numbers, using a codebook. So if the first word of
the message is "defense," this might become 3765. The figure
3765 is then added to the first group on the one-time pad, say
1196, using the Fibonacci system, which makes 4851. It is, in
effect, a double encipherment. (The Fibonacci system is also
known as Chinese arithmetic, where numbers greater than 9 are
not carried forward. All cipher systems work on the Fibonacci
system, because carrying numbers forward creates nonrandom
distribution.)

The VENONA codebreak became possible because during the
early years of the war the Russians ran short of cipher material.
Such was the pressure on their communications system that they
made duplicate sets of their one-time pads and issued them to

different embassies in the West. In fact, the chances of compromising their communications were slim. The number of messages being transmitted worldwide was vast, and the Russians operated on five channels—one for Ambassadorial communications, one for the GRU, another for the Naval GRU, a fourth for the KGB, and lastly a channel for trade traffic connected with the vast program of military equipment passing from West to East during the war, which on its own comprised about 80 percent of total Russian messages. A set of pads might be issued to the KGB in Washington for their communications with Moscow, and its duplicate might be the trade traffic channel between Mexico and Moscow.

Shortly after the end of the war a brilliant American cryptanalyst named Meredith Gardner, from the U.S. Armed Forces Security Agency (the forerunner of the NSA), began work on the charred remains of a Russian codebook found on a battlefield in Finland. Although it was incomplete, the codebook did have the groups for some of the most common instructions in radio messages—those for "Spell" and "Endspell." These are common because any codebook has only a finite vocabulary, and where an addresser lacks the relevant group in the codebook—always the case, for instance, with names—he has to spell the word out letter by letter, prefixing with the word "Spell," and ending with the word "Endspell" to alert his addressee.

Using these common groups Gardner checked back on previous Russian radio traffic, and realized that there were duplications across some channels, indicating that the same one-time pads had been used. Slowly he "matched" the traffic which had been enciphered using the same pads, and began to try to break it. At first no one would believe him when he claimed to have broken into the Russian ciphers, and he was taken seriously only when he got a major breakthrough in the Washington-to-Moscow Ambassadorial channel. He decrypted the English phrase "Defense does not win wars!" which was a "Spell/Endspell" sequence. Gardner recognized it as a book on defense strategy published in the USA just before the date the message was sent. At this point, the Armed Forces Security Agency shared the secret with the British, who at that time were the world leaders in cryptanalysis, and together they began a joint effort to break the traffic, which lasted forty years.

Operation BRIDE (as it was first known) but later DRUG and VENONA, as it was known in Britain, made painfully slow progress. Finding matches among the mass of traffic available took time enough. But even then there was no certainty the messages on each side of the match could be broken. The codebook was incomplete, so the codebreakers used "collateral" intelligence. If, for instance, they found a match between the Washington-to-Moscow KGB channel and the New York-to-Moscow trade channel, it was possible to attack the trade channel by using "collateral," information gathered from shipping manifests, cargo records, departure and arrival times, tide tables, and so forth, for the date of the message. This information enabled the codebreakers to make estimates of what might be in the trade traffic. Once breaks were made in one side of a match, it provided more groups for the codebook, and helped make inroads on the other side.

The British and Americans developed a key device for expanding the VENONA breaks. It was called a "window index." Every time a word or phrase was broken out, it was indexed to everywhere else it appeared in the matched traffic. The British began to index these decrypts in a more advanced way. They placed two unsolved groups on each side of the decrypted word or phrase and after a period of time these window indexes led to repetitions, where different words which had been broken out were followed by the same unsolved group. The repetition often gave enough collateral to begin a successful attack on the group, thus widening the window indexes. Another technique was "dragging." Where a "Spell/Endspell" sequence or name came up, and the cryptanalysts did not know what the missing letters of the spelled sequence were, the groups were dragged, using a computer, across the rest of the channels, and out would come a list of all the repeats. Then the cryptanalysts would set to work on the reverse side of the repeat matches, and hope to attack the "Spell/Endspell" sequence that way.

It was an imperfect art, often moving forward only a word or two a month, and then suddenly spilling forward, like the time the Americans found the complete text of a recorded speech in the Ambassadorial channel. Often terrible new difficulties were encountered: one-time pads were used in unorthodox ways, up and down, or folded, which made the process of finding matches infinitely more problematic. There were difficulties, too, with the codebooks. Sometimes they changed, and whereas the Ambassadorial, GRU, and trade channels used a straightforward alphabetically listed codebook, rather like a dictionary, so that the codebreakers could guess from the group where in the codebook it appeared, the KGB used a special multivolume random codebook which made decrypting matched KGB channels a mindbending task. The effort involved in VENONA was enormous. For years both GCHQ and NSA and MI5 employed teams of researchers scouring the world searching for "collateral"; but despite the effort less than 1 percent of the 200,000 messages we held were ever broken into, and many of those were broken only to the extent of a few words.

But the effect of the VENONA material on British and American intelligence was immense, not just in terms of the counterintelligence received, but in terms of the effect it had on shaping attitudes in the secret world. By the late 1940s enough progress was made in the New York/Moscow and Washington/Moscow KGB channels to reveal the extent of massive Russian espionage activity in the USA throughout and immediately after the war. More than 1200 cryptonyms littered the traffic, which, because they were frequently part of "Spell/Endspell" sequences, were often the easiest things to isolate in the traffic, even if they could not be broken. Of those 1200, more than 800 were assessed as recruited Soviet agents. It is probable that the majority of these were the low-level contacts which are the staple currency of all intelligence networks. But some were of major importance. Fourteen agents appeared to be operating in or close to the OSS (the wartime forerunner of the CIA), five agents had access, to one degree or another, to the White House, including one who, according to the traffic, traveled in Ambassador Averill Harriman's private airplane back from Moscow to the USA. Most damaging of all, the Russians had a chain of agents inside the American atomic weapons development program, and another with access to almost every document of importance which passed between the British and U.S. governments in 1945, including private telegrams sent by Churchill to Presidents Roosevelt and Truman.

Using leads in the decrypted traffic, some of these cases were solved. Maclean was identified as one of the sources of the Churchill telegrams, and many others besides; Klaus Fuchs and the Rosenbergs were unmasked as some of the nuclear spies; while comparison of geographical clues in the decrypts with the movements of Alger Hiss, a senior U.S. State Department official, over a lengthy period made him the best suspect as the agent on Harriman's plane. But despite frenzied counterintelligence and cryptanalytical effort, most of the cryptonyms remain today unidentified.

In Britain the situation was equally grim, but with one major difference. Whereas the Americans had all the Soviet radio traffic passing to and from the USA during and after the war, in Britain Churchill ordered all anti-Soviet intelligence work to cease during the wartime alliance, and GCHQ did not begin taking the traffic again until the very end of the war. Consequently there was far less traffic, and only one break was made into it, for the week September 15 to September 22, 1945, in the Moscow-to-London KGB channel.

There was a series of messages sent to a KGB officer in the London Embassy, Boris Krotov, who specialized in running high-grade agents. The messages came at a time of some crisis for the Russian intelligence services in the West. A young GRU cipher clerk in the Russian Embassy in Canada, Igor Gouzenko, had just defected, taking a mass of material incriminating spies in Canada and the USA, and in Britain a nuclear spy, Alan Nunn May. Most of the messages to Krotov from Moscow Center concerned instructions on how to handle the various agents under his care. Eight cryptonyms were mentioned in all, three of which were referred to as the "valuable *argentura* [spy ring] of Stanley, Hicks, and Johnson," two who were routinely referred to together as David and Rosa, and three others. By the end of the week's traffic all contact with the eight spies had been put on ice, and reduced to meetings, except in special circumstances, of once a month.

When I was indoctrinated into VENONA, I remember my first sight of the GCHQ copies of the Moscow-to-London KGB channel. Every time GCHQ broke a few more words in a message, they circulated to the very few users drop copies of the new decrypt. The copies were stamped TOP SECRET UMBRA VENONA, and listed the addresser and addressee, the date and time of the message, the channel and direction (for instance, KGB Moscow/London), and the message priority (whether it was routine or urgent). Underneath would be something like this:

TEXT OF MESSAGE
YOUR COMMUNICATION OF 74689 AND 02985 47199 67789 88005 62971 CONCERNING SPELL H I C K S END-SPELL 55557 81045 10835 68971 71129 EXTREME CAU-TION AT PRESENT TIME 56690 12748 92640 00471 SPELL S T A N L E Y ENDSPELL 37106 72885 MONTHLY UNTIL FURTHER NOTICE. SIGNATURE OF MESSAGE

(This is not a verbatim decrypt; merely a very close approximation of the kind of challenge we were faced with.)

VENONA was the most terrible secret of all; it was incomplete. It was obvious from the decrypts that each of the eight cryptonyms was an important spy, both from the care the Russians were taking to protect them all in September 1945, and because we knew that Krotov specialized in that type of agent. But there was precious little evidence from the traffic which could help us identify them. GCHQ circulated only translations which they had verified, and included the verbatim unsolved groups where they occurred, but they often attached to the copy a separate page of notes giving possible translations of the odd group, which had not yet been verified. Often a message would be repeated several times, as more groups were got out, and it was recirculated.

Stanley, we were sure, must be Philby. Golitsin had heard the code name Stanley, and associated it with KGB operations in the Middle East, but there was no proof of this in the traffic. Hicks, therefore, was almost certainly Burgess because of the reference to the *argentura*, and because of a veiled reference to Hicks' temperament. Johnson was probably Blunt, although again there was no proof of it in the traffic. But the identity of the five other spies remained a mystery. Maclean was obviously not one of these, since he was in Washington in September 1945. The consequences for the Mitchell investigation were obvious. Any one of the five unidentified cryptonyms could be the spy inside MI5. I remember wondering, as I read the tantalizing decrypts, how on earth anyone at the top of MI5 has slept at night in the dozen years since they were first decrypted.

Perhaps the most extraordinary thing in the whole VENONA story was the fact that it was closed down on both sides of the Atlantic in 1954. After the initial surge of activity in the late 1940s and early 1950s, and the rash of prosecutions which followed, cryptanalytical progress slowed to a virtual halt. Hand matching had reached the limitations of the human brain, and computers were not then powerful enough to take the program much further. There was another reason too; in 1948 the Russians began to alter their code procedures worldwide, removing all duplicated pads. The last casualty of this was the Australian VE-NONA operation, which had been making so much progress that the British and Americans were virtually reading the Russian ciphers continuously as the messages were produced. The Australians were never told at the time but were brought into it some years later, although when the extent of Soviet espionage penetration, especially of the Department of External Affairs, became apparent, they were provided with the intelligence in bowdlerized form, and it led to the establishment of ASIO (Australian Security Intelligence Organization) with MI5's help.

The reason for the change in Soviet codes became apparent in the early 1950s. The secret of the break had been leaked to the Russians by a young Armed Services Security Agency clerk, William Weisband. In fact, Weisband did not know the extent of the Russian mistake and it was only when Philby was indoctrinated in 1949 that they knew the breadth of their disaster, although other people, such as Roger Hollis, were indoctrinated in 1948, when the match suddenly ceased in Australia after he returned from organizing the setting up of ASIO. Although the duplicate one-time pads were withdrawn, the Russians could do nothing to prevent the continuing work on the traffic they had already sent up until 1948. But thanks to Philby's posting to Washington in 1949, they were able to monitor the precise progress that was being made. Once the Russians knew the extent of the VENONA leak, and the technical difficulties of finding more matches multiplied, it was only a matter of time before priorities moved on. In 1954 most of the work was closed down.

Years later, I arranged for Meredith Gardner to visit Britain to help us on the British VENONA. He was a quiet, scholarly man, entirely unaware of the awe in which he was held by other cryptanalysts. He used to tell me how he worked on the matches in his office, and of how a young pipe-smoking Englishman named Philby used to regularly visit him and peer over his shoulder and admire the progress he was making. Gardner was rather a sad figure by the late 1960s. He felt very keenly that the cryptanalytical break he had made possible was a thing of mathematical beauty, and he was depressed at the use to which it had been put.

"I never wanted it to get anyone into trouble," he used to say. He was appalled at the fact that his discovery had led, almost inevitably, to the electric chair, and felt (as I did) that the Rosenbergs, while guilty, ought to have been given clemency. In Gardner's mind, VENONA was almost an art form, and he did not want it sullied by crude McCarthyism. But the codebreak had a fundamental effect on Cold War attitudes among those few indoctrinated officers inside the British and American intelligence services. It became the wellspring for the new emphasis on counterespionage investigation which increasingly permeated Western intelligence in the decades after the first break was made. More directly, it showed the worldwide scale of the Soviet espionage attack, at a time when the Western political leadership was apparently pursuing a policy of alliance and extending the hand of friendship. In the British traffic, for instance, most of the KGB channel during that September week was taken up with messages from Moscow detailing arrangements for the return of Allied prisoners to the Soviet authorities, groups like the Cossacks and others who had fought against the Soviet Union. Many of the messages were just long lists of names and instructions that they should be apprehended as soon as possible. By the time I read the messages they were all long since dead, but at the time many intelligence officers must have been struck by the sense that peace had not come in 1945; a German concentration camp had merely been exchanged for a Soviet Gulag.

In 1959, a new discovery was made which resuscitated VENONA again. GCHQ discovered that the Swedish Signals Intelligence Service had taken and stored a considerable amount of new wartime traffic, including some GRU radio messages sent to and from London during the early years of the war. GCHQ persuaded the Swedes to relinquish their neutrality, and pass the material over for analysis. The discovery of the Swedish HASP material was one of the main reasons for Arthur's return to D1. He was one of the few officers inside MI5 with direct experience of VENONA, having worked intimately with it during the Fuchs and Maclean investigations.

There were high hopes that HASP would transform VENONA by providing more intelligence about unknown cryptonyms and, just as important, by providing more groups for the codebook, which would, in turn, lead to further breaks in VENONA material already held. Moreover, since powerful new computers were becoming available, it made sense to reopen the whole program (I was never convinced that the effort should have been dropped in the 1950s), and the pace gradually increased, with vigorous encouragement by Arthur, through the early 1960s.

In fact, there were no great immediate discoveries in the HASP material which related to Britain. Most of the material consisted of routine reports from GRU officers of bomb damage in various parts of Britain, and estimates of British military capability. There were dozens of cryptonyms, some of whom were interesting, but long since dead. J.B.S. Haldane, for instance, who was working in the Admiralty's submarine experimental station at Haslar, researching into deep diving techniques, was supplying details of the programs to the CPGB, who were passing it on to the GRU in London. Another spy identified in the traffic was the Honorable Owen Montagu, the son of Lord Swaythling (not to be confused with Euan Montagu, who organized the celebrated "Man Who Never Was" deception operation during the war). He was a freelance journalist, and from the traffic it was clear that he was used by the Russians to collect political intelligence in the Labor Party, and to a lesser degree the CPGB.

The extraordinary thing about the GRU traffic was the comparison with the KGB traffic of four years later. The GRU officers in 1940 and 1941 were clearly of low caliber, demoralized and running around like headless chickens in the wake of Stalin's purges of the 1930s. By 1945 they had given way to a new breed of professional Russian intelligence officers like Krotov. The entire agent-running procedure was clearly highly skilled, and pragmatic. Great care was being taken to protect agents for their long-term use. Where there seemed poor discipline in the GRU procedures, by 1945 the traffic showed that control was exerted from Moscow Center, and comparison between KGB and Ambassadorial channels demonstrated quite clearly the importance the KGB had inside the Russian State. This, in a sense, was the most enduring legacy of the VENONA break—the glimpse it gave us of the vast KGB machine, with networks all across the West, ready for the Cold War as the West prepared for peace.

When I finished studying the VENONA material in the special secure office where it was stored on the fifth floor, I moved into an office with Evelyn McBarnet, Arthur's research officer, who was already busy on the case. The Mitchell investigation came at an awkward time for D Branch. Hollis had moved Furnival Jones from his post to become head of C Branch, in preparation for his appointment as Deputy Director-General on Mitchell's retirement. F.J.'s replacement was Malcolm Cumming. It was not a popular appointment among the bright young men of D Branch, who were laboring to build on the achievements of the Lonsdale case. Arthur himself had hopes that he might have been offered the job. He certainly deserved it, in terms of achievement, but he had never been popular among the Directors for the stand he took in the early 1950s. He was seen as truculent, temperamental, too unwilling to tolerate fools gladly, which unfortunately was a prerequisite for advancement in the Service. When the Mitchell investigation was sanctioned, Hollis decided not to indoctrinate Cumming, who theoretically was a potential suspect. Oversight of the case was given to F.J., who supervised things from C Branch headquarters in Cork Street.

Evelyn McBarnet was a strange woman, with a large birthmark running down one side of her face. Like a hothouse plant, she lived all her life in the enclosed space of the office, and had no perceptible existence outside.

"Are you a Freemason?" she asked me almost as soon as I joined her in her office.

"No," I replied, "and I don't approve of it."

"I didn't think you looked like one, but you'd better join if you want to be a success in this place," she told me darkly.

Evelyn had always believed there was a penetration of MI5. She had spent years working in counterespionage as a research officer, far longer than Arthur or I. She was a walking compendium of office life and shrewd, if somewhat morbid, judge of character.

"I always knew there would have to be an investigation," she told me, but she had a disturbing conviction that the course of the investigation was preordained. The worst, she was sure, was yet to come.

"Arthur will never last, if he pushes this issue," she told me, "and neither will you, if you associate yourself with him."

"What on earth do you mean, Evelyn?" I asked, in genuine surprise.

She opened her safe and pulled out a small exercise book with a black cover.

"Read this," she told me.

I opened the book. It was neatly written in a woman's hand. I flicked through the pages quickly. It listed details of cases from the 1940s and 1950s, some of which I knew about vaguely, and others I did not, which the author had collated from the MI5 Registry. Each one contained an explicit allegation about a penetration of MI5 or MI6.

"Whose is this?" I asked, aghast.

"Anne Last's, a friend of mine. She used to work with me," said Evelyn. "She did it after Burgess and Maclean went, then she left to have a family, you know. She married Charles Elwell. Before she left she gave me the book, and told me that I would understand."

"Does Arthur know . . . ?"

"Of course."

"But have you shown it to anyone else?"

"And get chopped too . . . ?"

I carried on reading. Maxwell Knight's name figured frequently in the first few pages. During the war he was convinced there was a spy inside MI5, and had minuted to that effect, although no action was taken. There were literally dozens and dozens of allegations. Many of them were fanciful—offhand comments drawn from agent reports; but others were more concrete, like the testimony of Igor Gouzenko, the young Russian cipher clerk who defected to the Canadians in 1945, and whose defection triggered such alarm in the single week of British VENONA KGB traffic. According to Anne Last, Gouzenko claimed in his debriefing that there was a spy code-named Elli inside MI5. He had learned about Elli while serving in Moscow in 1942, from a friend of his, Luibimov, who handled radio messages dealing with Elli. Elli had something Russian in his background, had access to certain files, was serviced using Duboks, or dead letter boxes, and his information was often taken straight to Stalin. Gouzenko's allegation had been filed along with all the rest of his material, but then, inexplicably, left to gather dust.

"People didn't believe him," said Evelyn, "they said he got it wrong. There couldn't be a spy inside MI5 . . ."

On the last page was what appeared to be a kind of "last will and testament." "If MI5 is penetrated," it said, "I think it is most likely to be Roger Hollis or Graham Mitchell."

"How the hell can we investigate these?" I gasped. "We'll have to turn the whole place upside down to do it properly."

"That's what they said in 1951," said Evelyn bitterly.

Anne Last's book was only the first of many secrets Evelyn shared with me over the first weeks we worked together. Gradually she filled in much of the forgotten history of MI5, the kinds of stories you never heard on the A2 tapes: stories of doubts and suspicions, unexplained actions, and curious coincidences. I soon learned that I was by no means the first person to come to suspect the office had been deeply penetrated. The fears were as old as the office furniture.

That evening I joined the commuters thronging down Curzon Street toward Park Lane, my head humming with what I had learned from Evelyn. Here was a consistent unbroken pattern of allegations, each suggesting there was a spy in the office, stretching from 1942 to the present day. For too long they had gone uninvestigated, unchallenged. This time the chase would be long and hard and unrelenting. I paused to look back at Leconfield House.

"This time," I thought, "this time there will be no tip-offs, no defections. This one will not slip away . . ."

14

FOR ALL MY HIGH HOPES, THE MITCHELL INVESTIGATION WAS A wretched affair. It began with a row, it ended with a row, and little went right in between. It was clear to me that to stand any chance at all of clinching the case one way or the other before Mitchell retired, we would have to turn on the taps, and use every technical resource at our disposal. Hollis vehemently opposed any request for home telephone taps and the full watching facilities, saying that he was not prepared to indoctrinate any further MI5 officers into the case, and certainly had no intention of approaching the Home Secretary for permission to bug or burgle his own deputy's house.

Arthur reacted badly to the setbacks. His temper by now was on a short fuse, and he erupted at a meeting in Hollis' office when his precise, quiet request for facilities was refused point-blank by the Director-General. Arthur said it was intolerable to be restricted when such a grave issue was at stake, and threatened to approach the Prime Minister himself to alert him to the situation. Hollis always reacted smoothly to any threats, and merely said he noted Arthur's comment, but that his decision stood.

"Under no circumstances will I authorize an extension of this investigation!"

Arthur stalked out of the room, obviously fully intending to carry out his threat.

That evening Furnival Jones and I went to my club, the Oxford and Cambridge, to try to find a way of averting catastrophe. Relations had been swiftly deteriorating between Hollis and Arthur ever since Cumming had been appointed to the Directorship of D Branch, and with the Mitchell case poised so perilously, any hint of the turmoil inside the organization would be disastrous.

Furnival Jones was in a dreadful position. He knew as well as I that he would be Hollis' deputy himself within a few months, yet I could tell that he felt Hollis was indeed being obstructive.

"It'll mean the end of the Service, if Arthur does something stupid," said Furnival Jones gloomily into his glass.

I asked him if he could not approach Dick White privately to see if some pressure could be exerted on Hollis to relent. Furnival Jones looked at me almost in anguish. He could see that he was slowly being ground between competing loyalties—to Hollis, and to those who were conducting a very difficult and emotionally fraught inquiry. It was close to one in the morning before we came to any firm decision. Furnival Jones promised that he would make an appointment to see Dick White, if I undertook to restrain Arthur from any rash course of action. I telephoned Arthur from my club; it was late, but I knew he would be up, brooding over a Scotch bottle. I said I had to see him that night, and took a taxi around to his flat.

Arthur was in a truculent mood.

"I suppose you've come to tell me you've decided to throw your hand in too!" he said acidly.

For the second time that evening I settled down to a long drinking session, trying to talk Arthur around. He looked desperately strained. He had been seriously overworking since before the Lonsdale case, and was putting on weight drastically. His flesh was gray, and he was losing his youthfulness. He railed against the obstructions that were being put in his way. I could see that the specter of 1951 haunted him, when he had allowed himself to be shunted out to Malaya.

"I should have fought then, but I agreed with them at the time. It seemed best to leave it. But not this time," he said.

In the end he saw the sense of F.J.'s approach. An open breach with Hollis would get us nowhere, and there was at least hope that Dick would talk him around to agreeing to some of our requests for more facilities.

The following day I got a call from F.J. He said he had spoken to Dick, and we were all to assemble in his flat in Queen Anne's Gate on the following Sunday afternoon.

"He wants to see a presentation of the case, then he'll decide what to do."

Dick White's flat backed onto MI6 headquarters in Broadway, and I arrived there promptly at the appointed time. Dick answered the door; he was dressed casually, with an open shirt and cravat. He showed us into his study, an elegant book-lined room, decorated in seventeenth-century style. Paintings from the National Gallery collection lined the walls, and an ornamental mirror stood gleaming above the fireplace.

"Shall we have some tea?" he asked, anxious to break the tension which was apparent on everyone's face.

"Now," he said, looking at Arthur, "I think you had better make your case . . ."

Arthur explained that I had brought my charts tabulating access to the thirty-eight cases, and suggested that it might be better if, in the first instance, I made the presentation. For a moment there was confusion. The charts were too large to spread on the delicate tea table, but Dick saw the problem.

"No, no," he said, "that's quite all right—spread them on the floor."

Within two minutes we were sprawling across the carpet, and the elegant Sunday-afternoon reserve was lost as we began to go through the litany of fears once more. I explained that I had submitted two previous papers, one on Tisler, the other on Lonsdale, but that these had both been rejected. Dick looked at me sharply, but made no comment.

"The whole point is that we can't look at this problem piecemeal," I told him, "and the basis of these charts is to try to take an overall view, to see if there is any evidence of Russian interference in the cases . . ."

"Sounds like a bad case of induction to me, but go on," said Dick skeptically.

I went through the cases one by one, and explained how it always came down to the same five names.

"Did you at any stage discuss this with Arthur, before you drew this together?" he asked, looking me squarely in the eye.

"How could I? I was over in the Directorate most of the time."

Dick turned to Arthur.

"You mean to tell me that you both came to this conclusion?" He obviously found it hard to believe.

Arthur took over and explained the problem with facilities. Dick asked F.J., who so far had remained silent, for his opinion. He paused, and then committed himself irrevocably.

"Roger has refused to extend the investigation. Personally, I think it's a mistake. When you put together the lack of following with the lack of technical aids, there really is little chance of finding an answer to this case."

Dick was impressed with F.J.'s sensible appraisal.

"There are two factors here," he said after thinking for a while. "We have to do this investigation, and we have to be seen to do this investigation, and that's almost just as important."

He told us that some changes would certainly have to be made. He thought the investigation should be coordinated from an unofficial house, rather than a government building, and offered us the use of an MI6 safe house in Pavilion Road, near Sloane Square.

"I'll think overnight about what I am going to say to Roger, and you will hear from him."

The following day F.J. informed us that Hollis had given permission for a team of MI6 Watchers to be used on the case, although they would still not be allowed to trail Mitchell beyond the London railway station, in case their presence was noticed. We were allowed to indoctrinate Winterborn, and were given carte blanche to install a closed-circuit television system behind a two-way mirror in Mitchell's office. That afternoon we moved the burgeoning files across London to a tatty unfurnished upstairs flat in a small mews house in Pavilion Road, which for the rest of the case became our headquarters.

In the early stages of the investigation, we made a complete reexamination of the circumstances of Philby's defection. It yielded one vital discovery; I asked the CIA to check their computer records of the movement of all known Russian intelligence officers around the world, and we discovered that Yuri Modin, a KGB officer we strongly suspected had been Philby's controller during the 1940s, and of having arranged the Burgess/Maclean defections, had visited the Middle East in September 1962, just after Flora Solomon's meeting with Arthur in London. A further check showed Modin made a previous visit in May of the same year, shortly after the three Golitsin serials relating to the Ring of Five arrived at Leconfield House. Finally the CIA established that Modin had made no other trips abroad since the early 1950s. Eleanor Philby, Kim's wife, was interviewed at this time, and told us that Philby had cut short a family holiday in Jordan in September, and from then onward until his disappearance exhibited increasing signs of alcoholism and stress. It was obvious to us that Modin had gone to Beirut to alert Philby to the reopening of his case. Once the KGB knew of Golitsin's departure, it was an obvious precaution, but the odd thing was the fact that Philby seemed apparently unmoved until after Modin's second visit in September, which coincided exactly with the time when the case against him became unassailable.

We turned to the tapes of Philby's so-called "confession,"

which Nicholas Elliott brought back with him from Beirut. For many weeks it was impossible to listen to the tapes, because the sound quality was so poor. In typical MI6 style, they had used a single low-grade microphone in a room with the windows wide open. The traffic noise was deafening! Using the binaural tape enhancer which I had developed, and the services of Evelyn McBarnet and a young transcriber named Anne Orr-Ewing, who had the best hearing of all the transcribers, we managed to obtain a transcript which was about 80 percent accurate. Arthur and I listened to the tape one afternoon, following it carefully on the page. There was no doubt in anyone's mind, listening to the tape, that Philby arrived at the safe house well prepared for Elliott's confrontation. Elliott told him there was new evidence, that he was now convinced of his guilt, and Philby, who had denied everything time and again for a decade, swiftly admitted spying since 1934. He never once asked what the new evidence was.

Arthur found it distressing to listen to the tape; he kept screwing up his eyes, and pounding his knees with his fists in frustration as Philby reeled off a string of ludicrous claims: Blunt was in the clear, but Tim Milne, an apparently close friend of Philby's, who had loyally defended him for years, was not. The whole confession, including Philby's signed statement, looked carefully prepared to blend fact and fiction in a way which would mislead us. I thought back to my first meeting with Philby, the boyish charm, the stutter, how I sympathized with him; and the second time I heard that voice, in 1955, as he ducked and weaved around his MI6 interrogators, finessing a victory from a steadily losing hand. And now there was Elliott, trying his manful best to corner a man for whom deception had been a second skin for thirty years. It was no contest. By the end they sounded like two rather tipsy radio announcers, their warm, classical public-school accents discussing the greatest treachery of the twentieth century.

"It's all been terribly badly handled," moaned Arthur in despair as the tape flicked through the heads. "We should have sent a team out there, and grilled him while we had the chance . . ."

I agreed with him. Roger and Dick had not taken into account that Philby might defect.

On the face of it, the coincidental Modin journeys, the fact that Philby seemed to be expecting Elliott, and his artful confession all pointed in one direction: the Russians still had access to a source inside British Intelligence who was monitoring the progress of the Philby case. Only a handful of officers had such access, chief among them being Hollis and Mitchell.

I decided to pay a visit to GCHQ to see if there was anything further that could be done with the VENONA program to assist the Mitchell case. The VENONA work was done inside a large wooden hut, number H72, which formed a spur off one of the main avenues in the central GCHQ complex. The work was supervised by a young cryptanalyst named Geoffrey Sudbury, who sat in a small office at the front of the hut. Behind him dozens of linguists sat under harsh lamps, toiling for matches, and hoping to tease out the translations from a thousand anonymous groups of numbers.

Sudbury's office was a joyous menagerie of cryptanalytical bric-a-brac. Huge piles of bound VENONA window indexes piled up in one corner, and tray upon tray of decrypts stood on his desk, ready for his approval before they were circulated up to MI5 and MI6. Sudbury and I had a long talk about how the whole program could be pushed forward. The principal problem was that VENONA, up until then, had been hand matched, and computers were used only for specific pieces of work, such as dragging for a cryptonym. Most of the effort had gone into attacking the KGB and GRU channels directory; the trade traffic channels had been used wherever they formed the back of a match, but otherwise the bulk of it had been left unprocessed. A comprehensive computer-matching program was needed, using the new computers

which were becoming available by the early 1960s, in the hope
that more matches might be found.

It was a vast undertaking. There were over 150,000 trade traffic
messages, and very few were even in "punched" form, suitable for
processing through a computer. This alone was a huge task. Each
individual group had to be punched up twice by data processors,
in order to "verify" that the processed traffic was free from errors.
Then the first five groups of each message were computer
matched against the whole of the rest of the traffic, involving
something like 10 billion calculations for each message.

When I discussed the project with Willis at the Directorate of
Science, he was skeptical about the whole thing, so I went to see
Sir William Cook at the Atomic Weapons Research Establishment again, with Frank Morgan. I knew that AWRE had the
biggest computer facility in the country, bigger at that time than
even GCHQ. I explained what I wanted to do. We needed at
least three months on his computer to find the matches; once
that was done, we could farm them out to NSA and GCHQ for
the cryptanalytical work of trying to break the matches out.
Cook, as always, was marvelous. I told him of Willis' skepticism,
which he brushed aside.

"This is one of the most important contributions AWRE can
make," he said, lifting the telephone. He spoke immediately to
the AWRE head of Data Processing.

"There's a vital job I want you to start straightaway. I'm sending a chap down with the details. You don't need to know where
he works. Please do as he says . . ."

In two months we had punched up and verified every message,
and for the next three months the AWRE computers worked on
the VENONA for six hours a night.

At first it looked as if the AWRE computerization program
might transform the British VENONA. Early on we got a new
match for a message just after the existing week's traffic in mid-
September, which we had already broken. The message, when it

was partially decrypted, concerned Stanley again. He was to carry no documents which might incriminate him to his next meeting with Krotov. Then, in the midst of a haze of unbroken groups, there was a fleeting reference to a crisis in KGB affairs in Mexico. Krotov was told to refer to Stanley for details, since his "section" dealt with Mexican matters.

At the time of this message Philby was the head of the Iberian section of MI6, which controlled a large swath of Hispanic countries, including Mexico. It was a bitter moment. The categoric proof that Stanley was Philby had come just a matter of months after he defected. Had we broken it out a few years earlier, we could have arrested Philby on one of his regular trips back to London to visit the *Observer*. This merely intensified fears about the integrity of MI5, since it made the decision in 1954 to close down the VENONA program look deeply suspect. When we checked, we found that the officer who ordered the closedown was the then head of Counterespionage, Graham Mitchell.

Sadly, the Philby fragment was the only real assistance the computerization program gave the British VENONA effort. Matches were made in Mexican KGB traffic and elsewhere in South America which were of enormous interest to the CIA and the RCMP, since Mexico was a principal area where the KGB introduced illegals into North America. But the matches made in British VENONA were almost all trade to trade traffic, rather than trade traffic to the KGB or GRU, which was what we needed. The cryptanalytical effort in Hut H72 went even more intensely than before, but there was to be no new shortcut.

There was little in Mitchell's Record of Service to help us either. Born in 1905, educated at Oxford, he then worked as a journalist and later as a statistician in Conservative Central Office. This did surprise me, as I recalled that when arguing with Mitchell about the Lonsdale case, he had claimed that he could not understand my argument since he was "no statistician." He joined MI5 as a result of contact made through the Tory Party, and worked on the anti-Fascist side during the war, latterly with some involvement, too, in the CPGB. Thereafter his progress was swift: he became head of F Branch (Domestic Subversion) in the late 1940s, and Dick White's first head of Counterespionage in 1953, before Hollis appointed him his deputy in 1956. There were only two really striking things about Mitchell's career. One was the way it was intimately bound up with Hollis'. They had been contemporaries at Oxford, joined MI5 at around the same time, and followed each other up the ladder in complementary positions. The second was the fact that Mitchell seemed to be an underachiever. He was a clever man, picked by Dick White to transform D Branch. He signally failed to do so in the three years he held the job, and indeed, when the decision to close VENONA down was taken into account, it seemed almost as if he had willfully failed.

The intense surveillance of Mitchell in the office revealed very little. I treated his ink blotter with secret-writing material, and every night it was developed, so that we could check on everything he wrote. But there was nothing beyond the papers he worked on normally. The closed-circuit television was monitored continuously by the MI6 Watchers. It was an unpleasant task; every morning Mitchell came in and picked his teeth with a toothpick in front of the two-way mirror, and repeated the meticulous process again before lunch, after lunch, and then again before he went home. By the end of the case, I began to feel that the only parts of Mitchell that we knew at all well were the backs of his tonsils!

I arranged to feed him barium meals. I circulated to him the bound volumes of my analysis of clandestine Soviet radio communications, with all their classifications and group count schedules, which I had recently updated for GCHQ. If Mitchell was a spy, it was the sort of priceless intelligence he could not afford to ignore. I watched on the monitor as Mitchell looked at the report in a desultory sort of way. Later James Robertson, an old adver-

sary of mine who had run Soviet Counterespionage for a period in
the 1950s, came into his office, and they began talking about me.
Robertson never forgave me for the changes I made in D Branch
when he was there. He thought I was a jumped-up newcomer,
who should have learned to respect my elders and betters before
presuming to offer advice. He and Mitchell discussed my radio
analysis. Neither man understood its purpose.

"That bloody man Wright," said Robertson tartly, "he thinks
he knows it all. Wants his wings clipped!"

Mitchell nodded sagely, and I could not help smiling at the
irony of it all.

But the lighter moments were few and far between in what was
a grim vigil, watching and waiting for a man to betray himself on
the other side of a mirror. Only once did I think we had him.
One Friday afternoon he began drawing on a scrap of paper. He
concentrated intensely for perhaps twenty minutes, referring to
notes on a piece of paper he took from his wallet, and then
suddenly tore the piece of paper up and put it in his waste bin.
Every night, since the beginning of the case, Hollis arranged for
me to search his office, and Hollis' secretary was instructed to
retain his burn bag, containing his classified waste, so that it
could be checked as well. That evening I retrieved the scraps of
paper from the bin, and reconstructed them. It was a map of
Chobham Common, near where Mitchell lived, with dots and
arrows going in various directions. In the middle of the map were
the letters "RV" and the siting of two cars, one at either end of
the path across the common which passed the rendezvous site.

For days Pavilion Road was deserted, as the entire focus of the
case shifted to the isolated spot on the common indicated by
Mitchell's map. But Mitchell never went close to the spot, nor
did anyone else.

When I first began searching Mitchell's office, Hollis was
highly nervous.

"There are some highly sensitive documents inside, Peter, and I want your word that they will remain undisclosed."

Hollis was worried in particular about personnel reports, and other embarrassing, rather than secret, papers which have by necessity to pass across the Deputy Director-General's desk. He need not have worried. There was nothing remotely interesting that I saw in Mitchell's office, which only confirmed me in my view that being DDG under a man as autocratic as Hollis must have been one of the very worst jobs in the world.

Every night for some months Hollis and I met after hours. At first he expressed distaste at having to pry into a close colleague's affairs, but I never felt the sentiment was genuine. When I told him about the frequency with which Mitchell picked his teeth on the closed-circuit television, he laughed like a drain.

"Poor bugger should go to a decent dentist!" he laughed.

I, for my part, felt determined, even ruthless. I had waited for years for the chance to grapple with the penetration problem, and I felt few scruples.

It was in those evenings that I first came to know Hollis as a man. Although I had worked for him for close on eight years, we had rarely talked outside the strict confines of official business. We had moments of tension, but by and large our relationship was correct. Only once did we have a major confrontation, when I was in A2 with Hugh Winterborn in the late 1950s. An Argentine delegation came over to negotiate a meat contract with the British Government. Hollis passed down a request from the Board of Trade for any intelligence, and instructed us to arrange for microphone coverage of the Argentines. Winterborn and I were outraged. It was a clear breach of the Findlater-Stewart memorandum, which defined MI5's purposes as strictly those connected with national security. The rest of the A2 staff felt exactly as we did, and Hollis' instruction was refused. For a few hours we all anticipated mass dismissals, but then Hollis withdrew his instruction, and it was never discussed again. The only strike in MI5's history ended in total victory for the strikers!

Occasionally, during the searches of Mitchell's office, Hollis talked about his early years. He told me about his travels in China during the 1930s, where he worked for British American Tobacco.

"Dreadful business out there. Any damn fool could see what the Japanese were doing in Manchuria. It was perfectly obvious we'd lose China if we didn't act," he used to say.

As with many older MI5 officers, the roots of his dislike of the Americans lay prewar. He said the Americans could have helped out in the Far East, but refused to because they were gripped with isolationism. The French in the Far East were, he said, effete, and would rather have seen the whole place go down than help us. That left only the Russians.

"They watched and waited," he told me, "and they got it in the end after the war, when Mao came."

He rarely mentioned his family life, although many people in the office knew he was having a long-standing affair. Just occasionally he talked about his son Adrian, who was a gifted chess player, which evidently was a source of great pride for him. (Adrian used to go to Russia to play chess.)

On one occasion we were talking about the case when I ventured an opinion that, whatever the result, it demonstrated a weakness in our protective security. Hollis became huffy.

"What do you mean?" he asked.

I told him that procedures for vetting MI5 recruits were clearly less strict than those the Service laid down throughout other Whitehall departments.

"Look at me," I told him, "I still haven't had a vet since I joined in 1955."

The next day the forms were sent down for me, and the issue was never discussed again, although shortly after this the vetting procedure changed, and candidates had in future to provide more referees, one of which could be nominated by the Service.

The most memorable thing about those evenings with Hollis was his extraordinary supply of the filthiest jokes I had ever heard. It was almost is if they were a defensive mechanism, an excuse for talking, or else a way of easing the burden when he stepped down from the Olympian heights of power to mix with the troops. I asked him once where he had amassed such a fund of stories.

"China," he told me. "Everyone drank and told jokes. It was the only way to pass the time."

Early on I decided to search a small desk in the corner of Mitchell's office, and I asked Hollis for the key.

"It was Guy Liddell's desk," he said. "He left it when I took over from him. It's been there for years . . ."

I asked him for his consent to pick the locks of two of the drawers which were locked. He agreed and I brought the lockpicking tools the next day, and we inspected the insides of the two drawers. They were both empty, but one caught my attention. In the dust were four small marks, as if an object had been very recently dragged out of the drawer. I called Hollis over, and showed him the marks. He seemed as nonplussed as I, especially when I inspected the lock mechanism and found scratch marks, as if the drawer had recently been opened.

Hollis went back to his office through the interconnecting door which ran between Mitchell's office and his own. I finished the search alone.

"Only Hollis and I knew I was going to open that drawer," I thought to myself, "and something has definitely been moved. Could even be a tape recorder. Why not Mitchell? Because he didn't know. Only Hollis knew. Guy Liddell's desk. Hollis took over the Deputy's office from him. No key? A man like Liddell doesn't leave the desk, and take the key. Only Hollis knew. Only Hollis . . ."

I looked up. Through the door Hollis was staring at me. He said nothing. He just stared, and then bent over his file again.

Throughout the summer months of 1963, as Mitchell's retirement neared, the investigation continued at full pitch. But the whole thing was hopelessly compromised. It had all been too hasty, and too ill-planned. Battling the deadline, and lacking the support of Hollis, it was inevitable that the security of the operation began to crumble at the seams. Mitchell realized that something was wrong. For a start, he noticed that the circulation of papers through his in-tray became erratic, as Hollis sought to restrict his access. Then he began to take evasive action against the Watchers, doubling back on himself, and practicing standard countersurveillance. There was little doubt that he knew he was being followed. Through the television monitor, Mitchell exhibited all the signs of a man under terrible stress, as if he were sunk in a massive depression. He was a tall, thin man at the best of times, but he looked positively cadaverous toward the end, with dark, sunken eyes. When people were in the room with him he made an effort to appear normal, but as soon as he was alone, he looked tortured.

"Why are they doing this to me?" he moaned one day, gazing at Hollis' office door.

In the final month the whole affair became almost a farce. There was no chance of finding anything under those circumstances, so Arthur and I pressed Hollis to sanction an interrogation to resolve the case one way or the other. Hollis refused to commit himself, but a few days later he arrived unannounced at the small house in Pavilion Road.

"I have been to see the PM," he said stiffly to the half dozen of us who were in the room, "and I am afraid an interrogation is quite out of the question."

Out of the corner of my eye I could see Arthur brewing for another outburst.

"Another defection at this stage would be calamitous," he said.

He thanked us all briskly for our efforts and disappeared down to his waiting car. It was typical Hollis mismanagement of personnel. Here were experienced officers, working at a pitch of desperation, and he could barely spare us two minutes. The dirty work was done. Best leave it to the dirty workers!

It was, as well, a naive approach. The MI6 Watchers, led by a hot-headed and overimpressionable young officer named Stephen de Mowbray, were appalled by Hollis' decision, and immediately took it to be a crude attempt at in-house suppression, the very thing MI5 accused MI6 of with the Philby affair. Moreover, no closedown could remove the fact that the Mitchell case had been done. A full report on the investigation had been written by Ronnie Symonds, a senior D1 officer assigned to handle the paperwork in the case. Symonds' report outlined the history of allegations of penetration of MI5 and concluded that there was a strong likelihood that a spy existed at a high level inside the Service. It raised the obvious question of whether the Americans should be alerted.

Symonds' report was sent to Hollis and Dick White, and after private consultations between the two chiefs, we were summoned for another Sunday-afternoon council-of-war, this time at Hollis' house in Camden Square. The contrast between Dick White and Roger Hollis was never clearer than in their homes. Hollis' was a tatty, bookless townhouse, and he appeared at the door wearing his dark pinstripe weekday suit. He showed us into the dingy breakfast room, and launched straight into business. He wanted to hear our views. He gathered there was some concern about the Americans. Consultation never came naturally to Hollis, and there was more than a trace of irritation in his voice now that it had been forced on him.

Arthur acerbically said that we had to find a way of telling them now, in case it became necessary to tell them later, when the effect, if the case against Mitchell was ever proved, would be much more traumatic. Hollis was utterly opposed. He said it would destroy the alliance, especially after Philby.

"For all we know," I reminded Hollis, "the Americans might have sources or information which might help resolve the case. But we'll never get it unless we ask."

For the next hour Hollis debated the issue with the two of us, tempers fraying on all sides. The others in the room—Ronnie Symonds, Arthur's desk officer for the Mitchell case, Hugh Winterborn, and F.J. —tried desperately to keep the temperature down. Symonds said he wanted to keep his options open. Perhaps Mitchell should be interrogated, but then again, it was always possible to regard the issue as closed. As for America, he said he did not know the scene out there well enough to have a view. Winterborn was solid and sensible, supporting Arthur's view that the bigger disaster would be to say nothing now, only to find the case proved later. F.J. finally burst out in exasperation.

"We're not a bloody public school, you know. There's no obligation for us all to 'own up' to the Americans. We run our Service as we think fit, and I wish some of you would remember that!"

But even F.J. acknowledged that there was a problem which had to be resolved. He said that on balance he felt it would be quite prudent to keep the Americans informed, the question was how to do it. Hollis could see he was outnumbered, and suddenly announced that he would visit Washington himself.

"Wouldn't it be better done at working level?" asked F.J., but Hollis' jaw was set firm, and although Arthur tried to move him, it was clearly a waste of time.

"I have heard the arguments. My decision is made," he snapped, glowering at Arthur across the table.

Hollis left for the United States almost immediately, where he briefed John McCone, the new Director of the CIA following the removal of Allan Dulles after the Bay of Pigs, and Hoover. Shortly afterward Arthur followed on to brief the Bureau and the Agency at working level. He got a rough reception. The Americans simply failed to understand how a case could be left in such an inconclusive state. Here, allegedly, was one of the most dangerous spies of the twentieth century, recently retired from one of the prime counterespionage posts in the West, and yet he had not even been interrogated. The whole affair smacked, to them, of the kind of incompetence demonstrated by MI5 in 1951, and in a sense they were absolutely right.

Hollis returned, determined to resolve the case. He ordered a new review to be written by Ronnie Symonds, and Symonds was specifically instructed not to communicate or cooperate with either Arthur or me in the research and drafting of the new report.

When the Mitchell case was handed over to Symonds, I returned to the Directorate of Science, where I was informed that Willis had made a change in procedures. He felt the Directorate need no longer involve itself in GCHQ's affairs, and wanted me to relinquish all contacts with the organization. I was incensed. I knew that unless MI5 hunted and chivvied for facilities and cooperation from GCHQ, things would soon slip back to the desperate state that existed before 1955. Few officers inside MI5 had any real idea of what could be done for them by GCHQ, and, equally, few GCHQ people bothered to think what they could do for each other, a job which I felt was vital for the Directorate to continue. But Willis could not be shifted. He wanted me to leave Counterclan, and join the bureaucrats. It was the final straw. I went to see Hollis, and I told him that I could no longer continue to work in the Directorate. I told him I wanted to join D Branch if possible, or else return to A Branch. The Mitchell case gave me a taste of research, and I knew that the position as head of D3 was still vacant. To my surprise, Hollis offered me a transfer to D3 immediately. There was just a small caveat. He wanted me to return to the Directorate to finish one final special project for Willis, before taking up my new post in January 1964.

Willis' special project turned out to be one of the most important, and controversial, pieces of work I ever did for MI5. He wanted me to conduct a comprehensive review, to my knowledge the only one that was ever done inside British Intelligence, of every scrap of intelligence provided by yet another defector to appear in the West in the early 1960s—Oleg Penkovsky.

Penkovsky was, at the time, the jewel in MI6's crown. He was a senior GRU officer who spied in place for MI6 and the CIA during 1961 and 1962, providing massive quantities of intelligence about Soviet military capabilities and intentions. It was hailed on both sides of the Atlantic as the most successful penetration of Soviet Intelligence since World War II. Penkovsky alerted the West to the presence of Soviet missiles in Cuba, and his information about the Soviet nuclear arsenal shaped the American approach to the subsequent Cuban missile crisis. He also provided the evidence for the identification of the Russian missiles in Cuba. But in late 1962 Penkovsky and a British businessman, Greville Wynne, who was his cutout to MI6, were both arrested by the KGB, and put on trial. Wynne was given a long prison term (although he was eventually exchanged for Gordon Lonsdale and the Krogers) and Penkovsky, apparently, was shot.

I had been involved in the Penkovsky case during the time it was running. Penkovsky visited London on a number of occasions, as a member of a Soviet trade delegation, and had a series of clandestine debriefings with MI6 and CIA officers in the Mount Royal Hotel. At the time Hugh Winterborn was absent for a prolonged period through ill-health, and I was Acting A2, and was asked by MI6 to provide the technical coverage for the London Penkovsky operations. I arranged for continuous Watcher coverage of him and for the sophisticated microphoning system needed to capture every drop of intelligence that spilled out of him during the tense all-night sessions with his controllers.

The Penkovsky case ran counter to everything which was alleged about the penetration of MI5. Arthur and I often discussed this during the Mitchell case. If there was a high-level penetration, then Penkovsky had to be a plant, because news of him was known to the handful of senior suspects, including Mitchell, from a relatively early stage. When I was arranging the Mount Royal operation, Hollis asked me for the name of the agent MI6 were meeting, and I gave it to him. Cumming also asked, but since he was not on the MI6 indoctrination list, I refused to give it to him. This provoked a furious row, and Cumming accused me of becoming too big for my boots. He seemed to resent the fact that I did not consider myself in his debt for the role he played in hiring me into the Service.

Penkovsky seemed to fit into the most far-reaching of the allegations made by Golitsin. Golitsin said that in December 1958 Khrushchev transferred the head of the KGB, General Serov, to run the GRU. His replacement in the KGB was Alexander Shelepin. Shelepin was a much more subtle, flexible man than Serov, who was an old-style Beria henchman, a "nuts and bolts" man. The problem set to Shelepin was that Khrushchev and the Politburo had come to the conclusion that an all-out war with the West was not on. Khrushchev wanted to know how Russia could win without doing this. Shelepin took six months to survey the problem. He then called a large conference in Moscow of all the senior KGB officers the world over and discussed ways in which KGB methods could be modernized. Shelepin, according to Golitsin, boasted that the KGB had so many sources at its disposal in the West that he favored returning to the methods of the OGPU and the "Trust" as a means of masking the real nature of Soviet strategic intentions.

As a result of the Shelepin conference, Department D of the First Chief Directorate of the KGB (responsible for all overseas operations) was formed, a new department charged with planning deception of disinformation exercises on a strategic scale. Department D was put under the control of I. I. Agayants, an old, much respected KGB officer. In 1959, Golitsin said, he approached a friend who worked in this new Department to see if he could get a job there. The friend confided in him that Department D was planning a major disinformation operation using the GRU, but that it could not be implemented for some time because the GRU was penetrated by the CIA and this must be eliminated first. This penetration was almost certainly Colonel Popov, a high-ranking GRU official who spied in place for the CIA before being captured, tortured, and shot in 1959.

In fact, Golitsin never went back, as by then he was planning his defection, so he never learned any more details about the planned disinformation plan, other than the fact that it was basically a technical exercise, and involved all resources available to the First Chief Directorate. When Golitsin reached the West he began to speculate that the Sino-Soviet split was the Department D plan, and that it was a ploy designed to mislead the West. Some of Golitsin's admirers, like Arthur, believed (and continued to believe) this analysis, but although I was, during this early period, one of Golitsin's fervent supporters in the Anglo-American intelligence community, it has always seemed to me that the Penkovsky operation is a far better fit for the type of task Department D was set up for, than the inherently unlikely Sino-Soviet hypothesis.

Strategic deception has become an unfashionable concept in Western intelligence circles, largely because of the extremes to which some of its adherents, myself included in the early days, pushed it. But there is no doubt that it has a long and potent history. The "Trust" operations of the GPU and OGPU in the early years of the Bolshevik regime are a powerful reminder to any KGB recruit of the role these operations can play. At a time when the Bolshevik regime was threatened by several million White Russian émigrés in the 1920s, Feliks Dzerzhinsky, the legendary founder of the modern Russian Intelligence Services, masterminded the creation of a fake organization inside Russia dedicated to the overthrow of the Bolshevik regime. The Trust attracted the support of White Russian émigré groups abroad, and the Intelligence Services of the West, particularly MI6. In fact, the Trust was totally controlled by the OGPU, and they were able to neutralize most émigré and hostile intelligence activity, even kidnapping and disposing of the two top White leaders, Generals Kutepov and Miller, and the Trust persuaded the British not to attack the Soviet Government because it would be done by internal forces.

Strategic deception has also played a major part in the history of Western intelligence, most notably in the Double Cross operations of the war, which enabled the Allies to mislead the Germans about our intentions at D-Day.

Looking at the intelligence balance in 1963, there was no doubt that the Soviets had the necessary conditions to begin a major disinformation exercise. They had large-scale and high-level penetrations in the West, especially in Britain and the USA, and had possessed them almost continuously since the war. Hiss, Maclean, the nuclear spies, Philby, Burgess, Blake, and the many others gave them a very intimate knowledge of the very organizations which needed to be deceived. Secondly, and often overlooked, the Soviets had continuous penetrations of the Western Signals Intelligence organizations since the war, from Philby and Maclean until 1951, but closer to the early 1960s through the defection of the NSA operatives Martin and Mitchell in 1960, and the suicide in 1963 of Jack Dunlap, a chauffeur at NSA who betrayed details of dozens of the most sensitive discussions by senior NSA officials in his car.

As I read the files, a number of reasons made me believe that Penkovsky had to be the deception operation of which Golitsin had learned in 1959. The first thing that struck me about Penkovsky was the sheer coincidence of his arrival. If ever an organization needed a triumph it was MI6 in the early 1960s. It was rocked by the twin blows of Philby and George Blake, its morale desperately low after the Crabbe affair, and the disastrous Suez operations, and Dick White was trying to rebuild it. He removed the post of Deputy Director, sacked a number of senior officers most closely associated with the Sinclair regime, and tried to introduce some line management. He was never entirely successful. Dick was not a particularly gifted administrator. His achievements in MI5 stemmed from intimate knowledge of the office and its personnel, and a deep knowledge of counterespionage, rather than a flair for running organizations.

Deprived of these, his first years in MI6 were, almost inevitably, marked by expediency rather than clear strategy. This was never so well illustrated as with his decision to retain Philby as an agent runner in the Middle East, even though he believed him to be a spy. I asked him about this later, and he said that he simply felt that to sack Philby would create more problems inside MI6 than it might solve. Looking at MI6 in the early 1960s, I was reminded of Lenin's famous remark to Feliks Dzerzhinsky.

"The West are wishful thinkers, we will give them what they want to think."

MI6 needed a success, and they needed to believe in a success. In Penkovsky they got it.

There were three specific areas of the Penkovsky case which made me highly suspicious. The first was the manner of his recruitment. Toward the end of 1960, Penkovsky visited the American Embassy in Moscow in connection with his ostensible job, which was to arrange exchange visits with the West on scientific and technical matters. Once inside the Embassy he offered to provide intelligence to the Americans, and was interviewed by the CIA in their secure compound. He told them that he was, in fact, a senior GRU officer, working for the GKNIIR, the joint organization between the KGB and the GRU on scientific and technical intelligence. The Americans decided Penkovsky was a provocation, and refused his offer. By the time I read the files, the Americans had discovered through another defector, Nossenko, that the rooms used for the interview with Penkovsky had been clandestinely microphoned by the KGB. It was obvious that even if Penkovsky had been genuine, the Russians must have learned of his offer to spy for the Americans.

Early in 1961 Penkovsky made another attempt. He approached a Canadian businessman named Van Vleet in his apartment in Moscow. Van Vleet interviewed Penkovsky in his bathroom, with the water taps running to shield their conversation from eavesdropping. There was no proof that Van Vleet's apartment was bugged, but both he and Penkovsky assumed it to be so, because of his connections with the RCMP. Later, at Penkovsky's trial, evidence against him was produced in the form of tape recordings of conversations between Penkovsky and Wynne which had also taken place in bathrooms with water taps running. It was clear that the Russians had technical means of defeating this type of countercoverage.

Penkovsky's third approach, to Wynne, was successful, and as a result he was run jointly by MI6 and the CIA. But the second suspect area in the Penkovsky case was the type of intelligence which he provided. It was split into two types: ARNIKA, which was straight intelligence, and RUPEE, which was counterintelligence.

The RUPEE material consisted mostly of identifications of GRU officers around the world, nearly all of which were accurate and most of which were already known to us. But beyond that there were no leads at all which identified any Soviet illegals in the West, or to past or present penetrations of Western security. It made no sense to me; here was a man in some ways fulfilling a function analogous to my own, who had spent years at the summit of the GRU, and in regular contact with the KGB, and yet he had apparently picked up not one trace of intelligence about Soviet intelligence assets in the West. I compared Penkovsky's counterintelligence with that of the last major GRU source, Colonel Popov, who spied for the CIA inside the GRU during the 1950s. Popov provided identifications of nearly forty illegals operating in the West, before he was captured and shot.

ARNIKA was different; Penkovsky handed over literally thousands of documents dealing with the most sensitive Soviet military systems. But there were two oddities. Firstly, he sometimes handed over original documents. It seemed to me beyond belief that a spy would risk passing over actual originals, or that the Russians would not miss them from the files. Secondly, Penkovsky's most important documents, which enabled the Americans to identify the Russian missiles in Cuba, were shown to him by his uncle, a senior GRU commander of missile forces. Penkovsky claimed that he copied the document while his uncle was out of the room. Once again, this seemed to me to smack more of James Bond than of real life.

The third area which made me suspect Penkovsky was the manner in which he was run. The tradecraft was appallingly reckless for such a sensitive source. The problem was that his intelligence was so valuable, and at the time of the Cuban missile crisis so current, that he was literally bled for everything that could be got, with little attempt made to protect him or preserve him as a long-term asset. I counted the distribution list for Penkovsky's intelligence. Seventeen hundred people in Britain alone had access to Penkovsky's material during the time he was running in place. MI6, MI5, GCHQ, the various branches of Military Intelligence, the JIC, the Service chiefs and their staffs, the Foreign Office, various scientific research establishments—they all had their own lists of people indoctrinated for various parts of Penkovsky's material, although few people saw the whole range. Of course, like all source reports, there was no hint as to how the intelligence had been acquired, but by any standards it was an astonishingly large distribution, and raised the question of whether it would have been detected by the ever-vigilant Russian Intelligence Services, who at that point in 1963 had demonstrated a consistent ability to penetrate British security at high levels.

Arrangements in Moscow were even more extraordinary. MI6 arranged for Penkovsky to hand over exposed films to Mrs.

Chisholm, the wife of a local MI6 officer, Rory Chisholm, in a Moscow park. This procedure was followed more than a dozen times, long after both Penkovsky and Mrs. Chisholm had detected KGB surveillance of their movements. By the time I read the Penkovsky files, we also knew from George Blake's prison debriefings that Chisholm's identity as an MI6 officer was well known to the Russians. I was certain of one thing: even MI5, with our slender resources, and the restrictions placed on us by custom and the law, could not have failed to detect the Penkovsky operation, had the Russians run it in London the same way MI6 ran it in Moscow.

When I circulated my Penkovsky paper it was greeted with howls of outrage. The operation was marked with great courage and daring, and seemed, on the face of it, such a triumph, that people simply became overemotional when criticisms were voiced. Harry Shergold, Penkovsky's case officer, practically went for me at a meeting in MI6 one day.

"What the hell do you know about running agents?" he snarled. "You come in here and insult a brave man's memory, and expect us to believe this?"

The question remains, of course, why should the Russians have sent Penkovsky as a disinformation agent, if such he was? The answer, I think, lies in the politics of Cuba, and the politics of arms control. The Russians had two major strategic ambitions in the early 1960s—to preserve Castro in Cuba, at a time when the Americans were doing all in their power to remove him, by either coup or assassination, and to enhance and develop the Soviet intercontinental ballistic missile (ICBM) capability without arousing suspicions in the West. This was the era of the "missile gap." The fear that Russia was moving ahead in the production of nuclear weapons was a major plank in John Kennedy's 1960 presidential election campaign, and he committed his administration to closing the gap. The Soviets were desperate to convince the

West that the missile gap was an illusion, and that, if anything, the Soviets lagged behind the West.

Part of the reason for the fears about Soviet missile capability was the fact that, intelligence-wise, the West was blind at this time, because the U2 surveillance flights were cancelled after Gary Powers was shot down in May 1960, and photoreconnaissance over the Soviet Union did not become available again until the launch of the first satellite toward the end of 1962. During that time the only intelligence available to the West was the interception of telemetry signals and radio communications from the rocket-testing ranges in Soviet Asia, and, of course, Penkovsky.

The essence of Penkovsky's information was that the Soviet rocket program was nowhere near as well advanced as the West had thus far suspected, and that they had no ICBM capability, only intermediate-range ballistic missiles, IRBMs. Armed with that knowledge, Kennedy was able to call the Soviet bluff when the Americans detected IRBM facilities under construction in Cuba. The fact that the Russians were seen to be installing what, according to Penkovsky, were their state-of-the-art rockets in Cuba tended to confirm to the Americans the validity of Penkovsky's message that the Russians had no ICBM capability. Khrushchev was forced to withdraw, but achieved his major aim—an eventual acceptance from the USA that Cuba would remain unscathed.

Penkovsky's message was later confirmed by the two defectors from the Soviet delegation to the UN who contacted the FBI in the early 1960s, Top Hat and Fedora, the latter of which, like Penkovsky, was allegedly a scientific and technical officer. Both agents, but especially Fedora, gave intelligence which supported Penkovsky's message that Soviet rocketry was markedly inferior to the West's. Fedora gave immensely detailed intelligence about weaknesses in Soviet rocket accelerometers.

The confidence which Penkovsky's intelligence, and that of

Fedora and Top Hat, gave to the Americans was a crucial factor increasing the climate which gave rise to the SALT I arms control negotiations, and the era of détente, and that, I believe, was his purpose. He helped to lull suspicions in the West for more than a decade, and misled us as to the true state of Soviet missile development.

In the mid-1970s the climate began to change, and doubts began to emerge. Satellite photoreconnaissance was dramatically improved, and when the accuracy of Soviet ICBMs was analyzed using sophisticated measurements of the impact craters, the missiles were found to be much more accurate than had been detected by telemetry and radio intercepts. The only explanation was that a bias had been introduced into Russian signals, with the intention of misleading American detection systems.

While Penkovsky retained his status as MI6's finest postwar achievement, Fedora and Top Hat, for reasons which are too lengthy to detail here, were officially recognized by all sections of the U.S. intelligence community as provocations. Fedora's information about the accelerometers was found to be wrong, and there was even some evidence that the Russians had introduced a fake third gyro on their missiles to make them appear less accurate than they in fact were.

Findings like these cast doubt on the validity of previous arms control agreements, and fears about the ability of the USA to accurately assess Soviet missile capabilities in the end sounded the death knell for the SALT talks in the last 1970s. There was a growing realization in the U.S. defense community that on-site inspections were vital in any future negotiations, a concession which the Soviets have resolutely refused to concede. Today a consensus is beginning to emerge among Western defense strategists that the West was indeed overconfident in its assessment of Soviet missile strength in the 1960s, and that the Soviet used the era of détente as the cover for a massive military expansion. The idea that Penkovsky played some role in that is not now as far-fetched as it once sounded.

When I first wrote my Penkovsky analysis Maurice Oldfield (later chief of MI6 in the 1970s), who played a key role in the Penkovsky case as Chief of Station in Washington, told me:

"You've got a long road to hoe with this one, Peter, there's a lot of K's and Gongs riding high on the back of Penkovsky," he said, referring to the honors heaped on those involved in the Penkovsky operation.

Perhaps not such a long road today.

15

BY THE BEGINNING OF 1964 BOTH ARTHUR AND I WERE CONVINCED that Hollis, rather than Mitchell, was the most likely suspect for the spy we were certain had been active inside MI5 at a high level. Only this hypothesis could explain the incongruities in the Mitchell investigation. Hollis' long-standing refusal to entertain any possibility of a penetration of the Service, his unwillingness to authorize technical facilities during the Mitchell case, his refusal to sanction the interrogation, or brief the Americans until his hand was forced, all seemed to us to point in one direction.

Then suddenly, as we waited for Symonds' second report on Mitchell, an old case fell into our laps. Sir Anthony Blunt, Surveyor of the Queen's Pictures, international art historian, and former wartime senior officer for MI5, confessed in April 1964 to having spied for Russia throughout the war. It brewed up in late 1963, when MI5 were informed by the FBI that an American citizen, Michael Whitney Straight, had told them that Blunt had recruited him for the Soviets while they were both at Cambridge University in the 1930s. Arthur Martin flew over to interview Straight, who confirmed the story, and agreed to testify in a British court if necessary.

The question of how to handle the Blunt case was considered at a series of meetings in Hollis' office. The management saw it as a dreadful embarrassment. In the everlasting game of inter-Secret Service rivalry, the fact that MI6 had harbored proven traitors,

but thus far MI5 had not, was of enormous importance to the
Service's prestige in Whitehall. Hollis, in particular, craved the
respect of mandarins in the Cabinet and Home Office, and feared
the effect the Blunt case would have on MI5's status. Beyond
this, there was a terror of scandal. Hollis and many of his senior
staff were acutely aware of the damage any public revelation of
Blunt's activities might do to themselves, to MI5, and to the
incumbent Conservative Government. Harold Macmillan had finally resigned after a succession of security scandals, culminating
in the Profumo affair. Hollis made little secret of his hostility to
the Labor Party, then riding high in public opinion, and realized
only too well that a scandal on the scale that would be provoked
by Blunt's prosecution would surely bring the tottering Government down.

Arthur and I had simple motivations. We wanted to get our
hands on Blunt as soon as possible, to see if he could shed any
light on the question of further penetration of MI5. A trial involving Straight would in any case be unlikely to succeed, and
would delay, if not jeopardize entirely, our chances of ever gaining his cooperation. The decision to offer Blunt immunity was
possibly the only decision of note concerning the penetration of
MI5 where all parties agreed, and after the matter had been
cleared with the Attorney-General, Blunt was confronted by Arthur Martin and almost immediately admitted his role as Soviet
talent spotter and spy.

A few days after Blunt confessed, I was buzzed by Hollis' secretary early one evening and told to come to the DG's office at
once. Hollis and F.J. were sitting on either side of his desk, looking solemn; Victor Rothschild was standing at the window staring
out across Green Park.

"Hello, Victor," I said, a little surprised that he had not
warned me of his visit to the building.

"Thank you for coming, Peter," he replied in a brittle voice,
turning to face me. He looked distraught.

"I have just told Victor about Anthony," said Hollis, interrupting quickly.

Little wonder Victor looked devastated. Blunt and he had been close friends for nearly thirty years, first at Cambridge, and then during the war, when both men served inside MI5. After the war their careers took them on different paths. They were both men of extraordinary gifts in an increasingly gray world, and their relationship remained close. Like Blunt, Victor also fell under suspicion after the Burgess/Maclean defections. He had been friendly with Burgess as an undergraduate, and had originally owned the lease on a house off Welbeck Street, No. 5 Bentinck Street, where Blunt and Burgess both lived during the war. But while the suspicions against Victor swiftly melted, those against Blunt remained, particularly after Courtney Young interviewed him in the mid-1950s.

Victor's main concern, as soon as he was told the truth, was how to break the news to his wife, Tess. He knew as well as I did that news of Blunt's treachery would, if anything, have a more traumatic effect on her than on him. I had got to know Tess Rothschild well since first meeting Victor in 1958. She was a woman of great charm and femininity, and was closer to Blunt in many ways than Victor had ever been. She understood the vulnerable side of his character, and shared with him a love for art. In the 1930s she moved in that same circle of gifted left-wing intellectuals who studied in Cambridge, partied in London, and holidayed at Cap Ferrat, as the world tottered into World War II.

When war broke out, Tess Mayer, as she then was, joined MI5, where she served with great bravery and distinction alongside her future husband. During this period, she too had rooms in No. 5 Bentinck Street along with Blunt and Burgess. Tess' other roommate was Pat Rawdon-Smith, later Lady Llewellen-Davies. Tess was well aware of MI5's doubts about Blunt after the Burgess/Maclean defections, but she defended him to the hilt. Both she and her husband, Victor, knew how it felt to be innocent, yet fall under suspicion through having been friendly with Guy Burgess. To her, Blunt was a vulnerable and wonderfully gifted man, cruelly exposed to the everlasting burden of suspicion by providence and the betrayals of Guy Burgess.

"Anthony used to come back tight to Bentinck Street, sometimes so tight that I had to help him into bed," she used to say. "I would have known if he was a spy . . ."

Victor realized that we would need to interview Tess now that Blunt had confessed, but he dreaded telling her the truth.

"That is why I asked you up to Roger's office," he said quietly. "I think it would be better if the news came from you."

I knew that he needed to get away from Leconfield House, and gather his thoughts alone.

"Of course," I said, as gently as I could, suggesting that I bring Evelyn McBarnet as well, since Tess knew her.

A few days later Evelyn and I took a taxi over to St. James's Place. We were shown up to Victor's study, a light, scholarly room overlooking Green Park and stamped with his extraordinary character—paintings, scientific diagrams, musical instruments, books ancient and modern, and on the wall a huge self-designed slide rule. There was also a piano, on which Victor played jazz with great skill and élan. Victor was ill-at-ease, and I could tell that Tess sensed something was wrong. After a few minutes, Victor said I had some news for her, then slipped out of the room.

"Is there anything wrong, Peter?" she asked nervously.

"It's Anthony," I told her, "he has confessed at last."

"What to? You are not saying he was a spy?"

"Yes, I am, Tess."

For a second she raised her hand to her mouth as if in pain; then she let it slip gently onto her lap. I told her the story as best I could: of how he had admitted being recruited in 1937, a year or two after Philby, Burgess, and Maclean, and how he had given a long and detailed account of his espionage activities throughout the war. Tess did not cry; she just went terribly pale, and sat hunched up and frozen, her eyes staring at me as she listened. Like Victor, she was a person for whom loyalty in friendship was of surpassing importance; to have it betrayed shook her, as it had him, to the core.

"All those years," she whispered, "and I never suspected a thing."

I began to understand for the first time the intensity of feelings which had been forged in the crucible of those strange, long-ago years in Cambridge in the 1930s.

The Blunt confession had a drastic effect on Arthur's behavior. After years of toil, here finally was proof that he had been right all along. From the beginning he suspected Blunt, even though many people in the office, like Dick White, who had been close friends with Blunt during the war, initially doubted that it was possible. Arthur became even more driven, even more difficult to handle. He had the look of a man who could smell red meat, a ravenous, voracious manner as he collected his ancient scalp.

The confession dramatically sharpened attitudes toward penetration. The unthinkable, that there could be a spy inside MI5, became suddenly much more real. Arthur was convinced that if only we could keep the momentum up, the new D Branch team could get to the heart of the 1930s conspiracy. He felt that while things were running our way, and defectors and confessions were coming thick and fast, he might still resolve the greatest riddle of all—the identity of the mole inside MI5 today. But as Arthur pressed for speed and urgency and action, he was faced by the new D Branch Director, Cumming, who favored a slow and cautious approach.

The relationship between the two men deteriorated in an alarming way during the early part of 1964. Arthur had little respect for Cumming: he felt his approach was out of date. Arthur had been largely responsible for rebuilding Soviet Counterespionage since 1959, and because of his reputation, his influence spread way beyond D1. He was an ambitious man, and understandably so, but he lacked tact. He felt he should have been D Branch Director rather than Cumming, and made little secret of the fact that he expected the job very shortly. To him, Cumming was mishandling the whole penetration issue. Cumming deeply resented Arthur's attitude, which was rarely hidden, as well as the intrusions on his authority. He was bitter, also, about the way he had been kept out of the Mitchell inquiry, and suspected that Arthur harbored secret suspicions about Hollis. A showdown was clearly only a matter of time in coming.

Shortly after Blunt confessed, it occurred. In May 1964 I visited Washington to try to persuade the CIA to help our fledgling Movements Analysis program. Hal Doyne Ditmass, who ran the Movements Analysis, and I wanted the CIA to provide computer effort to process the mass of material which the program was producing (7 million movements a year) and my request to the CIA had Hollis' approval. Angleton was totally supportive, and Helms agreed to send over not just one or two technicians, but a twenty-man team and a guarantee of all the computer time in the CIA that the program required. As soon as I got back, with the CIA computer team due to arrive the following week, Arthur told me that Hal Doyne Ditmass was being transferred. I exploded.

"How the hell can we do any planning if vital staff are transferred just as soon as they familiarize themselves with an area?" I raged. "Hal and I have spent four years developing this work, and just when it really starts to produce results, he gets a transfer!"

Arthur was just as upset as I. He had handpicked many of the staff in D1, and resented any attempt to move them, especially at this time of maximum activity in the Soviet counterespionage field. Arthur stormed into Cumming's office, believing he should have opposed the move. The row filtered down the corridor, as months of pent-up resentment poured out. Cumming accused Arthur of riding slipshod over the Branch, and exceeding his authority. Arthur, for his part, made little secret of his belief that the Branch was being badly handled. Inevitably, the argument focused on the recent Mitchell case. Cumming accused Arthur of being obsessed with what was, in his opinion, a dead case, and, moreover, one which had done enormous damage to the morale of the Service. Arthur responded by indicating that, so far as he was concerned, the case still had a very long way to go. Cumming reported the row to Hollis, who promptly requested a full written report on the matter. The following day Cumming sent Arthur a draft copy of the report he intended submitting to Hollis.

Arthur was appalled by what he read. Cumming's report made no mention of the implications for the CIA visit of Doyne Ditmass' removal from the Movements Analysis program. It was an explicit attack on Arthur, culminating in the suggestion that Arthur harbored suspicions about the identity of the spy inside MI5 which he was not willing to share with his Director.

Arthur was by now at breaking point with Cumming.

"Not bloody true!" he scrawled in the margin, and continued to deface every line of Cumming's report, before sending it back from whence it came. Cumming, sensing his chance for a decisive victory, promptly sent the copy as it stood to Hollis, who summarily suspended Arthur for a fortnight for indiscipline.

I was in a hopeless position: I had twenty CIA technicians arriving at Leconfield House any day, expecting to enter important negotiations with Hal Doyne Ditmass, me, and Arthur Martin, and as things stood, there would only be me on the MI5 side of the table. I went to see Hollis privately and explained, with as little rancor as I could, the nature of the problem. I reminded Hollis that the approach to the CIA had been done in his name, and he agreed to reinstate Doyne Ditmass for another year.

"But what about Arthur?" I asked, hoping that Hollis might change his mind on that too.

"I am not prepared to discuss the matter," he retorted.

"But what about Blunt?" I pleaded. "We can't just leave him out in the cold when we've just broken him . . ."

"It's about time Arthur learned that he's not the DG yet," said Hollis grimly. "When he's sitting in this chair, he can make the decisions. Until then, I do!"

When Arthur returned, we began the debriefing in earnest, systematically identifying his every controller and recruitment, and checking every item of intelligence that he handed over to the Russians. Arthur met Blunt regularly and questioned him on the basis of detailed research briefs which D3 and Evelyn drew up. Each session was taped, and the transcripts processed by D3 to check for inaccuracies and points which needed further questioning.

Blunt swiftly named as fellow spies Leo Long, a former officer in British Military Intelligence, and John Cairncross, who had served in the Treasury in 1940, before joining the Government Code and Cipher School (GC&CS) at Bletchley with access to ENIGMA SIGINT material, and, in 1944, MI6. Long, informed by Arthur that a prosecution was most unlikely provided he cooperated with MI5, swiftly confessed, as did Cairncross, who was seen by Arthur in Rome.

But after his initial leads, Blunt ran out of things to say. He sat and listened to Arthur's questions, helped where he could, but there was nothing like the wealth of detail we expected. Arthur and I decided to confront him together. The plan was to introduce me as the officer analyzing Blunt's confession. I would then play nasty to Arthur's nice, and tell Blunt I had serious doubts about the veracity of his confession. It was an old interrogation trick, but it had worked before. There was one further twist. We set the meeting up in Maurice Oldfield's flat in Chandos Court, Caxton Street, Westminster, which had a concealed taping system. Usually when Blunt and Arthur met, Arthur recorded the conversation openly on a hand tape recorder. We decided that we would turn off the visible tape recorder when I went for Blunt, to give him additional security. Hollis was extremely reluctant about the plan. From the beginning he instructed that no pressure was

to be applied to Blunt, in case he should defect. But we managed
to persuade him that on this one occasion the risk was worth
taking.

We met Blunt several nights later. He was tall and extremely
thin, wearing a tweed suit with a large bow tie. He looked distinguished, if slightly effeminate. He was friendly but guarded, especially toward Arthur. I could tell there was a tension between
them; neither man could forget that they had sat down together
ten years before, and Blunt had lied through his teeth. They
talked in a businesslike fashion for half an hour, mainly about
documents which Blunt removed from the Registry. Every now
and then Blunt snatched a look across at me. I could tell he knew
what was coming. Finally, Arthur brought me into the conversation.

"Peter has been doing the analysis. I think he has something to
say . . ."

I switched off the tape recorder and paused for effect.

"It's quite clear to me, reading the transcripts, that you have
not been telling us the full truth . . ."

Blunt flinched as if I had struck him. He was sitting in an easy
chair with his pencil-thin legs crossed. His outstretched leg kicked
involuntarily.

"I have told you everything which you have asked," he replied,
looking me straight in the eye.

"That's nonsense, and you know it is, too. You say you only
know about Long and Cairncross, those were the only ones. I
don't believe you!"

He purpled, and a tic began to flicker on his right cheek. He
poured himself another gin, playing for time.

"We've been very fair with you," I went on. "We've been
polite, and we've kept our side of the bargain like gentlemen. But
you have not kept yours . . ."

He listened intently as I made my play. Where was he not
telling the truth? he wanted to know. I pointed out areas where

we felt he was holding back. I knew he was trying to gauge whether I had fresh evidence or information which could put him on the spot, or whether we were just working from gut feelings. After a few minutes' discomfort, he began to resume his poise. The tic began to settle down. He knew we had nothing to throw at him.

"I've already told you, Peter," he muttered, "there was nobody else!"

I switched tack, and began to press his conscience.

"Have you ever thought about the people who died?"

Blunt feigned ignorance.

"There were no deaths," he said smoothly, "I never had access to that type of thing . . ."

"What about Gibby's spy?" I flashed, referring to an agent run inside the Kremlin by an MI6 officer named Harold Gibson. "Gibby's spy" provided MI6 with Politburo documents before the war, until he was betrayed by Blunt and subsequently executed.

"He was a spy," said Blunt harshly, momentarily dropping his guard to reveal the KGB professional. "He knew the game; he knew the risks."

Blunt knew he had been caught in a lie, and the tic started up again with a vengeance. We wrestled for an hour, but the longer it went on, the more he realized the strength of his position. The session broke up with ill-concealed temper.

"The truth is, given the choice, you wouldn't betray anyone you thought was vulnerable, would you?" I asked, as Blunt prepared to leave.

"That's true," he said, standing to his full height, "but I've already told you. There are no more names . . ."

He said it with such intensity that I felt he almost believed it himself.

There had been an incident which was perturbing. The tape recorder which we overtly had in the room decided to scramble up its tape. I knelt on the floor and proceeded to straighten the tape out and got it going again. While I was doing this, Blunt said to Arthur, "Isn't it fascinating to watch a technical expert do his stuff?"

Now, Blunt had not been told by either Arthur or me that I was a scientist. I had been introduced as the man processing what he, Blunt, had told us. I looked Blunt straight in the eye and he blushed purple. Somebody had told him who I really was.

"You take him on," snapped Arthur when Blunt had left. "He's played out . . ."

Arthur was keen to strip the bones of his other carcasses, Long and Cairncross.

Long was in the Apostles Society at Cambridge, a self-regarding élite club of intellectuals, many of whom were left-wing and homosexual. When war broke out he joined Military Intelligence, where he was posted to MI14, responsible for assessing Oberkommando Wehrmacht SIGINT and hence military strength. Throughout the war he met clandestinely with Blunt and handed over any intelligence he could lay his hands on. After the war he moved to the British Control Commission in Germany, where he eventually rose to become deputy head of Military Intelligence before leaving in 1952 to pursue a career in commerce. He left Intelligence because he was getting married and did not wish to have to tell his wife that he had been a spy.

I met Long several times with Arthur, and disliked him intensely. Unlike the other members of the Ring, he lacked class, and I often wondered how on earth he was accepted into the Apostles. He was an officious, fussy man with a face like a motor mechanic's, and seemed still to regard himself as a superior Army officer, despite his treachery. Far from being helpful in his debriefing, his attitude, when challenged on a point, was invariably to say that we would just have to take his word for it. He went through his story with us briskly. No, he knew of no other spies, and claimed that he gave up all espionage activities in 1945. This failed to tally with what Blunt had told us. He said that in 1946 he went to Germany to persuade Long to apply for a post inside MI5. Long agreed, and Blunt, then a trusted and well-respected recent departure from the Service, wrote a recommendation for him. Luckily for MI5, Guy Liddell had a marked prejudice against uniformed military officers, and blackballed him at the Board, even though Dick White supported him, much to his later embarrassment. But despite this attempt to join MI5, and Long's continuing secret work in Germany, he denied all further contact with the Russians, which was clearly rubbish.

Cairncross was a different character entirely. He was a clever, rather frail-looking Scotsman with a shock of red hair and a broad accent. He came from a humble working-class background but, possessed of a brilliant intellect, he made his way to Cambridge in the 1930s, becoming an open Communist before dropping out on the instructions of the Russians and applying to join the Foreign Office.

Cairncross was one of Arthur's original suspects in 1951, after papers containing Treasury information were found in Burgess' flat after the defection. Evelyn McBarnet recognized the handwriting as that of John Cairncross. He was placed under continuous surveillance, but although he went to a rendezvous with his controller, the Russian never turned up. When Arthur confronted Cairncross in 1952 he denied being a spy, claiming that he had supplied information to Burgess as a friend, without realizing that he was a spy. Shortly afterward, Cairncross left Britain and did not return until 1967.

After Cairncross confessed, Arthur and I traveled to Paris to meet him again for a further debriefing in a neutral venue. He had already told Arthur the details of his recruitment by the veteran Communist James Klugman, and the intelligence from GCHQ and MI6 which he had passed to the Russians, and we were anxious to find out if he had any other information which might lead to further spies. Cairncross was an engaging man.

Where Long floated with the tide, Communist when it was fashionable, and anxious to save his neck thereafter, Cairncross remained a committed Communist. They were his beliefs, and with characteristic Scottish tenacity, he clung to them. Unlike Long, too, Cairncross tried his best to help. He was anxious to come home, and thought that cooperation was the best way to earn his ticket.

Cairncross said he had no firm evidence against anyone, but was able to identify two senior civil servants who had been fellow Communists with him at Cambridge. One was subsequently required to resign, while the other was denied access to defense-related secrets. We were particularly interested in what Cairncross could tell us about GCHQ, which thus far had apparently escaped the attentions of the Russian intelligence services in a way which made us distinctly suspicious, especially given the far greater numbers of people employed here.

Cairncross told us about four men from GCHQ who he thought might repay further investigation. One of these worked with him in the Air Section of GCHQ, and had talked about the desirability of enabling British SIGINT material to reach the Soviet Union. Cairncross, although amused by the irony of the man's approach, was in no position to judge his seriousness, so he kept quiet about his own role. The second man, according to Cairncross, had been sacked after returning to Oxford and telling his former tutor full details of his work inside GCHQ. The tutor, appalled by the indiscretion, reported him to GCHQ, and he was sacked. A third man named by Cairncross, like the first, had long since left GCHQ for an academic career, so effort was concentrated on the fourth, a senior GCHQ official in the technical section. After a full investigation he was completely cleared.

GCHQ became highly agitated by the D Branch inquiries resulting from Cairncross' information, as did C Branch; both protected their respective empires jealously, and resented what they saw as interference, particularly when I made some caustic comments about how they could improve their vetting.

As my D3 section pursued these leads, I wrestled with the problem of how to handle Blunt, now that he was my responsibility. Before I began meeting Blunt I had to attend a briefing by Michael Adeane, the Queen's Private Secretary. We met at his office in the Palace. He was punctilious and correct, and assured me that the Palace was willing to cooperate in any inquiries the Service thought fit. He spoke in the detached manner of someone who wishes not to know very much more about the matter.

"The Queen," he said, "has been fully informed about Sir Anthony, and is quite content for him to be dealt with in any way which gets at the truth."

There was only one caveat.

"From time to time," said Adeane, "you may find Blunt referring to an assignment he undertook on behalf of the Palace—a visit to Germany at the end of the war. Please do not pursue this matter. Strictly speaking, it is not relevant to considerations of national security."

Adeane carefully ushered me to the door. I could not help reflecting on the difference between his delicate touch and the hysterical way MI5 had handled Blunt, terrified that he might defect, or that somehow the scandal might leak. Although I spent hundreds of hours with Blunt, I never did learn the secret of his mission to Germany. But then, the Palace had had several centuries to learn the difficult art of scandal burying. MI5 have only been in the business since 1909!

When I took over Blunt I stopped all meetings with him while I considered a new policy. Confrontation was clearly never going to work, firstly because Hollis was vehemently opposed to anything which might provoke a defection, or a public statement from Blunt, and secondly because Blunt himself knew that our hand was essentially a weak one, that we were still groping in the dark and interrogating him from a position of ignorance rather than strength. I decided that we had to adopt a subtle approach, in an attempt to play on his character. I could tell that Blunt wanted to be thought helpful, even where it was clear that he was not. Moreover, he disliked intensely being caught in a lie. We had to extract the intelligence from him by a slow process of cumulative pressure, advancing on small fronts, rather than on any large one. To do that we needed a far more profound knowledge of the 1930s than MI5 at the time possessed.

I decided, too, that we had to move the interviews onto his patch. He always came to Maurice Oldfield's flat in a confrontational mood, defensive, on edge, sharpened up, and aware that he was being recorded. I felt moving to his place would lessen the tension, and enable us to develop something of a relationship.

Every month or so for the next six years Blunt and I met in his study at the Courtauld Institute. Blunt's study was a large room decorated in magnificent baroque style, with gold-leaf cornicework painted by his students at the Courtauld. On every wall hung exquisite paintings, including a Poussin above the fireplace, bought in Paris in the 1930s with 80 pounds lent to him by Victor Rothschild. (He was supposed to have left this painting to Victor's oldest daughter, Emma, but he failed to do this. The picture was valued at 500,000 pounds for his estate and went to the nation.) It was the perfect setting to discuss treachery. For every meeting we sat in the same place: around the fireplace, underneath the Poussin. Sometimes we took tea, with finely cut sandwiches; more often we drank, he gin and I Scotch; always we talked, about the 1930s, about the KGB, about espionage and friendship, love and betrayal. They remain for me among the most vivid encounters of my life.

Blunt was one of the most elegant, charming, and cultivated men I have met. He could speak five languages, and the range and depth of his knowledge was profoundly impressive. It was not limited solely to the arts; in fact, he was proud of telling me, his first degree at Cambridge was in mathematics, and he retained a lifelong fascination with the philosophy of science.

The most striking thing about Blunt was the contradiction between his evident strength of character and his curious vulnerability. It was this contradiction which caused people of both sexes to fall in love with him. He was obviously homosexual, but in fact, as I learned from him, he had had at least two love affairs with women, who remained close to him throughout his life. Blunt was capable of slipping from art historian and scholar one minute, to intelligent bureaucrat the next, to spy, to waspish homosexual, to languid establishmentarian. But the roles took their toll on him as a man. I realized soon after we began meeting that Blunt, far from being liberated by the immunity offer, continued to carry a heavy burden. It was not a burden of guilt, for he felt none. He felt pain for deceiving Tess Rothschild, and other close friends like Dick White and Guy Liddell (he was in tears at Guy's funeral), but it was the pain of what had to be done, rather than the pain of what might have been avoided. His burden was the weight of obligation placed on him by those friends, accomplices, and lovers whose secrets he knew, and which he felt himself bound to keep.

As soon as we began our meetings at the Courtauld I could see Blunt relax. He remained canny, however, and since he knew all about SF, I soon noticed that the telephone was placed discreetly at the far end of the hall. On the first afternoon we met there I noticed it as he went out to fetch some tea.

"Bring the tea cozy to put on the telephone," I shouted.

He laughed.

"Oh no, Peter, you'll never be able to hear us down there with that thing."

At first I took notes in a small notebook, but it became difficult to take everything down, so I had to plan a way of obtaining clandestine coverage of the meetings. Eventually the premises next to the Courtauld were modernized, and I arranged for a probe microphone to be inserted through the wall into Blunt's study. It was a ticklish job. The measurements needed to be perfect to ensure that the probe emerged at the right spot on Blunt's side of the fireplace close to where we sat. A2 arranged for an artist friend of Blunt's to telephone him at a prearranged time when I was visiting him, and while he was out in the hall talking, I produced my tape measure and made all the necessary measurements for the microphone, which was successfully installed and working beautifully until the end. For all I know, it is probably still there now.

For our first sessions I relaxed things. I tried not to press him too hard, content simply to run through the old memories. He talked of how he had joined the Soviet cause, recruited by the then youthful, brilliant Guy Burgess. Guy was still a painful subject for Blunt; he had just died in Moscow, alone, his once virile body broken by years of abuse.

"You probably find this impossible to believe," he told me as he poured the tea, "but anyone who knew Guy well, really well, will tell you that he was a great patriot."

"Oh, I can believe that," I said. "He only wanted Britain to be Communist! Did you hear from him, before he died?"

Blunt sipped his tea nervously, the cup and saucer shaking slightly in his hand. Then he went to his desk and fetched me a letter.

"This was the last one," he said. "You didn't miss it; it was hand delivered . . ." He left the room.

It was a pathetic letter, rambling and full of flaccid sentimental observations. Burgess talked of Moscow life, and tried to make it sound as if it was still as good as ever. Now and again he referred to the old days, and the Reform Club, and people they both knew. At the end he talked of his feelings for Blunt, and the love they shared thirty years before. He knew he was dying, but was whistling to the end. Blunt came back into the room after I finished reading the letter. He was upset, more I suspect because he knew I could see that Burgess still meant something to him. I had won a crucial first victory. He had lifted the veil for the first time, and allowed me a glimpse into the secret world which bound the Ring of Five together.

Blunt joined the Russian Intelligence Service in the heyday of the period now known in Western counterintelligence circles as "the time of the great illegals." After the ARCOS raid in London in 1928, where MI5 smashed a large part of the Russian espionage apparatus in a police raid, the Russians concluded that their legal residences, the embassies, consulates, and the like, were unsafe as centers for agent running. From then onward their agents were controlled by the "great illegals," men like Theodore Maly, Deutsch, "Otto," Richard Sorge, Alexander Rado, "Sonia," Leopold Trepper, the Piecks, the Poretskys, and Krivitsky. They were often not Russians at all, although they held Russian citizenship. They were Trotskyist Communists who believed in international Communism and the Comintern. They worked undercover, often at great personal risk, and traveled throughout the world in search of potential recruits. They were the best recruiters and controllers the Russian Intelligence Service ever had. They all knew each other, and between them they recruited and built high-grade spy rings like the "Ring of Five" in Britain, Sorge's rings in China and Japan, the Rote Drei in Switzerland, and the Rote Kapelle in German-occupied Europe—the finest espionage rings history has ever known, and which contributed enormously to Russian survival and success in World War II.

Unlike Philby and Burgess, Blunt never met "Theo," their first controller, a former Hungarian priest named Theodore Maly. Maly understood the idealism of people like Philby and Burgess, and their desire for political action. He became a captivating tutor in international politics, and his students worshipped him. In 1936–1937 Maly was replaced by "Otto," and it was he who orchestrated Blunt's recruitment by Burgess. Like Theo, "Otto" was a middle-class East European, probably Czech, who was able to make the Soviet cause appealing not simply for political reasons but because he shared with his young recruits the same cultured European background. Blunt admitted to me on many occasions that he doubted he would ever have joined had the approach come from a Russian.

For some reason, we were never able to identify "Otto." Philby, Blunt, and Cairncross all claimed they never knew his real name, although Philby in his confession told Nicholas Elliott that while in Washington he recognized "Otto" from a photograph in the FBI files as a Comintern agent named Arnold Deutsch. But when we checked we found that no picture of Deutsch existed in FBI files during Philby's time in Washington. Moreover, Deutsch had fair curly hair. I used to bring Blunt volume after volume of the MI5 Russian intelligence officer files in the hope that he might recognize him. Blunt treated the books as if they were catalogues from the National Gallery. He would study them carefully through his half-moon spectacles, pausing to admire a particularly striking face, or an elegantly captured figure on a street corner. But we never identified "Otto" or discovered the reason why the Ring were so desperate to conceal his identity so many years later.

In 1938 Stalin purged all his great illegals. They were Trotskyists and non-Russians and he was convinced they were plotting against him, along with elements in the Red Army. One by one they were recalled to Moscow and murdered. Most went willingly, fully aware of the fate that awaited them, perhaps hoping that they could persuade the demented tyrant of the great services they had rendered him in the West. Some, like Krivitsky, decided to defect, although even he was almost certainly eventually murdered by a Russian assassin in Washington in 1941.

For over a year after "Otto's" departure, the Ring remained in limbo, out of touch and apparently abandoned. Then Guy Burgess and Kim Philby reestablished contact with the Russians through Philby's first wife, Litzi Friedman, a long-time European

Comintern agent. According to Blunt, the Ring was run through a complex chain of couriers: from Litzi Friedman messages passed to her close friend and fellow Comintern agent, Edith Tudor Hart, and thence to Bob Stewart, the CPGB official responsible for liaison with the Russian Embassy, and thence on to Moscow. Until Blunt confessed we were entirely unaware of this chain, and it had enormous implications. Each member of the chain almost certainly knew the identities of the Ring, claimed Blunt, and it had always puzzled him that the Ring was not detected at this point by MI5. We had always assumed the Ring had been kept entirely separate from the CPGB apparatus, which was thoroughly penetrated in the 1930s by agents run by Maxwell Knight. But now it appeared that we had missed the greatest CPGB secret of all. In 1938 MI5 were basking in the success of the Woolwich Arsenal case, where evidence from Maxwell Knight's best agent, Joan Gray (Miss X), secured the conviction of senior CPGB officials for espionage in the Woolwich Arsenal Munitions Factory. Had we run the case on longer, we might well have captured the most damaging spies in British history before they began.

At the end of 1940, the Russians finally reestablished contact with the Ring, and from this period onward they were directed into the intelligence world. Their controller during this period was "Henry," a Russian intelligence officer named Anatoli Gromov, or Gorski, who was working under diplomatic cover. Gromov ran all the spies in the Ring, almost certainly the eight whose cryptonyms appear in the VENONA traffic, until he left for Washington in 1944 to run Donald Maclean, who was posted to the British Embassy. Those who were left in London were taken over by Boris Krotov, the KGB officer whose VENONA messages revealed the existence of the eight spies. Blunt said he had a great respect for the professionalism of his KGB controllers, but they never really stimulated him in the way that "Otto" had. Gromov and Krotov were technocrats of the modern Russian intelligence machine, whereas to Blunt, the talented European controllers of the 1930s were artists.

"Was that why you left MI5?" I asked.

"Oh, that partly," he said. "I was tempted to stay. But they didn't need me. Kim would serve them well. He was rising to the top, I knew that. And I needed my art. After all, if they had wanted me, they could so easily have blackmailed me to stay."

The onset of the Cold War and the spread of McCarthyism reinforced Blunt's conviction that he had made the right choice in the 1930s, and he continued to be totally loyal to those who remained in the game. In 1951 he opted to stay and brazen it out, rather than defect with Burgess and Maclean. He was pressured to defect at this time by Modin ("Peter"). He told me a life of exile in Moscow would have been intolerable for him. He had visited Russia in the 1930s. It was a fine and admirable tragic country, but the place which appealed to him most was the Hermitage, Leningrad's magnificent gallery.

After 1951 Blunt was left alone with Philby. He was much less close to him than to Burgess. Philby was a strong, dominant personality, yet he needed Blunt desperately. Blunt still had the ear of his former friends in MI5, and was able to glean scraps for Philby of how the case against him was developing. They used to meet to discuss their chances of survival. Philby seemed bereft without his career in MI6, and had little understanding of the importance of art and scholarship to Blunt, even while the net closed on them both.

"Kim and I had different outlooks on life," Blunt told me. "He only ever had one ambition in life—to be a spy. I had other things in mine . . ."

Blunt admired Philby, but there was a part of him that was frightened by his utter conviction, his ruthlessly one-dimensional view of life. Blunt needed love and art and, in the end, the comfort of life in the Establishment. Philby, on the other hand, lived his life from bed to bed; he had an Arabian attitude to women, needing only the thrill of espionage to sustain him. Isaiah Berlin once said to me, "Anthony's trouble is that he wants to hunt with society's hounds and run with the Communist hares!"

"Kim never wavered," he said. "He always remained loyal, right to the end."

By late 1964 I was submerged by the weight of material emanating from the Long, Cairncross, and Blunt confessions, as well as the enormous task of collating and systematically reexamining all the material which had reached MI5 since 1960 from the various defectors. It was at this point that Symonds' second report on the Mitchell case finally reached me.

One morning, about a fortnight before the October 1964 general election, Hollis' secretary handed me a thick file, and told me to report to the DG's office that afternoon to discuss it. There was precious little time to read the report, let alone study it. Symonds had followed Hollis' instructions zealously, and during the eight months it took him to prepare the document, he never discussed its contents with either Arthur or me. But its thrust was clear enough. Symonds reassessed the Mitchell case in the light of the Blunt confession, which, of course, we had not possessed at the time of the first report. According to Symonds, the case against Mitchell was not strong. Symonds was not prepared to rule out the possibility of a more recent penetration, but he felt the likelihood was considerably diminished.

Arthur also received Symonds' report that morning; he knew he was being outflanked, and that the decision to circulate the report at such a late stage was a deliberate device to prevent any counterattack. He told me that he intended at the meeting to take the line that he could not comment until he was given adequate time to study it. For the first part of the meeting he was a silent, smoldering presence at one side of the conference table.

Hollis opened briskly.

"I don't propose to waste too much time," he began. "I have read this paper, which strikes me as most convincing. I would like your views before reaching a decision. As you know, gentlemen, an election is due very soon, and I feel it is much better for the Service if we can resolve this case now, so that I do not have to brief any incoming Prime Minister."

Everyone knew what he meant. He did not want to brief Harold Wilson, the Labor leader, who looked increasingly likely to beat the Tories at the forthcoming contest. Hollis' attitude was quite simple: Blunt, Long, and Cairncross tied up some useful loose ends, the Mitchell case fell, and everything was neatly resolved. He wanted to close the case and minute the file that the question of penetration had been dismissed.

Hollis asked for opinions around the table. There was surprisingly little comment at first. The Mitchell inquiry had been so badly botched on all sides that few of us felt it a strong wicket to defend, particularly since Arthur and I both now had strong suspicions that Hollis was the culprit. I said simply that if Symonds' first report was the case for the prosecution, then this latest was the case for the defense, and that without an interrogation I could not accept a verdict of "not guilty," and wanted my views recorded in the minutes. Hollis made a small note on the pad in front of him, and turned to Cumming. Cumming delivered a lecture on the lack of discipline exhibited during the Mitchell investigation. It was clear to all of us that the decision to exclude him from the indoctrination had shattered his self-esteem. F.J. said only that the best that could be said for the Mitchell case was that it was nonproven.

"And you, Arthur . . . ?" asked Hollis.

Arthur looked up from the report.

"Well," he said, "there is a third possibility. Someone could be running Mitchell as their stalking horse."

There was silence around the table. He and Hollis stared at each other for a brief moment. Everyone in the room knew exactly what Arthur meant.

"I should like that remark clarified," said Cumming from the other end of the table. Symonds flicked anxiously through his report, as if he were looking to see if somehow Arthur's hypothesis had crept into it undetected.

Hollis merely picked up where he left off, ignoring Arthur's comment as if he had not heard it.

"Well, we have to make a decision," he said, "and therefore I propose to close this case down, and minute the file to that effect . . ."

His pen paused above the file. Arthur could contain himself no longer.

"Intellectually, you simply cannot do this," he burst out in his most precise manner. "You're neglecting virtually all the Golitsin allegations about penetration. There's the question of the leak about the Crabbe operation. There's the Technics Department—we don't even know yet which document Golitsin is referring to. Whatever the status of the Mitchell case, it cannot be right to ignore them."

Hollis tried to deflect the attack, but Arthur pressed forward. He knew Hollis had overreached himself. Symonds admitted he knew too little about the Golitsin material to present authoritative opinion. F.J. was inclined to agree that further work on Golitsin would be prudent. Hollis could feel the meeting ebb away from him. He threw down his pen in exasperation and instructed Patrick Stewart to conduct a final review of all Golitsin serials outstanding. In the meantime, he ordered, the Mitchell case was closed.

After the meeting I approached F.J. It was intolerable, I said, for the DG to assign a research task to an officer without consulting me, the head of Research, when I was already wrestling with the mass of material pouring in from Blunt, Long, and Cairncross, as well as from defectors in Washington.

"Things are difficult enough as it is," I said, "but if we start splitting the work up, there will be chaos!"

F.J. could see the problem. The system was approaching overload, and he agreed with me that more coordination was needed, not less. I suggested that we try to establish some kind of inter-Service working party to research the entire range of material concerning the penetrations of British Intelligence reaching us from confessions or defectors. F.J. said he would see what he could do.

Shortly afterward he called me into his office and said that he had discussed the whole matter with Dick White, who agreed that such a committee should be established. Dick prevailed upon Hollis, who finally gave his reluctant agreement. The committee would be formed jointly from D Branch staff of MI5, and the Counterintelligence Division of MI6. It would report to the Director, D Branch, and the head of MI6 Counterintelligence, and I was to be its working chairman. The committee was given a code name: FLUENCY.

Hollis used the row over the Symonds report as the pretext for clipping Arthur's wings. He divided the now burgeoning D1 empire into two sections: D1, to handle order of battle and operations; and a new D1 (Investigations) Section, to handle the investigations side of counterespionage. Arthur was left in charge of the truncated D1, and Ronnie Symonds was promoted alongside him as an assistant director in charge of D1 (Investigations).

It was a cruel blow to Arthur, for whom investigations had been his lifeblood since the late 1940s and into which most of his effort had gone since his return in 1959. He had been upset not to be asked to chair the Fluency Committee, although he understood that this was essentially a D3 research task. But to be supplanted in his own department by Symonds, his former junior, who for a long time had viewed Arthur as his mentor, was a bitter pill to swallow. Arthur felt betrayed by the Symonds report. He could not understand how Symonds could write two reports within such a short space of time which seemed to contradict each other. He believed that MI5 had made a desperate mistake.

Arthur became reckless, as if the self-destructive impulse which always ran deep in him suddenly took over. He was convinced that he was being victimized for his energetic pursuit of penetration. To make matters worse, Hollis specified that although the two sections were to be run independently of each other, Arthur was to have some kind of oversight of both areas, in deference to his vast experience and knowledge. It was an absurd arrangement, and bound to lead to catastrophe. The two men rowed continually. Arthur believed that oversight meant control while Symonds wanted to go his own way. Finally things boiled over when Arthur abruptly ordered Symonds to bring his case officers to a conference, and Symonds refused. Arthur told him he was making it impossible for him to do his coordinating job; Symonds retorted that Arthur was interfering, and placed a written complaint before Cumming. Cumming took the complaint to Hollis and recommended Arthur's immediate dismissal, to which Hollis enthusiastically agreed.

The matter was discussed at the next Directors' meeting. Arthur had no allies there; too many Directors felt threatened by his forceful, sometimes intemperate style. The only friend he had among the Directors, Bill Magan, who staunchly defended Arthur to the end, was conveniently absent when the decision was taken.

I remember Arthur came to my office the day it happened, steely quiet.

"They've sacked me," he said simply. "Roger's given me two days to clear my desk." In fact, he was taken on straightaway by MI6, at Dick White's insistence and over Hollis' protests. But although this transfer saved Arthur's pension, his career was cut off in its prime.

I could scarcely believe it. Here was the finest counterespionage officer in the world, a man at that time with a genuine international reputation for his skill and experience, sacked for the pettiest piece of bureaucratic bickering. This was the man who since 1959 had built D1 from an utterly ineffectual section into a modern, aggressive, and effective counterespionage unit. It was still grossly undermanned, it was true, but that was no fault of Arthur's.

Arthur's great flaw was naiveté. He never understood the extent to which he had made enemies over the years. His mistake was to assume that advancement would come commensurately with achievement. He was an ambitious man, as he had every right to be. But his was not the ambition of petty infighting. He wanted to slay the dragons and fight the beasts outside, and could never understand why so few of his superiors supported him in his simple approach. He was temperamental, he was obsessive, and he was often possessed by peculiar ideas, but the failure of MI5 to harness his temperament and exploit his great gifts is one of the lasting indictments of the organization.

"It's a plus as far as I'm concerned," he said the night he was sacked, "to get out of this."

But I knew he did not mean it.

I tried to cheer Arthur up, but he was convinced Hollis had engineered the whole thing to protect himself, and there was little I could do. The stain of dismissal was a bitter price to pay after the achievements of the previous twenty years. He knew that his career had been broken, and that, as in 1951, all he had worked for would be destroyed. I never saw a sadder man than Arthur the night he left the office. He shook my hand, and I thanked him for all he had done for me. He took one look around the office. "Good luck," he said and stepped out for the last time.

16 ———————————————

BY THE TIME ARTHUR LEFT I WAS IN THE MIDST OF A MAJOR reconstruction of the D3 Research section. When I took it over it had no clear sense of purpose in the way I wanted it to have. I was convinced that it had a central role to play if MI5 were finally to get to the bottom of the 1930s conspiracy. An intelligence service, particularly a counterespionage service, depends on its memory and its sense of history; without them it is lost. But in 1964 MI5 was quite simply overloaded with the mass of contradictory information flowing in from defectors and confessing spies. Loose ends are in the nature of the profession of intelligence, but we were overwhelmed by the weight of unresolved allegations and unproven suspicions about the 1930s which were lying in the Registry. We needed to go back to the period, and in effect positively vet every single acquaintance of Philby, Burgess, Maclean, Blunt, Long, and Cairncross.

It is difficult today to realize how little was actually known, even as late as 1964, about the milieu in which the spies moved, despite the defections in 1951. The tendency had been to regard the spies as "rotten apples," aberrations, rather than as part of a wider-ranging conspiracy born of the special circumstances of the 1930s. The growing gulf in the office between those who believed the Service was penetrated and those who were sure it was not was echoed by a similar division between those who felt the extent of Soviet penetration in the 1930s had been limited, and those who felt its scope had been very wide indeed, and viewed the eight cryptonyms in venona as the best proof of their case. Throughout the late 1950s tension between the two sides grew, as Hollis resisted any attempts by those like Arthur and me to grapple with the problem.

The reasons for the failure to confront the conspiracy adequately are complex. On a simple level, little progress was made with the two best suspects, Philby and Blunt, and this made it difficult to justify deploying an immense investigative effort. There was, too, the fear of the Establishment. By the time the defections occurred, most of those associated with Burgess and Maclean were already significant figures in public life. It is one thing to ask embarrassing questions of a young undergraduate, quite another to do the same to a lengthy list of rising civil servants on the fast track to Permanent Under Secretary chairs.

At heart it was a failure of will. Politicians and successive managements in MI5 were terrified that intensive inquiries might trigger further defections or uncover unsavory Establishment scandal, and that was considered an unacceptable risk during the 1950s. Moreover, in order to conduct a no-holds-barred investigation MI5 inevitably would have to show something of its hand. This ancient dilemma faces all counterespionage services; in order to investigate, you have to risk approaching and interviewing people, and thus the risks of leakage or publicity increase exponentially the more intensive the inquiries you make. This dilemma was particularly acute when facing the problem of investigating Soviet recruitment at Oxford and Cambridge in the 1930s. Most of those we wanted to interview were still part of a closely knit group of Oxbridge intellectuals, with no necessary allegiance to MI5, or to the continuing secrecy of our operations. News of our activities, it was feared, would spread like wildfire, and faced with that risk, successive managements in MI5 were never willing to grasp the nettle. We opted for secret inquiries, where overt ones would have been far more productive.

Philby's defection and the confessions of Blunt, Long, and Cairncross swept away many of these reservations, although the fear of Establishment scandal remained just as acute as ever. Hollis agreed to the drastic expansion of D3, and it was given a simple, yet massive task—to return to the 1930s, and search the files for clues which might lead us to spies still active today, to vet a generation, to clear up as many loose ends as possible, and to provide the Service with an accurate history for the first time. The guiding principle of my D3 section was a remark Guy Liddell made to me on one of his frequent visits back to the office after he retired.

"I bet 50 percent of the spies you catch over the next ten years have files or leads in the Registry which you could have followed up . . ."

I was sure he was right. I thought back to Houghton, and his wife's report on him, to Blake, and to Sniper's early lead to Blake, to Philby and to Blunt, where evidence existed but was never pursued relentlessly enough. Perhaps most amazing of all, I read the Klaus Fuchs file, and discovered that after he was caught MI5 found his name, his Communist background, and even his Party membership number, all contained in Gestapo records which MI5 confiscated at the end of the war. Somehow the information failed to reach the officers responsible for his vetting. But also in 1945–48 an officer, Michael Sorpell, had researched Fuchs and recorded on the file that Fuchs must be a spy.

There were several obvious places to look in the inert mass of papers lying in the Registry. First there were the Gestapo records. The Gestapo was an extremely efficient counterespionage service, and operated extensively against European Communist parties and the Soviet intelligence services. They had a trove of information about them, developed at a time when our knowledge of Europe was virtually nonexistent because of the conditions of war. They had invaluable intelligence on the most important of all European Soviet rings—the Rote Kapelle, or Red Orchestra.

This was a series of loosely linked self-sustaining illegal rings controlled by the GRU in German-occupied Europe. The Rote Kapelle was run with great bravery and skill, relaying by radio vital intelligence to Moscow about German military movements.

The most important of all the Gestapo records for the British were the Robinson papers. Henry Robinson was a leading member of the Rote Kapelle in Paris, and one of the Comintern's most trusted agents. In 1943 he was captured by the Gestapo and executed. Although he refused to talk before dying, papers were found under the floorboards of his house which revealed some of the Ring's activities. The hand-written notes listed forty or fifty names and addresses in Britain, indicating that Robinson had also been responsible for liaising with a Rote Kapelle ring in Britain. After the war Evelyn McBarnet did a lot of work on the Robinson papers, but the names were all aliases, and many of the addresses were either post-boxes or else had been destroyed in the war. Another MI5 officer, Michael Hanley, did a huge research task in the 1950s, identifying and listing every known agent of the Rote Kapelle. There were more than five thousand names in all. But since then the trail had gone dead. Perhaps, I thought, there might be clues among all this material which might take us somewhere.

Another place to look was among the records of defector debriefings. Work was already in progress with the recent defectors like Golitsin and Goleniewski, but there were still many loose ends in the intelligence provided by prewar and wartime defectors. Walter Krivitsky, the senior NKVD officer who defected in 1937, told MI5, for instance, that there was a well-born spy who had been educated at Eton and Oxford, and joined the Foreign Office. For years everyone assumed this to be Donald Maclean, even though Maclean was educated at Gresham Holt's and Cambridge. He just did not fit, but rather than confront the problem, the allegation had been left to collect dust in the files.

Then there was Konstantin Volkov, a senior NKVD officer

who approached the British Consulate in Istanbul and offered to reveal the names of Soviet spies in Britain in return for money. He gave an Embassy official a list of the departments where the spies allegedly worked. Unfortunately for Volkov, his list landed on Kim Philby's desk at MI6 headquarters. Philby was then head of MI6 Soviet Counterintelligence, and against the wishes of Director C he persuaded him to let him go to Turkey, ostensibly to arrange for Volkov's defection. He then delayed his arrival by two days. The would-be defector was never seen again, although the Turks thought that both Volkov and his wife had been flown out strapped to stretchers. One of Volkov's spies was thought to be Philby himself, but there were several others who had just never been cleared up—like the spy Volkov claimed was working for MI6 in Persia.

Lastly there was the VENONA material—by far the most reliable intelligence of all on past penetration of Western security. After Arthur left I took over the VENONA program, and commissioned yet another full-scale review of the material to see if new leads could be gathered. This was to lead to the first D3-generated case, ironically a French rather than a British one. The HASP GRU material, dating from 1940 and 1941, contained a lot of information about Soviet penetration of the various émigré and nationalist movements who made their headquarters in London during the first years of the war. The Russians, for instance, had a prime source in the heart of the Free Czechoslovakian Intelligence Service, which ran its own networks in German-occupied Eastern Europe via couriers. The Soviet source had the cryptonym Baron, and was probably the Czech politician Sedlecek, who later played a prominent role in the Lucy Ring in Switzerland.

The most serious penetration, so far as MI5 were concerned, was in the Free French Government lad by Charles de Gaulle. De Gaulle faced persistent plots in London masterminded by his two Communist deputies, André Labarthe, a former *Chef du Cabinet* who was responsible for civilian affairs, and Admiral Mueselier, who controlled military affairs. MI5 kept a close eye on these plots during the war at Churchill's instigation, and Churchill ordered the arrest of both Labarthe and Mueselier when de Gaulle had gone to Dakar to free that territory for the Free French; but in 1964 we broke a decrypt which showed conclusively that Labarthe had been working as a Soviet spy during this period, moreover at a time when the Molotov–von Ribbentrop pact was still in existence.

The U.S. VENONA also contained material about Soviet penetration of the Free French. The CIA had done no work on it, either because they thought it was too old or because they had no one with sufficient grasp of French history. When I studied it, I found that another senior French politician, Pierre Cot, the Air Minister of Daladier's prewar cabinet, was also an active Russian spy.

This discovery came at a time of great tension between the French and British intelligence services. Anti-French feelings ran strongly inside British Intelligence. Many officers of both services had served in the war and remembered the supine French surrender. Courtney Young always claimed that he formed lifelong views on the French when traveling back from Dunkirk on a boat. Even Blunt, for all his reverence for French art and style, was vituperative on the subject of French cowardice.

Relations were not helped by the arrival of Anatoli Golitsin. Some of his best intelligence concerned Soviet penetration of SDECE, the French equivalent to MI6. Golitsin said there was a ring of highly placed SDECE agents known as the Sapphire Ring. Shortly after Golitsin defected, the deputy head of SDECE threw himself out of a window. Angleton persuaded the head of the CIA to get President Kennedy to write to de Gaulle warning him about Golitsin's allegations, but de Gaulle felt the Americans and the British were manipulating Golitsin to cast aspersions on French integrity. This remained the official French view even after Golitsin gave the information which led to the arrest and conviction of Georges Paques, a senior French Government official, in 1965.

To complicate matters still further, the DST (the French counterespionage service) and MI5 were collaborating on a case involving a double agent, Air Bubble. Air Bubble was an industrial chemist named Dr. Jean Paul Soupert. Soupert was an agent runner for East German Intelligence and the KGB, but the Belgian *Sécurité d'Etat* doubled him. He revealed that two of his agents were employees of the Kodak Company in Britain who were passing him details of sensitive commercial processes. The Belgians informed MI5, who began an intensive investigation of both Kodak employees, Alfred Roberts and Godfrey Conway. Soupert also told the Belgians about an East German illegal named Herbert Steinbrecher, who was running agents inside the French Concorde assembly plants, and this information was passed on to the DST to investigate in collaboration with MI6.

Unfortunately both cases ended in catastrophe. Although Conway and Roberts were caught, they were acquitted. Far worse for Anglo-French relations, the inquiries into Steinbrecher revealed that MI6 had recruited a French police chief, whose police district ran up to the German border. He was a "blanche" agent, that is to say MI6 had deliberately concealed him from their hosts, the French, and were using him to spy on both French and German nationals. The French, for their part, were forced to admit that Steinbrecher's agents had acquired for the Russians every detail of the Anglo-French Concorde's advanced electronic systems. The result, inevitably, was a spectacular row.

I approached Angleton and Louis Tordella of NSA, and got their agreement to provide the DST with the VENONA intelligence which proved Cot and Labarthe to be Russian spies. They were old, but still politically active, and it seemed to me a sensible precaution. I traveled to Paris in early 1965 to DST headquarters, where I was met by Marcel Chalet, the deputy head of the service. Chalet was a small, dapper Frenchman who joined the DST after the war, having served with great courage in the Resistance under Jean Moulin, narrowly escaping arrest by the Gestapo on the day Moulin himself was lifted. Like all French Resistance veterans, Chalet wore his pink ribbon with conspicuous pride. He was a militant anti-Communist, and yet he admired Moulin, a dedicated Communist, more than any other man in his life. Several times he and I discussed the Resistance, but even in the 1960s he could not discuss his former commander without tears coming to his eyes.

I explained to Marcel that we had obtained new information which indicated the true roles of Cot and Labarthe, and showed him the relevant VENONA decrypts. He was astonished by the material, and immediately pledged a full investigation.

"You don't think they are too old, then . . . ?" I asked.

Marcel fixed me with a withering glance.

"Until you see a French politician turning green in his coffin, you cannot say he is too old!"

Unfortunately Labarthe died of a heart attack as Marcel interrogated him, and Cot was left to die in peace, but the exchange of information did much to ease tension between the DST and MI5, and made Marcel and me friends for the rest of our careers.

The night before I left Paris he took me out to dinner. The restaurant was discreet, but the food was excellent. Marcel was an attentive host, providing bottles of the best claret, and regaling me with a string of waspish anecdotes about the perils of Gallic intelligence work. We discussed VENONA, and he was fascinated to learn about the scale of our success.

"They had some success with us recently," he told me, and described how in Washington they had discovered a fuse in the French Embassy cipher room modified to act as a transmitter.

"It was non-Western specification, and the range was perfect for the Russian Military Attaché's house across the road," he said, noisily tucking into his plate of oysters in typical French style. My ears pricked up. The STOCKADE operation against the French Embassy ciphers in London and Washington had recently ended precipitately, when teams of French technicians went into both embassies with sheets of metal and copper tubes, and began screening the cipher rooms. Obviously the Russians, too, had realized that radiations could be picked up from poorly screened machines. Still, I thought, at least the French had not discovered our operation.

Chalet obviously found the whole affair amusing, and even offered to send the fuse over to Leconfield House, so that we could examine it. Still smiling, he casually dropped a question below the belt.

"And you, my dear Peter, have you had any luck with radiations . . . ?"

I choked momentarily on my claret.

"Not much," I replied.

Marcel filled my glass, patently disbelieving my every word. Like true professionals, we turned to other things, and never discussed the matter again.

But for all the enjoyment of the French interlude, research into the Ring of Five was the most pressing task facing D3. I asked Hollis for the 8D branch interrogators to be placed inside D3, so that I could use them for an extensive program of interviews with every known acquaintance of Philby, Burgess, Maclean, Blunt, Long, and Cairncross. Hollis agreed, but instructed that I myself had to conduct any interview deemed sensitive, which normally meant it was with a lord, a knight, a politician, a top civil servant, or a spy suspect.

In all, I saw more than a hundred people. Labor politicians like Christopher Mayhew and Dennis Healey, then Secretary of State for Defense, who refused even to meet me, were unwilling to discuss their memories of the Communist Party in the 1930s. But others, like historian Isaiah Berlin and writer Arthur Marshall, were wonderfully helpful, and met me regularly to discuss their contemporaries at Oxford and Cambridge. Berlin insisted we meet at the Reform Club. He thought it appropriate to discuss Guy Burgess at the scene of his greatest triumphs. He had a keen eye for Burgess' social circle, particularly those whose views appeared to have changed over the years. He also gave me sound advice on how to proceed with my inquiries.

"Don't go to see Bowra," he told me, referring to Maurice Bowra, the distinguished Professor of Literature at Oxford University. Bowra was a homosexual as well as a close friend of Guy Burgess, and was close to the top of my list of those who I thought could help me.

"Why not?" I asked.

"Because he'll have it all around every high table in Oxford if you do," he said.

I took Berlin's advice and gave Bowra a wide berth.

Marshall, or "Artie" as he was known to everyone, knew practically everyone in Cambridge in the 1930s, particularly the secret network of homosexuals at King's and Trinity. Artie had a prodigious memory for gossip, intrigue, and scandal, and, most important of all, he knew who was sleeping with whom in the Burgess and Blunt circles.

Blunt, too, loved to discuss the scandalous side of Cambridge life in the 1930s. He relished gossip, and never tired of telling me of the time he blackballed Sir Edward Playfair, in later life Permanent Secretary at the Ministry of Defense, for the Apostles Society. Blunt thought Playfair crushingly dull, and, having met the man, I could not disagree with his judgment. His funniest story concerned Guy Burgess and Churchill's niece Clarissa Churchill. Apparently Burgess was tasked by his Soviet controllers to wed Clarissa Churchill, to ensure him perfect cover for his espionage activities. Burgess was appalled by the task. For one thing, he was an inveterate homosexual; for another, Clarissa Churchill was scarcely better-looking than her uncle; and lastly, it was known that James Pope-Hennessy, later to become a distinguished writer, had become infatuated with her.

But Burgess was nothing if not game. Within a month he was pursuing Clarissa Churchill, causing upset and outrage in equal measure. James Pope-Hennessy was desperately upset by Burgess' attentions to her. One evening he arrived at Burgess' flat with a revolver, threatening to shoot them both before attempting to commit suicide. Blunt loved the story, and it was made all the better, in his eyes and mine, by the fact that, shortly afterward, Clarissa Churchill married Anthony Eden and later became Lady Avon.

I soon realized that the Ring of Five stood at the center of a series of other concentric rings, each pledged to silence, each anxious to protect its secrets from outsiders. There was the secret ring of homosexuals, where loyalty to their kind overrode all other obligations; there was the secret world of the Apostles, where ties to fellow Apostles remained strong throughout life; and then there was the ring of those friends of Blunt and Burgess who were not themselves spies, but who knew or guessed what was going on. Each ring supported the others, and made the task of identifying the inner core that much more difficult.

It was hard not to dislike many of those I interviewed. Funnily enough, I did not mind the spies so much; they had made their choice, and followed it to the best of their abilities. But those on the periphery were different. When I saw them they were clothed in the respectability of later life. But their arrogance and their cultured voices masked guilt and fear. It was I who was wrong to raise the issue, not they; it ought to be left alone, they would tell me. I was being McCarthyite. Things were different then. Of course, spying was wrong, but there were reasons. They were a Lotus Generation, following political fashions as if they were a clothes catalogue, still pledged in the 1960s to vows of silence they made thirty years before. They in turn disliked me. I had seen into the secret heart of the present Establishment at a time when they had been young and careless. I knew their scandals and their intrigues. I knew too much, and they knew it.

One of the first D3 tasks was to reexamine a lead which had lain uninvestigated in the files since Burgess and Maclean's defection in 1951. It was given by Goronwy Rees, a friend of both Burgess and Blunt. He first met them at Oxford in the 1930s, and during the war, while serving in Military Intelligence, was a regular visitor to Bentinck Street. Shortly after the defections he approached Dick White, then the head of Counterespionage, and told him that he knew Burgess to have been a longtime Soviet agent. Burgess, he claimed, had tried to recruit him before the war, but Rees, disillusioned after the Molotov–von Ribbentrop pact, refused to continue any clandestine relationship. Rees also claimed that Blunt, Guy Liddell, a former MI6 officer named Robin Zaehner, and Stuart Hampshire, a brilliant RSS officer, were all fellow accomplices. But whereas Blunt was undoubtedly a Soviet spy, the accusations against the other three individuals were later proved groundless.

Dick White disliked Rees intensely, and thought he was making malicious accusations in order to court attention, if not publicity. The four men were all close friends, and it was for this reason that he found it hard to share Arthur Martin's suspicions about Blunt. Dick's view of Rees seemed confirmed when, in 1956, Rees wrote an anonymous series of articles for a popular newspaper. Orgies and espionage made as good copy in the 1950s as they do today, and the Rees articles, detailing some of the salacious activities of Burgess and those close to him, caused a sensation.

But when Blunt confessed, the color of Rees' 1951 testimony changed. I thought it at least prudent to reexamine it, if only to satisfy myself that Rees had not been lying when he claimed to have given up all thoughts of the Soviet cause before the war. At first he was reluctant to talk to me, and his wife accused me of Gestapo-type tactics in trying to resurrect the past after so many years. They had both suffered grievously for the newspaper articles. Rees' authorship became known, and he was sacked from

academic life. Since 1956 they had eked out a miserable existence, shunned by the Establishment. Eventually Rees agreed to
see me, and went through his story again. He had no proof that
any of those he named were fellow conspirators. But all, he said,
had been close friends of Burgess in that crucial prewar period.

The accusation against Guy Liddell was palpably absurd. Everyone who knew him, or of him, inside MI5 was convinced that
Liddell was completely loyal. He had left his diaries, known as
"Wallflower," when he left MI5. Reading those, nobody could
believe that he was a spy. But the accusation against Robin
Zaehner, who had served for MI6 in the Middle East, cross-
checked with Volkov's spy in the Middle East.

I studied Zaehner's Personal File. He was responsible for MI6
counterintelligence in Persia during the war. It was difficult and
dangerous work. The railway lines into Russia, carrying vital military supplies, were key targets for German sabotage. Zaehner was
perfectly equipped for the job, speaking the local dialects fluently,
and much of his time was spent undercover, operating in the
murky and cutthroat world of countersabotage. By the end of the
war his task was even more fraught. The Russians themselves
were trying to gain control of the railway, and Zaehner had to
work behind Russian lines, constantly at risk of betrayal and murder by pro-German or pro-Russian Arabs. On the face of it, the
very fact that Zaehner survived gave a touch of credibility to
Rees' allegation.

After the war Zaehner left intelligence work, and became Professor of Ancient Persian at Oxford University. I made an appointment to see him at All Souls. The cords which bind Oxford
and British Intelligence together are strong, and it was the first of
many trips I was to make to that city during the next five years.

Zaehner was a small, wiry-looking man, clothed in the dis-
tracted charm of erudition. He poured me a drink and chatted
easily about old colleagues in the secret world. I wondered, as he

chatted, how I could broach the subject of my visit in a tactful way. I decided there was none.

"I'm sorry, Robin," I began, "a problem has come up. We're following up some old allegations. I'm afraid there's one that points at you . . ."

At first he rallied. Pointed at him? he protested. Of course, I must be mistaken. Had I checked his record? Which allegation?

I told him about Volkov, and the spy in Persia.

He crumpled. I knew then, from his reaction, that Rees had been terribly, vindictively mistaken.

"I spent six years in the desert," he said limply. "I stayed behind two years after Yalta, when everyone else went home. I got no honors, but I thought at least I had earned a degree of trust."

Zaehner spoke quite without rancor; just a kind of sadness. After all that he had done, all that he had risked, to be accused of this, years later, wounded him to the quick. He dabbed tears from his eyes. I felt a heel, like a policeman who breaks bad news to parents in the night.

When Zaehner composed himself he was a paragon of professionalism. Of course, he understood why I had to come see him. He went through his career at MI6 and searched his memory for a clue as to the identity of Volkov's spy. We talked for hours as the shadow of the spires of All Souls faded across the lawns.

"I cannot think of an Englishman who could be this spy," he said, tapping his foot on the floor as if to trigger his memory. "There weren't many of us, and I'd vouch for every one."

He thought it was likely to be an agent, rather than an officer. Agents were often shared between MI6 and the KGB in the latter stages of the war, and the possibility of a plant was obvious. One name fitted perfectly, a man called Rudi Hamburger. After MI6 recruited him, he was arrested by the Russians, then turned loose, before being reemployed by MI6 again. The dates tallied perfectly with the time Volkov had access to files in Moscow, and it seemed obvious that Hamburger had simply been turned in prison, and tasked to find out whatever he could about his British employers. (Rudi Hamburger was the first husband of "Sonia," who later was an illegal in Switzerland and England.)

Zaehner and I parted friends, but I felt bitter at the ease with which the accusation had been made, and anger at those who had left such an accusation lying in the files for so many years before clearing it up. Driving back to London I began to wonder about the cost of clearing up "loose ends." Was it fair, I thought, to drag these things up? Perhaps, after all, it was better to leave them in the files undisturbed and unresolved.

That Christmas Zaehner sent me a friendly Christmas card, and not too many years later he died. I sent a wreath, anxious to make amends; but I could never forget the look on his face when I asked him if he was a spy. In that moment the civilized cradle of Oxford disintegrated around him; he was back behind the lines again, surrounded by enemies, alone and double-crossed.

The last name Rees gave me was that of Sir Stuart Hampshire. Hampshire was a brilliant wartime codebreaker and analyst for the Radio Security Service, one of the élite team who broke the ISOS Abwehr codes, and laid the foundations for the Double Cross System. After the war he pursued a career in the Foreign Office, before leaving for a distinguished academic career as a philosopher at Oxford and Princeton. Rees had no evidence whatsoever for the charge he made in 1951; it was based solely on the fact that Hampshire had been extremely close to Burgess during the 1930s. I knew from my own interviews that Hampshire was considered by contemporaries to have been strongly left wing, although non-Communist, and I was amazed to find that no one had even bothered to interview him on what he knew about Guy Burgess.

However, there was an extraordinary complication with the Hampshire case. Although long since retired from the secret world, he had been invited by the Cabinet Secretary, Burke

Trend, to conduct a major review of the future of GCHQ. Concern about the escalating cost of SIGINT had been growing ever since NSA moved into the satellite age. The Americans were pressing GCHQ to share the costs of spy satellites. The incoming Labor Government was already faced with annual bills in excess of 100 million pounds, and the Prime Minister, Harold Wilson, instructed Trend to conduct a review to see if such costs were justified. Trend consulted Dick White, who suggested Hampshire for the review in light of his previous RSS work. When I looked at Hampshire's file I was amazed to find that despite Rees' allegation, Hampshire had not been vetted. Dick White, who had known Hampshire for years, simply wrote Hollis a letter for the file, and that was it.

Hampshire's inquiry lasted the best part of a year, during which time he had full access to GCHQ, as well as a six-week visit to NSA. There were a number of fundamental issues raised in Hampshire's report. The first was whether, in light of the growing costs, Britain could afford to maintain its share of the UKUSA agreement, which guaranteed us so much exchanged information from the Americans. The second, more immediate issue was whether Britain should opt in with the Americans on a new generation of spy satellites; and the third area was how far GCHQ should support the Counterclan activities.

The answers in short were Yes, No, and Yes. We could not possibly afford to lose the UKUSA exchange, but on the other hand, we could remain in without necessarily funding every technical development pound for dollar. As for Counterclan, Hampshire endorsed it strongly. The only major change he requested was a termination of airborne RAFTER on the grounds that it was not cost effective. I opposed this at the time, but with hindsight it was a sensible economy, and the RAF were, in any case, beginning to resent the demands we were making on them. Hampshire and I spent a good deal of time discussing MI5's relationship with GCHQ. I pressed strongly for him to recommend the creation of a new Radio Security Service, an organization independent of GCHQ, which would be controlled by MI5, and responsible solely for the detection of domestic spy radios. I thought Hampshire, with his background, would welcome such an idea, and I told him that it was the only way that we would ensure the facilities that we needed. Hampshire disagreed, not, I think, with the principle, but more with the practicalities. He concluded, probably rightly, that such an initiative would be fought tooth and nail by both GCHQ and MI6, and would, therefore, be very unlikely to succeed.

Interviewing Hampshire about the Rees allegation was obviously out of the question until his review was complete, but in 1967 I obtained permission, and traveled to Princeton University in the USA, where Hampshire was the Visiting Professor. I knew Princeton well. I had often visited there in my days as a scientist. Rudi Kompfner, the man who invented the traveling wave tube (the radio valve used in most microwave links), gave me the best description of its bizarre architecture. He called it "pseudo-Gothic-Cotswold."

I talked to Hampshire for some time about his memories of Guy Burgess. He told me that he now thought in retrospect that perhaps he himself had been the target of a recruitment approach by Burgess, though he had not realized it at the time. He described how in 1935 he and Anthony Blunt had traveled to Paris together, and one evening they had dinner with James Klugman and the artist Ben Nicholson. After dinner Klugman took the lead in a lengthy session in which Hampshire was quizzed as to his political beliefs.

Some months later he was invited to dine alone with Guy Burgess at his flat in Chester Square. Both men drank heavily, and in the small hours Guy made a pitch at him, asking him to work for peace. It was dangerous work, he said, but worth it. There was much talk of the intellectual ferment of the times, the Nazi menace, and the need to take a much more Marxist line in

academic studies. At the time Hampshire thought this was the
prelude to an invitation to join a left-wing debating society, then
the vogue among young Oxbridge intellectuals, but no specific
proposition was made. "In retrospect," said Hampshire, "perhaps
Burgess was trying to recruit me."

When I got back to Britain I checked this story with Blunt. He
remembered the Klugman dinner, which he confirmed was a
looking-over operation, but said he knew nothing of Burgess'
pitch. Neither could he resolve whether the dinner had occurred
in 1935 or 1937. The dates were important; in 1935 Blunt and
Burgess were still mere Party members, but in 1937 both were
spies and thus any recruitment would have been for the Russians.
I sent one of my staff to see Ben Nicholson. Luckily he kept
complete diaries for each year of his professional life, and was able
to establish beyond any doubt that the dinner had, in fact, taken
place in 1937.

I went to see Dick White and gave him the Hampshire papers
to read. I was puzzled as to why Hampshire had never told MI5
about his dealings with Guy Burgess after Burgess defected in
1951. Dick confirmed that Hampshire had never mentioned this
to him. I went to see Hampshire again when he returned to
London. He seemed slightly embarrassed. He told me that Burgess' approach was so muddled that he could hardly be sure of its
importance. As for Blunt, it never occurred to him to connect
Blunt's presence at the dinner with Burgess' approach, and since
Blunt was on such personal terms with people like Dick White
and Guy Liddell throughout the war, he assumed he was entirely
trustworthy. Anyway, he was not alone in wanting to close the
chapter.

Both Dick and Hollis were desperately embarrassed at the revelation that the man whom they had chosen to conduct the most
secret review of Anglo-American intelligence sharing should himself have been the unwitting target of a Soviet recruitment approach. They knew that the arrangements for Hampshire's vet-

ting would, at the very least, look seriously inadequate to American eyes, particularly at a time when they were already up in arms at what they saw as the "old school tie" approach to intelligence in Britain. They could hardly own up, and the Hampshire case was carefully buried forever.

The unsuccessful recruitment of Hampshire was also interesting for the light it cast on James Klugman's role in Soviet Intelligence recruitment in the 1930s. He had clearly been instrumental in arranging the looking-over dinner in Paris. Cairncross had also told us that it was Klugman who had recruited him. Until then, MI5 had tended to assume Klugman was merely an overt Party activist, rather than a covert agent recruiter or talent spotter. It was obvious that Klugman could tell us much about the 1930s, if we could persuade or pressurize him to confess. I knew Klugman would never accept a direct approach from MI5, so we struck a deal with Cairncross; if he came back to Britain, confronted Klugman, and persuaded him to meet MI5 and tell all, we would allow him to come back to the country permanently.

Cairncross accepted our offer with alacrity, and visited Klugman in London. Klugman was an old man, a hard veteran of the class war, busy writing a history of the Communist Party as a last testament to a lifetime's work. He laughed when Cairncross asked him to meet MI5, and shrugged him off when Cairncross threatened to expose him if he did not. The attempt failed miserably and Cairncross was forced back into exile. Shortly afterward, Klugman took his secrets to the grave.

There were other loyal party servants who refused our approaches. Bob Stewart and Edith Tudor Hart, both of whom were involved as couriers for the Ring of Five in 1939–40, were approached. Neither would talk. They were disciplined soldiers, and had spent too long in the game to be broken. The public rarely realizes the weakness of MI5's position with inquiries of this sort. We cannot compel people to talk to us. Almost everything we do, unless an arrest is imminent, depends on coopera-

tion. For instance, Blunt told us that he knew of two other spies
—one of whom he had discovered after the man made a recruitment approach to Leo Long, whom Blunt was already running.
The situation was additionally complicated by the fact that Blunt
was having an affair with the potential recruiter, although neither
told the other about his designs on Long. Both of these men, who
are still alive and living in Britain today, were working on the
Phantom Program during the war, although they left afterward to
pursue academic careers. Despite many efforts, neither would
agree to meet me to discuss their involvement with Russian Intelligence. The only positive action was to warn a senior police chief,
who was friendly with one of the spies, and their relationship
ceased.

17 ——————————————

AFTER I HAD BEEN MEETING BLUNT FOR A YEAR, AN OBVIOUS PAT-
tern emerged. I was able to tease things out from him—mostly
pillow talk he had gathered from Guy Burgess. He claimed a
writer on *The Times* had been approached. I traced him, and he
confirmed that Burgess had tried to recruit him, but that he
turned him down, fearful of the consequences of being caught.
Another contact Blunt identified was Tom Wylie, a War Office
clerk, long since dead. Wylie, said Blunt, used to let Burgess see
anything which came into his hands. But although Blunt, under
pressure, expanded his information, it always pointed at those
who were either dead, long since retired, or else comfortably out
of secret access and danger.

I knew that Blunt must know of others who were not retired,
who still had access. These were the people he was protecting.
But how could I identify them? I decided to draw up lists of all
those who were mentioned by interviewees as having noted left-
wing views before the war, or who interviewees felt would have
been likely to have been the target for a recruitment approach
from Guy Burgess.

One name stood out beyond all the others: Alister Watson.
Berlin mentioned him, the writer Arthur Marshall mentioned
him, Tess Rothschild mentioned him. He was, they all said, a
fervent Marxist at Cambridge in the 1930s—a sure sign that he
was likely to have been approached.

I began to make inquiries into his background. I knew him quite well from the war. He worked currently as a scientist in the Admiralty Research Laboratory, and actually lived for two years with my brother in Bristol. I never cared for Watson at the time. He was tall and thin, with a pinched, goatlike face and a strange affected tiptoed walk. Watson considered himself one of the greatest theoretical physicists of his day, yet most of his colleagues thought his grasp of practical work distinctly ropey and that he had made serious mistakes in theoretical work. He was, I thought, a bit of a fraud.

Watson was a failure. At Cambridge he was considered a brilliant student, destined for the highest academic honors, until his thesis was found to contain a massive fundamental error. He failed to gain a fellowship, and took a job in the Admiralty instead. After service in the Radar and Signals Establishment of the Navy, he became head of the Submarine Detection Research Section at ARL. It was one of the most secret and important jobs in the entire NATO defense establishment, but it was obscure work, particularly for one who had promised so much in his youth.

At Cambridge, Watson was an ardent Marxist; indeed, many of those I interviewed described him as the "high priest" of Marxist theory among the Apostles. Marxism had a beautiful logic, an all-embracing answer to every question, which captivated him. He was drawn to _Das Kapital_ as others were drawn to the Bible and, like a preacher manqué, he began to proselytize the creed among his friends, particularly when his hopes of an academic career began to fade. Blunt later admitted that Watson schooled him in Marxism.

When I studied his file, his departure from Cambridge struck me as most peculiar—just at the time of Munich, when radical discontent with the Establishment was at its height. It bore all the hallmarks of Burgess' and Philby's move to the right at the same period. There was one other item of interest. Victor Rothschild wrote a letter to Dick White in 1951 suggesting that Watson should be investigated in view of his Communist affiliations in the 1930s. Inexplicably, Victor's suggestion had never been pursued, and since then Watson had been successfully vetted no less than three times, and made no mention of his political background.

I decided to try Watson's name out on Blunt at our next meeting. I knew it would be a waste of time to approach the matter directly, so I prepared a list of all known members of the Apostles including Watson, and asked him to pick out those he had known, or felt I should take an interest in. He went down the list, but made no mention of Watson.

"What about Alister?" I asked him finally.

"No," said Blunt firmly, "he's not relevant."

The time had come to confront Blunt. I told him he was lying again, that he knew as well as I did that Watson was a close friend and fellow Communist at Cambridge. Blunt's tic started again. Yes, it was true, he admitted. They were friends. They still saw each other regularly at Apostles dinners and the like, but he had not recruited him, and nor had Guy so far as he knew.

Alister, he said, was a tragic figure, whose life had gone terribly wrong. He was a man who promised so much, yet had achieved so little, whereas his undergraduate friends, like Blunt himself and Turing, had achieved eminence, and in Turing's case immortality.

"I learned my Marxist theory at Alister's feet," Blunt told me.

"I suppose you know where he works?" I asked.

"The Admiralty, isn't it?"

"You said there were no more, Anthony. You said you were telling me the truth . . ."

Blunt raked the fire vigorously.

"I could never be Whittaker Chambers," he said after a while, referring to the famous American Communist who renounced his creed in the 1950s and named his former accomplices, including

Alger Hiss, in a series of sensational appearances before Congressional committees.

"It's so McCarthyite," he went on, "naming names, informing, witchhunts . . ."

"But, Anthony, that's what you are—that's why we gave you immunity. It was your choice. It's no good putting the hood on, if you won't point the finger . . ."

Blunt fell silent. Years had passed since 1937, but the weight never lifted.

"I suppose you'll turn the works on him," he said finally.

I wrote a lengthy report on Watson in early 1965, recommending an urgent investigation. I submitted it to Hollis and F.J. via the head of D Branch, Alec MacDonald, who had replaced Cumming when the latter retired, aware at last that he would never attain the Deputy's chair. MacDonald was a sensible former Indian policeman, with a taste for cordon bleu cooking and the other good things in life, and a dislike of excessive administration. He was good to be with, but could be infuriating to work for.

Nothing happened for five months, and finally, when I attended my D3 annual review meeting with Hollis and F.J., I raised the subject. Why, I asked, had an investigation not been sanctioned? At first there was a lot of talk about priorities, and limits on resources. I reminded them that the whole rationale for D3 was that it should produce leads, which were then to be taken on by D1 (Investigations) if their strength warranted it. Here was a strong lead to a suspect currently enjoying prime access to NATO secrets. I said that if this was to be the procedure, they might just as well close down D3 entirely.

F.J. was very sensible. Hollis was surly and defensive. The mistake had occurred at D Branch level. Somehow or other, in the confusion of the handover from Cumming to MacDonald, the case had not been given the priority it needed. Hollis instructed there and then that the case be activated.

Patrick Stewart, then D1 (Investigations), took it on. He was a great friend as well as a brilliant officer, with an uncomplicated, clear mind. He was a man of great personal courage. During the war he was severely crippled, but despite his wheelchair he continued working at MI5 until ill-health finally drove him into early retirement. Watson was immediately placed under full surveillance, and we soon discovered that his wife and daughter were both current Communists, and from the tenor of his conversations, so was Watson himself, although he had declared none of this during his vettings.

The investigation, however, was limited. Watson was due to visit the USA to be indoctrinated into the latest American anti-submarine-detection techniques, and the Admiralty insisted that the case be clarified before his departure. We decided to interrogate him. Every day for six weeks Watson reported to the Ministry of Defense, where he was questioned by MI5's top interrogator, and today the Deputy Director-General of the Service, Cecil Shipp.

Watson began by acting like an affronted senior civil servant. What right had we to question him? he wanted to know. But this soon disappeared as Shipp probed his story.

Did he know Guy Burgess?

Of course.

Did he ever visit Guy Burgess' flat?

On occasions, yes.

Whom did he meet there?

Guy, Anthony . . .

Anyone else?

Yes, a foreigner. He couldn't remember his name . . .

Could he describe him?

At first he couldn't. Then he could. He was Central European. He had dark hair, slicked down, he thought. It sounded very like "Otto," the controller of the Ring of Five in the late 1930s.

"Does the name 'Otto' mean anything to you?" asked Shipp.

"Yes—that was the man's name. That's right, Otto . . ." answered Watson, a shade too enthusiastically.

For a while Shipp pursued other areas of questioning, but then he returned to Otto. Had Watson ever met him again? At first Watson couldn't remember. Then he thought perhaps he had met him, but he could recollect no details. Then he remembered that they used to meet in parks, and under lampposts on street corners, and on tube trains.

"Did he give you anything?"

"No, I'm quite sure of that . . ."

"Did you give him anything?"

"No, I don't think so . . ."

"Tell me, Mr. Watson, why did you meet him like that? Why not at your flat, or at a restaurant?"

No answer.

A long, long pause.

"I was interested in these people," he said lamely. "I wanted to find out more about Russia . . ."

"You were interested in these people . . ." reiterated Shipp with crushing sarcasm.

The next day Shipp showed Watson thirty photographs spread out in a neat fan on the table in front of him. They contained portraits of some of the most important KGB officers since 1945, who had been in Britain.

"Do you recognize any of these people?" he was asked.

Watson stared at the photographs, fingering one or two hesitantly. He muttered to himself as he sorted them, resorted them, stacked them in piles, and unstacked them again, every word captured on the hidden microphones. We were certain, from his answers about Otto, that Watson feared or suspected that we had direct evidence against him, perhaps a surveillance photograph of him meeting a KGB officer, or a confession which implicated him. At night he went home, and we could hear him mumbling there via the SF we had installed on his telephone.

"They've got something," he kept whispering. "They've got something, but I don't know what it is . . ."

After several hours, Watson picked out three photographs. The first was Yuri Modin, Philby's controller; the second was Sergei Kondrashev, George Blake's controller; and the third was Nikolai Karpekov, Vassall's controller. Watson admitted meeting all three regularly, sometimes close to the Admiralty Research Laboratory at Teddington during his lunch hour, but he denied passing any secrets. Golitsin said that he knew that Karpekov had two Naval spies, one of whom was a Naval scientist. Also that Kondrashev had had two spies, one of whom was Blake, the other a Naval spy.

Shipp tore into him. Did he really expect us to believe that he just happened to meet four top KGB controllers, by chance, for no reason? Did he think we were stupid? Naive? It was all secret, wasn't it? They were clandestine meetings? He was a spy, wasn't he? It all fitted, didn't it—friendship with Burgess, Marxism in the 1930s, concealed Communism and entry into secret work, meeting Russians? It was time to confess.

Day after day Shipp pursued him. Let's take it from the beginning again, he would say, and Watson would tell the same incredible story. The mark of a good interrogator is his memory, and Shipp had one like an elephant. Every variation, every omission in Watson's narrative was stored and thrown back at him hours, and sometimes days, later. But Watson stuck doggedly to his story. He had never passed anything over. His lips quivered, he was red and sweaty, but like a punch-drunk boxer he refused to take the count.

After six weeks of daily interrogation Watson was visibly wilting. He came into sessions drugged with tranquilizers, rambling incoherently, barely aware of the questions that we asked. In desperation almost, Cecil Shipp began to skirt the issue of immunity. At the time we had not obtained the Attorney-General's permission, so he phrased his questions hypothetically.

"Would it change your story," Watson was asked, "if we were to offer you immunity?"

But Watson was too far gone. He seemed unable even to understand the offer that was made to him, and the interrogation was suspended.

No one who listened to the interrogation or studied the transcripts was in any doubt that Watson had been a spy, probably since 1938. Given his access to antisubmarine-detection research, he was, in my view, probably the most damaging of all the Cambridge spies. One detail, in particular, clinched the case. Watson told a long story about Kondrashev. He had met him, but did not care for him. He described Kondrashev in great detail. He was too bourgeois, claimed Watson. He wore flannel trousers and a blue blazer, and walked a poodle. They had a row and they stopped meeting.

This clicked exactly with one of Golitsin's early serials. He said Kondrashev was sent to Britain to run two very important spies—one in the Navy and one in MI6. The MI6 spy was definitely George Blake, and we always assumed the Naval spy to be Blake too, since he served in the Navy before joining MI6. Golitsin had one more fragment. He said Kondrashev fell out with the Naval spy. The spy objected to his bourgeois habits, and refused to meet him. Golitsin recalled that as a result Korovin, the former London KGB resident, was forced to return to London to replace Kondrashev as the Naval spy's controller. It was obviously Watson.

At MI5's insistence, Watson was removed from secret access overnight, and transferred to the Oceanographic Institute, where he worked on until retirement. In the absence of a confession, we relied on our legal justification on Watson's failure to declare his Communist background, and those of his wife and daughter, on his vetting forms. He made no protest.

After Watson's interrogation I decided to have one more try at breaking him. I arranged for him to meet Blunt at a neutral venue—Brown's Hotel in London. There were two reasons for this; firstly, I was not at all sure that Watson understood the meaning of our immunity offer, and I wanted Blunt to explain it. Secondly, I wanted to resolve, if possible, the question of whether or not Watson was a member of the Ring of Five. Golitsin said the members of the Ring all knew each other, and all knew they were all spies. As far as Blunt was concerned, he claimed it was only ever a Ring of Four—himself, Burgess, Philby, and Maclean, with other recruits like Cairncross and Long existing independently of the central Ring members. Watson seemed by far the best starter for the fifth.

Blunt was very reluctant at first to go along with the plan.

"Alister has suffered enough," he pleaded, when I first raised it.

I had arranged meetings between Blunt and previous conspirators on a number of occasions. The sessions with Long and Straight were mild encounters; Blunt even told Straight that exposing him was the best thing he ever did. But when I suggested he contact Baron zu Putlitz, Klop Ustinov's wartime spy, who had returned to East Germany, he became distinctly agitated. Zu Putlitz and Blunt were lovers during the war, after Klop Ustinov brought zu Putlitz out of Holland and back to London. In 1945 Blunt accompanied zu Putlitz back to East Germany, and they had remained in touch ever since. Zu Putlitz had also been working for the Russians before and after the war, in order to smooth his return East, and I was interested to see if he could be turned our way again. I asked Blunt to write him a letter asking him if he would be prepared to meet me in Helsinki or Berlin.

"That's not fair, Peter, that's dirty. He's done enough for this country."

But Blunt knew he could not refuse. He wrote the letter, although much to his relief zu Putlitz turned my offer down.

Watson was like zu Putlitz. There was something about acknowledging the relationship which caused Blunt deep unease, in a way that did not occur with Long or Straight or others. It was a deep-seated desire to protect them, to deny us any knowledge of their activities, and also a desire to hide his confession. He dreaded being seen by them, I think, as an informer.

I picked Blunt up from the Courtauld one evening and we drove over to Brown's Hotel, where Patrick Stewart had booked a room for us all. He and Watson were waiting. Blunt was desperately anxious.

"I hope you've got something to drink," he said when we arrived at the hotel.

He and Watson greeted each other nervously, afraid to show any warmth in front of either Patrick or me. Watson was frail, like a man just out of hospital, but eventually we coaxed him into telling the story of his dealings with the Russians again. It was a pathetic story in the interrogation room, but it looked even more ridiculous in front of Blunt.

They both talked about Cambridge most of the time, and Otto, and the move to the left in the 1930s. It struck me as an odd way for the idealism and activism of the 1930s to end: in a small hotel suite, with a bottle of Scotch and a bottle of gin. They wanted to change the world, but ended up changing only themselves.

"I'm through with it now, Alister," said Blunt. "I've confessed," he kept saying, "and I'm still here. You've got nothing to worry about."

But Watson scarcely listened to Blunt's entreaties. They were talking at cross-purposes. Watson was overpoweringly jealous of Blunt and clearly always had been for thirty years. It came to the surface in a drunken attack on his friend. Treachery, for him, seemed almost the secondary issue. He was much more interesting in talking, now that his life had failed, about where it went wrong.

"You've been such a success, Anthony, and yet it was I who was the great hope at Cambridge. Cambridge was my whole life," he said, practically in tears, "but I had to go into secret work, and now it has ruined my life . . ."

Blunt left the table, upset and embarrassed. He walked over to the drinks cabinet on the other side of the room. He had drunk almost a complete bottle of gin, but still needed more. I walked over to him.

"Well . . . ?" I asked.

Blunt stood, his shoulders sagging with strain.

"I suppose you're right," he said, his eyes gleaming with emotion. "I suppose he must be one of us, but I never recruited him, and Guy never told me he had."

There was no gin left, so Blunt poured himself a tumbler full of sherry and added soda water. He gulped it down.

"Sometimes," he said, "I think it would have been easier to go to prison."

Victor and Tess Rothschild were a constant help during the D3 inquiries into the 1930s. Both knew so much about the personalities and the hidden relationships of the period, and were often able to prevail upon otherwise reluctant inhabitants of the Ring of Five's menagerie to meet me. Victor was also able to make a number of vital introductions for me. For instance, one of the questions which fascinated me after the Watson case was the degree to which other scientists besides Watson had been targets for recruitment. Burgess, Blunt, Philby, and Maclean were all classically educated, but I wondered whether rings had been recruited at, for instance, the world-famous Cambridge University Cavendish Laboratory.

My suspicions fell on the renowned Soviet scientist Peter Kapitza, father of the Russian atomic bomb. Kapitza came to Cambridge in the 1920s, financed by the British Royal Society, where he built the Mond Law temperature laboratory attached to the Cavendish. Kapitza remained close to the Soviet Government, and on several occasions was observed receiving Russian intelligence officers in his rooms. In the 1930s the Soviet Government, alarmed by growing international tension, insisted Kapitza return to work in Russia, and he was allowed to take all his machinery back with him. But both before and after the war he remained in touch with British scientists, often receiving those who visited Russia in his well-appointed dacha outside Moscow. For years it was rumored inside MI5 that Kapitza had talent-spotted potential recruits inside the Cavendish. But no one had ever really traced through the story. No one knew who, or how many, or whether Kapitza was ever successful. It was just another loose end, left in the files, seeping doubt and suspicion.

The one man who was in a position to know more about Kapitza, who he was friendly with, who his contacts were during his time at Cambridge, was Lord Adrian, who knew Kapitza when he was in Britain, and in the 1960s was Chancellor of the University of Cambridge and President of the Royal Society. Victor promptly arranged a dinner party at which I was able to meet Adrian, and from there guide him gently onto the subject of the Russian scientist.

Adrian was entirely cooperative, and could well understand the suspicions we had about Kapitza, even though he admired his achievements tremendously. He began to reel off names of those who had been especially close to Kapitza. More names for my black books. More names to be checked in the Registry. More names to be traced, interviewed, assessed, cleared, and in one or two cases, removed from access. All to be sure, finally, that no one had slipped through the net.

The most important help Victor gave was persuading Flora Solomon to meet MI5 again. I knew from her session with Arthur that she knew far more than she was saying. She had obviously been in the thick of things in the mid-1930s, part inspiration, part fellow accomplice, and part courier for the fledgling Ring of Five along with her friends Litzi Philby and Edith Tudor Hart. After her meeting with Arthur she refused to meet MI5 again. She had a typically Russian paranoia about conspiracy and treachery. She was convinced we would double-cross her, and put her in prison, or that she would be assassinated by the Russians, as she believed had happened to Tomas Harris. I asked Victor if he could intercede on my behalf, and eventually, in mid-1965, she agreed to see me.

"Does the name Dennis Proctor mean anything to you?" she growled.

It did indeed. Dennis Proctor was then the Permanent Secretary at the Ministry of Fuel and Power, having joined the Civil Service in the 1930s, when he had served as Stanley Baldwin's private secretary. In my travels around Cambridge and Oxford nearly a dozen people had picked out Proctor as a notable left-winger, although not a Communist, during his undergraduate days. He had the classic Cambridge Comintern recruit's profile—he was a close friend of Burgess, Blunt, Philby, and Watson and a member of the Apostles.

There was one other odd thing about Proctor which had puzzled me. Shortly before the 1951 defections he suddenly left the Civil Service for no apparent reason to take a job with a shipping company in Copenhagen. In 1953, just as suddenly, he reappeared in London and resumed his Civil Service career.

I asked Flora why she mentioned Proctor.

"Kim used to bring people to see me," she said. "He valued my opinion. I would never join, but I used to tell him what I thought of his recruits."

"And what did you tell him about Proctor . . . ?"

"Kim brought him around for dinner one night. I didn't like him. I told Kim he was no good. He had no backbone. 'How will he stand up to stress?' I asked him."

Proctor was another name which Blunt had clearly deliberately avoided giving me. I went to Hollis and requested permission to interview Proctor, but he refused. It would cause too much fuss in Whitehall, he said, and there were enough problems there as it was. I would have to wait until he retired. After all, said Hollis, it's only a few months.

Proctor retired to a delightful rustic French farmhouse in the rolling countryside outside Avignon with his second wife and children, and in February 1966 I traveled to France to visit him.

Proctor was a distinguished-looking man, with a hook nose, receding hairline, and just a touch of the cleric about him. He greeted me with the easy charm and familiarity which upper-class Englishmen use to set their visitors at a distance. I explained that MI5 were looking back into the 1930s.

"We're just tying up loose ends, you know, that sort of thing . . ."

Proctor talked about the period in crisp civil servant's shorthand. He rarely mentioned himself at first. Like the model civil servant, he was the modest observer of other people's lives and decisions. But beneath his reserve, I could detect an enthusiasm, as if he were recalling a better world.

"And how did you feel about things then yourself?" I asked.

"You mean what were my politics?" he countered, smiling at my euphemism. "Well, you presumably know I have been left-wing all my life?"

"Really?"

"Oh yes," he went on, "but never Communist. I wanted to go into Government service too much to join the Party, and besides I didn't have the courage of people like Guy Burgess, who did it openly."

I asked him if Guy had ever approached him to work for peace, or for the Comintern, or anything like that.

He shook his head.

"No, I don't think so . . . No, I don't remember anything like that at all."

"But Guy knew what your political views were?"

"Why, yes. We were very close. Guy, myself, Anthony. The Apostles, you know . . ."

"Don't you think it's odd he never tried to recruit you?"

He paused for thought.

"I suppose it is, now you come to mention it. In fact, I'm really rather insulted he didn't . . ."

He laughed. I laughed too, and he suggested we take a walk before dinner. It was still just winter, but the earth was thawing, as if spring lay just beneath the surface. We talked about other things—about England, and the Civil Service, and the way things had changed.

"Most of us, you know, have spent our lives escaping from the thirties," he told me, as we looked back down the valley toward his house.

"We were all so exquisitely happy then. It was our world. But we lost it in 1939, and we've been looking to escape ever since."

He pointed to the farmhouse, shrouded in late-afternoon mist.

"That's my escape . . ." he said.

That evening we had a splendid dinner, and afterward retired to his study with the port. Proctor was drunk, and I could see he was finding my visit a strain. He knew that sooner or later I would return to Burgess.

For a while he seemed to doze off over his port, and woke up perspiring heavily. He began to dab his forehead nervously with his handkerchief.

"Why do you think it was Guy never bothered to approach you?" I asked as I filled his glass again.

Proctor gulped his down, and poured himself another.

"I admired Guy very much," he said, after a pause. "People forget, you know, just how gifted Guy was. They don't remember how he was before the war. The looks, the vitality, the intellect. They just think of him afterward."

I said nothing, waiting for him to fill the silence.

He began again, talking more urgently.

"You see, I had no secrets from him. Whenever I had a problem, no matter how secret, I used to discuss it with him, and his advice was always sound. I think the real truth of the matter is

that Guy had no need to recruit me. He could get to know anything he wanted. All he had to do was ask."

"What about 1951?" I asked, anxious to press him while he
was talking.

"No, no, no," he clucked, "you've got that all wrong. I left in
1950 for personal reasons, nothing to do with this—to do with
Varda, my first wife. She committed suicide, you know, in 1951."

"Did you see Guy before he went?"

"No—but my wife did, about six weeks before. She and her
father were very close to him. I was in Copenhagen at the time."

"And she killed herself afterward?"

"Not long after, yes . . ."

He sat up and looked at me, suddenly sober.

"I'd rather not talk about it, if you don't mind. But there's no
connection, I promise you."

He slumped back again in the chair, disheveled like a de-
frocked priest.

"They were both terrible, shocking events," he said quietly. "A
year or two later, when I recovered, Edward Bridges invited me
back into the Civil Service, and I came back to England." (Edward Bridges was then Permanent Secretary at the Treasury and
Head of the Home Civil Service.)

I never did discover why Proctor's first wife, Varda, committed
suicide, or what she and Guy Burgess discussed. The truth about
Proctor was difficult to judge. I was inclined to believe his claim
that he was never formally recruited, while disbelieving his asser-
tion that Burgess had nothing to do with his departure to Denmark in 1950. But whatever the case, I am absolutely sure that
during the time he was Baldwin's private secretary, and probably
right up until 1950, he shared with Guy every secret which
crossed his desk.

The next time I saw Blunt I told him about my discussion with
Proctor.

"You didn't tell us about him, Anthony," I said, reproachful rather than angry. It always upset Blunt more if he felt the deceit was a matter between friends.

"You kept quiet again—to protect him."

He got up and went to the window, and gazed through it as if he could see back into the past.

"What about Dennis?" I asked again.

"All I can say is he must have been the best source Guy ever had. But I didn't know what role he was playing," he said finally. "All I knew was that he was still in Government . . ."

"But you could have guessed . . ." I sighed with irritation.

Blunt pulled the curtains, as if faintly disappointed with the noise and dust and fashions of the square outside.

"Unless you lived through it, Peter, you cannot understand . . ."

"Oh, I lived through it, Anthony," I said, suddenly angry. "I know more about the thirties probably than you will ever know. I remember my father driving himself mad with drink, because he couldn't get a job. I remember losing my education, my world, everything. I know all about the thirties . . ."

One of the most interesting things to emerge in the D3 researches was the existence of the Oxford Ring. In the past, Soviet recruitment was associated mainly with Cambridge University, but once Blunt opened up, it was obvious that Burgess and James Klugman had targeted Oxford in the same way. The first hard source on the Oxford Ring came from a colleague of Blunt's at the Courtauld Institute, Phoebe Pool. Blunt admitted that she had been his courier during the 1930s, and I was anxious to interview her. She and Blunt were close; they had even written a book together on Picasso.

Blunt told me she was a neurotic, and already in the process of a nervous breakdown. He said that she would clam up, or worse, if I spoke to her directly, so he organized a cutout for me—another senior figure at the Courtauld, Anita Brookner, to whom I could relay questions for Pool. A degree of deception was inevitable.

Pool was told that new inquiries were being made into the 1930s, and Anthony wanted to know if there was anybody else he should warn.

Phoebe Pool told Anita Brookner that she used to run messages for Otto to two brothers, Peter and Bernard Floud. Peter, the former Director of the Victoria and Albert Museum, was dead, but his brother Bernard was a senior Labor MP. Pool also said a young woman, Jennifer Fisher Williams, was involved, and urged Brookner to ensure that "Andy Cohen," the senior diplomat Sir Andrew Cohen, was warned too, as he also was at risk. All these names were well known to me. All except Andrew Cohen (Cohen was an Apostle and Cambridge student) were connected with the Clarendon, a left-wing dining and discussion club in Oxford during the 1930s, but this was the first hard evidence that the club had been a center for Soviet espionage recruitment.

Ironically, Jennifer Fisher Williams was married to a former wartime MI5 officer, Herbert Hart, by the time her name emerged, so I visited her husband at Oxford, where he was pursuing a distinguished academic career as Professor of Jurisprudence, and asked him if he would approach his wife on my behalf. He rang her up there and then, assured her there was no threat to her position, and she agreed to meet me.

Jennifer Hart was a fussy, middle-class woman, too old, I thought, for the fashionably short skirt and white net stockings she was wearing. She told her story quite straightforwardly, but had a condescending, disapproving manner, as if she equated my interest in the left-wing politics of the 1930s with looking up ladies' skirts. To her, it was rather vulgar and ungentlemanly.

She said she was an open Party member in the 1930s, and was approached by a Russian, who from her description was definitely Otto. Otto instructed her to go underground, and she used to meet him clandestinely at Kew Gardens. She told us that she was merely part of the Party underground, and that she gave up meeting Otto when she joined the Home Office in 1938, where she worked in a highly sensitive department which processed applications for telephone intercepts. She told us, too, that she had never passed on any secret information.

She had two other contacts, she said. One was Bernard Floud, who recruited her, and the other man who controlled her for a short time she identified from a photograph as Arthur Wynn, a close friend of Edith Tudor Hart and her husband, who was active in trade union circles before joining the Civil Service.

There was no doubt in my mind, listening to Jennifer Hart, that this was a separate Ring based exclusively at Oxford University, but investigating it proved enormously difficult. Almost at once, Sir Andrew Cohen (who was at Cambridge and became a diplomat) died from a heart attack, so he was crossed off the list. Peter Floud was already dead, but his brother looked more hopeful when the Prime Minister, Harold Wilson, named him to a junior ministerial post in the Labor Government. MI5 were asked to provide him with security clearance. We objected and requested permission to interrogate Floud about Jennifer Hart's allegation. Wilson had, at the time, a standing ban on any inquiries relating to MPs, but when he read the MI5 brief, he gave clearance for the interview.

Floud's attitude, when I began the interview, was extraordinary. He treated the matter as of little importance, and when I pressed him on Jennifer Hart's story he refused to either confirm or deny that he had recruited her.

"How can I deny it, if I can't remember anything about it?" he said repeatedly.

I was tough with him. I knew that his wife, an agoraphobic depressive, had recently committed suicide, but Floud was eager to conclude the interview, presumably lured by the scent of office. I explained to him in unmistakable terms that, since it was my responsibility to advise on his security clearance, I could not possibly clear him until he gave a satisfactory explanation for the Hart story. Still he fell back lamely on his lack of memory. The session ended inconclusively, and I asked for him to attend a further interview the following day. I did not make any progress with him, he maintaining that he had no recollection of recruiting Jennifer.

The next morning I got a message that Floud had committed suicide, apparently with a gas poker and a blanket. Not long after, Blunt telephoned me with more bad news.

"Phoebe's dead," he said.

"Good God, how?" I gasped.

"She threw herself under a tube . . ."

Three deaths, two of which were suicides, in such a small group of people, at a time when we were actively investigating them, seemed far more than bad luck. MI5 was terrified that it would be linked publicly with the deaths, and all further work was suspended. Newspapers were already vigorously pursuing the story of Philby's role as the Third Man, and had discovered for the first time the seniority of his position in MI6. Rumors of Blunt's involvement were also beginning to surface in Fleet Street. The entire scandalous tapestry was in danger of unraveling. That still left the problem of Arthur Wynn, who, by coincidence, was also due for promotion to the Deputy Secretary's job at the Board of Trade, which also required security clearance.

"What shall we do?" asked F.J. nervously.

"We should tell him we'll give him clearance, if he tells the truth about the Ring. Otherwise no clearance . . ."

"But that's blackmail," he said, doing his best to sound shocked.

I saw nothing unfair about my offer, but then, as I told F.J., I was never destined to be a diplomat or a politician.

"All these suicides," he said, "they'll ruin our image. We're just not that sort of Service."

The Oxford Ring completed my inquiries into the 1930s conspiracy. By the end of the 1960s the task was virtually complete, those involved nearing or well past retirement. We had identified every member of the Ring of Five and a number of others and their controllers. We knew how the Ring worked at various times, we knew what their communications were, whom they depended on, and where they went for help. We had also identified one major undiscovered spy, Watson, and another crucial source for the Russians during the period 1935–51, Proctor, as well as an important new Ring at Oxford. Altogether we had identified, dead or alive, nearly forty probable spies. Beyond that we had scrutinized carefully the records of dozens of people in every sphere of British public life. Most were given a clean bill of health, but some were found to be secret Communists or associates, and were removed from access or quietly encouraged to retire.

Of course, there were still loose ends. Klugman took his secrets with him, Otto was never identified, and the British end of the Rote Kapelle we never found. But we knew the most important thing of all—we knew how far the conspiracy extended. We knew our history, and we had no need to be afraid again. The vetting of a generation had been painful, certainly, more painful probably than it need have been had the inquiries been conducted at the right time, when the trails were still fresh. But we had exorcised the past, and we could at last return to the present again, not forgetting that there might be descendants from the people of the 1930s.

18 ————————————

ONE OTHER UNRESOLVED QUESTION REMAINED THROUGHOUT THE
1960s, perhaps the most important of all—whether or not there
was an undiscovered mole inside MI5. The FLUENCY Working
Party's research into the history of penetration of British Intelligence continued in parallel with the D3 inquiries. Hollis took
little interest in FLUENCY, principally because it was not due to
report until after his scheduled retirement in December 1965. He
still considered the penetration issue closed after the meeting to
discuss the second Symonds report in October 1964, and he ordered that none of those officers involved in the Mitchell case
should discuss it even among themselves. It was a hopeless request. For one thing, Hollis' visit to the USA and Canada in
1963, to brief the CIA, FBI, and RCMP that Mitchell might
possibly have been a spy, caused predictable fury and alarm.
Shortly after Hollis' visit, I traveled to Canada myself. The DEW
WORM microphones, which had lain undisturbed in the walls of
the Soviet Embassy since 1956, were suddenly dug out by a team
of Russian sweepers. No preliminary searches were made; the
Russians knew exactly where the microphones were, and we
heard them take them out before the lines went dead.

The RCMP wondered if Mitchell had perhaps compromised
the operation. Jim Bennett, who by now was head of Counterespionage in the RCMP, began to sound me out. It was impossible
to deflect his interest, and I gave him a brief résumé of the

evidence which pointed toward a high-level penetration. In fact, I had my own theory. I was sure the presence of the DEW WORM microphones was blown to the Russians in 1956, hence their refusal to use the rooms for anything other than occasional consular business. But they clearly learned the exact locations of the system only in 1964. This coincided exactly with the Mitchell investigation, which considered in great detail the possibility that FLUENCY might have been betrayed by Mitchell in 1956. Both Mitchell and Hollis also received the detailed file in 1956, including the details about the way the DEW WORM system worked. The operation was undoubtedly blown then. Whether it was Mitchell or Hollis who had done it, the Russians could not afford to take the microphones out unless the sweepers found them without being told exactly where they were. Despite over twenty days of searching, they failed to do so, even though they knew the exact area that had been bugged.

F.J. blasted me when he heard that I had talked about the penetration issue in Canada, but I told him that it was impossible to avoid discussion after Hollis' abortive visit. To ignore the problem only made it worse in the eyes of our allies.

In Washington interest was just as acute. I remember a house party at Michael McCaul's, the man who in 1964 became the SLO in Washington in succession to Harry Stone. Angleton and I detached ourselves, and he quizzed me hard on the state of affairs inside MI5.

"What the hell's got into you guys," he kept saying. "Hollis comes out there with some cock-and-bull story about Mitchell. He doesn't seem to know the first thing about the case. There's been no interrogation, and now he says there's nothing in it! . . ."

I tried to talk him through the case. Mitchell, I told him, was in the clear, we thought, but I stated that as far as Arthur and I were concerned, Hollis was our next suspect. I asked him if he had any information which might help us break open the case.

He said he would see what he could do. It was a difficult time for the CIA. Kennedy had just been assassinated and the Warren Commission of inquiry was sitting, and Angleton had pressing problems of his own.

In 1965, British security seemed once again catastrophically bad to American eyes. In just four years a succession of spy scandals and disasters had engulfed both MI5 and MI6. First Houghton was unmasked, having betrayed vital parts of NATO's underwater-detection systems. Although the Houghton case was a triumph for MI5's new counterespionage capability, it caused outrage in the U.S. Navy, which had long fostered hostility to its British counterpart. The enmity surfaced at a National Security Council meeting, soon after the Houghton trial, at which the U.S. Navy had sought a complete break in the British-American intelligence and secrets exchange. Jim Angleton and Al Belmont from the FBI nipped the Navy ploy in the bud.

"The only difference between us and them," said Belmont dryly, "is they catch spies, and we don't."

But nothing Belmont said could possibly mitigate the string of disasters which followed. Blake was tried and convicted in 1961, casting doubt on virtually every European CIA operation including the Berlin Tunnel. Vassall was caught the next year, 1962; once again, valuable NATO Naval secrets had gone East because of a British spy. In January 1963 Philby defected, with the British authorities apparently mute and impotent. There were the security implications of the Profumo affair in the same year, with its suggestions, taken seriously at the time in the FBI, that the Russians were obtaining nuclear secrets from Profumo via Christine Keeler. Blunt, Long, and Cairncross confessed in 1964, while other cases simply collapsed humiliatingly in court. The Kodak case in 1964 was one, but far worse in American eyes was the Martelli case in early 1965.

The Martelli case had started in 1963 with an allegation by Fedora that the KGB had a foreign ideological source inside an

English nuclear research establishment. He had been operational only in the last one to two years. While this meant that the defector, Golitsin, did not know about him, it severely limited the field of likely candidates. After a few false steps, the investigation closed in on Giuseppe Martelli, who had come to the Dulham Laboratory in the autumn of 1962 from Euratom. But Martelli was not cleared for secret atomic material. Despite this, the investigation went ahead. It was possible that, like Houghton in the Lonsdale case, when he was at Portland, Martelli got his secrets from a girlfriend who did have access. When it was found that Martelli *had* a girlfriend who had access to secrets it became *certainly* possible that Martelli also had access to secrets that he should not have had.

Further investigation did not produce any evidence that Martelli was able to acquire secrets. A search of his office at Culham produced rendezvous information from a locked drawer in his desk. At this time Martelli was away in Europe on holiday. When he returned he was picked up at Southend airport. He was questioned by Special Branch and identified Karpekov as a Russian he knew. He also had a map in his possession which indicated rendezvous arrangements. As a result his house at Abingdon was searched and a concealment device was found which contained miniature one-time pads à la Lonsdale. Part of a page of one pad had apparently been used. A diary was found which had the details of a grid for transforming letters, and therefore words, into numbers for the one-time pad to be used to encipher a message.

A long meeting was held by Hollis, with Mitchell present, to decide what to do. The crucial factor was that no evidence had been found that Martelli had access to secrets or was passing them to a foreign power. The Official Secrets Act (OSA) did have a clause which made it a crime to prepare to commit espionage. But it would be very difficult to prove that Martelli was doing this. There was no proof that he had been in clandestine communication with a foreign power. GCHQ could attest that the cipher pads were similar to those used by spies to communicate with their Russian masters but, unlike in the Lonsdale case, they could not prove that Martelli had done so. It is not often realized that it was the GCHQ testimony in the Lonsdale case that ensured the defendants were convicted. Without this evidence Lonsdale and his associates would have got off either scot-free or with a minor sentence.

I, as the MI5 SIGINT expert, pointed out to the management at the meeting that the evidence MI5 had was not sufficient to prove even the intention to communicate secrets to a foreign power. The Legal Branch of MI5 were keen to try to get Martelli on "the act preparatory" clause of the OSA to establish it as a valid reason to prosecute under the OSA. To the astonishment of the professional counterespionage officers present, Hollis and Mitchell pressed for the prosecution of Martelli to go ahead. The result was that the Attorney-General did go ahead and MI5 suffered the damage.

Even today I find it very difficult to understand why the Martelli case went ahead, unless one remembers the date of the trial—July 2, 1963. This was at the height of the Mitchell case. It is obvious that at this juncture it would have suited the Russians and Hollis for the CE side of MI5 to be knocked down.

The other case to be considered here is that of Frank Bossard. Early in 1965 Top Hat, the FBI-GRU agent, produced photocopies of documents from the Ministry of Supply of the highest security grading in the guided weapons field, involving high-level secrets of the USA. It was relatively easy to narrow the field of suspects to a few people. The suspects were put under all kinds of surveillance. It was discovered that Bossard, one of the suspects, occasionally during his lunch hour would collect a suitcase from the Left Luggage Office at Waterloo Station. He would go to a hotel in Bloomsbury and book himself into a room under a false name. He would stay there alone for about half an hour. On leaving he would take the suitcase back to the Left Luggage Office and return to work. MI5 in due course removed the case from Waterloo. In it were found document-copying cameras, cassettes of film, and two gramophone records on which there were about eight Russian songs. The details of the Russian songs were copied. The entire contents of the case were photographed and restored to the case, which was then returned to Waterloo. I rang up GCHQ and gave them the details of the records. It took GCHQ less than an hour to identify five of the tunes as having been transmitted by a Russian transmitter, found to be in the Moscow area by direction-finding. This transmitter was known to be a GRU Russian Intelligence Service transmitter.

We decided to arrest Bossard next time he took his case from Waterloo and went to a hotel with it. This took place on March 15, 1965. He was caught in the act of photographing Top Secret documents. When confronted with the fact that MI5 knew all about the tunes on the records, he admitted that he had been supplying photographs of secret documents to the Russians for money through dead letter boxes, i.e. secret caches. He received his money the same way. After his initial recruitment, he had met a Russian only once in nearly five years. He said that the individual tunes broadcast indicated which dead letter box to fill, or not to fill any. MI5 had all they wanted for a Section One prosecution. On May 10, 1965, Bossard was sentenced to twenty-one years in jail.

Since we now know that Top Hat, the source of the information, was a plant, why did the Russians decide to throw away Bossard? To understand the case, it is necessary to go into various aspects. First, the Russians had succeeded in damaging MI5 through Fedora and the Martelli case in 1963. This had resulted in increased suspicion, particularly in MI5, that Fedora was a plant. In 1964 Top Hat had given MI5 a story about technical eavesdropping coverage of the British Prime Minister's office, which, unless the Russians had a much more sophisticated system than we knew of in the West, was very unlikely. All efforts to find such a system in use had failed. This had led the British to consider that the story was phony, and both MI5 and the FBI had begun to question Top Hat's bona fides.

Top Hat's production of photographs of British documents of the highest classifications not only made it very difficult to believe that he was a plant (people ask the question: Would the Russians throw away such a source?); it would also result in the Americans once again becoming very suspicious of British security and in an outcry in the USA to cut Britain off from their secrets. Now if one had to choose a spy to risk, Bossard was ideal. He had practically no physical contact with Russians. His Moscow radio control was via innocent tunes. If it had not been for GCHQ's detailed traffic analysis, we would have been unaware of the significance of the records and we would not have been able to prove communication between the Russian Intelligence Service and Bossard. He would have been prosecuted only on the illegal copying of classified documents, a technical crime with relatively small penalties. Once again the professional and technical skill of GCHQ and MI5 had caught the Russians out. This success had two major effects. It enabled the American Intelligence Services to protect British interests in the American Government and it increased and did not diminish the doubts about Top Hat.

But the fundamental question has to be asked: Why did the Russians consider that they had to boost the bona fides of Top Hat? He had been operational since the end of 1962 and without a source at high level in either MI5, the FBI, or the CIA, there would have been nothing to alert the Russians that he was a suspect. At the end of 1964, MI5 had become very suspicious. Only Sullivan, the head of Domestic Intelligence in the FBI, had any fears of Top Hat's bona fides and he, Sullivan, was certainly not a Russian spy. In the CIA only Angleton and one or two close associates were suspicious. But the few people in MI5 who knew about Top Hat did not believe he was genuine. Hollis knew that these people had grave doubts about Top Hat.

There were other strains, too, on the alliance. There was deep-seated hostility in the American intelligence community to the accession to power of Harold Wilson and the Labor Government in 1964. Partly this was due to anti-Labor bias, partly to the Labor Government's commitment to abandon Polaris—a pledge they soon reneged on.

Hanging over everything from late 1963 onward, when Hollis made his trip to Washington, was the Mitchell case, and the fear that MI5 itself was deeply and currently penetrated at or near the summit, with the Secret Service apparently incapable of wrestling with the problem. The sacking of Arthur Martin only compounded American suspicions. They knew he was committed to hunting down Stalin's Englishmen wherever they were hiding, and to American eyes it seemed as if a public-school cabal had seen him off.

In mid-1965 matters came to a head. President Johnson commissioned a review of British security from the President's Foreign Intelligence Advisory Board (PFIAB), a committee of retired intelligence notables, bankers, industrialists, and politicians, formed to advise the President on improvements in national security. Two men were given the task of conducting this Top Secret review—Gordon Gray, a former Secretary of Defense under President Eisenhower, and Governor of North Carolina, and the Secretary of the PFIAB, Gerald Coyne, a former senior FBI officer who ran PFIAB for fifteen years.

Gray and Coyne came to London secretly in the summer of 1965 and began reviewing the Anglo-American intelligence relationship, and in particular the effectiveness of MI5. The work was delicate in the extreme. No one in British Intelligence was to be told that the review was even taking place. In any other country the review would be known by a cruder name—espionage. Most of Gray and Coyne's material was supplied by Cleveland

Cram, the CIA officer in charge of liaison in London with MI5. Cram was a brilliant and levelheaded CIA officer who had served in London for many years, and knew the weaknesses of MI5 only too well. Cram brought Gray and Coyne into Leconfield House and MI6 headquarters on a number of occasions, introducing them merely as colleagues. At this time CIA officers of Cram's stature had open access to all British Intelligence establishments, and the subterfuge was easy to perform on us.

I first heard about the Gray and Coyne review when I visited Washington in 1965. Angleton briefed me on the contents of the finished report. I was thunderstruck. Gray and Coyne had produced a devastating critique of MI5. They cited the inadequate size of British Counterespionage, and said that many individually talented officers were betrayed by poor organization and lack of resources. The report was especially critical of the quality of leadership inside MI5, particularly that provided by Hollis and Cumming, then the head of Counterespionage. Gray and Coyne concluded that Hollis had evidently lost the confidence of his senior officers (which was true) as well as that of his peers in Whitehall, which was also true.

Angleton was thrilled by the report, and told me that it would form the basis of a new relationship between British and American counterintelligence. He told me that the CIA intended making a direct approach to Harold Wilson, along with the American Ambassador in London, David Bruce, to brief him on the findings.

"Everything'll change now," he said, "we're going to have a beefed-up CIA London station, and half those officers are going to work directly inside MI5. We'll have access to everything, and help you where we can."

Once I had heard about the Gray-Coyne report, I was in an invidious position. Angleton had briefed me in confidence, but I was duty-bound to report the existence of such a document, and the planned approach to Wilson. Angleton's ambitions were obvious: he wanted the CIA to swallow MI5 up whole, and use it as an Agency outstation. I returned to London and told Hollis and F.J. everything I knew. It was one of the few occasions when Hollis showed any visible sign of shock. He ordered a check of records, and within a few hours got confirmation that Gray and Coyne had indeed visited virtually every British Intelligence establishment without ever declaring their true purpose.

Later that afternoon I saw both men sweep out to a waiting car at the front of Leconfield House.

"Thank you for your help, Peter," said F.J. grimly. "Never can trust the bloody Americans to play it by the rules!" I thought this was a touch sanctimonious, but I judged it better to keep clear of the flak which was rapidly building. F.J. and Hollis were off to see the Foreign Secretary to protest at this blatant abuse of the UKUSA agreement, and there was no telling where the row might end.

Poor Cleve Cram was hauled over the coals. He opposed the approach to Wilson, yet Helms and Angleton insisted he begin sounding out George Wigg, Wilson's security adviser. But Hollis was in no mood for excuses. He had been humiliated in front of the entire intelligence establishment in London and Washington, and Cram was threatened with expulsion if there were any further transgressions. I saw Cram a few days later skulking around the fifth floor of Leconfield House. He looked a little sheepish.

"You nearly got me PNG'd," he said, smiling ruefully. He knew the CIA had been trying it on, and had been caught fair and square. The Gray-Coyne report was a terrible indictment of Hollis' tenure as Director-General of MI5, and he knew it. But the Americans, typically, had handled the affair with all the finesse of a bull in a china shop. The essence of their plan was well-meant—to provide the resources and manpower which MI5 lacked. Of course they had other motives. They wanted MI5 as a supplicant client, rather than as a well-disposed but independent ally.

Improvements did flow from the report. For the first time MI5 management conceded the need to drastically expand D Branch, and the old colonial appendages, like E Branch, withered on the vine. Henceforth D Branch had first call on all resources. It was inevitable that new management would be sought for the revamped D Branch. Alec MacDonald, a former colonial policeman, was brought in, and Malcolm Cumming, realizing that he would never become Deputy DG, opted for early retirement.

The other important initiative which flowed from the report was the recognition which followed that a mechanism was needed to secure closer cooperation between Western counterintelligence services. GCHQ and NSA had a formal exchange under the terms of the UKUSA agreement. MI6 and the CIA regularly exchanged foreign intelligence assessments via the Joint Intelligence Committee in London and the National Security Council in Washington. But counterintelligence was still basically ad hoc. Angleton and I had often discussed the value of creating a forum for the regular free exchange of counterintelligence. So much counterintelligence, particularly when it flowed from defectors, ranged across national borders, and access to each country's files was essential if the best progress was to be made. But Angleton was an autocratic man; he wanted to use the Gray-Coyne report to force a one-way flow. But finally he became converted to the virtues of a genuinely mutual forum and, at his urging, a conference of senior counterintelligence officers from the USA, Britain, Australia, Canada, and New Zealand was organized to take place roughly every eighteen months. The conferences were called CAZAB, and the first was held in Melbourne, Australia, in November 1967.

The Gray-Coyne report was not the only epitaph to Hollis' career. As he approached retirement, the shape of the FLUENCY conclusions became clear. The Working Party consisted of Terence Lecky and Geoffrey Hinton from MI6 Counterintelligence, as well as Arthur Martin when he was transferred over in mid-

1965. The MI5 contingent was Patrick Stewart, Anne Orr-Ewing, and Evelyn McBarnet from D3, with me in the chair. The papers were circulated direct to the Director D, Alec MacDonald, and the head of Counterintelligence, Christopher Phillpotts. We met every Thursday in my office or a fifth-floor conference room at Leconfield House.

The mood was tense to begin with, each member aware of the awesome significance of the task at hand—to review in detail every single allegation which had ever been made about the penetration of British Intelligence. The first decision FLUENCY made was to change the approach to penetration which Arthur and I had adopted in the Mitchell case. In 1963, when we presented the case for penetration to Dick White, we relied heavily on analysis of the oddities and discrepancies in technical and double-agent cases, known in the jargon as "manifestations," FLUENCY decided to dispense with all manifestations. They were felt to be an overlay of specific allegations of penetration which had been made by defectors. These were the primary evidence, and we concentrated solely on them.

The first task was to collate the allegations. This was relatively straightforward, as much of the work had already been done during the Mitchell inquiry, and continued at my instigation as part of D3's overall program of research.

After six months' work we had compiled a large file, which contained the full list of allegations—over two hundred in all, some dating back to World War I. The allegations were then apportioned to various officers around the table. Those that came from Polish sources, like Goleniewski, were given to Terence Lecky. Evelyn McBarnet handled the old MI5 allegations, Patrick Stewart took the Golitsin material, and I looked at Krivitsky, Volkov, and VENONA.

Once the allegations were gathered we set about assessing them. We examined each allegation carefully, and made a decision about its validity—that is to say, whether we believed it to be true. In some cases, for instance, a defector might have said a spy existed in MI5 or MI6, but we were able to satisfy ourselves that they were mistaken. Where we satisfied ourselves that an allegation was true, it was termed, in counterintelligence jargon, "a true bill." Then we checked whether each allegation had ever been attributed to a known spy, such as Philby, Burgess, or Blunt, and if it had, the attribution was reexamined to see if it was still valid in view of any intelligence which might subsequently have come to light.

Assessing allegations depended on the quality of our records, and we faced a major problem with MI6 archives. They were in a mess. Each of the Geographical Divisions and the Counterintelligence Department kept their own records. MI6 were producers of intelligence, not collaters of it, and little thought had been given to an effective system of record-keeping. Indeed, this was a principal reason why so many allegations were simply left unresolved, and one of the by-products of the FLUENCY inquiries was a general recognition of the need to improve the MI6 Registry. In 1967 Arthur finally left Counterintelligence to take over the MI6 Registry, where he made one last major contribution to British Intelligence by totally overhauling the system.

After thorough review, each of the two hundred allegations was placed in one of six categories:

a. the allegation was a true bill, and was definitely attributable to a known spy;

b. the allegation was a true bill, and was almost certainly attributable to a known spy;

c. the allegation was a true bill, but it was not possible to attribute it to a known spy;

d. it was not possible to ascertain whether the allegation was or was not a true bill, because there was insufficient information;

e. the allegation was doubted;

f. the allegation was not a true bill, i.e. rubbish.

As Hollis approached retirement, FLUENCY began to uncover

an entirely new picture of the history of the penetration of British Intelligence. Many allegations which previously had been attributed to known spies like Philby or Blunt were found on detailed inspection to have been wrongly attributed. Twenty-eight of the two hundred allegations we examined were in the all-important C category—they were true bills, but they pointed to as yet undiscovered spies.

Of those twenty-eight, there were ten really important allegations, all of which related to MI5:

1. Volkov's "Acting Head," dated September 1945;

2. Gouzenko's "Elli," also dated September 1945;

3. Skripkin's betrayal, dated 1946 (information came from Rastvorov in 1954);

4. Goleniewski's "middling grade agent," dating from the mid-1950s;

5. Golitsin's information about the Skripkin investigation, also dated 1946;

6. Golitsin's information about the special safe in KGB headquarters to house material from British Intelligence;

7. Golitsin's information about the index to files in KGB headquarters containing material from British Intelligence;

8. Golitsin's information about the "Technics" Document;

9. Golitsin's information about the special arrangements for protecting the Soviet colony in London; and

10. Golitsin's information about the betrayal of Crabbe's diving mission.

Each of the Golitsin allegations dates from 1962–63.

The really startling thing about this list was the way it followed a clear chronological pattern from 1942 to 1963. The Golitsin material, although more recent, was not specific enough to point in the direction of any one officer, beyond the fact that it had clearly to be a high-level penetration to account for the allegations. But the first three serials, even though dated, transformed the FLUENCY work, and pointed in Hollis' direction for the first time.

19

KONSTANTIN VOLKOV'S LIST WAS THE FIRST SERIAL WHICH WE IN-
vestigated. This was already the subject of intensive D3 inquiries
to trace the second of the two Foreign Office spies mentioned in
the list. I decided to have the entire document retranslated by
Geoffrey Sudbury, the GCHQ officer who ran the VENONA program. Sudbury was a fluent Russian speaker, but most important
of all, from the VENONA program he was familiar with the kind of
Russian Intelligence Service jargon in use at the time Volkov
attempted to defect, whereas the British Embassy official in Turkey who had made the original translation was not.

One entry in Volkov's list puzzled me in particular. In the
original translation it referred to his knowledge of files and documents concerning very important Soviet agents in important establishments in London. "Judging by their cryptonyms, there are
seven such agents, five in British Intelligence and two in the
Foreign Office. I know, for instance, that one of these agents is
fulfilling the duties of head of a department of British Counterintelligence."

When the case against Philby was first compiled in 1951, MI5
assumed that the last spy referred to by Volkov was Philby, who
in 1945 was indeed fulfilling the duties of head of a department
of MI6—Counterintelligence, responsible for Soviet counterintelligence. But I knew enough Russian from VENONA myself to
see that there were two words in the Russian which did not

appear in the original translation—the word *otdel*, which means "section," which was closely followed by the word *upravalenie*, meaning "directorate" or "senior division." In any case, there was no irresistible reason why this particular entry by Volkov had to be Philby. There were five spies in British Intelligence in all, and any of those could just as easily have been Philby.

A few days after I gave Sudbury the Volkov list he rang me up excitedly, almost forgetting for a moment to switch over to his scrambler.

"The translation's wrong," he said, "it's all NKVD idiom. The man who wrote it was obviously quite senior. He's written it very carefully, with pride in his professional skill and knowledge. The real translation should read: 'I know, for instance, that one of these agents is fulfilling the duties of head of a section of the British Counterintelligence Directorate.'

"Actually, I rather think this man's position is temporary. He's 'fulfilling the duties' rather than in the job itself, which suggests to me he's the acting head, or something very like it . . ."

"I'm sorry," I replied cautiously.

"But don't you see," shrieked Geoffrey through the electronic haze, "the British Counterintelligence Directorate is MI5, it's not MI6!"

The meaning was crystal clear. If Sudbury was right, this was not Philby, and it could not be Blunt either, since he was never acting head of anything. Only one man had been acting head of a section of the British Counterintelligence Directorate in 1944–45. His name was Roger Hollis.

The second allegation was Igor Gouzenko's MI5 spy "Elli," which I had first seen in Anne Last's notebook during the Mitchell investigation. FLUENCY reexamined the case of Elli in great detail. The extraordinary thing about Gouzenko's Elli was the fact that it came in September 1945 in exactly the same period that Volkov made his "Acting Head" allegation, and also on the same date that we made the crucial break into the VENONA traffic.

The essence of Gouzenko's story was simple. He said he knew there was a spy in "five of MI." He had learned this from a friend, Luibimov, who had worked alongside him in the main GRU cipher room in Moscow in 1942. Elli's communications were handled through dead letter boxes, one of which was a crack in a tombstone. There was something Russian about Elli, said Gouzenko, either in his background, or because he had visited Russia, or could speak the language. Elli was an important spy because he could remove from MI5 the files which dealt with Russians in London.

Luibimov showed him parts of the telegrams from the spy, whose code name was Elli. Gouzenko said that when Elli's telegrams came in, there was always a woman present in the cipher room who read the decrypts first and, if necessary, took them straight to Stalin. I invited Ismail Akhmedov, a senior GRU officer who defected to the West at the end of the war, to Britain, and asked him who this woman could be. He said her name was Vera, and she controlled all GRU illegals in the West and worked directly under him, although security procedures were such that she never disclosed the identities of her agents to him. Alexander Foote, who worked for the GRU as an illegal in Switzerland during the war before defecting in the late 1940s, also described Vera (in his book *Handbook for Spies)* as the woman who was in charge of him when he visited Moscow for training in 1945.

The first problem with Gouzenko's story was that over the years since he had first told it in 1945, he varied the details. "Give of MI" became MI5. The distinction was vital. Theoretically, "five of MI" could be taken as referring to Section V of MI. And, of course, in 1942 Philby was working in Section V of MI6. The other problem with Gouzenko was that by the mid-1960s he was an irretrievable alcoholic. His memory was at best unreliable for events which occurred more than twenty years before. I sent a request to the Canadian RCMP for permission to interview Gouzenko once more, but we were told that Gouzenko had been causing problems for the Canadian authorities through his alcoholism and badgering for money. They feared that further contact with him would exacerbate the problems, and that there was a high risk Gouzenko might seek to publicize the purpose of our interview with him.

I asked the RCMP if they had the original notes of the debriefing of Gouzenko, since they were the best evidence for what precisely he had said about Elli in the first days after defecting. The RCMP officer who had looked after Gouzenko was long since dead and his notes had not been filed but almost certainly destroyed.

The evidence in British Intelligence files only complicated the validity of Gouzenko's story still further. When Gouzenko defected, an MI6 officer, Peter Dwyer, traveled up to Canada from Washington to attend his debriefing. Dwyer sent back daily telegrams to MI6 headquarters in London outlining Gouzenko's information. Dwyer's cables were handled by the head of Soviet Counterintelligence in MI6, Kim Philby. Philby, in the following week, was to have to face the pressing problem of Volkov's almost simultaneous approach to the British in Turkey. By good luck he asked that his opposite number of MI5, Roger Hollis, should go to Canada to see Gouzenko instead of him. Was this coincidence, we wondered, or an arrangement made in the knowledge that Hollis was a fellow spy and could be trusted to muddy the waters in the Gouzenko case? We have it from VENONA, however, that the KGB was unaware of the existence of a GRU spy in MI5 when Hollis traveled to Canada and interviewed Gouzenko. The most specific and important material Gouzenko possessed related to possible spies in the atomic weapons development program, and Hollis' report dwelt on this aspect at length. The spy Elli in "five of MI" was almost a footnote. Hollis judged Gouzenko to be confused about the structure of British Intelligence. Gouzenko was wrong, and the matter was buried. This was a mistaken judgment.

Nevertheless, the lead registered in the mind of Guy Liddell, then head of Counterespionage. In his diaries he speculated about the possible identity of Elli. Oddly, I learned of this only after Liddell's old secretary brought the diaries to me, asking that I preserve them, as Hollis had ordered that they be destroyed. Once again I paused for thought. Was this chance, or did Hollis have some other reason for suppressing Liddell's diaries?

In 1965 we managed to break a new message out of the VE-NONA, which transformed the FLUENCY assessment as to whether Gouzenko's Elli was a true bill. The one week of VENONA traffic which we had broken into began on September 15, 1945, with a message to Krotov discussing, with no sense of panic, the precautions he should take to protect valuable *argentura* in the light of problems faced by the "neighbors" in Canada. This was clearly a reference to Gouzenko's defection, which had taken place in Canada the previous week. The "neighbors," we already knew, was the KGB jargon for the GRU, for whom Gouzenko worked. The KGB had no reason to fear that any of its agents in Britain had been compromised by Gouzenko. The GRU knew no KGB secrets and, in any case, Philby was there to monitor any unforeseen developments on a daily basis.

However, by the end of the week's traffic, September 22, the tone of the messages is markedly different. The relaxed tone disappears. Krotov is given elaborate and detailed instructions on how to proceed with his agents. "Brush contact only" is to be employed, and meetings are to be reduced to the absolute minimum, if possible only once a month.

The question we needed to answer was: Why had Moscow Center suddenly become so worried about the implications of Gouzenko's testimony? Gouzenko had actually defected on September 5, two weeks previously, and almost immediately the GRU would be making provisional damage assessments and the requisite precautionary arrangements for any assets they feared Gouzenko might have betrayed. By September 12 details of what

Gouzenko was saying to his debriefers in Canada were flowing from Peter Dwyer back to Kim Philby in MI6 headquarters in London. Yet is is not until a week later that the KGB became suddenly worried.

The answer lay in the MI6 files for the relevant period. On September 18–19 a telegram reached Philby's desk which first detailed Gouzenko's description of the spy code-named Elli. This was the first time Philby would have been aware of any reference to the spy in "five of MI." The actual copy of the telegram, when we examined it in the 1960s, was folded into four, with grimy edges, as if it had been placed in an inside pocket, and was initialed off HARP (Philby's initials) two days after he received it. Clearly he had removed the telegram during those two days and shown it to his Russian controller in London. No other telegram in the file dealing with Gouzenko had been treated in this manner. This was obviously the telegram which had caused such worry at the tail-end of the week's VENONA.

I asked GCHQ to conduct a search of all KGB traffic flowing from London to Moscow. We could read none of this traffic. The only matches in the VENONA we had were coming the other way, from Moscow into the KGB in London. Sudbury told me that the only noticeable thing GCHQ could detect in the traffic was a message sent on September 19–20, which they could tell was a message of the highest priority because it overrode all others on the same channel. The significance was obvious—it was sent the day after Philby had received the MI6 telegram containing Gouzenko's description of the spy Elli in "five of MI." Indeed, when GCHQ conducted a group-count analysis of the message, they were able to conclude that it corresponded to the same length as a verbatim copy of the MI6 telegram from Canada which Philby removed from the files.

Once we realized London had sent a high-priority message to Moscow, we searched for the reply. There was only one high-priority message in the line going the other way, from Moscow to

London. So far we had never been able to read this particular message properly. It was dated at the very end of the week's traffic, but because it was flashed high priority, it was received in London somewhat earlier than other messages which we read. In late 1965 Sudbury and I made a determined attack on this message, using as collateral the guess that it was a reply to a message containing the information in Philby's telegram. Eventually we succeeded in breaking it out. It read: "Consent has been obtained from the Chiefs to consult with the neighbors about Stanley's material about their affairs in Canada. Stanley's data is correct."

I remember sitting in Sudbury's office puzzling over this translation. It made no sense. I wondered at first if we had made a mistake, but Sudbury checked the translation against the other side of the VENONA, and the trade traffic read off perfectly. There was no mistake. Philby, by the time this message was sent, had been a top-class KGB agent and head of Counterespionage in MI6 for the best part of ten years, yet it appeared as if they doubted his intelligence. Why did it need checking? What was it about Stanley's data which had thrown the KGB into such confusion?

Only one explanation could account for all these oddities. The KGB must have been ignorant of the spy in "five of MI" controlled by the GRU. Thus, when Philby relayed to them news of this spy, and the threat to him by Gouzenko, the KGB had to obtain permission from the "Chiefs," the Politburo, to consult with the "neighbors," the GRU, to ask if they did indeed have such an asset in London. Having received assurance from the GRU that they did have such a spy, the KGB realized that the heat was likely to come on in London, so they sent back the message confirming Stanley's data, and followed it up with urgent orders to increase security.

But who was Elli, and where did he work? He was obviously not Blunt or Philby, since we knew that they were never controlled at any time by the GRU. I asked every Russian defector in the West what the phrase "five of MI" signified. All assured me it meant MI5, not Section V of MI6 or anything else. Whoever Elli was, he must have had access to files on Russians, which placed him indisputably in F Branch, where this material was handled. The senior officer in F Branch was Roger Hollis, the very same suspect defined by Volkov's "Acting Head" allegation.

FLUENCY spent years trying to unravel the riddle that lay in the three connected threads of Volkov's "Acting Head"; Gouzenko's "Elli"; and the VENONA with its eight cryptonyms, each of which came together in that one week in September 1945. Was it Mitchell or Hollis? Both or neither? The resemblances between these strands was uncanny. The "Acting Head" and Elli both pointed to the same two men, but the first allegation was KGB and the second GRU. The VENONA had eight spies; Volkov's list talked of seven in London, two in the Foreign Office, and five in British Intelligence. Maclean had been in Washington for a year, so he could not be one of the Foreign Office spies. Burgess probably was one of these. He was working in the Foreign Office Press Department at the relevant time. The best bet for the other seemed to be Krivitsky's "Eton and Oxford" Foreign Office spy, whom Philby used to decoy MI5 away from Maclean as the net closed on him in 1951.

But what of the five spies in British Intelligence? One was Philby, another was Blunt, and a third Cairncross. Long might theoretically have been a fourth Volkov spy, but he was not in London at this time and he could not possibly be one of the eight VENONA cryptonyms, since he was in Germany in September 1945. That still left one Volkov spy, the "Acting Head," unaccounted for, as well as four VENONA cryptonyms, of which presumably the "Acting Head" was one, and Volkov's second Foreign Office spy another. As for Elli, there was no trace of him anywhere.

The third FLUENCY allegation was the Skripkin case. This was given to us by Yuri Rastvorov, a second secretary at the Russian

Embassy in Tokyo, who was in fact a Lieutenant-Colonel in the
KGB. British Naval Intelligence made contact with Rastvorov in
autumn 1953, and began negotiations for his defection.
Rastvorov eventually agreed to come, provided only that he was
taken straight to a British colony, such as Australia(!), rather than
back to Britain. He said his reluctance to come back to Britain
was because he knew that British Intelligence was penetrated,
although he did not elaborate further.

The Naval Intelligence Department (NID) arranged to fly the
KGB man by RAF Transport Command plane from Tokyo to
Singapore, where they intended to hand him over to the joint
MI5-MI6 establishment SIFE (Security Intelligence Far East).
Rastvorov was not told of these plans, but unfortunately, as the
aircraft taxied to the end of the runway, a snowstorm hit Tokyo
and the plane was unable to take off. While waiting for the storm
to abate, the chatter of the crew revealed to Rastvorov that the
plane was going to Singapore rather than Australia. He panicked
and fled the aircraft, went immediately to the American Embassy, and defected to them instead.

Sometime later the CIA reported that Rastvorov had given
further details of his reasons for believing British Intelligence was
penetrated. He said that a friend of his, a Lieutenant Skripkin,
had approached the British in the Far East in 1946, and offered
to defect. Skripkin made arrangements to return to Moscow,
fetch his wife, and then defect on his next visit out of the country. However, back in Moscow, Skripkin was somehow detected
by the KGB. He was approached by two KGB officers who pretended to be MI6 officers. He gave himself away, was tried and
shot.

When we looked Skripkin up in the Registry we found that he
did indeed have a file. It contained copies of two reports from
British Naval Intelligence in the Far East dealing with plans for
Skripkin's defection, one dated May 1946, and the other July
1946. They had been stapled together and sent from SIFE for

MI5's information, arriving in London during the first half of August. The file was dealt with by Roger Hollis, the Assistant Director of F Branch, and a junior officer. Hollis instructed the junior officer to make a file and place it in the Registry, where it lay until Rastvorov told his story in 1954. When the file was retrieved it was automatically attributed to Philby by MI5.

When FLUENCY reexamined the case several new facts came to light. Firstly, when Golitsin defected in 1961, he asked us what we knew about the Skripkin case. He said that he had worked on the case in 1946, when he was a junior officer in the Counter-intelligence Branch of the First Chief Directorate. He remembered that the report came to him from London, and definitely not from the Far East, at the end of 1946, when the snow was on the ground in Moscow. Without prompting, Golitsin told the story of how the two KGB men tricked Skripkin by posing as MI6 officers. Golitsin was also asked to describe the two documents he had seen. Golitsin was astonishingly accurate. The first, he said, was an account of Skripkin's sounding out, and an assessment of his worth. The second was a résumé of his future plans, including an address in Moscow where he could be contacted. Golitsin also said he was certain the papers had been stapled together at the time the agent had photographed them.

The second new fact FLUENCY had was that Philby, when questioned by Nicholas Elliott in Beirut, was asked if he had betrayed Skripkin. Philby vehemently denied having done so, not having known about the case even when given more details of it. This was most odd, because we assumed it would be in Philby's interest to claim credit for the case. Perhaps Philby was telling the truth on this occasion.

I arranged for a complete search of the entire distribution of both Skripkin reports, to see if it could shed any further light on the case. The results were extremely revealing. The May report went to Naval Intelligence (Hong Kong), SIFE at Singapore, and the Naval Intelligence Department in London. They placed the report in a Naval docket and circulated it within NID, and passed a copy routinely to the Naval Section of R Division in MI6. They, in turn, passed it to Section V, who filed it. Extensive searches in the MI6 records showed that Philby was never on the distribution list.

The July document followed the same distribution trail, except at SIFE in Singapore. It was at this point that they decided to staple together both reports, and send them routinely to MI5, where they arrived on August 8. This was the first occasion MI5 knew anything about the affair, and it was also the only place where both reports were stapled together, a fact which chimed perfectly with Golitsin's recollection. Whoever betrayed Skripkin must have been inside MI5, not MI6. That ruled out Philby, and Blunt had already left MI5 the previous year. Once again the finger pointed toward Roger Hollis, the F Branch Assistant Director who handled the Skripkin file.

Once the shape of the FLUENCY allegations became clear I began the most dangerous task I ever undertook. Without authorization I began to make my own "freelance" inquiries into Hollis' background. I had to be cautious, since I knew that the slightest leak back would inevitably lead to the sack. I traveled down to Oxford, and visited the Bodleian Library. There I discovered in the university records that Hollis, although he went up to Oxford in the 1920s, never took a degree. He left inexplicably after five terms. It seemed an odd thing for so conventional a man to do. I visited Hollis' old college, Worcester, and searched the records there to find out who had lived on the same staircase. In his fourth term Hollis moved to digs in Wellington Square, and I checked through the Oxford Calendars, which list the addresses of every student resident at Oxford, to find those students with whom he shared a house. I even tried the records of the University Golfing Society in the hope that somewhere there would be a clue to the enigma of Hollis' personality.

Working without Hollis' record of service, I was forced to work blind. I knew from talking to Hollis that he had visited China, so I ran a trace through the Passport Office for the dates of his arrivals and departures from Britain. I made discreet inquiries at the Standard Chartered Bank, where Hollis worked before leaving for China, but apart from an old forwarding address at a bank in Peking, they had no records.

I wanted to find some evidence of a secret life, a careless friend, a sign of overt political activity. Every man is defined by his friends, and I began to draw up a picture of those to whom Hollis was close in those vital years in the late 1920s and 1930s. Two men in particular were of interest at Oxford—Claud Cockburn and Maurice Richardson. Both were left-wing: in Cockburn's case, when I ran a check on his file I noticed that Hollis had retained the file throughout the war, and never declared his friendship on the file as the Service customs demand. Did he, I wondered, have a reason to hide his relationship with Cockburn, a man with extensive Comintern contacts?

Out in China there was a similar pattern. China was a hotbed of political activity in the 1930s, and was an active recruiting ground for the Comintern. Hugh Winterborn told me that an old retired colonel he had known in Japan knew Hollis while in China, having shared a flat with him for a year, and he made an appointment for me to visit him. Tony Stables was a brusque, old-fashioned military officer, and he remembered Hollis well. He said he never knew his political opinions, but always assumed they were left-wing because he mixed with people like Agnes Smedley, a left-wing journalist and Comintern talent spotter, as well as another man called Arthur Ewert, whom Stables described as an international socialist.

The other person who was visited (by Arthur Martin) was Jane Sissmore. Jane Sissmore was responsible for bringing Hollis into MI5 before the war. She eventually transferred from MI5 to MI6, married an MI6 officer, and became Jane Archer. She was a formidable, intellectual woman who ran the old MI6 Communist

Affairs research section. I often used to see her on D3 inquiries. She was always helpful, and told me the inquiries should have been embarked on years before. One afternoon I broached the subject of Mitchell and Hollis, who had both worked closely with her during the war. Jane was a wily old bird, and knew exactly why I was tapping her.

"Could either be a spy, would you say?" I asked her.

"They were both untrustworthy," she told me, "but if I had to choose the more likely candidate I would pick Roger."

In November 1965 Hollis buzzed down to me and asked me to come up to his office. It was unlike him to be so informal. I had never before visited his office without being summoned by his secretary. He greeted me warmly by the door.

"Come over and sit down," he said, smiling broadly.

He brushed imaginary dust off the sofa, and sat opposite me in the easy chair. That, too, was odd. Hollis usually sat in a straight-backed chair. Hollis was anxious to put the meeting on an informal footing. He made rather clumsy small talk about his imminent retirement.

"Difficult time," he said, "the pension's not much, and every bit counts . . ."

"What are your plans?"

"Oh, down to the country I think. I have a little place down there. Get right away from it all. A bit of golf, a few walks . . . that kind of thing."

He laughed in a gurgling sort of way.

"Funny to think my picture will be up there in a few weeks' time," he said, looking up at the portraits which stared down at him. They were all such different-looking men: Kell's stiff military bearing; Petrie's detached pose; Sillitoe, the hunch-shouldered policeman; and Dick, with his easy charm and soft charisma.

Hollis turned to face me, hunching forward, with his hands on his knees. He was smiling again, like a Cheshire cat.

"Peter, there is just one thing I wanted to ask you before I go. I wanted to know why you think I'm a spy."

I had to think very fast. If I told him a lie and he knew I had, I was out that day. So I told him the truth.

Hollis made it sound so natural. Ever since he and I discussed Tisler nearly ten years before, we had been building for this confrontation. But now that it was out in the open, lying on the table between us like an inanimate object, words seemed so inadequate in the face of all the secretly nursed suspicions which had gone before.

"It's all based on the old allegations, sir," I told him, "and the way things have been going wrong. You know my views on post-war failure. It's just a process of elimination. First it was Mitchell, and now it's you."

"Oh yes—but surely you've been looking at new things . . . ?"

"Yes, the old allegations, sir."

For an hour I went through the Volkov list, the retranslation, Gouzenko's Elli, the Skripkin report.

"Well, Peter," he said, laughing gently, "you have got the manacles on me, haven't you . . . ?"

I began to interrupt. He held his hands face up to quiet me.

"All I can say is that I am not a spy."

"But is there anything definite, sir, anything I can put before the FLUENCY meeting, anything at all . . . ?"

"I can probably dig out the notes of the Gouzenko interrogation . . ." He sounded unsure. "I don't really recollect Skripkin, to be honest. And Volkov . . ."

He drummed the edge of his seat with his sharpened pencil, and clicked his teeth.

"I don't think you've got Volkov right. Why should Kim go all the way out to Turkey? He'd check first."

He sighed, as if it was all too long ago.

"It's useful, is it, the FLUENCY thing . . . ?" he asked suddenly.

"I think so, yes, sir. I think it's long overdue."

"Yes, I rather thought you would think that . . . MacDonald isn't so sure—well, I suppose you know that."

"He receives the reports, sir. I suppose he reads them."

"Oh, yes, I'm sure we all read them," replied Hollis. "They make fascinating reading. All that history. Always good to blow a few cobwebs off the pipes."

He smiled his Cheshire cat smile again.

"Well, thank you for your frankness, Peter," he said, rising from his seat. "I must be getting on. Good to have this chat, though . . ."

He strode stiffly back to his work. Like two actors we exited to different wings, our roles complete.

I never saw Roger Hollis again. Within a few days the new Director-General, Martin Furnival Jones, was installed in the office. His first decision was to remove the photographs from the wall and place them in his ante-office.

"Don't need an audience for the job," he muttered darkly when I asked why.

F.J. was a man of few words, and he grew into the job. He was a determined man who believed he faced one major problem— the scale of the Soviet assault, in terms of numbers of Russian intelligence officers in London, relative to his own pitiful forces. His tenure as Director-General was marked by his campaign to expand MI5 and reduce Soviet diplomatic personnel. He had some success with the first, and eventually triumphed with the second.

F.J.'s top priority was Russian counterespionage, and once he took over, the whole approach to the problem changed. Whereas before I had to be persistent to get anything approved, with F.J. I could buzz him, go right up to see him, and get a decision there and then. He supported the D3 inquiries unreservedly, and sanctioned all the important interviews without question. He never shrank from making value judgments in cases like Watson and Proctor. If the evidence convinced him, he would act on it. F.J. was a man of few complexities. He was a typical English gentleman on the surface, with a streak of toughness a mile wide just underneath. It made him few friends in Whitehall, but it was what the Service needed.

Sadly for me, he appointed Anthony Simkins as his deputy. Simkins was probably the one man in MI5 whom I actively disliked, and the feeling was reciprocated in full measure. I knew I would have trouble as soon as he was appointed. Simkins was a lawyer. He and I had already had a major argument some years before, when he was Director-General of C Branch, where he had had some modest success. I was asked to chair an interdepartmental working party consisting of MI5, MI6, the Foreign Office, and GCHQ to review technical security at the British Embassy in Moscow, following a fire in the radio room responsible for intercepting local Russian communications. It was clear from the investigation that not only had the Russians started the fire deliberately, but that they had had access to the radio room for some time. The Russians had been reading the radio receiver settings each night, thus they knew what we were intercepting. The Russians who cleaned the Embassy simply unscrewed the bolts (which were well oiled) on the security door lock and walked straight in.

During the course of the inquiry I was also able to solve one other riddle from Volkov's list. Volkov claimed that the Russians could read the Foreign Office ciphers in Moscow. Maclean certainly betrayed every code he had access to in the Foreign Office, but Foreign Office records showed that the Moscow Embassy used one-time pads during and just after the war, so Maclean could not have been responsible.

Remembering my work with "the Thing" in 1951, I was sure the Russians had been using a concealed microphone system, and we eventually found two microphones buried in the plaster above the cipher room. During the war, two clerks routinely handled the Embassy one-time pad communications, one reading over the clear text message for the other to encipher. The Russians simply recorded the clear text straight through their microphones. By the very good work of the Building Research Laboratory we were able to establish that the probable date of the concrete embedding of the microphone was about 1942, when the Embassy was in Kuibyshev.

The Working Party Report found an extraordinary and persistent level of appalling security inside the Embassy, and every member of the committee endorsed a highly critical conclusion, which demanded the installation of an MI5 officer to work fulltime in the Embassy on security. I circulated the trenchant report to F.J., who was then Deputy Director-General, and asked for his approval before I sent it to the Foreign Office. F.J. suggested I show it to Simkins as a courtesy, since he was Director C, responsible for Protective Security, and technically the Working Party covered his area. I sent Simkins a copy, and was surprised, a few hours later, to receive an angry summons to his office.

"You can't possibly send anything like this to the Foreign Office," he said, as if I were suggesting sending inquisition implements as a gift to the Pope.

"Why ever not?" I asked. "It's about time the bastards received a blasting. The whole place is a shambles!"

"Well, I'm sorry. It's the Foreign Office. It's a most important department of state, and you simply have no business sending them reports like this. I don't propose to approve it!"

To my amazement, he defaced the report with a blue pencil. I took the report to F.J. and showed him what Simkins had done. F.J. grunted, and told me to type it up and send it unchanged.

"Bloody Foreign Office," he growled, "I've had the bloody lot of them . . ."

The report was sent and a young MI5 officer, Tony Motion,

was sent out to Moscow, but from then on I knew Simkins was an enemy for life.

Shortly after F.J. took over as Director-General the FLUENCY Working Party submitted its first report to him and to Dick White, as chief of MI6. The report was in two sections. The first half listed each of the twenty-eight allegations which we were sure were true bills and investigatable but which could not be attributed to any known spy. The second half of the report contained the allegations written up as a narrative, starting with Gouzenko's Elli in 1942, and ending with Golitsin's information in 1962, to show the more or less continuous nature of the penetration. This report was submitted to both chiefs. But it was six months before the report was discussed again. Then we were told to resubmit our findings, listing only those allegations which we felt could be investigated, and giving the candidate who, in our judgment, best fitted the allegation.

The FLUENCY Working Party decided that Gouzenko's Elli and Volkov's "Acting Head" should both be investigated, and that because of their closeness in time, they should be considered together. The candidate was typed neatly at the bottom of the page. Stripped of title, stripped of rank, it was just a name: Roger Hollis.

The third allegation was included in our report was Goleniewski's "middling-grade agent," and it was potentially as damaging as the first two pointing toward Hollis. The "middling-grade agent" story began in November 1963. Goleniewski, Sniper as he was previously known, finally agreed to meet MI5 to clarify some of the details of the allegations he had made in anonymous letters from Poland. Previously Goleniewski was unwilling to meet anyone directly from MI5 because of our failure to catch Lambda 1, George Blake. But with Blake in jail, Goleniewski was seen by the head of the Polish section, who was himself half Polish by descent.

By the time MI5 saw Goleniewski, the CIA suspected he was

going clinically insane. He began to have delusions that he was descended from the Tsar, but despite that, his recall of intelligence remained remarkably accurate. One morning during the course of his interviews, Goleniewski announced that he had a story to tell which he had never told before. He said that he had not mentioned it before because the British had made such a mess of detecting Blake, but he knew there was a middling-grade agent inside MI5.

Goleniewski said he knew about the middling-grade agent because he, a friend, and his former superior, had a serious discussion in the 1950s about whether to defect to the West. Deciding between Britain and the USA was difficult. All three agreed that Britain was the better place to live because of the large Polish émigré community, but MI6 was obviously impossible to approach because of Lambda 1. Goleniewski suggested to the other two that they try to contact MI5 through the émigré community in London, which he knew was monitored extensively by D Branch. Goleniewski's chief said that this plan was equally dangerous, since he knew the Russians also had a spy inside MI5.

This spy had been recruited by the Third Chief Directorate of the KGB, responsible for the armed services. The Third Chief Directorate had been allowed to keep the agent because he was so important to them, and he was not transferred to the First Chief Directorate, which was the usual practice. The agent had served in the British Army, and held rank as a British officer when he was recruited. Goleniewski thought the recruitment had taken place in Eastern Europe, and named the Russian KGB colonel who had carried it out. The spy had provided the Russians with valuable Polish counterintelligence, probably because he worked in the Polish section of MI5.

There was one other detail. In the mid-1950s the British successfully exfiltrated the Polish premier, Hanke, to the West. This had resulted in an inquiry in Warsaw, which General Serov, then head of the KGB, conducted himself. For some reason the KGB

failed to gain advance warning of the exfiltration, and Goleniewski learned that this was because the middling-grade agent was
"on ice," either because he was under suspicion or because he was
abroad and out of contact, or perhaps simply because his nerve
was shaky. The spy was apparently on ice for two to three years
before resuming work in the Polish section in the late 1950s.
Later, when Goleniewski was in Moscow in 1959 he asked a
friend in the Third Chief Directorate who was responsible for
recruiting the agent, and if the operation was still active. His
friend expressed surprise that he even knew of the affair, and
advised him to remain quiet.

"This is a very dark affair," he said, "and I advise you to forget
all about it."

Goleniewski's allegation was extraordinarily detailed, but because of the overload in Counterintelligence from late 1963 onward, and because of the doubts about Goleniewski's credibility,
the allegation was not investigated properly until FLUENCY began
sitting. We divided the allegation up into its seven separate in-
dicators, and allotted marks to every candidate who fulfilled each
of the criteria. Eight people in MI5 partially fitted Goleniewski's
middling-grade agent, but one fitted every part of it exactly. His
name was Michael Hanley, the Director of C Branch, and a man
strongly tipped to become F.J.'s successor.

Solely because he was the proverbial "perfect fit," FLUENCY
unanimously recommended that Hanley be investigated in connection with Goleniewski's allegation, and he was given the code
name HARRIET.

Another six months went by before the second FLUENCY report
was finally discussed. another meeting was called after hours in
F.J.'s conference room, attended by me, Anne Orr-Ewing, Patrick Stewart, Evelyn McBarnet, Anthony Simkins, and F.J. It was
to be an entirely internal MI5 discussion as each of the three
outstanding FLUENCY cases was an MI5 rather than an MI6 matter.

It was the sort of meeting which began quietly. F.J. had a bottle of Scotch on the table. The lights cast dramatic shadows across the room. F.J. was striding up and down, his pipe clenched ferociously between his teeth.

He spun around.

"Do you really stand by these candidates?" he asked. "You realize the implications of what you are saying . . . ?"

"Certainly I do," I said, shaken nevertheless by the force of his approach.

"It's grotesque," he muttered, stabbing at the Hollis pages, "you can't expect me to accept that . . ."

He threw the report down onto the desk.

"Where's this going to end, Peter—you've sent me a paper which says that my predecessor and most likely my successor are both spies. Have you thought it through? Have you stopped to think of the damage that will be done if we act on these recommendations? It will take a decade to recover from this, even if there's nothing at the end of it."

"I stand by what we have written, F.J., and what's more, so does every other member of the FLUENCY Working Party, and I can assure you if there were other candidates, you would have had them."

Simkins was sitting at the other end of the table. I could feel him chafing at the bit. He wanted to tear into me, but this was F.J.'s interrogation, and he wanted no distractions.

"You've wanted this on the record for years—you and Arthur, haven't you? Have you any idea what this kind of thing did to Roger?"

"I talked with him about it shortly before he left," I told F.J. "He was quite calm about it."

F.J. was taken aback as I described my last confrontation with Hollis.

"He must have been a tough man," he said grimly.

Finally, Simkins saw his chance.

"It's simply outrageous," he spat in a shrill voice, his public-school vowels stretching to breaking point, "everyone knows you and Martin had it in for Roger. You go around criticizing the Foreign Office, this person, that person, and then you let fly with accusations, spreading rumors, spreading poison. It's so undisciplined. If there is a criticism of Roger, it's that he let you go too far."

"All I want is the truth, Anthony," I said, trying with difficulty to maintain civility.

"Truth! You don't know the meaning of it. You need a bit of respect! It's scandalous! The man has scarcely set foot outside the office and you blackguard his name and reputation, a man with thirty years' service in the office, who did more for the place than you will ever do."

Luckily, Patrick Stewart rallied back on my behalf.

"It's all very well, Anthony, to sound off, but you've only just come into this."

He gripped the sides of his wheelchair, his knuckles turning white.

"Some of us have been struggling with this problem for years. It's not easy. It's not pleasant, but we all felt that it had to be done, and the least we expect when we have completed a report as difficult as this is a little rational debate."

But Simkins was determined to press on.

"What about America—you spread the poison out there too. When I was out there all they wanted to discuss was bloody penetration. It's intolerable. We'll be made the laughingstock of the world."

"And you don't think we are when Philby goes or Blunt confesses . . ." I shot back.

F.J. chewed his pipe energetically, occasionally pausing to light it with a match, almost as if he were not listening to the row ebbing and flowing. Then after half an hour he suddenly interrupted.

"Right, here's my decision. I am sure you will agree, Peter, that we have to solve the middling-grade agent as the top priority. He's still in here if he exists."

I nodded.

"Well, I want Hanley looked at." He slapped the page with the back of his hand. "He's such a perfect fit, and the Americans know all about the allegation. But I want the others who score highly looked at as well . . . I want it run down to the ends of the earth, and then we'll tell the Americans. As for the other"— he was glaring at he now— "I won't change my view, it's grotesque . . ."

F.J. dismissed the meeting, and everyone trooped out, leaving him alone with the cares of office on his shoulders. He was the Pope, trying to reconcile a divided Church.

20

HANLEY WAS A HUGE, FLORID MAN, WITH AN OUTWARDLY BULLY-
ing manner, which concealed a shy man underneath. Ever since
his promotion as Director C in 1960, he was seen as a potential
Director-General. He was the right age, mid-forties, with a supple
civil servant's mind, which endeared him to Whitehall, and a
brusque military exterior which made him popular with the board
at MI5. By the time the HARRIET investigation emerged he was
the crown prince—certain to succeed F.J. when he retired in the
early 1970s.

It is always distressing to pursue an investigation into a colleague. With Hollis and Mitchell it was different. They were
distant figures, close to retirement by the time the suspicions
against them hardened. But Hanley and I knew each other well.
We were contemporaries, and although by no stretch of the imagination friends, we had served together amicably on committees
for over ten years. His career lay in front of him, and his future
was in my hands.

Patrick Stewart, the D1 (Investigations), and I handled the
investigation jointly. The first task was to provide a complete
picture of Hanley's life. We started backtracking through his family background, his entry into the Service, and his subsequent
career. Dozens of people who knew him were interviewed, all
under the guise of a routine positive vet.

The most difficult aspect of all in the HARRIET affair was that the investigation soon revealed that Hanley had had a most distressing childhood following the breakup of his parents' marriage. He was left with deep-seated feelings of inferiority, which, according to his record of service, required psychiatric treatment in the 1950s, when he was a young MI5 officer, a fact which Hanley made known to the office at the time.

That Hanley had visited a psychiatrist was not in itself unusual. Many senior officers in MI5 had counseling of one form or another during their careers to assist them in carrying the burdens of secrecy. But inevitably our investigation had to probe Hanley's old wounds, in case they revealed a motive for espionage. F.J., Patrick Stewart, and I discussed the problem, and F.J. wrote a personal letter to Hanley's psychiatrist asking him to lift the oath of confidentiality. I visited the psychiatrist in Harley Street. He knew Hanley's occupation, and showed no hesitation in pronouncing Hanley a determined, robust character who had learned to live with his early disabilities. I asked him if he could ever conceive of him as a spy.

"Absolutely not!" he replied with total conviction.

Neither was there any hint of espionage in Hanley's early life. At Oxford before the war he was the model of the sensible, mildly left-wing student. When the war came he stayed at Oxford for a year to get his degree and then joined a searchlight regiment in Home Defense as a subaltern, and remained there until 1945. It was important work, but not remotely adequate for someone of Hanley's considerable intellectual gifts. But everyone who knew him at this time remarked on his nagging sense of inferiority, and the consequent lack of ambition.

The first point in his life which aroused our interest was his decision, in 1945, to enroll for a crash course in the Russian language at the Joint Services Language School at Cambridge, which both our own operations and Golitsin had told us was a recruiting ground for the KGB (but there was not the slightest evidence from our sources that Hanley had been involved with them). The Russian language course was the first time Hanley came into contact with Russians, and from then on his career seemed an uncanny fit for Goleniewski's allegations. After service in Budapest, where he served on the Joint Allied Intelligence Committee with the KGB officer named by Goleniewski as having made the recruitment of the middling-grade agent, Hanley returned to London. He became the War Office liaison officer with the Soviet military attaché, and dealt mainly with returnee problems. During this time he began to have dealings with MI5, and when he was demobilized in the late 1940s, he applied for a full-time post, and joined as a research officer on Russian Affairs. His first task was the compilation of the index of agents of the Rote Kapelle which decades later I was to find so invaluable in my D3 work.

Within two years Hanley shifted to the Polish desk (D2) and his career took off. First he went to Hong Kong for two and a half years and then returned to E Branch (Colonial Affairs) before becoming head of D2, and in 1960 a member of the Board as Director C. It was a career with ever-increasing momentum, yet his background presented a possible espionage profile. Here was a man from a troubled childhood, with deep-seated feelings of insecurity, who comes into continuous contact with Russians at a delicate time of his life, when he is beginning for the first time to emerge from his shell. Perhaps, like Blake, he had a chip on his shoulder, and the Russians had played skillfully on his concealed feelings of resentment until they fanned into treachery.

The problem was that neither Patrick nor I believed it, despite the fact that on paper the surface fit with Goleniewski's allegation was so precise. It was the exact reverse of the case with Hollis, where we were both instinctively convinced of the case against him, even though on paper the connections looked far weaker.

As far as Hanley was concerned, too much weighed against the "chip on the shoulder" theory. From the start of his career in MI5, Hanley had been marked out as a flyer. He was valued by both his peers and his superiors, despite his often hectoring manner. He had married into the office, and enjoyed a close and devoted relationship with his wife. And lastly there was the evidence of the psychiatrist.

Espionage is a crime almost devoid of evidence, which is why intuition, for better or worse, always has a large part to play in its successful detection. All a counterespionage officer usually has when he confronts his suspect is a background, a trail, a set of coincidences which are open to a variety of interpretations but which, as Dick White used to say, lead to the epiphany—that moment when all the facts add up to only one conclusion. But with Hanley, the trail led one way, and intuition another. The only possible way to resolve the case was through interrogation, and when we submitted the papers to F.J. he agreed.

Mention interrogations, and most people imagine grueling sessions under blazing lamps: men in shirt-sleeves wearing down a sleep-deprived suspect with aggressive questioning until finally he collapses sobbing on the floor, admitting the truth. The reality is much more prosaic. MI5 interrogations are orderly affairs, usually conducted between 9:30 A.M. and 5 P.M. with a break for lunch.

So why do so many spies confess? The secret is to achieve superiority over the man sitting across the table. This was the secret of Skardon's success as an interrogator. Although we mocked him for years later for his willingness to clear suspects we subsequently learned to have been spies, he was genuinely feared by Blunt and other members of the Ring of Five. But his superiority in the interrogation room was not based on intellect or physique. Mainly, of course, it was the devastating briefs provided for him by Arthur Martin and Evelyn McBarnet which convinced men like Fuchs that Skardon knew them better than they knew themselves. It was not only the briefs that helped Skardon but also the skill of the eavesdroppers. In the Fuchs case, Skardon was convinced that he was innocent until they pointed out where Fuchs had lied. This information enabled Skardon to break him.

But Skardon himself played an important role too. He epitomized, in his manner, the world of sensible English middle-class values—tea in the afternoon and lace curtains—so much so that it was impossible for those he interrogated to ever see him as the embodiment of capitalist iniquity, and thus they were thrown off balance from the very start.

But none of this stood a chance against Hanley if he was a spy. He was an insider. He knew all the tricks too well. Like Philby, he would see the punches coming. The only way to proceed with a professional is to put him through an extremely thorough vet. A complete curriculum vitae of the suspect's life and career is drawn up, and he is taken through it in interrogation. If there are any deviations, omissions, or inaccuracies, these are then probed. If the suspect is guilty the pressure can often lead to further inaccuracies, until his secret life begins to unravel.

The MI5 technique is an imperfect sytem. But like trial by jury, it is the best yet devised. If has the virtue of enabling a man, if he has nothing to hide, and has the resilience to bear the strain, to clear himself. But its disadvantage is that hidden blemishes on an innocent man's record can often come to the surface during intensive investigation and render continued service impossible. It is a little like medieval justice: sometimes innocence can be proved only at the cost of a career.

F.J. elected to conduct Hanley's interrogation himself. He knew it would be a difficult encounter and that in the end Hanley's fate would rest in his own hands, and he felt it unfair to entrust the task to any other officer. But he ensured that Patrick and I monitored the entire interrogation from the D1 operations room in Leconfield House.

Hanley was summoned into F.J.'s office one morning, and informed that an allegation had been made, and that he was required to submit himself immediately for interrogation. The interrogation took place in the Director-General's office, with an overt microphone on the table. It was recorded in the room where Patrick and I were monitoring the interrogation. Throughout the first day F.J. took Hanley through his life. Hanley was scrupulously honest, sometimes painfully so. He ducked no questions, hid no details of his life or his inner feelings. On the second day he was given the details of Goleniewski's allegation. He was not shaken in any way. He agreed that he was a perfect fit, but calmly stated that he was not a spy, had never been, and had never at any stage been approached by a Russian or anyone else, although at least once a week in Budapest he had met the Russian officer who was alleged to have made the approach.

Hanley's interrogation proved that while secret service is a profession of deceit and intrigue, many of its practitioners are men of exceptional character. Here was a proud man, who cherished his achievements, and those that he felt might be his to come. One morning he is invited to undergo a trial by ordeal and is stripped apart, year by year, until his soul is bare. All the while he knows that faceless colleagues have dogged his every step, listening at home, listening at the office, listening now. The strain must have been more than most men could bear. No one listening could doubt for one moment that this was an honest man. Hanley was tough, and he showed the system could work. He walked through the fire and emerged unscathed.

That night F.J., Patrick Stewart, and I went to my club, the Oxford and Cambridge, to discuss the interrogation. F.J. settled down into a corner with a large Scotch. His eyes were pinched, as they always were when he was stressed.

"Are you satisfied?" he asked dully.

"He's in the clear," I agreed.

Patrick nodded silently.

"You'll inform FLUENCY, of course . . . ?" said F.J.

At that moment Hanley himself walked in unexpectedly. He and I shared the same club, and occasionally ran into each other, but I never expected he would come there so soon after his ordeal. We were in a quiet corner, and he walked past without noticing us, dragging his feet slightly, as if in shock. His normally florid face was white as a sheet.

After the HARRIET investigation was closed down, F.J. asked me to visit the CIA and inform them that MI5 considered Hanley cleared of the Goleniewski allegations. It was a job of enormous sensitivity. The CIA were already up in arms over the Mitchell and Hollis cases, and were themselves well aware of Goleniewski's allegations, and the fact that Hanley was a near-perfect fit. It was essential for the preservation of the alliance that they be left in no doubt about the veracity of our conclusion.

F.J. did not get on with Americans particularly well, and preferred to leave dealings to Michael McCaul and me. Partly it was antipathy toward Angleton, and partly it was residual upper-middle-class anti-Americanism. Dick White had something of the same prejudice. Neither was a wealthy man, while Helms and Angleton rarely hid the fact that they were paid handsomely for similar duties.

Both men had reason to distrust the Americans deep down. F.J. never forgave Helms and Angleton for the Gray and Coyne affair, while Dick had clashed repeatedly with the American military hierarchy when he controlled Counterintelligence in Europe at the end of the war, and was never forgiven. In 1953, when Sillitoe retired, the Americans stupidly tried to block his appointment as Director-General.

There was, in the end, a fundamental difference in approach. Both F.J. and Dick saw themselves as servants of the Crown, and their services as part of the orderly, timeless configuration of Whitehall. They were insiders, whereas Helms, Angleton, and Hoover were all outsiders. There was a streak of ruthlessness and lawlessness about the American intelligence community which disturbed many in the senior echelons of British Intelligence. They feared a future calamity, and wanted to keep their distance, so inevitably the weight of liaison often fell on the shoulders of officers like me.

I traveled to Washington in 1968 to brief Angleton on the results of the HARRIET case. We had a businesslike meeting. I outlined the course of the investigation, and told him we were unanimously of the view that Hanley was in the clear. Angleton then took me to see Dick Helms and explained to him what my mission was. Helms said that he did not wish to hear anything more; if I said that Hanley was in the clear, he unconditionally accepted my word. But the clearance of Hanley solved very little.

After we left Helms, Angleton said that he wanted to discuss with me the question of Goleniewski's being a plant. The HAR-RIET fit was so perfect that it did not need a suspicious man to believe the KGB had deliberately planted the allegation to discredit him. Angleton and Helms already suspected that Goleniewski had fallen back under Russian control shortly before he defected. Repeated analysis of the intelligence he provided showed a distinct change in its character from Polish to Russian matters, as if the Russians were deliberately feeding out barium meals of their own intelligence in order to isolate the leak. This analysis was shared by MI5, and was the main reason why Goleniewski's middling-grade agent story was ignored for such a long time. The clearing of HARRIET raised a major question mark over the validity of the middling-grade agent, and the validity of Goleniewski's information, particularly after he defected. The middling-grade agent story did not appear until November 1963. Goleniewski defected in January 1961. Now for the KGB to concoct the story in the detail they did, they would need access to Hanley's record of service. With his position, the only person who could acquire this would be Roger Hollis.

But if Goleniewski had been turned, or was the unwitting vehicle for disinformation, what were the implications for the other assets MI6 and the CIA held in Poland, which since the war had been the West's most consistently fruitful sphere of Eastern Bloc operations. I did some preliminary work on this subject during the HARRIET investigation. I found, to my horror, that for a long period all agents run by MI6 were met at a flat rented by a secretary in the Warsaw MI6 station. Over ninety meetings had taken place there. I speculated that perhaps the reason why the UB and the KGB apparently failed to detect this astonishing series of meetings was that they were planting false agents on us. MI6 hackles were raised again, as they had been over the Penkovsky affair.

The belief that defectors were being sent to deceive Western counterintelligence during the sudden flood of arrivals in the early 1960s obsessed all of us. Golitsin's central contention was that the KGB had embarked on a systematic disinformation campaign, and that false defectors would be sent to the West to discredit him. Almost immediately Yuri Nossenko arrived on the CIA's doorstep, appearing to deflect many of the leads Golitsin gave about Soviet penetration of American and British Intelligence.

Nossenko threw the CIA into turmoil. He told them he had seen the file belonging to Lee Harvey Oswald, the alleged assassin of President Kennedy. He claimed the KGB had no involvement in the assassination, and had made no contact with Oswald in Russia, despite the fact that he had worked on a Top Secret U2 surveillance base shortly before defecting. To many officers in the CIA, Nossenko's story was too pat, especially when it was found that he had lied about his rank and status in the KGB. But why had he been sent? The CIA set about trying to break Nossenko using methods of imprisonment and physical pressure which would never have been tolerated in MI5. But even by 1967 they were no nearer to solving the riddle.

Suspicions were also growing about the FBI sources Top Hat and Fedora, who were passing information while still in place, but refusing to disclose their provenance. They provided bona fides for Nossenko, as if to assure the Americans that he was genuine, even to the extent of supporting Nossenko's claim to a false rank.

But if Top Hat and Fedora were phony, what of the leads they gave to penetrations of British security?

Fedora had given the tip which led to Martelli, albeit that it resulted in the disastrous prosecution and his acquittal. Top Hat passed copies of documents detailing American weapons guidance systems to the Americans which, he claimed, the Soviets were obtaining from a source in Britain. After investigation we were able to catch Frank Bossard, an officer in the Missile Guidance Branch of the Aviation Ministry. He was arrested in 1965, and sent to prison for twenty-one years. If Fedora and Top Hat were plants, then the Russians were prepared to sacrifice huge assets in order to build up their bona fides. It must be taken into account that had it not been for the skill of GCHQ we probably would not have obtained the evidence which proved that Bossard was working for the GRU.

We were in the place Angleton called "the wilderness of mirrors," where defectors are false, lies are truth, truth lies, and the reflections leave you dazzled and confused. The idea of false defectors is a hard one to accept, unless you read the history books and learn how MI5 did it with the Double Cross System throughout the war. It is now an unfashionable theory. But there are very few intelligence officers who lived through those years of the 1960s who do not believe that during that period we were the victim of some kind of Soviet ploy involving defectors. Some may dispute whether it was successful, or debate the limits of its scale, but few would doubt that such a game was being played. Furthermore, it could be played only if the Russians had good feedback from MI5 of intelligence about the game.

Twenty years later the truth of those years is still impossible to tie down. Goleniewski, Penkovsky, Nossenko, Fedora, and Top Hat—all had signs of interference in one way or another. I do not mean that each was a conscious false defector, although Fedora and Top Hat certainly were, as even the FBI were forced to conclude in the 1970s, long after I retired. But I do think they were being used at various times—Penkovsky to influence our perception of Soviet missile technology; Nossenko to influence the American attitude to the Kennedy assassination. Goleniewski, Fedora, and Top Hat, I believe, were part of a systematic attempt to rupture the all-important Anglo-American intelligence alliance, and also to support the deception about the performance of the Soviet ICBMs until the mid-1970s.

Consider the timing of key pieces of intelligence from these three defectors. Goleniewski gave his information about the middling-grade agent in late 1963, nearly three years after his defection. This was at the time of Hollis' visit to Washington to brief the FBI and CIA on the results of the Mitchell investigation. Nothing could be better designed to precipitate the final breach in relations between British and American intelligence than another apparently undetected spy in MI5. Luckily, Angleton's doubts about Goleniewski ensured that the story did not have the drastic impact it might otherwise have had, and in fact only served to strengthen Anglo-American suspicions of both Goleniewski and Hollis.

Almost immediately Fedora made contact with the Americans, and gave the lead which led us to Martelli. Discovery of another nuclear spy was guaranteed to create the maximum possible strain between London and Washington, though the KGB could never have dreamed that MI5 would botch the prosecution as badly as they did.

Months later, as if part of a coordinated campaign, Top Hat led us to Bossard. Once again, American weapons technology was involved, which automatically meant that the American armed forces would take an active role in protesting at British security weaknesses. When we made the damage assessment for Bossard, we concluded that virtually the entire advanced American guidance systems had been betrayed. Patrick Stewart sent an advance copy to Angleton with a one-word memorandum attached. It read simply: "Help!"

Luckily for Britain, Angleton was able to protect us from the onslaught. But it was a close-run thing, and few realize today that the exchange came nearer to breakdown in the early years of the 1960s than at any time since the war.

The night before I returned to London, Angleton and I went to dinner at a small Chinese restaurant in Alexandria, where his son ate regularly. It was one of Angleton's favorite haunts when he felt the need to talk. We could be assured of privacy, he told me, because the Chinese kept the Russians out.

Angleton was at the zenith of his power, although the strain was beginning to tell on him. For years he had been waging a covert bureaucratic war with the Soviet Division of the CIA, to ensure the independence and expansion of his counterintelligence empire. He had been successful beyond all expectations, and achieved virtual veto influence over all operations and personnel within the Agency. He controlled the Israeli account, and made the CIA station in Tel Aviv redundant. He ensured that all important communications with British Intelligence went through him personally, bypassing the London station. He even succeeded in establishing his own counterintelligence cipher independent of CIA communications, which he claimed were insecure, although we all believed that the real reason was empire-building.

The CAZAB conferences were his outstanding achievement. The best, the brightest, and the most senior officers in Western intelligence came together once every eighteen months to discuss his agenda—the Soviet threat, the role of counterintelligence— and to conduct doom-laden future scenarios. In Angleton's mind, not unreasonably, the CAZABs were the first decisive step in creating a unified Western intelligence command capable of challenging the Soviet Bloc.

The CAZAB conferences suited Angleton's temperament perfectly, and he always seemed at his most relaxed in their super-secure, electronically swept environment, grappling with the endless ambiguities of the wildnerness of mirrors. I fully supported these meetings, which were very important.

Gambling was always a major feature of CAZAB conferences. Each daily session would usually end with a poker school, a game at which Angleton excelled, although I was sometimes able to "take him to the cleaners." Horse racing was also an occasional diversion. I remember at the New York CAZAB in the late 1960s–early 1970s, Angleton became the bookmaker for CAZAB for the Washington International horse race, featuring horses from all over the world, which was scheduled for the first afternoon. Before the meeting I asked Angleton to put $100 on the nose of the British horse. Lester Piggott was riding him and had ridden the winner the previous year. The British horse was unfancied, but the MI5 and MI6 contingent, anxious to be seen to fly the flag in even the most secret chambers, soon wagered around $500 between them.

That afternoon, as Angleton delivered a long paper on long-range Soviet disinformation techniques, most minds, on the British side at least, were down at the racetrack. After an hour Angleton's secretary walked in and nervously handed him a slip of paper. She handed him two chits; the first said, "How much do you want for your house, Jim?" and the second said, "The British horse won!"

"Jesus Christ!" cursed Angleton. "I forgot to lay the bets off, and that goddamn British horse has come in at 11 to 1!"

That night, as we flew back to Washington in a small CIA propeller plane, Angleton crawled around the belly of the fuselage, paying off his debts from a huge wad of $100 bills.

"The sacrifices I make for the West . . ." he said, as he paid me my whack.

But the humor could not mask the fact that he was making enemies throughout the CIA—in the Soviet Division, among other directors jealous of his power, and among those officers whose promotion prospects he had adversely affected. He was safe while Helms was Director, but the war in Vietnam was rapidly altering the face of the Agency, and the gathering political fashion for détente was beginning to undermine the foundations of Cold War suspicion upon which his empire was built.

One Cold War veteran, Bill Harvey, had already gone, driven into retirement by alcoholism. Angleton, too, was drinking far more than was good for him, and had begun to look not merely pallid but genuinely ravaged. His mood changed too. He became increasingly introspective, and the dry humor became less and less visible. He seemed pent-up and aggressive, trusting fewer and fewer people, who were turning more and more against him.

Drinking, smoking, and fishing were Angleton's main releases. Barry Russell Jones told me in amazement of accompanying him on a fishing trip to a stretch of river he owned in Idaho, and finding that Angleton had buried bottles of Jack Daniel's under the water at hundred-yard intervals, so that he could never be caught short. Back in Washington he found relief in growing exotic orchids (he was a world expert), crafting leatherwork, goldbeating, or making fishing lures for his friends and admirers.

Angleton and I talked until 4 A.M. We examined every possible scenario of the defections. Who was true, and who was false? Who defected, and who was sent? The lines were embedded like poetry in a child's mind. We were both on the rack. So much depended on making the right assumptions about the defectors— for him, the assassination of his President; for me, the next move in the hunt for the mole. Eventually we walked back through Alexandria toward the 44th Street bridge. Angleton had parked his car down behind the Okinawa Memorial, near the National Cemetery. Angleton was highly patriotic in that unique American way which expresses itself in reverence for the flag, and symbols of national heritage, like the Okinawa Memorial, fascinated him. He paused to look across at it. The cars swished past behind us on the freeway.

"This is Kim's work," he muttered. It was one of the few times I ever heard him mention his old friend Philby.

If there was a plot to deceive the West using defectors in the early 1960s, we were easy prey to it. Throughout those years there was a conscious policy in both London and Washington to do everything possible to attract defectors. They were seen as the secret weapon which could disrupt the smooth machine in Dzherzhinsky Square. In part this policy grew up through feelings of guilt. Early defectors like Gouzenko and Von Petrov had been poorly rewarded for their services, and felt bitter at the treatment they had received. They were paid a fee, and then pushed back out into the cold, and expected to make lives for themselves as best they could. Most failed. There was guilt, too, at the inadequate security arrangements which led to the deaths of Volkov and Krivitsky, and we feared that unless a conscious effort was made to show the benefits of defection, word would get back East and inhibit further approaches.

By the time Golitsin came over, the policy had hardened. Any means to secure defections were authorized, starting with immense payments, but including other methods also. I remember one particular operation which began in the mid-1960s involving a senior KGB officer named Sergei Grigovin (a pseudonym) which illustrates the lengths we were prepared to go to. Grigovin was already known to us, because he had served in Denmark, and the Danish intelligence service had alerted us routinely to his identity. They also provided us with a few snippets of intelligence about him—one in particular was that he had a reputation for enjoying the company of women. The source report was circulated through to D4, the agent-running section of D Branch, and they were instructed to keep an eye out for Grigovin's indiscretions, since he had left his wife in Moscow.

Any Russian, and especially a KGB officer, who is caught liaising with women in the West by the KGB security division, the "SK," is in serious trouble, and the case had distinct possibilities.

A year later a D4 agent runner received the first tip. An agent of his, a senior executive at the *Daily Mirror* newspaper, was in the habit of occasionally meeting Grigovin at dinner parties. A woman friend of his told him that Grigovin was having an affair with a friend to whom she had introduced the Russian. D4 raised the matter at the weekly meeting with D1 (Operations) and it was agreed that a much closer eye would be kept on the situation. The agent runner was told to encourage his agent gently to keep an eye on the evolving romance.

Eventually Grigovin finished with the girl, and when he next met the woman who had introduced them, he asked if she knew any other friends. The D1 realized immediately this was our chance. If we could introduce our own girl to Grigovin we would be in a perfect position to begin an entrapment operation. The plan was put up to F.J., who gave his consent, although the operation was kept secret from the Foreign Office, on the grounds that they would very likely veto it. D4 were instructed to produce a woman suitable for the job. They had a number of high-class call-girls they used for entrapments, and eventually one was successfully introduced to Grigovin at a party. He took the bait perfectly, and was soon engaged in an affair with her.

Events began to move toward their climax. He was placed under intensive surveillance, and we analyzed the various possibilities. It was obvious from the surveillance that Grigovin was purely interested in the girl for sex, and there was thought to be little chance of playing on his heartstrings. It had to be straightforward entrapment.

The plans for a defection are complex, and require weeks of careful planning. First a room was hired, and a two-way mirror and camera equipment installed. Then safe houses, and transport arrangements were made to safeguard Grigovin should he decide to defect. He had a family in Moscow, and checks were made on them in case he bargained for them to be exfiltrated as well.

Finally the day came. The D1 took charge of the operation

himself. Grigovin and the girl arrived, and we ensured we had a good ten minutes of film on them in bed before the D1 and two burly MI5 officers opened the door with one of Leslie Jagger's keys.

"One of ours, I'm afraid . . ." said the D1, as the girl was hustled out of the door.

Grigovin looked momentarily stunned. The D1 pointed to the mirror. For a moment the KGB man looked straight into the camera. Then he understood.

"I am a diplomat," said the Russian. "I demand to speak to the Embassy . . . I have my pass!"

He tried to reach across toward his trousers. One of our boys stood on them.

"Hardly diplomatic behavior," said the D1. He bent down and threw the naked Russian his underpants. Then he got down to business.

"Let's face it, you're finished, Grigovin. They'll send you back if they find out . . ."

He let the thought sink in.

"You look as if you're more suited to the West. We know, we've checked. Four years in America, three years in Denmark. Now London. You don't want to go back anyway, do you? Why don't you come over? We'll look after you. There's a good pension. You'll be safe."

The Russian brushed the offer aside with a wave of his hand, and again demanded to speak to his Embassy.

For two hours the D1 tried to reason with him. Think of the future, he told him. He would be stripped of his privileges and sent back to Moscow in disgrace, to serve his career out in some dreary Siberian outpost. No more foreign exchange, no more overseas perks.

"I am a diplomat," Grigovin kept saying. "I demand to speak to my Embassy."

He was like a World War II captured airman, reciting only his name, rank, and serial number. He was a crack soldier, and eventually we realized there was to be no defection. His clothes were returned and we dumped him back on the pavement near Kensington Park Gardens. Months of planning, years of patient waiting were wasted.

The next morning an anonymous brown package was delivered to the Embassy, addressed to the Ambassador personally. It contained photographs of Grigovin in bed. That evening Special Branch sighted the KGB man being escorted onto an Aeroflot plane. We did send a report to the MI6 station in Moscow advising them to keep an eye out for him in case he had second thoughts and managed to make contact. But we never heard from Grigovin again.

Defections are always tinged with tragedy, but none was as sad as the case involving a young man called Nadiensky—the defector who changed his mind. He worked for the shipping section of the Trade Delegation, and we identified him early on as a KGB officer. He was a quiet man, and his only claim to fame was that his wife was related to a senior Soviet official in the Politburo. He first came to our attention when the Watchers saw him meet a girl in a London park.

Initially all effort went into the girl. The Watchers tracked her home, and she was identified as a secretary in a minor government agency with no access to classified material. Michael McCaul went to see the girl, and asked why she was meeting a Soviet official. She convinced him that Nadiensky had no interest in her for espionage purposes. They were in love, and she had no idea that he was involved with the KGB. She said he was not at all how she imagined Russians. He was a romantic and rather frightened man, who talked constantly of making a new life for himself in the West.

Once again D1 (Operations) and D4 met to consider the best course of action. We decided to ask the girl to continue the affair normally, while we planned an approach to Nadiensky. It was obvious that the operation could not be sustained over the long term. The girl was already under great stress, and it seemed likely that she would soon betray herself. But the prize was a considerable one. Although Nadiensky himself was a low-level officer, almost certainly co-opted for the duration of his posting in London, he had enormous propaganda value. This was the time of Stalin's daughter Svetlana's defection, and we knew the embarrassment it would cause the Russians to have a relative of one of their senior politicians seek asylum in the West.

On the following Sunday Nadiensky was due to visit Harwich on official business. He was accompanying some Soviet sailors to their ship, which was due to sail that night, and he applied routinely for permission from the Foreign Office to leave the 80-kilometer restriction which is imposed on all Eastern Bloc diplomats. McCaul sat in his car outside Harwich docks with a team of Watchers and waited for Nadiensky to emerge. As he walked past, McCaul called him by name. He hesitated momentarily.

"We know about the girl . . ." hissed McCaul, "we know you want to stay. Get in the car quickly, and we can talk!"

Nadiensky looked up and down the street and then, seizing his moment, ducked into the back of the car. McCaul drove straight to my house in Essex. We gave him tea, and tried not to talk too much. We had the bird, but it was important not to panic him.

"I hear you want to join us . . . ?" I began, when Nadiensky had adjusted to his surroundings.

He nodded, at first nervously, and then decisively

"We believe you've been co-opted?" I queried.

He gulped his tea.

"The KGB, you mean?" he asked in good English.

"We assumed you were," I went on.

"You have no choice," he flashed suddenly with some bitterness, "if they want you to work for them, they simply order you. You have no choice."

I ran through the arrangements we could make. There would

be safety and protection, a pension, and later perhaps a job. There would be a short meeting with the girl, but then he would have to work hard for some months.

"For British Security . . . I know," he said. He half smiled. He knew the game, co-opted or not.

That evening we drove Nadiensky to a safe house near Wimbledon, and armed guards were posted inside with him. Twelve hours later the Foreign Office received a request from the Soviet Embassy asking if they had any information concerning the whereabouts of a certain junior diplomat who had disappeared while returning from a routine visit to Harwich.

The Foreign Office Northern Department had already been alerted to the defection of Nadiensky by the Deputy Director-General, then F.J. The Foreign Office treated the matter as they treated all matters which were likely to upset the Russians, as something to be avoided at all costs. They immediately sent an official down to the safe house to interview Nadiensky. He was asked if he was applying voluntarily, and whether he wanted to speak to anyone at the Soviet Embassy. He confirmed his decision was voluntary, and told him he had no wish to speak to any Russians. The Foreign Office broke the news to the Soviet Embassy.

Immediately Nadiensky's wife was seen leaving for Moscow. The following day the Soviet Embassy demanded that the Foreign Office arrange for Nadiensky's wife to be able to speak to him on the telephone from the Soviet Union. At first Nadiensky did not wish to speak to her, and we were very unhappy at this blatant attempt to pressure a man already under great strain. But the Foreign Office insisted on protocol.

The call was only the first of many which the Russians insisted on over the next four days. Mostly it was Nadiensky's wife, but other relations took their turn in tearfully pleading with him to reconsider his decision.

"Think of us," they told him, "think of the ruin and scandal that will befall us."

Nadiensky began to wilt visibly. Over in Whitehall the Foreign Office and MI5 practically came to blows. Why did the Foreign Office allow these calls, we wanted to know, when the Russians never allowed access to our people, like Greville Wynne, when they were arrested in Moscow. But the Foreign Office, with little regard for our priorities, and none for Nadiensky's interests, sat on the niceties of the diplomatic trade.

"We cannot deny the family humanitarian access," they said.

On the fourth day Nadiensky told us he had decided to go back. It was causing too much trouble for his family. McCaul tried to point out the dangers, but it was futile. He was like a patient on the operating table, hovering between life and death, and now we could feel him gently slipping away.

"Are you sure you want to go back?" I asked Nadiensky when I last saw him, shortly before he went back.

"What I want no longer matters," he said without emotion. "I have done my duty by my family."

Fatalism was Nadiensky's only refuge. He was one of the many faceless victims of the Cold War, his life ground down between the two great secret armies which face each other West and East.

But if it was our own fault that we had stumbled into the maze of intelligence provided by defectors, we desperately needed a way out. Angleton opted for blind faith in Golitsin to lead him to safety. In one way it made sense to turn to the architect of the maze to help us find a way out. But although I began as a fervent admirer of Golitsin and all his theories, by the end of the 1960s I was beginning to have my doubts.

The problem was Golitsin's obsession with his "methodology." He claimed that if he was given access to the files of Western intelligence services it would trigger associations in his memory which could lead him to spies. The theory was that since so much of the intelligence he saw in Dzherzhinsky Square was bowdlerized, in other words, source-disguised to protect the identity of the agent supplying the KGB, if he read the files he might be able to seize on points of familiarity with the material he had seen in the KGB Registry.

There were two ways of playing Golitsin. One was to accept his methodology, and allow him to dictate the entire thrust of counterintelligence policy. The other was to continue the frustrating task of trying to prize out from him the nuggets of fact, such as the sorts of information contained in the reports he had seen, the approximate location of an agent, and so forth, which could then be investigated by orthodox counterintelligence methods.

Where Western counterespionage services succeeded in obtaining from him these kinds of factual leads, Golitsin was of enormous help. This was how we finally put the finger on Vassall, and how Marcel Chalet was able to identify Georges Paques. It was the same with Golitsin's political intelligence. Where he stuck to what he saw and what he heard, he was impressive and believable. There is no question, for instance, that he attended Shelepin's famous conference at which Directorate D, responsible for Disinformation Operations, was established. But where Golitsin extrapolated from what he knew to develop broad theories, such as his forty-year grand disinformation program, or where he attempted to fit events which occurred after his defection into his theories, as he did with the Sino-Soviet split, he was disastrous.

Most of the Golitsin acolytes in MI5, of which I was one, soon broke with Golitsin's wilder theories and strict adherence to his methodology. Only Arthur, and more junior officers like Stephen de Mowbray, who was responsible for Golitsin during a spell of duty as an MI6 liaison officer in Washington in the early 1960s, remained loyal.

But in Washington the situation was very different. Angleton swallowed the "methodology" hook, line, and sinker and allowed

Golitsin to range freely across the CIA's files, picking traitors apparently at random, and often unable to justify his decisions on anything other than the flimsiest of grounds. The results were disastrous, and led to the worst excesses of counterintelligence misjudgment. A string of senior CIA officers, most notably Dave Murphy, the head of the Soviet Division, unfairly fell under suspicion, their careers ruined. In the end, the situation became so bad, with so many different officers under suspicion as a result of Golitsin's leads, that the CIA decided the only way of purging the doubt was to disband the Soviet Division, and start again with a completely new complement of officers. It was obviously a way out of the maze, but it could never justify the damage to the morale in the Agency as a whole.

Although MI5 avoided the excesses of the CIA, Golitsin was still badly handled. He was allowed to think himself too important. All defectors should be treated at arm's length, and made to earn their keep, and as little feedback as possible should ever be given to them, so that they are never able to assess their own significance in relation to the rest of the Intelligence Service's activities. Right from his first visit to Britain in 1963, we opened up to Golitsin, and I was responsible for that as much as anyone. When the Mitchell case got under way Arthur and I shared everything with him, with Hollis' and F.J.'s agreement. He even chose the code name for the case, SPETERS, after a famous old Chekhist intelligence officer. He knew from the start that we were hunting a high-level spy, and inevitably that must have colored the intelligence he gave us. In the tense and almost hysterical months of 1963, as the scent of treachery lingered in every corridor, it is easy to see how our fears fed on his theories.

But there is no question that he knew of many penetrations in the West. The record in Britain, Norway, and France proves it. But in our haste we were never able to get an uncorrupted version of all his leads, and this, I am sure, is still costing the West dear.

The tide finally turned against Golitsin in 1967. He was invited to address the first CAZAB conference in Melbourne, Australia. His appearance was eagerly awaited by all those present, since so much of the previous five years had flowed from him. Golitsin was cocky as ever, and soon launched into a lengthy oration on the failures of Western intelligence services to interpret his material correctly.

"I know of more spies," he boomed, "why are you not willing to cooperate with me?"

He laid special emphasis on Britain, and the many penetrations which, he claimed, were as yet undiscovered, and which only he could locate. F.J. was smiling the smile he reserved for particularly tiresome people. He always hated his linen to be washed in public. Finally his patience snapped.

"What is is you want?" he asked.

"The files . . . access to your files," replied Golitsin.

"All right, you can have them—anything you want. We'll see if you've got anything to give us."

Golitsin came over in spring 1968. I initially pressed him to come over straightaway, but it was winter in London, and he told me darkly that he had already seen too much snow in his life. He was set up in a safe house near Brighton, and Michael McCaul and his wife lived with him to keep house and provide him with company. Every week I came down from Leconfield House with a briefcase of files for him to study.

When I first gave him material I warned him that he could not take notes. Both F.J. and I were worried that part of the motivation behind his "methodology" was so that he could amass as much intelligence from each Western service as possible for some unknown future purpose.

"But of course," he replied huffily, "I am a professional, Peter, I understand these things."

For four months Golitsin roamed across the most secret files in MI5, and every month Michael McCaul went to Glyn Mills

Bank and drew out 10,000 pounds in cash, placed it in a small suitcase, and brought it down for Golitsin.

But for all the money, there was little that Golitsin had to give. F.J. had called his bluff. There were some useful things, of course. He studied the VENONA, and was able to fill in a few groups using his knowledge of KGB procedures. He spent a long time studying the files of the Joint Services Language School in Cambridge, looking through the curriculum vitaes of candidates to see if any caught his attention. We even conducted voice tests with some of those he was particularly interested in, to see if Golitsin could detect, from the idioms they used, whether or not they were picking up Russian words from KGB controllers. It was artful, but it never paid off, and in the end we decided that the only safe thing to do was to close the school down.

But in the crucial area—whether or not he could shed any light on the penetration problem—he was a complete loss. He filled in some more details in the Skripkin allegation and he did have one totally bizarre theory. He spent weeks studying the VENONA traffic to see if he could help us identify the unknown cryptonyms. There were two in particular which interested him—David and Rosa—who from the message already broken were obviously working together, probably as man and wife, or perhaps brother and sister. Golitsin asked for the files of all MI5 officers who had served during the time the VENONA traffic was taken. One day he announced he had an answer.

"Your spies are here. My methodology has uncovered them," he intoned darkly, pointing his finger like the witch-finder at two files on the table in front of him. I knew the files well. They belonged to Victor and Tess Rothschild.

"Don't be totally absurd, Anatole," I said. "Victor is one of the best friends this Service has ever had . . . how on earth did you jump at that conclusion?"

"They are Jewish. David and Rosa are Jewish names . . ."

It sounded like KGB anti-Semitism to me, and I could not help thinking that if this had been the CIA and I had been Angleton, Victor and Tess would almost certainly have been listed as spies on Golitsin's groundless interpretation.

The principal problem with Golitsin's methodology was that he interpreted the files as if he were still in the KGB. He looked for operations which went wrong, or mistakes which were attributable to a single officer.

"Where is that man now?" he would ask.

"Same job," I would reply.

Golitsin would say nothing for a few days, and then announce that he was sure the man was a traitor.

"But why, Anatole?"

"Because in KGB, failure is a serious offense. You would not be trusted, and that makes a man unhappy, and maybe then he thinks of turning."

He never understood the culture of the West, and because he himself was driven to defect because his career was damaged after his abortive visit to Stalin, he assumed that anyone in the West would act in the same way.

"But that's not how it is in the West," I used to tell him. "We don't act like that over here—it only happens in the FBI."

Golitsin would look blank. He was a man almost devoid of humor.

"Look, Anatole, we've been studying this for twenty years, and we don't know who the spies are, and your guessing isn't helping us at all."

He looked at me and down at the file, as if to make me guilty for doubting him.

"What do you know, Peter," he would growl, "you were not there in Dzherzhinsky Square, as I was."

But for all his vanity and greed, he was a genuine man, with that sudden sadness that all Russians have. I remember showing him the Volkov file one afternoon. As he read the story of the attempted defector whose file ended up on Kim Philby's desk, he began to weep.

"How could you be so careless, Peter?" he asked in anguish, only too well aware that but for the grace of God Golitsin would have suffered the same fate.

McCaul and I looked sheepish. There was no excuse we could give.

By the end of his stay my sessions with Golitsin had degenerated into tedious diatribes about disinformation, and recycled information which already existed in our Registry. He was a shadow of the man who captivated the best minds in Western counterintelligence with his photographic memory and his unerring eye for detail. Before he left he handed us a massive typescript which he had labored to produce himself, typing one-fingered on an old Olivetti portable. He told me it was the definitive study on disinformation theory. I handed it in to the Registry. The time when I waited on his every word had long gone. I did not even bother to read it.

I saw Golitsin once more in New York the following winter. We had lunch at an Italian restaurant near Central Park. It was a sad, furtive occasion. Golitsin still talked of his plans for an institute for the study of disinformation, and new leads he had discovered. But he knew he was finished. The Czechoslovakian invasion the previous summer had brought a flood of new defectors to the West—men like Frolik and August, whose information was less ambitious but easier to digest. He knew he was yesterday's newspapers, and I think he could tell I was humoring him.

He had recently suffered tragedy. His daughter, upon whom he doted, had fallen prey to the ultimate Western depravity—drug addiction—and had committed suicide. It was a terrible blow, and Golitsin blamed himself.

After lunch we walked across Central Park together in brilliant winter sunshine. He wanted me to visit his farm in upstate New

York, but I told him I had to get back to London. There was little left to say.

"Are you thinking of going home?" I asked him as we came to the parting.

"Oh no," he replied, after an unusual pause, "they would never forgive me."

Golitsin rarely talked about Russia, but it was clearly on his mind.

"Are you homesick?"

"Sometimes . . ."

We made our farewells, and his feet made a crunching sound as he walked across the snow. Like all defectors, Golitsin was feeling the cold.

21

WITH GOLITSIN UNABLE TO ADVANCE THE PENETRATION ISSUE ANY further, MI5 were trapped in the middle of a maze. The search for the high-level spy, for which FLUENCY considered Sir Roger Hollis the best suspect, had been suspended since 1966, so that all attention could focus on the hunt for the middling-grade agent. With Hanley's clearance there was no obvious road forward. Did we abandon the search for the middling-grade agent, and assume Goleniewski's story was planted, or did we continue to search for other candidates, of whom there were a number who were almost as good a fit as Hanley had been? If we assumed that Goleniewski's middling-grade agent story was planted, did we assume it was a lure to draw our attention away from another middling-grade agent, or from the high-level spy? Did both exist, or neither? To do nothing was clearly impossible, and thus, like actors in a Greek tragedy, we had no real choice but to continue widening our investigations, spreading the poison even further through the corridors.

The next best suspect was Gregory Stevens (a pseudonym), an extrovert and gifted officer with a puckish sense of humor. Stevens was about a 60 percent fit for the Goleniewski allegation. He had an even stronger Polish background than Hanley. He was half Polish by birth, and had risen to Hanley's old job as head of the Polish Section of MI5, where his knowledge of the language, culture, and history of his mother's country made him highly successful. Ironically, or perhaps sinisterly, Stevens was the officer who interviewed Goleniewski in 1963, and first heard the story of the middling-grade agent. Was this, like Hollis' visit to see Gouzenko, just another coincidence?

Like Hanley, too, Stevens had been in military uniform and there was also a connection with the KGB officer who Goleniewski alleged had made the recruitment. Both men attended the Yalta Conference in 1945, Stevens as a military translator assigned to assist Stalin with his translations into English, until Stalin complained that he spoke Russian with a Polish Accent.

Like Hanley, Stevens had also undergone psychiatric treatment, and once again I paid a discreet visit to Harley Street. But whereas Hanley had informed his doctor of the nature of his profession, Stevens had never hinted at his involvement in national security.

"I wouldn't have thought he was stable enough to be in that line of work," said the doctor.

"Do you find him trustworthy?" I asked casually.

"He's very clever," replied the doctor, "but I think his cleverness can sometimes lead him astray."

"How do you mean?"

"There's a touch of the Walter Mitty about him. I don't think you could always rely on what he said."

The more I looked at the case, the more I came to doubt whether Stevens should ever have been recruited in the first place. It seemed a hard thing to say. He was a good officer, and an asset to the Service, but in the end, if vetting meant anything, this man ought never to have been allowed in. The psychiatric problems were only a small part of it. The real worry was his Polish background. According to his record of service, he visited Poland regularly with office permission for private holidays to see his relations. His uncle, to whom he was particularly close, was an active member of the Polish Communist Party, and they occasionally met in London. For an organization that was routinely rejecting any applicant with even the faintest trace of the British Communist Party in his family background, the Stevens case presented an obvious problem. And the fact that he had been linked to the middling-grade agent investigation made the situation even more untenable, since in order to clear himself, he had to emerge clean from an exhaustive vet. With half his family living behind the Iron Curtain an adequate vet was impossible.

The investigation was conducted as far as it could possibly go, and then Stevens was summoned for an interrogation, which I conducted with Jim Patrick, a one-eyed Gurkha officer who worked as an interrogator for D3.

Stevens had obviously been half expecting the call ever since he had first heard Goleniewski talk about a middling-grade agent with Polish connections He was alternately truculent and defensive. He stared me nervously in the eye, as if to convince me he was telling the truth. He agreed that he was a good fit for the allegation and accepted that someone of his background was an odd recruitment for an organization like MI5.

"I always wondered when everyone would wake up to the Polish side of me," he said. "I suppose I'll fail the vet now, won't I?"

"I don't know," I replied, "but if it's any consolation, it won't be me that'll decide. It'll be F.J."

He obviously felt that whichever way the interrogation went, he could not possibly win. Unlike Hanley, he could not really hope to walk through the fire unscathed.

We had been going three days when he walked coolly into the room one morning and sat down at the table opposite me.

"It's time for me to tell you something," he said. "I've decided to confess . . ."

I flashed a glance over to Jim, who immediately began taking notes. It was only an additional precaution, since all the sessions were taped.

"Yes," he went on, "I've been wanting to tell someone about it for years. You're right . . . I'm the spy you're looking for."

He seemed to crumple up in front of us, his shoulders heaving, as if he were weeping. But it only lasted a moment or two, before he held his head up, and looked straight at me.

"Do you really mean this, Greg?" I asked.

"You have a witness, don't you?"

"You realize you'll have to give a statement to the Branch?"

He nodded. I leaned over to Jim and told him to inform the Director-General's security man, Tom Roberts, and arrange for Special Branch to come immediately. Stevens and I sat opposite each other, the files and questions in front of me suddenly redundant.

"It's all true, Peter," he said again, in a clear voice.

I told him that he had best not say anything until Tom Roberts arrived. Jim Patrick came back in. For a few seconds more we sat in silence, and then I noticed Stevens' shoulders going again. For a moment I thought he was weeping, perhaps even about to have a breakdown. It often happens.

"Damn," I thought to myself, "I should have had the office doctor stand by."

Then suddenly he began to roar with laughter.

"You really believed me, didn't you?" he cried.

For a second I felt the hot flush of embarrassment.

"I'm not sure I understand . . . ?"

"You wanted a spy, didn't you," he said, reddening suddenly, now that the joke was over. "I thought I'd give you one. I was going to get chopped anyway. I know that!"

"I don't think we should discuss the matter here," I replied. "Tom Roberts will be here in a minute, you can explain it all to F.J."

For all I knew, it was a real confession which he was trying to retract, although I felt I knew Stevens well enough to believe that he was only horsing about. But it was a stupid thing to do. Any chance he had of surviving the investigation had almost certainly gone.

F.J. was appalled when he heard what had happened. He was a lawyer, and had a venerable respect for the niceties of MI5's processes.

"What do you think?" he asked me when I got back to his office.

"Was the confession bogus, or do you think he retracted it?"

"You know my views," I replied. "I am sure he is in the clear because I think the middling-grade agent was a phony allegation from the start. I just think he had a brainstorm . . ."

F.J. grunted. Tales of false defectors were never very welcome to a man of his solidity.

"You don't suppose he made the whole thing up—Goleniewski's story, I mean?" he asked.

I told him we had checked the tapes before the interrogation.

"I even got Stevens to verify the translation. Oh, Goleniewski said it all right."

"Don't see how we can keep him," he muttered, chewing his pipe. "Man's obviously unstable. Polish thing grotesque as well. Sort of thing that gets into newspapers."

He waved me out.

Within an hour Gregory Stevens' career was terminated. He spent ten minutes with F.J., and Tom Roberts escorted him to the pavement outside Leconfield House. He didn't even have a chance to clear his desk.

A few days later Arthur came to see me. He and I had seen little of each other since his departure to MI6. He had aged and seemed less driven than he was before, though the past still held him. He wanted to know about Stevens. They were friends in D Branch in the old days, and Arthur, much the older man, had an almost paternal regard for him.

"Did you have to do it?" he asked.

I told him about the middling-grade agent, and the retracted confession, and the confusion and doubt which plagued us all.

"What else could we do?" I asked. "How can we tell Whitehall to do their vetting, and then turn a blind eye ourselves?"

Arthur knew we had been right, but the cost was becoming progressively higher.

"It's poisoning us all," he said quietly.

Gregory Stevens' departure caused great bitterness in the office. He was a popular officer, and inevitably I was blamed. No one, apart from a handful of senior officers, knew the context which had led up to his investigation—the long history of suspected high-level penetration of MI5, the Blunt confessions, the terrible secret of the FLUENCY conclusions which implicated Sir Roger Hollis, and the hunt for the middling-grade agent.

Word began to spread through the office that D3 was conducting vetting purges in the office, and that officers like Gregory Stevens were being victimized. There was talk of the Gestapo. Younger officers began to avoid me in the canteen. Casual conversation with many of my colleagues became a rarity. Those of us involved in the penetration issue were set apart, feared and distrusted in equal measure.

It was the same in MI6. After years of neglect, a new head of Counterintelligence, Christopher Phillpotts, was appointed in the mid-1960s, around the time FLUENCY got off the ground. Phillpotts looked to all intents and purposes like a figure from the *ancien régime* of British Intelligence. He was a charismatic war hero with a penchant for pink gins and cravats and bow ties. But he was a strict disciplinarian, who believed that in the wake of Philby's defection, the Augean stables needed cleaning. A thorough review of security procedures and personnel was the precondition for a return to self-respect for a Service which, despite Dick White's best efforts, had still to recover from the wounds of Philby, Suez, and Commander Crabbe. Those who could not satisfactorily account for their backgrounds would have to go. National security demanded that, at long last, the benefit of the doubt be given to the state.

Phillpotts supported *fluency* without reservation, and initiated his own program of vetting inside Century House. At least eight senior officers were forced to resign in the wake of Phillpotts' new regime. One officer, for instance, was forced to go when it was discovered that he had a long affair with Litzi Friedman without ever declaring it to the office. Friedman was Philby's first wife, and almost certainly the person who recruited him to the Soviet cause. Another senior officer to suffer had been a member of the Communist Party in the 1930s. Several officers who had been through the Joint Services Language School were also unable to account for discrepancies in their backgrounds, and chose to leave. Even Nicholas Elliott, for so long Philby's supporter, until finally traveling to Beirut to obtain his confession, was investigated, in case Philby had managed to extract intelligence from him. But after lengthy interrogation Elliott just convinced his interrogator, Arthur Martin, that he was in the clear.

None of this was a matter of treachery. But for so long the normal rules of vetting had been waived in the club world of intelligence that when the reckoning came it was abrupt and painful. Much of the blame for the purges inside MI6 was attributed to MI5, and to people like Patrick Stewart and me in particular. Many felt that MI5 were taking advantage of Philby's defection to even up a few old scores.

I had been unpopular inside certain sections of MI6 since my review of the Penkovsky case. But it was the Ellis case which really earned me the undying enmity of the MI6 old guard, and enmity which I wore as a mark of achievement.

The Ellis case caused friction between MI5 and MI6 for almost as long as the Philby case. It began in the aftermath of the Burgess and Maclean defections, when MI5 began to reanalyze the intelligence provided by the defector Walter Krivitsky. One of Krivitsky's serials concerned a White Russian émigré based in Paris named Vladimir Von Petrov, who, Krivitsky alleged, had been an important agent for the Fourth Department, the GRU, during the prewar period, with good sources in Britain as well as Germany, where he was operating as a double agent for the Germans and the Russians.

MI5 were interested to find out who those sources might be, so they studied Von Petrov's file and found a series of debriefing reports of Abwehr officers taken at the end of the war. The Abwehr officers confirmed that Von Petrov was being run by them as their agent, although, of course, they did not know that he was also working for the Russians. Several mentioned that Von Petrov had a source in British Intelligence who could obtain our order of battle, as well as details of vital operations, such as the tap on the secret telephone link between Hitler and his Ambassador in London, von Ribbentrop. One Abwehr officer even remembered the name of Von Petrov's source—it was a Captain Ellis, who was an Australian, a brilliant linguist, and who had a Russian wife.

Charles "Dickie" Ellis was then a senior MI6 officer, recently promoted from MI6 controller for Far Eastern Affairs to be in charge of all operations in North and South America. He joined MI6 in the 1920s, and was based in Paris, where he was responsible for recruiting agents in the White Russian émigré community. During this period he recruited an agent with access to Von Petrov.

The prewar Russian émigré community was a cesspool of uncertain loyalties, and when MI5 raised the query against Ellis, MI6 rejected any possibility that he could be a spy. They maintained that it was much more likely that Von Petrov was working for Ellis, than the other way around, and was lying to protect himself. In any case, Ellis had opted for early retirement, and was planning to return to Australia. Dick White, newly appointed to MI5, and not wanting to aggravate still further the tensions already strained to breaking point by the gathering suspicions against Philby, agreed to shelve the case, where it lay festering in the Registry until I took over as D3.

When Phillpotts took over as head of Counterintelligence, I approached him as chairman of FLUENCY and asked him if he was prepared to sanction a joint MI5-MI6 investigation into Ellis to finally resolve the case. He went to Dick White, who gave his agreement, and I began working with a young MI6 counterintelligence officer named Bunny Pancheff.

The real difficulty in the Ellis case was trying to determine whether he was working for the Germans or the Russians, or both. Early on we got confirmation of the Abwehr officer's story, when we traced the records of the prewar operation to tap the Hitler–von Ribbentrop link. The officer in charge of processing the product was Ellis. The question was whether he was providing the information to Von Petrov in the knowledge that he was a Russian spy, or whether he assumed he was working only for the Germans.

The first thing which convinced me Ellis was always a Russian spy was the discovery of the distribution of the Abwehr officer's report in which he claimed Von Petrov's British source was a Captain Ellis. The report was sent routinely to Kim Philby, in the Counterintelligence Department. He had scrawled in the margin: "Who is this man Ellis? NFA," meaning "No further action" before burying the report in the files. At the time Ellis' office was just a few doors down the corridor, but it seemed to me to be a most suspicious oversight by the normally eagle-eyed Philby.

That was only the first of a number of interesting connections between Philby's career and Ellis'. Within a year of Philby's falling under suspicion Ellis took early retirement, pleading ill-health. He travelled to Australia, and took up a job as a consultant to ASIS, the Australian overseas intelligence-gathering organization. While there he was briefed by the Australians on the impending defection of Vladimir Petrov, a Beria henchman who opted to stay in the West rather than take his chances in Moscow. Almost immediately Ellis returned to Britain and contacted Kim Philby despite being specifically warned against doing so by

Maurice Oldfield. No one knows what they discussed, but from that date onward Petrov fell under suspicion in Australia, and when he noticed his safe had been tampered with in the Soviet Embassy, he defected earlier than anticipated, eluding by hours two burly KGB officers who had been sent out from Moscow to bring him back. The reasons for Ellis' hasty flight from Australia have never been clear, but I have always assumed that he thought the Petrov who was about to defect was the same Von Petrov with whom he had been involved in the 1920s, and who must have known the secret of his treachery.

We look at his wartime record. He spent most of the war in the USA working as deputy to Sir Williams Stephenson, the Man Called Intrepid, at British Security Coordination. Some of the American VENONA showed clearly that the Soviets were operating a number of agents inside BSC, but although we tried exhaustive analysis to link Ellis with each of the cryptonyms, we could never be certain.

I began to search further back for more definite clues connecting Ellis to the Soviets in the prewar period. At the time I was studying the prewar period as part of the D3 researches, and was rereading Elizabeth Poretsky's autobiography, *Our Own People*, about her life as the wife of Ludwik Poretsky (also known as Ignace Reiss), one of the "great illegals" who worked along with Krivitsky as a Fourth Department agent runner for the Soviet GRU. He was murdered after he refused to return to Moscow and defected. I first read the book in its English translation, but this time I studied the original French text, titled *Les Nôtres*. I seized on an extraordinary statement which had not appeared in the English edition. Elizabeth Poretsky said that in the late 1920s Ludwik had an agent high up in British Intelligence.

In 1966 I traveled to Paris to see Mrs. Poretsky, a shrew who guarded her husband's memory jealously and remained suspicious of all agents of Western imperialism, I talked around the subject for a while, and then reminded her of the passage in the book.

Surely, I ventured, she had got her dates wrong, and presumably this agent was Philby? She became quite indignant, squawking at me for my ignorance.

"This was not Philby," she jabbered. "Ludwik ran this agent in Amsterdam in 1928 and 1929. Philby was just a schoolboy then."

"Do you think you could recognize the man?" I asked, trying hard to conceal my excitement.

She began to hedge. She told me she was still loyal to *Les Nôtres*. She could never inform.

"Oh no," I told her, "it's nothing like that—we just need it for our records."

I produced a spread of twenty photographs from my briefcase. Some were dummy photographs, others were of known colleagues of her husband, and one was of Ellis, dating from the mid-1920s. She picked out all those she ought to have known, and Ellis as well.

"I do not know this man's name," she told me, "but I am sure he is familiar."

From Paris I traveled by bus to Amsterdam to see a woman named Mrs. Pieck, the widow of a Dutchman, Henri Pieck, who worked as a Soviet illegal and recruited several spies in Britain during the prewar period, including John Herbert King, a cipher clerk in the Foreign Office. Elizabeth Poretsky had suggested I visit Mrs. Pieck in case she could throw any light on the photograph she had picked out. Mrs. Pieck was a woman from the same mold, and had clearly been warned of my imminent arrival. She too picked out Ellis' photograph, but refused to say why.

There was only one other lead. Elizabeth Poretsky told in her book how Richard Sorge, the great Soviet illegal who eventually built up one of the most important spy networks in history in China and Japan during World War II, had travelled to Britain during the late 1920s. His mission had been highly dangerous, but she told me she knew no more details, and tried too obviously to dissuade me from visiting Sorge's widow, Christiane, who was living in a seminary near New York. I cabled Stephen de Mowbray, then based in Washington as an MI6 liaison officer, and asked him to visit her.

Christiane Sorge placed the final piece in the jigsaw, but left the picture still infuriatingly unfocused. She did indeed remember Sorge's mission, and said it was to see a very important agent, although she knew nothing of his identity. She recalled just one fragment—a meeting on a street corner in London. She and Rickie had gone together to meet this agent, but he had told her to stand well back and cover him in case there was trouble. Could she recognize the man? Stephen asked her. She had seen him, but not well. He showed her the photographs.

"This man looks familiar," she said, "but I could not be certain, after over forty years."

It was Ellis' photograph.

Eventually Ellis was interrogated. He was old, and claimed to be in ill-health, so Bunny Pancheff and I were instructed to take the sessions extremely gently. Ellis denied everything for several days. He blustered and blamed the whole thing on jealous colleagues. But as we produced the evidence, the Abwehr officer's report, and the indoctrination list for the telephone tap, he began to wilt.

After lunch on the Friday he returned to the interrogation room in the basement of the old War Office, known as Room 055, with a typed sheet of paper. It was a confession of sorts. He claimed that he had got into trouble during the early years in MI6. He was sent out into the field with no training and no money, and began providing chicken feed, odd scraps of information about MI6 plans, to his agent Zilenski (his brother-in-law), who was in touch with Von Petrov, in order to obtain more intelligence in return. It was a dangerous game, and soon he was being blackmailed. He claimed that his wife was ill, and he needed money, so he agreed to supply Zilenski with more information.

Ellis' confession was carefully shaded at the edges to hide precisely what intelligence he had given, and where it had gone, so, under interrogation, we asked him to clarify it. He admitted passing over detailed order-of-battle plans for British Intelligence, as well as betraying the Hitler–von Ribbentrop telephone link, even though he knew this material was being passed by Von Petrov to the Germans. (Part of the Abwehr information came from Stevens and Best, who were captured by a trick on the Dutch-German border by the Gestapo. We were able to talk to them after the war, and they said that at their interrogation they were amazed how much the Abwehr knew about the organization of MI6. We asked Ellis when he last had contact with the Russian émigrés. He admitted that it was in December 1939, after the outbreak of war.

Ellis was a venal, sly man. He sat there, stripped of his rank, white-faced and puffy. But never once did I hear an apology. I could understand how a man might choose the Soviets through ideological conviction. But to sell colleagues out to the Germans for a few pounds in time of war? I told him that had he been caught in 1939–40 he would have been hanged.

Ellis clearly thought the interrogation was over. But it had just begun. We wanted to know about his involvement with the Soviets, we said. For a moment he wavered in front of us, then he fought back.

"Never!" he shouted, "never with the Communists . . ."

The next day we took him through the odd chain of events—his trip to Australia, and his rapid return to Britain, and the coincidence of Petrov's defection. But he denied everything, even when he was caught out in repeated lying about his actions until he retired. Not even an authorized offer of immunity could make him change his mind. But I have little doubt of Ellis' involvement with the Russians.

Bunny Pancheff and I wrote the case up, and concluded that in our opinion Ellis had certainly committed espionage for the Germans, including during the war, and that we believed him also to have been a long-term agent of the Russian Intelligence Service until his removal from secret access. The report was endorsed without reservation by Christopher Phillpotts, and submitted to Dick White and his deputy, Maurice Oldfield.

Oldfield was a shy and good man, with a wonderful grasp of the principles of counterintelligence. But he was a poor judge of character. At first he doubted the veracity of Ellis' confession, until eventually Bunny Pancheff played the crucial exchanges to him. But even though we had uncovered a traitor of major proportions, I sometimes felt as if it were I who was being blamed. Oldfield despised the climate of fear engendered by Phillpotts' vetting purges, and campaigned hard to change Dick's mind. The fact that Ellis had confessed seemed to weigh hardly at all on his thinking. As far as he was concerned, it was all a long time ago, and best forgotten.

As the climate against investigations turned in the late 1960s, I wanted desperately to have some of the FLUENCY conclusions circulated more widely inside both Services. I felt sure that this was the only way we could restore some general consent for a continuation of the work. At the moment, people knew nothing of the cases, and to them our activities seemed like blind Mc-Carthyism. D3 had become such a massive section, embracing FLUENCY and the D3 researches into the 1930s. Inevitably, other senior officers resented its priority call on resources and personnel, and since they had no way of judging the importance of the work we were conducting, their resentments grew. I was accused of being suspicious of everybody. F.J. would defend me if the attacks were public. On one occasion he turned around and said to my attacker, "It is Peter's job to be suspicious." Like Angleton, I could sense my enemies multiplying. It was a curious sensation. After years of being the hunter, I suddenly felt myself hunted.

Matters came to a head in 1969 at the annual conference attended by senior MI5 officers at the Sunningdale Civil Service

College in Berkshire. A number of officers launched bitter attacks on me, and others involved in D1 (Investigations), as well as on the work we were doing. What had D3 ever achieved? they asked. They talked of the bonds of trust between fellow officers ruptured by the climate of suspicion. Innocent men suffering, they said.

"Which innocent men?" I said. "That's a lie. Who? You name them!"

My hands were tied. I could not talk in specifics or generalities, and was forced to defend myself by stressing that every move we made in relation to a case was endorsed by F.J. personally. But without my explaining to them the long history of the search for penetration, they could not possibly understand.

Afterward I applied to F.J. to publish a paper on the FLUENCY assessments. I outlined the sort of thing we could circulate to the top seventy officers: a résumé of the continuous allegations of penetration since the war, including the attributions to the known spies wherever possible, and indicating the large number of still unexplained allegations. F.J. refused even to consider it.

"If I do this, Peter," he said, "it will break the heart of the Service. We would never recover."

"But these people don't even know Blunt was a spy. How can they possibly sympathize and support our work, if they aren't told something?"

"In my view," he said, "it would be better if no one knew, ever!"

"But how can we go on?" I asked him. "We've got young people coming into the Service every year. They listen to the tapes, they read the office histories, and they learn nothing about this, and it's the most important subject there is. How can you expect them to live a lie? You might as well not have done any of this work, unless you face up to it, and show people we have by explaining to them how it all happened, and say to people, 'Look, there are these gaps, and that's why we've got to carry on.' "

F.J. would have none of it. There were moments, not many it is true, but this was one, when he was immutable.

"What about me?" I asked finally. "How do I go on in the office, facing this level of hostility?"

He suddenly became steely.

"That is a price you have to pay for sitting in judgment on people."

In 1968, following his clearance, Michael Hanley was appointed head of Counterespionage. Even since the traumatic events of the previous year Hanley and I had barely spoken. He had never said anything, but I could tell he blamed me for the decision to investigate him. When he took over he lost no time in trying to clip my wings. At first it was public slap-downs.

"Oh, Peter," he would say mockingly, "that's just another one of your mad theories."

But then his assault became more serious. He began to remove staff and resources from D3 wherever possible. At first I fought my corner, and went to F.J. to get them reinstated, but after a while I began to wonder whether it was worth the fight. The D3 research task was nearing completion. Only the high-level penetration issue remained unsolved, and that had been shelved for more than three years, with little sign that it would ever be revived. The constant strain of the work was taking its toll on my health. My thoughts turned toward retirement and to my first love—farming.

I decided that at least I should confront Hanley personally before giving up, I went to see him and asked him point-blank why he was trying to drive me out of the Service. He claimed there was no persecution. It was just that D3 had got too big, and there were increasing complaints that some of its less glamorous, but no less important tasks, like security assessments for ministers and the like, were being neglected.

"Well, give me an officer to look after the paperwork, then," I countered.

But Hanley refused.

"I know I'm a poor administrator," I admitted, "but are you sure the real reason for this isn't because you bear a grudge against this type of work?"

Hanley became red-faced. He knew what I was driving at, but denied his own experience was coloring his judgment.

"I suppose you know it was me?" I said. "Have you ever seen the file?"

The ice was broken. I went back to my office and pulled out the file on the HARRIET investigation. I showed Hanley everything —the way the search for the middling-grade agent arose from the FLUENCY report, the shelving of the hunt for the high-level spy, the D3 inquiries, the Watson and Proctor cases, the investigations, the visit to his psychiatrist.

"I never realized," he said, as he studied the files.

"We're the people who were asked to do the dirty work," I told him bitterly, "and now when we've done most of the work, they want to brush it under the carpet and forget us, and forget the things we did."

Indoctrination into the burden of terrible secrets which so few have shouldered had a profound effect on Hanley. He realized that he had no experience of any of this, and his only knowledge of D Branch was from his time on the Polish desk in the 1950s. In order to make a success of D Branch he had to have guidance. One day he called me into his office and explained his problem. He was quite straightforward, and I respected him for it. He still wanted to break down D3. Its mammoth task was almost finished, he told me, and in any case, he wanted me to become his personal consultant on the whole reorganization of D Branch which he was planning. I was to have sight of every paper, and access to all cases in the Branch with the brief to guide him with my intimate knowledge of the previous fifteen years. Unlike any other officer, I had never moved from D Branch. As Dick White promised at my interview, I received no promotion, but then I was not forced to play musical chairs, switching from department to department every second year. D Branch had been my life. I knew every case and file. It was a fair offer, and I accepted immediately.

But that still left the problem of penetration.

"Who is going to continue that work? We can't let the thing slip again, otherwise another backlog of unresolved cases will build up," I said.

I had been convinced for more than a year that we needed some formal mechanism for looking at the whole question of internal penetration. The problem of the 1960s was that there was no department in the Service where allegations of penetration could be investigated. Everything was ad hoc. FLUENCY had no formal status, it was just a working party. The work did not sit easily inside D1 (Investigations), because their correct job was to investigate penetrations that occurred outside the Service. It was precisely this lack of a mechanism which contributed to the accusations of "the Gestapo" in the office. We were seen to be people pursuing investigations outside the normal channels, and in an organization as conscious of hierarchy as MI5, that was a considerable problem. With a proper section devoted to the work, the Service would be able to see that the management had given its full backing. It would, in other words, have legitimacy.

There was one other factor in my mind. I knew that if the issue of high-level penetration was ever to be solved, it could be done only by giving fresh minds access to the problem. Over the past ten years the subject had become intimately bound up with personalities—principally mine and Arthur's. We were seen as men with grudges, or as men with obsessions, unable to conceive of any interpretation other than Hollis' being guilty. I lobbied Hanley and F.J. furiously, trying to persuade them to set up such a section, and staff it with people who had no connection with either Arthur or me, or with the terrible events of the previous ten years.

Hanley was doubtful, but F.J. seized on the idea immediately, and persuaded Hanley to incorporate it into his plans. By late 1968 the reorganization was complete. D Branch became K Branch, which was split into two separate units: KX, which handled all investigative work, and had its own director on the Board; and KY, which was responsible for order of battle and operations, also with its own director. KX incorporated D1 (Investigations) and much of the old D3, and comprised three sections: K1 and K2, which were Soviet and satellite investigating sections; K3, which was now a research section cut out of D3, a section servicing the investigation sections; and a new unit, K7, charged with sole responsibility for investigating allegations of penetration of the Intelligence Services. KY comprised K4, order of battle; K5, which was agent running and operations; and K6, which assumed responsibility for all security assessments and compiling the specialist records, ministerial briefings, special indexes, and record collection which previously had been under my control in D3.

Duncum Wagh was the first officer appointed to head K7. He was a good choice—a sensible, levelheaded officer who was always thorough in his reasoning and, once his mind was made up, doubly impressive in justifying his proposed course of action. His career had suffered unduly from his mistake in clearing Houghton after his wife's complaint ten years previously. But solid hard work, some of it on my Moscow Embassy Working Party, had earned him a major chance, and K7 was certainly that. He was supported by a forceful ex-marine officer named John Day. I strongly advised that nobody involved in the penetration issue to date should work in K7.

I had one meeting with Duncum Wagh, and handed over to him everything in my safe which related to FLUENCY all the records from my own freelance inquiries into Hollis' background, my analyzes of the Lonsdale case, some work on the middling-grade agent. It was only when he took them that I realized what a burden those small green combination boxes had been all those years.

"Here," I said, "it's your problem now, thank God!"

I had very little to do with K7 in the early days. Neither
Duncum Wagh nor John Day wanted me around, for fear it
would prejudice their won freedom of maneuver and credibility,
and I understood that. I did introduce John Day to Blunt, and
talked again through the whole question of why he had been
allowed to leave MI5 by the Russians in 1945. Blunt always
thought it was odd.

"I think if they had pressured me, I probably would have
stayed on, at least for a bit. I loved the work, and adored Guy
Liddell and Dick White, and I expect I could still have pursued
my art . . . but they never asked me."

Blunt could shed no light on whether there was already a replacement for him in the office, although he knew that was what
concerned us. We showed him the VENONA message with the
eight cryptonyms. But they meant nothing to him. The only
fragment he had was a lunch he attended with Guy Burgess and
Graham Mitchell at the Reform Club. It was clearly another
looking-over session, but as to whether Guy had actually made an
approach, Blunt claimed he knew nothing. A little later I was told
that John Day had interrogated Mitchell at long last, and they
were quire satisfied he was in the clear. As I always suspected, it
came down to Hollis.

For a long time I heard nothing. Then one day John Day came
to see me. He brought with him the first K7 report on high-level
penetration. It concluded categorically that Hollis was the best
candidate, and recommended his immediate investigation and
interrogation.

"I always thought you saw reds under the beds," said John Day
after I had read the report, "but I wanted to tell you that I think
you were right all along."

This time there was no escape—not for myself, for F.J., or for
the man in the black suit playing golf in quiet retirement in the
Somerset village of Calcott.

22

IT WOULD HAVE BEEN NICE TO HAVE CROWNED MY CAREER WITH A triumph. It would have been nice to have solved the riddle. Better he was innocent than the continuing uncertainty. But the secret world is not so simple, and at the end the shadows remained, as dense as before, shrouding the truth.

One morning in 1969 I made my way up to a small operations room in what had once been the D3 offices. The desk earphones whispered gently as A2 technicians checked the microphones in our safe house in South Audley Street. For them it was another day, another interrogation, but for me it was the final act in a tenyear drama. The brief lay on the table, as big as a thick telephone directory. On the inside front cover was the curious single word "Drat," Hollis' code name. It was issued to me years before, when I was doing my D3 private inquiries, by the small office in B Branch which allocated cover names. I laughed at the time. "Drat" seemed so absurd. I never realized what pain would be associated with it.

Anne Orr-Ewing was an extremely thorough officer who had risen from the Transcription Department to D3 as a research officer before joining K7. The K7 case was substantially the same as my own freelance inquiries of 1965 and 1966. It was more detailed, of course. They had access to Hollis' Record of Service, and had traced and interviewed his contemporaries at Oxford, searched the Shanghai Special Branch records, but no crucial proof had been found. In the end, as always, it came down to a matter of belief.

A small white envelope inviting Hollis back up to the office was sent a few days before the interrogation. The final plans were laid. There was a row, too, of course. We assumed that Hollis would be placed under continuous surveillance during the period of the interrogation, in case, like Blake, he panicked and made a move to contact his Russian controllers, if he had any. But F.J. would have none of it. He gave no reasons, but we could tell by his face that he was immovable. Even Hanley protested about this, point-ing out to F.J. that he had not been spared the full works. But F.J. felt he had been backed into a corner in sanctioning the interrogation, and this was a final indignity he was not prepared to impose on his predecessor.

John Day was told to conduct the interview Anne Orr-Ewing and I were to listen in to provide analysis as the interrogation proceeded. F.J. knew he was too committed on the subject to be a fair choice, and he realized that, after so many years' delay, he had to be seen to be allowing the troops their chance.

A door opened in South Audley Street. Hollis was shown in.

"Where do you want me?" he asked, his familiar voice still strong after all the years.

John Day began to explain the procedure of the interview.

"Yes, I'm familiar with the procedure . . . but I need pencil and a paper, if you please."

I tried to imagine the scene in the room in South Audley Street. I could see Hollis in there, sitting upright. I rather thought he would miss his desk. Of course the pencils would be essential. And he would be wearing his Cheshire cat smile. Would he feel humiliated? I wondered. Or frightened? I somehow doubted it. Emotion was never something I associated with him. I remembered something he always used to say to me.

"Peter, you're too emotional on the subject."

I was doing my best to control my excitement.

John Day began by going through routine details of Hollis' career and early life. Hollis knew the procedure, and began running ahead of the brief.

"We'll take it a little slower, if you don't mind," said John Day.

Hollis showed faint irritation.

"This is a little laborious, if you don't mind me saying so. You must have this information on my R/S."

But John Day was not to be intimidated.

"I think we had best follow procedure in this instance, if you don't mind."

Hollis told a simple story. He said he left home because he realized he was not religious. But Oxford, he claimed, was no escape. It, too, reminded him of his religious upbringing.

"I wanted to get away, do something with my life in the outside world. The only ambition I had was to play golf, and I realized early on at Oxford that I could never make a career out of it. So I decided to travel."

The Far East had always attracted him. Originally he thought he might travel with some friends—Maurice Richardson was one. But the plan fell through. In retrospect, said Hollis, he was glad. They had far too little in common to make good traveling companions.

China fascinated him. Of course, he met the odd left-wing person out there, but then that was normal. Everyone knew Agnes Smedley was left-wing. It was the same at Oxford. He had been friendly with Maurice Richardson and Claud Cockburn, both of whom were best described as pink.

He said his health was a constant problem. TB afflicted him throughout this period, and in the end it forced his return to Europe. He traveled back via Moscow.

"I wanted to see what it was like. Awful place. Dirty, depressing. Nobody smiled. Intellectuals were making a tremendous fuss about the place. But I hated it."

"Did you meet anybody there?" asked John Day.

"On buses and trains. That sort of thing. But otherwise no. You don't meet Russians like you do people in other countries, like China, for instance."

At a lunch, Anne Orr-Ewing, John Day, F.J., and I met back at Leconfield House. Hollis' performance had been calm and flawless.

"He'll clear himself, if he goes on like this," said Anne Orr-Ewing.

After lunch we went on to his return to Britain. Suddenly the crisp focus disintegrated. The delivery was still resolute, but all the detail disappeared. He could not remember where he had lived, whom he had met, what plans he had, and yet we had all the answers in the brief. We knew what he had been doing. For instance, he had lived virtually next door to an old MI6 officer named Archie Lyall, who had been a close friend of Guy Burgess. But although they must have seen each other numerous times, Hollis had no recollection of him at all. For an hour or more Hollis stumbled, until he reached the point in his career where he joined MI5 before the war. Suddenly, and as abruptly as it had disappeared, precision returned.

That night the interrogating team met again at the Oxford and Cambridge Club to debate the day's session.

"What about this blank year?" I asked.

F.J. placed his pipe on the table wearily.

"You've got that all wrong," he said.

He told us that Hollis was in a mess when he came back from China—his health was shot, he had no career, no prospects. It did not seem to occur to him that this would have made Hollis much more vulnerable to recruitment. He was drifting, and it was a period in his life he had long wanted to forget. Little wonder, said F.J., that he can't remember where he lived.

"Well, it's a pretty odd state of mind to start applying for a job in MI5 or MI6 for that matter," I remarked. I meant it seriously, but it sounded sarcastic. F.J. bridled.

"For God's sake, Peter!" Then he cut himself short. There was still another session to go.

The following day Hollis sat down again.

"Are we ready?" Hollis asked patronizingly. John Day waited in silence. It was a nice touch, and reminded Hollis that, for once, he was not in charge.

Day began on a different tack.

"I want to ask you again about Claud Cockburn's file . . ."

This had come up the previous morning. Hollis volunteered his friendship with Cockburn at Oxford, and was asked why he had never declared the fact on Cockburn's file, as any MI5 officer was supposed to do if he handled the file of an acquaintance. Hollis brushed the question aside. He said there was no general requirement at that time to record personal friendships on files.

It was a lie, only a small one, true, but a lie nonetheless. The brief contained a full annex proving that it was indeed current practice in MI5 prewar to record friendships, and that Hollis would have known of the regulation.

Day began to challenge Hollis on his answer the previous day. Why had he lied? Hollis was never a stammerer, or a flusterer. There was a slight pause, and then he acknowledged his mistake. Yes, he admitted, there was another reason. He knew that Cockburn was of interest to the Service as a prominent left-winger and Comintern agent, and since he was a recent arrival, and wanted very much to pursue a career inside MI5, he chose to ignore the regulation in case his friendship with Cockburn were seen as a black mark against him.

"I am sure I wasn't the first or the last officer to break that particular rule."

"What about other friends," pressed Day. "What about Philby? Were you friendly with him?"

"Not really. He was too much of a drinker. We had good professional relations, but nothing more."

"And Blunt?"

"More so, particularly during the war. I thought he was very gifted. But I saw him less after he left the Service. Now and again we would meet at the Travelers. Small talk—that sort of thing. He loved to gossip."

Gouzenko, Volkov, and Skripkin he dispatched swiftly. Gouzenko was unreliable. He still doubted that Elli really existed. As for his trip to Canada, there was nothing sinister in Philby's sending the file on to him.

"I was the acknowledged Soviet expert at the time. It would be natural for Philby to refer it to me, particularly because it was a Commonwealth matter."

"And Volkov?"

"I see no reason to disbelieve Philby. He thought Volkov's spy was himself . . . Why should he go all that way to protect someone else?"

Only once did a trace of the old Director-General break through, when John Day began to ask him about events in the early 1960s. He was asked about the sacking of Arthur Martin. A harsh tone crept into his voice.

"He was being thoroughly undisciplined. I never knew what he was doing. Take Blunt. We agreed on a formal immunity offer relating to events before 1945. Martin goes in to see him, and offers him *carte blanche* immunity. The Attorney-General was incensed, and so was I. There was no controlling him. He and Wright were busy setting up a privileged Gestapo, and something had to be done to break it up. I don't regret it for one moment. I think it was absolutely justified in the circumstances and, if anything, should have happened much earlier."

John Day asked him why he had not allowed Mitchell to be interrogated in 1963.

"It's in the files. The Prime Minister would not sanction it."

"Did you actually ask him for permission?"

"Of course I did," replied Hollis testily.

"But he has no recollection of the meeting," countered Day.

"That's absurd! The situation was critical. The Profumo business was as its height. The whole question of the exchange with the Americans had to be considered. Another scandal would have brought the Government down. That's why consultation was vital."

It was all shadow-boxing. Day moved and jabbed, but he could never really land a blow. Somehow he never got close enough to street-fight, to grapple and gouge him, and make him confess. Time had slipped away. It was all old, too old, to ever find the truth.

By the end of the afternoon only the routine questions for the record were left.

"Have you at any stage communicated official information to any unauthorized person?"

"No," replied Hollis firmly.

"Have you ever been approached by anyone clandestinely to pass information?"

"Never."

The chairs scraped as Hollis got up He said goodbye, and meant it. He traveled back to Somerset, back to his golf, and his cottage. He left the interrogation room as unknown as when he entered—an enigma, an apparently sober man, with a streak of filthy humor. The autocrat with crippling insecurity.

F.J. met us again at the Oxford and Cambridge Club that night. There was an air of resignation around the table. We knew that we had not brought the case home. But equally we felt adamant that there was enough doubt to keep the case alive. F.J. was silent. He felt the interrogation vindicated his faith in Hollis.

"I hope we can move on to other things," he said.

Once again the case was closed. But nothing, and certainly not Hollis' interrogation, could paper over the deep chasm which divided those who believed penetration had occurred, and those, like F.J., who had finally come to doubt it. I could not help remembering all the wasted years, the years when it could have been investigated, the years of neglect and drift, the years when files gathered dust, when reports went unanswered, the years when fear of the unknown prevented us from ever knowing the truth. Only a chance breakthrough, a defector or a cipher break, could help us solve the case now. A desperate sense of failure gripped me—failure and frustration and a desire to get away and forget. Looking back, my retirement began that night as I traveled home on the train to Essex. What came after was mostly going through the motions.

Hollis' interrogation signaled the end of one decade, and ushered in the new. The 1970s were to be the years of reckoning, when the secret armies of the West were finally and painfully exposed to the searing searchlight of publicity. For thirty years West and East had fought a nocturnal battle, hidden and protected by custom and necessity. But within four years the secrets would come pouring out.

Ironically, the 1970s opened well for MI5. We finally got a defector we believed in. His name was Oleg Lyalin. He was recruited by two of the best officers in MI5, a bluff Yorkshireman named Harry Wharton, and a former SIS undercover officer of conspicuous courage, Tony Brookes, who with his wife had operated in France and survived. The operation was managed by the head of KY, a calm, dependable officer by the name of Christopher Herbert. Lyalin was having an affair with a girl, and when Wharton and Brookes made contact with him he said he wanted to defect. They managed to persuade him to stay in place, and for six months he provided MI5 with a detailed run-down of the KGB order of battle in London. He was only a relatively low-level KGB officer connected to the Sabotage Department, but any breach in the KGB's armory is invaluable.

As soon as the Lyalin case began we realized that this was the best possible test as to whether high-level penetration of MI5 still existed. If Lyalin survived we were in the clear. From 1966 until at least 1976 we had no evidence of Russian interference with our operations. We had five spy cases, and the Lyalin case and the expulsion of the 105 Russian diplomats, both of which had been in existence for at least six months. Yet up to the end of 1965, every case for twenty years or more was tainted by Russian "sticky fingers." We should note that Hollis retired at the end of 1965. The secret was known to only ten people, and to no one outside the office apart from Dennis Greenhill, Permanent Secretary at the Foreign Office. Greenhill was a good friend of MI5, and I enjoyed especially warm relations with him. He too had been to Bishop's Stortford College, along with Dick White and me. I first dealt with him over the French STOCKADE operation, but we began to have much more to do with each other when I took over D3, and routinely provided security briefings for his senior diplomats.

Lyalin soon began to exhibit the strain of leading a double life. Brookes and Wharton arranged safe houses where he could meet his girlfriend for love sessions. The arrangements for these visits were laborious, and each time one or the other had to sit outside the room monitoring events inside for telltale signs of stress or betrayal. Lyalin began to drink too heavily, and when he was posted back to Moscow we decided to bring his ordeal to an end. Lyalin himself was quite game to return to Russia and continue to spy in place, but we had already concluded that he would never survive. Lyalin was attached to the Trade Delegation but had no diplomatic immunity, so we decided that we would simply arrest him as he walked through customs at Heathrow Airport, and force his hand.

Almost immediately our plans fell apart. I was living in London during the week, and one night in February 1970, at 3 A.M., I received a telephone call from the Duty Officer.

"Get in quick," he said, "we need access to your safe."

I dressed and took a taxi to the office, to find Tony Brookes waiting for me.

"We need the antidote kit," he told me. "Lyalin's blown. He

was arrested for drunken driving a few hours ago, and he's in the clink at Marlborough Street!"

I unlocked my safe and produced a small roll like a toolkit which Dr. Ladell of Porton Down had given me ten years previously toward the end of my time as Scientific Officer. I contained antidotes to all the known poisons used by the KGB. Whenever a defector came out we had the case near him twenty-four hours a day, but otherwise it remained in my safe. No one else cared to hold it so close.

I quickly described to Brookes the basic symptoms of nerve gas or toxic poisoning, and told him how to administer the antidote. He rushed off to the prison to guard Lyalin, while I hoisted the deputy head of Special Branch out of bed, and got him to alert Marlborough Street to the identity of the drunk in their basement cell. Meanwhile the MI5 Legal Department applied to the Home Secretary and the Attorney-General for formal immunity for Lyalin from his drunken charge, explaining that there was serious risk of assassination if he was brought before an open court.

The successful defection of Lyalin presented MI5 with a unique opportunity. Ever since F.J. became Director-General he had nursed the dream of decisively changing the balance of forces ranged against him. He knew that the central problem facing MI5 was the massive superiority in the numbers of Soviet intelligence officers in London. Throughout the 1960s he had struggled to get the Treasury to agree to an expansion of MI5's counterespionage capability, but they were always reluctant. He had been able to achieve a certain amount by redirecting resources internally in favor of D Branch, but we were still outnumbered by a factor of more than three to one. With Edward Heath in power, F.J. put the case for a major reduction of intelligence officers to him, citing the order-of-battle figures for intelligence officers. This was before Lyalin came on the scene. Heath's reaction was "throw the lot out." The Foreign and Commonwealth Office

(FCO) protested, but we were not to do this either since we wanted a number here to retaliate with if the Russians were vindictive. However, the whole arrangement was agreed between us and FCO by March 1971. We delayed action until the autumn because Lyalin had come on the scene and we did not want to disturb things until he either defected or had gone home.

In his debriefing, Lyalin identified dozens of KGB officers active under diplomatic cover. Most of these identifications were already known for us through the Movements Analysis program, which I had helped establish in the early 1960s with Arthur Martin and Hal Doyne Ditmass.

Calculating KGB strength has always been a contentious business, and yet it lies at the heart of a rational assessment of the threat posed by hostile intelligence. When I ran D3 I made a series of analyses of Soviet strength in 1945, based on the VENONA material. Although we broke only a small fraction of the traffic, GCHQ were able to statistically assess the total number of spies active in Britain at between 150 and 300. (The statistical analysis was conducted using methodology devised by one of the top cryptographers, I. J. Good.) By the 1960s, through rough analysis of the VENONA, and through comparing intelligence provided by defectors, as well as Blunt and Cairncross, with our own passport records, we were confident that there were between forty-five and fifty Russian intelligence officers in London in 1945, of whom about twenty-five were agent runners. Dividing this into the number of spies demonstrated in the VENONA gave a median figure of around eight to nine spies per agent runner, which dovetailed neatly with the one week of VENONA traffic which demonstrated that Krotov was running eight spies.

Now the real question is how far those figures can be extrapolated into modern times. By the late 1960s the Movements Analysis program was indicating between 450 and 550 Russian intelligence officers active in Britain. But what percentage of those were agent runners? Even if we assumed that the number of agent runners had remained static over a twenty-year period, at around twenty-five, and that the rest were there to provide cover, countersurveillance, internal security, and analysis, this still left us facing a huge problem. It meant that there were upward of 200 spies currently active in Britain. If we took the figure of agent runners to have expanded commensurately with the rise in total numbers of intelligence officers, the situation was even more alarming—more than a thousand spies! Of course, the vast majority of those spies would be low level contacts among the Communist Party and various trade unions, but if even 1 percent were penetrations of the level of Houghton or Vassall, the implications were disastrous.

Whenever I placed these analyses forward to the Home Office for inclusion in the routine threat assessments, there was strife. John Allen, a former lawyer, and fast rising in K Branch, repeatedly disputed my analysis.

"You can't say that, there can't be that many IOs in London, the Home Office will never believe it!"

But Lyalin's defection removed all the objections. He confirmed the Movements Analysis figure of around 450 intelligence officers based in London, and maintained that a large percentage were active agent runners. He proved beyond any shadow of doubt that the Movements Analysis program was quite correct and my statistical arguments valid. It was also apparent that not all the increase was in low-level spies. With greater determination that I ever saw him pursue anything, F.J. put to the Foreign Office the case for mass expulsions of a large number of the Russian diplomats. In the end, Ted Heath and the Foreign Secretary, Alec Douglas-Home, agreed, after a discreet approach by Home to the Soviet Foreign Minister, Alexei Kosygin, suggesting the Russians remove some of their intelligence officers without publicity was brushed aside imperiously.

The expulsions were seen as a brilliant coup throughout the Western intelligence world, and we received telegrams of congratulation from the heads of every Service. It was F.J.'s greatest triumph, made sweeter because the fact that the plan had clearly not leaked to the Russians proved that, whatever the truth of the past, high-level penetration of MI5 was definitely at an end.

Angleton supported the expulsions unreservedly, and confessed that he had long wanted to engineer something similar in Washington. But Henry Kissinger was a firm opponent. Angleton told me that Kissinger had exploded when he learned of the British expulsions. He was desperately pursuing détente with the USSR, and minuted the CIA angrily, telling them that had he known of the proposal he would have used every power at his command to get it quashed. Luckily, the CIA were able to state truthfully that they had known nothing of the plan.

But Angleton was deeply suspicious of Lyalin. After the defection Angleton paid a secret visit to London. He looked worse than ever, consumed by the dark, foreboding role he was committed to playing. He viewed himself as a kind of Cassandra preaching doom and decline for the West. He thought Lyalin was a plant, and told us all so at a meeting Marlborough Street.

"Oh come on, Jim," I said, "Lyalin's just not that big. He's a KGB thug, what possible disinformation interest could they have in him?"

Angleton felt betrayed. We had not told him about Lyalin while we were running him in place, and he told us stiffly that the whole purpose of UKUSA was the full exchange of intelligence. Patience with Angleton was rapidly wearing thin in London in 1970. Maurice Oldfield had an ill-concealed hostility to all his ideas and theories, and even inside MI5 he had begun to make enemies.

We learned later just how far he was prepared to go to discredit Lyalin. As Lyalin was debriefed, we routinely sent over our intelligence digests containing his material to the FBI for circulation through to the CIA, and on to the National Security Council and up to the President.

Some months later, J. Edgar Hoover took a vacation in Florida, and took the opportunity to call on President Nixon at his holiday home on Key Biscayne.

"How do you like the British reports from their source Lyalin, Mr. President?"

"What reports?" replied Nixon. He had never received them.

When Hoover checked back with Kissinger, he had not received them either. Kissinger got on to the CIA and instituted a full search. They were finally found in Angleton's safe. He had concluded Lyalin was a provocation, and simply refused to circulate the documents. Tom Karamasines, the CIA Director of Plans, issued a stern rebuke, and it was the beginning of Angleton's slide from power.

The roots of his demise lay much earlier in the Golitsin-Nossenko feud. For Angleton it became an article of faith that Nossenko was a plant, since that ensured Golitsin primacy among all the defectors who arrived in the early 1960s. I remember in 1967, after the first CAZAB conference, telling Angleton that I was travelling back to Britain via the USA. My daughter was living in Boston, and I thought I would combine some business with a purely personal visit. As soon as I told Angleton I was visiting Washington he became quite aggressive. He told me I had no right to visit Washington unless he was in town. At the time I thought his worry was to do with the Israelis. The Middle Eastern situation was brewing up, and Angleton always jealously protected his relations with the Israeli secret service, Mossad. He knew of my close friendship with Victor Rothschild, and often tried to break it off. On one occasion he even wrote to F.J. to try to curtail it as an interference in the CIA Mossad liaison, but F.J. treated the letter with the contempt it deserved.

But Angleton's distress had nothing to do with Israel. I learned the truth. Just before the CAZAB conference an internal CIA inquiry led by a security officer named Bruce Solie had concluded that Nossenko was almost certainly a genuine defector, although it could offer no explanation for the curious contradictions in his story. Angleton had never told the British this fact, despite its implications for Nossenko's and Golitsin's information. He was obviously frightened that if I visited Washington I might get to hear of Solie's report through another channel.

Incidents like these began to undermine Angleton's credibility. The Nossenko and Lyalin incidents did much to shake the faith of even those who knew him best and defend him longest. We began to doubt whether, after all, the secret sources to which Angleton claimed he had access actually existed. Perhaps it was, after all, just a three-card trick.

In 1970 Angleton suffered the greatest blow of all. He lost his administrative officer and effective number two, Jim Hunt. Hunt was a hard man, who treated Angleton's obsessions with balanced skepticism. He had his feet on the ground, and he made things happen. Angleton, like myself, was a hopeless administrator, and Hunt ensured that papers were circulated, requests replied to, and the day-to-day routine, upon which an efficient intelligence service relies, was maintained. Without him, Angleton became a ship without anchor, drifting slowly toward the abyss.

Lyalin's defection and the expulsion of the 105 Russian diplomats were not the only signs of a new dawn which seemed to be breaking for British Intelligence in the 1970s. Following his election as Prime Minister in 1970, Edward Heath appointed Victor Rothschild as head of Central Policy Review Staff (CPRS)—the Think Tank. Never was a man more perfectly suited to a job. Victor had the right qualities of inspiration and radicalism to provide the kind of challenging policy unit Heath wanted. The call came at just the right time for Victor. I could tell that he was becoming slightly bored toward the end of the 1960s. He had no regard for Harold Wilson, and there was no role for him in public life. He maintained his links with British Intelligence, utilizing his friendship with the Shah of Iran, and running agents personally for Dick White in the Middle East, particularly Mr. Reporter, who played such a decisive role in MI6 operations in the 1950s. It was exciting, but he hankered after a real challenge, and the Think Tank was exactly what he needed.

As a head of the Think Tank, Victor Rothschild took a close interest in security, and Heath encouraged him to do so, much to the irritation of the Home Office, and in particular the powerful Permanent Secretary of the time, Philip Allen (now Lord Allen of Abbeydale, and a member of the Security Commission). Victor became, in effect, the Lord Wigg of Heath's Government. Once inside the Cabinet Office Victor teamed up with Dick White, the newly installed Cabinet Intelligence Coordinator following his retirement from MI6. Together they combined to give British Intelligence its highest ever postwar profile.

Victor's finest achievement for MI5 was securing F.J.'s succession. F.J. was never a popular figure in Whitehall. He was too much his own man, and too secret even for that bastion of secrecy. Normally the outgoing Director-General has the right to choose his successor, but as F.J. approached retirement in 1972, the Home Office, and especially Philip Allen, decided it was time to exert authority. Allen was convinced that an outsider should be appointed. He had become suspicious of MI5 and feared they had become a dangerous repository of scandal. He knew only sketchy details of the full extent of the traumas of the mole hunts, but he knew about Blunt and Long, and he knew enough to be worried. He was alarmed by what seemed to him to be the cavalier use of immunities, and the undoubtedly poor caliber of MI5 management. He wanted a safe pair of hands at the helm of the organization—someone who could tell him what was going on, someone he could trust.

Simkins finally retired, to my great relief, about a year before F.J.'s scheduled retirement, and was replaced by Michael Hanley. As far as Allen was concerned, Hanley was neither experienced enough nor independent enough to be entrusted with the top job. Allen's preferred candidate was Sir James Waddell, a deputy sec-

retary at the Home Office, who was responsible for Police and
Security Affairs, and handled all day-to-day liaison between MI5
and the Home Office. Waddell was a dependable mandarin who
had somehow missed out on a permanent secretary's job. Allen, to
whom he had given loyal service, wanted to install him as a Director-General of the Security Service.

Waddell's prospective appointment was viewed with considerable concern inside MI5. He was a finicky man who insisted on
the last dot and comma on intercept warrant applications. He
lacked the experience as an intelligence officer to gain the respect
of its senior officers. Many of us felt his candidacy was pure
Whitehall expediency, which would set the Service back a decade, in the same way that Rennie's appointment as C just a few
years before had caused a massive slump in morale in MI6.

Of course, there was another consideration as well. There were
many secrets which MI5 had kept from their political and Civil
Service masters, and the last thing anyone in MI5 wanted at that
stage was the explosive story of the mole hunts to receive an
airing around Whitehall.

The first I heard of the problem of succession was when F.J.
mentioned it in late 1971. He told me he was determined to stop
Waddell taking over the Service, and said he had already approached Dick White to ask for assistance. But the situation
looked gloomy. A committee of top permanent secretaries
chaired by the Cabinet Secretary and attached to the Senior Appointments Selection Committee had already recommended
Waddell, and although F.J. had put forward Hanley's name he
had received no votes at all. He was too new, too inexperienced,
and the mandarins knew too little about him.

"Is there anything you can do with your powerful friend?"
asked F.J., referring in his customary manner to Victor.

At the time I used to see Victor informally once a week—
sometimes in his room at the Cabinet Office, more often at his
home. On my next visit I raised the question of the succession. It

had all the right elements to fire Victor's imagination—a heady brew of intrigue and secrecy.

He told me he had already been alerted to the situation by Dick White, who had told him that he supported Hanley for the job. Dick had initially given some thought to supporting Maurice Oldfield for the job. Sir John Rennie, anxious to remove the man who effectively ran MI6, even though he himself was the titular head, had put Oldfield's name forward, but Oldfield had made it plain he preferred to sit it out and wait for another chance as Director C if Rennie retired. (Rennie did retire prematurely after the disclosure that his son had been convicted of a drugs charge, and Oldfield succeeded him.)

"Do the Service want Hanley?" asked Victor. He often used me as a sounding board for Service as opposed to management opinion.

"Certainly," I replied.

"Do you have anything against him?"

I told him the story of the HARRIET affair. Although Victor already knew of my suspicions about penetration, and I had discussed both Hollis and Mitchell with him, the fact that Hanley had once been a suspect was new to him.

I told him I was quite convinced he was in the clear, and so were the Americans. I told him the Service were dead set against Waddell, and that there would undoubtedly be serious trouble if he were appointed.

"We need all the help we can get, Victor!"

"Ted won't like it," he told me, for the moment assuming the *gravitas* of a senior civil servant. Then he cast the somehow inappropriate mantle aside, and fell into his more natural conspiratorial manner.

"Let's see what we can do," he muttered, and asked me to arrange for him to meet Hanley as soon as possible.

By this time Hanley and I had established a reasonable working relationship. HARRIET was always a block to any warmth, but he dealt with me in a straightforward manner, and I tried to be as much help as I could, guiding him around the previous twenty years of counterintelligence rather like an accomplished chauffeur, pointing out the sights to admire, and the potholes to avoid. I knew he would bridle when I told him of my meeting with F.J. and Victor. There was just a trace of socialism about Hanley, which showed itself in utterances about achieving the job on his merits, not through the old boy network. But in the end ambition was the better master, and he agreed to go with me one evening to Victor's elegant flat in St. James's Place. I had one drink and made a tactical withdrawal to my club to allow them to talk freely. The next day Victor rang me up.

"He's a very good choice," he said. "We must meet tonight and make our plans."

That night, over a particularly fine claret, we drew up our campaign. Dick White had obviously failed to impress his choice either on his mandarin colleagues or on Ted Heath. Dick was always diffident when it came to staff matters, and had not been able to summon up the gumption to bang the table. Of course, that was never his style. Undoubtedly his one failure in his career was his inability to make good appointments. Too often he was betrayed by sentiment or orthodoxy. He overpromoted Hollis and Cumming in MI5, and he failed to order the decisive purge necessary in the Philby-infected MI6 until much too late. It was the same with Hanley. He knew what was best for the Service, but he seemed unable to grasp the nettle and act.

To be fair, he never enjoyed good relations with Edward Heath. Their styles were so dissimilar. Dick worshipped Harold Macmillan, and the grand old man had a very high regard for his chief of Intelligence. Similarly, he got on well with Harold Wilson. They shared a suppleness of mind, and Wilson appreciated Dick's reassuring and comforting manner on vexed issues such as Rhodesia. But Heath was a thrusting, hectoring man, quite alien to anything Dick had encountered before, and he found himself increasingly unable to stamp his personality on the Prime Minister.

Victor and I went through all the options, even at one point considering whether we could run Victor himself as an alternative candidate. I knew he had secretly hankered after the job for years, but although his appointment would have been a brilliant and popular one, he knew he was too old, and in any case, the Think Tank was the real challenge for a man of his intellectual horizons.

We discussed casting around for support in the scientific community, and we decided that Victor would approach people like Sir William Cook to gain their support for Hanley. Victor also told me he would contrive a safe meeting with Heath.

"It's no good bringing it up formally at No. 10," he told me. "As soon as Robert Armstrong sees it, or hears of it, word will get back to the bloody Permanent Under Secretaries!"

Robert Armstrong, Heath's Principal Private Secretary (today Cabinet Secretary and head of the Home Civil Service), was a key figure in the power struggle, since no one else had closer or more continuous access to Heath. Any hint of special pleading by Victor would certainly be reported by him to the Permanent Secretaries' Committee. Victor decided that the best plan was to get to Heath in an unguarded moment when Armstrong was not there. The best opportunity was the next Think Tank weekend conference, scheduled for Chequers in a few weeks' time.

"I'll take Ted out for a walk in the garden, where Robert can't hear, and I'll bend his ear . . ."

As it happened, I was beginning to see a good deal of Robert Armstrong myself. I had recently been reviewing the American VENONA, and one unidentified cryptonym in particular had begun to interest me. It appeared in the traffic as "Agent Number 19." Agent 19 was clearly a very important Soviet asset, who passed over details of a succession of significant wartime discussions between Churchill and Roosevelt during the Trident Talks in June 1943.

The Americans had assumed the identity of Agent 19 was Eduard Beneš, the former Czechoslovakian President, whose reward for a lifetime's work as a Soviet stooge was to be toppled from power ignominiously in 1948. Beneš attended the Trident Talks, and was well known as a conduit of intelligence to the Russians. However, when I looked at the text of the messages themselves, I became distinctly skeptical about this explanation. The conversations Agent 19 was reporting were clearly informal discussions between Churchill and Roosevelt about plans for the Second Front, and in particular naval and shipping dispositions. It struck me as improbable that Beneš would have been permitted into these discussions, especially since Czechoslovakia had no ships at all, being a landlocked country.

I began to wonder if Agent 19 were perhaps someone closer to home. The first task was to locate any available British records of the meetings between Roosevelt and Churchill at the Trident Talks to see if I could find a record of the particular meeting referred to by Agent 19 and, if possible, a list of who attended it.

The search for the phantom Trident discussion was quite the most bizarre experience of my career. Victor arranged for me to meet Robert Armstrong. He was keen to help. He was a fast-rising mandarin, already tipped as a future Cabinet Secretary, and since he would need the support of the intelligence community to obtain the job, he was anxious to build up friendly relations. He threw himself boyishly into the task of searching No. 10 Downing Street for any available records. But after several weeks we drew a blank.

Armstrong suggested I call on Lord Ismay, Churchill's former Chief of Staff, and Sir John Colville, his former Private Secretary, but although both men remembered the Trident Talks, they had not been present at these particular discussions. I tried Mary Churchill, but she had no records either. Lastly, Armstrong arranged for me to see Martin Gilbert, Churchill's historian. For each day Churchill was Prime Minister, one of his private secretaries kept a record of his engagements and Gilbert had all the volumes. Perhaps here there would be a record. I gave Gilbert the relevant date, and he searched through the indexed diaries.

"Good God," he said, "the diary for that date is blank!"

The search for Agent 19 had run into the sand, and it remains unsolved to this day.

The row over the succession to F.J. fell at the height of my search for Agent 19, so I suggested to Victor that I, rather than he, sound out Robert Armstrong. It was important to maintain Victor's position of neutrality, but no one could blame me for partisanship in the matter of the succession. On my next visit to No. 10 I made a light reference to the fears inside MI5. He smiled.

"The cards are stacked against you," he said. "I don't think it's worth pushing on this one."

I told him that if the wise men were intent on Waddell, they were making a mistake.

"We aren't being civil servants," I told him, "and Waddell will be out of his depth in the job . . . he'll play it too much by the rules."

Armstrong betrayed little himself, beyond telling me what I already knew, that the Permanent Secretaries were firmly behind Waddell.

"They just want to reward him, and they can't find him a top job in any of the other ministries!" I said bitterly.

Armstrong laughed.

"Oh no, Peter, we're not that conspiratorial!"

A few weeks later I saw Victor again. He had managed to have his talk with Heath in the sunshine at Chequers, and he told him of the strong resistance inside MI5 to the appointment of an outsider. Heath was sympathetic, but explained that he would have to have a very good reason to reject unanimous Civil Service advice. But eventually Victor managed to persuade him to interview both candidates personally.

It was a major breakthrough. We were all certain that Hanley would impress Heath with the force of his personality, whereas Waddell's diffidence would be sure to tell against him. When Hanley got the news his demeanor changed. He could see events were moving in his direction. Rather pompously he came into my office and told me that he was to see the Prime Minister the following day.

"And I don't need a briefing, thank you very much."

I thought the announcement would come quickly, but the days passed and we heard nothing. Throughout the Whitehall village, antennae were out to catch signs of a result. On every visit I made to the Home Office I checked on the latest state of play. But there was no news, apart from the insistent refrain: "Philip Allen will not have Hanley at any price."

At the weekend my wife and I traveled to Dolgellau in Wales, to buy cows at an auction for the farm we had recently purchased in Cornwall for our retirement. Ever since Hollis' interrogation, and my departure from D3, I had begun planning a return to agriculture, and a less painful future away from the whispering corridors and paper mountains of MI5. Whitehall was the last thing on my mind as the auctioneer rattled on in an impenetrable Welsh dialect. Steers and heifers were slapped in and out of the small crowded ring, their owners croaking and whistling to keep their animals alert.

Suddenly across the loudspeaker I heard a voice.

"Can Mr. Wright from London please come to the office for a telephone call . . ."

I struggled to make my way through the crowded terrace, past a hundred tightly pressed Welsh farmers each craning for a view of the ring. Eventually I reached the tiny office and picked up the telephone. It was Victor.

"Do you know what the buggers done now?" he roared.

"What are you talking about, Victor?"

"They've switched horses. They want to appoint some chap called Graham Harrison. Does the name mean anything to you?"

"They will never accept him," I yelled back. "The man was a friend of Burgess and Maclean."

I suddenly remembered where I was. But I had no need to worry. The auctioneer's clerk continued to work on his figures, oblivious to my conversation. I told Victor I would call on him as soon as I got back to London.

Francis Graham Harrison was also a deputy secretary at the Home Office. Although there was no suggestion that he was a spy, he was a close friend of Guy Burgess, and had moved in the Oxford set which included Jennifer Hart and Arthur Wynn. To appoint a man with those connections would have been, to borrow F.J.'s phrase, grotesque, and I told Victor that the Service would never wear it.

Early the following week Victor rang again.

"An announcement will be made tomorrow," he said. "I think you will be pleased . . ."

"How did you swing it?"

"I took Dick by the ear and took him in to see Ted. We both told him there would be a mutiny unless he appointed Hanley. He soon got the point!"

The next day F.J. summoned in a couple of the senior officers to tell us that Hanley had finally been appointed.

"It's been a difficult campaign," he told me gravely, "but I have finally won through."

"I am very pleased to hear that, sir," I replied with a straight face.

Shortly before F.J. retired he and I had a short meeting to discuss the looming situation in Northern Ireland. It was clearly going to be the major problem facing his successor. He feared that it would threaten all that he had done since 1965 to build up MI5's counterespionage capability. He had lobbied the Treasury to provide more resources, but they had refused. They wanted

F.J. to shift resources away from counterespionage and into
counterterrorism. As far as they were concerned, the expulsion of
the 105 diplomats had eradicated the KGB threat for a generation. But F.J. believed that complacency was precisely the way to
fritter away the advantage he had achieved.

F.J. looked tired, as if he longed to put the burdens aside. He
was a man of few words but I could tell he wanted to talk. He was
glad to be going, he said. The pleasure of the work had all but
disappeared. He was worried, too, about money. Although he
cultivated the air of a gentleman, he was not a wealthy man. He
had an attractive house in Hampstead, but he had a young daughter still to educate, and he talked bitterly of having to sell himself
in the marketplace as a security consultant, when he should be
retiring to his beloved bird-watching. (In fact, he became a
consultant to Imperial Chemical Industries [ICI].)

"Well, how do you think I've done?" he asked me as he
cleaned his pipe, sucking and scraping at it almost nervously.

"What, you want to know, honestly?" I asked.

He nodded.

"You got on top of the Russian problem, but I don't think you
ever made contact with the ordinary officer."

He looked surprisingly wounded. "You should have told me,"
he said.

"I'm sorry. I didn't feel it was my place."

I always liked F.J. and I think most of the senior officers did
too. He was never a wag, but he saw the absurdity of life and his
profession. I will always treasure traveling to Australia with him
for the first CAZAB conference in 1967. As we approached the
passport barrier a party of ASIO officials was waiting to meet us
on the other side. F.J. handed in his passport.

"What's this?" drawled the passport officer, pointing to the
entry in F.J.'s passport under "Occupation."

F.J. had entered "Gentleman."

"That is my occupation," uttered F.J. in his most patrician

manner, "I have no other. I am a gentleman. Don't you have them here?"

The Australian drew himself up to his full height, but luckily I had managed to attract the attention of the ASIO party, who hurriedly explained the situation and whisked us both through to the other side. F.J. beamed for the rest of the day, as if he had won a great team match single-handed.

F.J. ran the office as a democracy of the elect. If you were a trusted senior officer, his door was always open, his manner always familiar. But he remained a remote figure to the younger generation of officers, and he was consequently blind to many of the resentments, which were building up below.

Few in Whitehall mourned his passing. At the height of the row over his succession, he offered to stay on another year to give Hanley extra time to play himself in as deputy. But the Home Office would have none of it. He told the truth and politicians and civil servants hated him for it. He also kept the secrets, and that made him an object of fear and suspicion.

Within a year Dick White had also left, and British Intelligence had lost its two most important executives. Their contribution is hard to overvalue. They were a perfect match. Dick was the subtle interpreter of intelligence, smoothing feelings in Whitehall and Downing Street; F.J. was the tough man, sounding warnings and bringing bad news.

I broke with them on only one issue in twenty years—high-level penetration. I think history will judge that they were never prepared to force the issue through. Consequently they allowed decisions to go unmade and the issue to fester so that it caused more damage than it ever need have done. But in other ways their contribution was massive. They became a link between the Old and the New World, and together they made British Intelligence respected throughout the world.

23 —————————————————

HANLEY SEEMED ILL AT EASE WHEN HE FIRST MOVED INTO THE Director-General's office. He knew he was a controversial appointment, and this made him move with a greater degree of caution than ought otherwise to have been the case. He wanted to please and reassure his political and Whitehall masters, and he made compromises a more secure man might not have.

Hanley was a bright man, intellectually superior to F.J. But he lacked F.J.'s strength of character. I didn't have faith in him, as I had in F.J., and my separation from the office began once F.J. left. The Service began to change and those last four years were an extended farewell.

At first the changes were slight—silly things, like the fact that Hanley, unlike F.J., never offered lifts in his chauffeured car. But then they were more pronounced. We moved offices from Leconfield House, first to Marlborough Street and then to the drab premises on Gower Street. I suggested to Hanley that we go for a greenfield site, perhaps in Cheltenham, but he was insistent that we had to stay in London. He began to promote his own men. They were young and keen, but they were civil servants: men of safety rather than men of arms. I began to realize that a generation was passing. For all our differences, those of us involved in the great mole hunts, on whichever side, were fast disappearing. The age of heroes was being replaced by the age of mediocrity.

Hanley summoned me in soon after taking over to talk about my position.

"I have faith in you, Peter, and as long as I am in this job, there will be work for you here," he told me, referring to the rising resentment which had plagued my last year in D3.

He told me he thought I should leave my job as K Branch consultant, and come and work for him personally.

"I want you as my personal consultant on counterespionage," he told me. "You'll have an office next to mine, and you'll see every paper as before. But I want you to look at some fresh problems for me. I don't want you wrapped up in the current K Branch cases—I want you to be looking ahead."

We drew up a new agenda, some of it to my liking, other parts not. He wanted me to continue to control the VENONA program, and agreed that we should finally initiate a comprehensive worldwide search for any remaining traffic.

He wanted me to look at Northern Ireland.

"I need one of your bright ideas, Peter," he told me, "see what you can do . . ."

He wanted me to sit on the Computer Working Party, which was planning the transition of the MI5 Registry into the computer age, a leap into the future due to take place in the mid-1970s. D3 had given me a special insight into the use of the Registry to trace leads, and he wanted me to apply these techniques to computerization.

At first I thought Ireland might give me a new lease on life. I made a couple of trips. It reminded me a lot of Cyprus. A fierce, insoluble conflict made worse by a vacillating British policy. At the time I first went, the Government were telling the world that the situation was getting better. I spent a fortnight reviewing the records of all explosions over a twelve-month period. I drew a graph and proved conclusively that the weight of explosives being detonated was a steeply ascending curve. So much for an improved security situation! But, as in Cyprus, the Army and the politicians simply refused to face reality.

The only major recommendation I made was that we should devise a system to tapping the telephone lines of the Irish Republic. Lines across the border were well covered, but vital Provisional IRA communications flowed back and forth from the west coast of the Republic to Dublin. I devised a scheme for intercepting the microwaves from the attic of the British Embassy in Dublin using a device no larger than a packing case, but although MI5 endorsed the plan, the Foreign Office vetoed it. This was in the period leading up to what became the Sunningdale Agreement, and the Foreign Office were terrified that news of the plan might leak. I pointed out to them that the basic lesson from Cyprus had been the inherent instability of political solutions negotiated without a decisive security advantage, but they would not listen. It was no surprise to me when Sunningdale collapsed.

I lost heart once the Dublin scheme fell through. It seemed to me a measure of how far the bureaucrats had taken control. Twenty years before, we would have tackled it without any worries at all. I did suggest examining the possibilities of planting booby-trapped detonators on the Provisionals. It would have been a feasible operation in conjunction with MI6, along the same lines as the Cyprus plan to plant fake receivers on Grivas. But even the MI5 management took fright, and refused to investigate the plan any further.

"That's murder," I was told.

"Innocent people are being killed and maimed every day," I said.

"Which policy do you think the British people would like us to pursue?"

The Irish situation was only one part of a decisive shift inside MI5 toward domestic concerns. The growth of student militancy in the 1960s gave way to industrial militancy in the early 1970s. The miners' strike of 1972, and a succession of stoppages in the

motorcar industry, had a profound effect on the thinking of the
Heath Government. Intelligence on domestic subversion became
the overriding priority.

This is the most sensitive area a Director-General of MI5 can
get into, and it requires a strong man to maintain his own independence and that of the Service. Hanley, through the circumstances of his appointment, was ill-equipped to deal with this
pressure. Whereas F.G. was always a champion of MI5's independence, Hanley resolved to do what his masters wanted, and he
set about providing them with as professional and extensive a
source of domestic intelligence as was possible.

Traditionally, K Branch was MI5's prestige department and F
Branch its poor relation, shunned by the brightest officers, and
run shambolically by an amiable tippler. But Hanley began to
pour resources and men into F Branch and away from K Branch.
A whole string of brilliant counterespionage officers, including
Michael McCaul, was lost forever.

The most significant pointer to this change occurred after I
retired, when Sir John Jones was appointed Director-General in
1981. He was the rising star of F Branch in Hanley's new reorganization, and when he secured the top job he was the first Director-General since Hollis to have achieved it without any personal
counterespionage experience. He was an F Branch man through
and through, and his appointment perfectly illustrated the decisive shift in MI5's center of gravity.

Early on in his tenure as Director-General, Hanley called a
meeting of senior staff in A Branch and F Branch to discuss the
changing shape of MI5's priorities. The meeting began with a
presentation from Hanley on the climate of subversion in the
country, and the growth of what he termed the "far and wide
left." The Prime Minister and the Home Office, he said, had left
him in no doubt that they wanted a major increase in effort on
this target. He then handed over to a young and ambitious F
Branch officer, David Ransome, who outlined the activities and

structure of a host of left-wing splinter groups, like the Workers' Revolutionary Party (WRP) and the Socialist Workers' Party (SWP).

Hanley loved seminars, and the meeting went on for most of the day. The F Branch people wanted a relaxation in the restrictions governing the use of telephone taps and letter intercepts, and a much closer relationship with the Post Office. The enemy was diffuse, and its communications so widespread, that this was the only way they could get to grips with the problem. John Jones was a forceful advocate. F Branch needed all the technical resources currently at the disposal of K Branch, he claimed. Agent running was no longer viable as the principal means of coverage. For a start, he could not infiltrate his officers into these left-wing groups since many of them lived promiscuous lives, and there were some sacrifices even an MI5 officer would not make for his country. If, on the other hand, he recruited agents, there was obviously a much higher risk of publicity and scandal. The only answer was to use massive technical resources. I could see from Hanley's face that he agreed.

I, on the other hand, pushed the value of agents.

"Use agents if you want to keep an eye on these groups," I told Hanley later in private, "you'll be storing up problems for the future if you commit all our technical resources against them. The Post Office can't in the end be trusted as much as our own people. It's bound to go wrong."

It was the same with the Computer Working Party. I soon realized that the main interest F Branch had in the Computer Working Party was to establish widespread computer links, principally with the National Insurance computer in Newcastle. In the past, of course, we had always been able to get material from the National Insurance records if we really wanted it. We had a couple of undercover officers posted up there who could be contacted for our files. But establishing a direct computer link was something completely different.

I was not alone among the old guard, anti-Soviet officers in being disturbed by these new developments. We could see all that we had worked to achieve frittered away chasing these minor left-wing groupings. But more than that, the move into the computer generation signaled the relegation of the role of the individual officer. From now on we were to be data processors, scanning tens of thousands of names at the press of a button.

"The fun has gone" was a sentiment I heard more and more in those last few years.

Hanley himself was unable to grasp the difficulties he was getting himself into. It was easy to believe that we had the public's consent when we broke into a Soviet diplomat's house. But the wholesale surveillance of a large proportion of the population raised more than a question mark. "Big Brother" loomed.

Veterans of D Branch viewed groups like the WRP, SWP, and Campaign for Nuclear Disarmament (CND) as largely irrelevant pieces of the jigsaw. Certainly an eye should be kept on them, but we were quite satisfied they were not the major objects of KGB attack. These were the Intelligence Services, the Civil Service, and increasingly in the 1960s, the trade unions and the Labor Party.

Since the 1960s a wealth of material about the penetration of the latter two bodies had been flowing into MI5's files, principally from two Czechoslovakian defectors named Frolik and August. They named a series of Labor Party politicians and trade union leaders as Eastern Bloc agents. Some were certainly well founded, like the case of the MP Will Owen, who admitted being paid thousands of pounds over a ten-year period to provide information to Czechoslovakian intelligence officers, and yet, when he was prosecuted in 1970, was acquitted because it was held that he had not had access to classified information, and because the Czech defector could not produce documentary evidence of what he had said at the trial.

Tom Driberg was another MP named by the Czech defectors.

I went to see Driberg myself, and he finally admitted that he was providing material to a Czech controller for money. For a while we ran Driberg on, but apart from picking up a mass of salacious detail about Labor Party peccadilloes, he had nothing of interest for us.

His only lasting story concerned the time he lent a Cabinet Minister his flat so that the Minister could try and conduct an affair in strict privacy. Driberg was determined to find the identity of the woman who was the recipient of the Minister's favors, and one evening after the Minister had vacated, he searched the flat and found a letter addressed to a prominent female member of the Labor Party. Driberg claimed to be horrified by his discovery and raised it with the Minister concerned, suggesting that he ought to be more careful in case word of his activities ever became public! Since Driberg was certainly providing the same stories to his Czech friends, his concern for Labor Party confidentiality seemed hollow, to say the least.

John Stonehouse was another MP who the Czech defectors claimed was working for them, but after he was interviewed in the presence of Harold Wilson, and denied all the charges, the MI5 objections against him were withdrawn.

This was the context which shaped the fraught relations between MI5 and the Prime Minister for much of this period. Much has been written about Harold Wilson and MI5, some of it wildly inaccurate. But as far as I am concerned, the story started with the premature death of Hugh Gaitskell in 1963. Gaitskell was Wilson's predecessor as Leader of the Labor Party. I knew him personally and admired him greatly. I had met him and his family at the Blackwater Sailing Club, and I recall about a month before he died he told me that he was going to Russia.

After he died his doctor got in touch with MI5 and asked to see somebody from the Service. Arthur Martin, as the head of Russian Counterespionage, went to see him. The doctor explained that he was disturbed by the manner of Gaitskell's death.

He said that Gaitskell had died of a disease called lupus disseminata, which attacks the body's organs. He said that it was rare in temperate climates and that there was no evidence that Gaitskell had been anywhere recently where he could have contracted the disease.

Arthur Martin suggested that I should go to Porton Down, the chemical and microbiological laboratory for the Ministry of Defense. I went to see the chief doctor in the chemical warfare laboratory, Dr. Ladell, and asked his advice. He said that nobody knew how one contracted lupus. There was some suspicion that it might be a form of fungus and he did not have the foggiest idea how one would infect somebody with the disease. I came back and made my report in these terms.

The next development was that Golitsin told us quite independently that during the last few years of his service he had had some contacts with Department 13, which was known as the Department of Wet Affairs in the KGB. This department was responsible for organizing assassinations. He said that just before he left he knew that the KGB were planning a high-level political assassination in Europe in order to get their man into the top place. He did not know which country it was planned in but he pointed out that the chief of Department 13 was a man called General Rodin, who had been in Britain for many years and had just returned on promotion to take up the job, so he would have had good knowledge of the political scene in England.

We did not know where to go next because Ladell had said that it wasn't known how the disease was contracted. I consulted Jim Angleton about the problem. He said that he would get a search made of Russian scientific papers to see whether there there was any hint of what the Russians knew about the disease. A month or two later he sent us a paper about lupus which he had had translated from a Russian scientific journal. The paper was several years old and Angleton reported that there were no other papers in the Russian literature that they could find. This paper described the use of a special chemical which the Russians had found would induce lupus in experimental rats. However, it was unlikely that this particular chemical could have been used to murder Gaitskell because the quantities required to produce lupus were considerable and had to be given repeatedly. I took the paper to Ladell and, while surprised by this area of Soviet expertise, he confirmed that it was unlikely that Gaitskell could have been poisoned by the coffee and biscuits. But he pointed out that the paper was seven years old and if the Russians had continued to work on it they might have found a much better form of the chemical which would require much smaller doses and perhaps work as a one-shot drug. He told me there was no way of proving it without doing a lot of scientific work and Porton was unable to do the necessary work as it was already overloaded.

I said I would take the matter home and discuss it with my management. Once again I wrote an account of what Ladell had said and confirmed its accuracy with him personally. Back in MI5 we discussed the problem at length in the office and it was agreed that nothing could be done unless we had further evidence of the Russians' using such a drug to assassinate people. Over the next few years I watched out for any evidence and asked Ladell also to watch out for it. Needless to say we had no further example of anybody who was in a vulnerable position dying of lupus. However, if there was a high-level leak in MI5 to the Russians, they would have been informed of our suspicions and I am sure they would have ensured that no other case came our way.

Harold Wilson meanwhile had become Prime Minister. It was inevitable that Wilson would come to the attention of MI5. Before he became Prime Minister he worked for an East-West trading organization and paid many visits to Russia. MI5, well aware that the KGB will stop at nothing to entrap or frame visitors, were concerned that he should be well aware of the risk of being compromised by the Russians. When Wilson succeeded Gaitskell as Leader of the Labor Party, there was a further source of friction between himself and MI5. He began to surround himself with other East European émigré businessmen, some of whom had themselves been the subject of MI5's inquiries.

After Harold Wilson became Prime Minister in 1964, Angleton made a special trip to England to see F.J., who was then director of counterespionage. Angleton came to offer us some very secret information from a source he would not name. This source alleged, according to Angleton, that Wilson was a Soviet agent. He said he would give us more detailed evidence and information if we could guarantee to keep the information inside MI5 and out of political circles. The accusation was totally incredible, but given the fact that Angleton was head of the CIA's Counterintelligence Division, we had no choice but to take it seriously. Not surprisingly the management of MI5 were deeply disturbed by the manner in which Angleton passed this information over. After consideration, they refused to accept Angleton's restrictions on the use to which we could put the information, and as a result we were not told anything more. However, Angleton's approach was recorded in the files under the code name Oatsheaf.

After Hollis retired and Furnival Jones became Director-General, I went to F.J. and said I was paying a visit to the USA and asked whether I should tackle Angleton on the Oatsheaf information, with a view to getting more details. He said that I could, but again insisted that we could not give Angleton any guarantee about any information which he gave us. I tackled Angleton in Washington. He put up a vintage performance. There were dark mutterings about "clandestine meetings" with the Russians. But when he was pushed for details, there were none, and I knew from bitter experience that Angleton was more than capable of manufacturing evidence when none existed.

But if the Oatsheaf affair was nothing more than a diversion, by the end of the 1960s information was coming to MI5's attention which suggested that there almost certainly was Soviet penetration of the Labor Party. First the Czechoslovakian defectors,

Frolik and August, arrived in the West and named a series of Labor MPs and trade unionists as successful recruits. Then we received the most damaging information of all from Oleg Lyalin. While Lyalin was still in place, he told MI5 about a friend of his called Vaygaukas. Vaygaukas was a KGB officer working under cover in the Soviet Trade Delegation in London. Lyalin told us that Vaygaukas had claimed to him to be in contact with a man called Joseph Kagan, a Lithuanian émigré who was a close friend of Harold Wilson's. Kagan had helped finance Wilson's private office, and had even lent him an aircraft during elections, and Wilson had been much photographed wearing Kagan's raincoats, which he manufactured in a factory near Leeds.

Inevitably MI5 were extremely anxious to discover whether or not Kagan had any relationship with Vaygaukas. We placed him under intensive surveillance and attempted to recruit agents inside his factory. Then, following the expulsion of the 105 Soviet diplomats in 1971, we finally got the opportunity to discuss the matter with both men. Harold Wilson, by then out of office, approached Sir Arthur Young, head of the City of London police and a consultant to one of Kagan's companies. Wilson asked to be put in touch with MI5 because he wished to discuss Kagan. Furnival Jones thought this approach bizarre, but agreed to send Harry Wharton, who was then handling Lyalin. Wharton briefed Wilson on Lyalin's information about Kagan's alleged dealings with Vaygaukas. Wilson told him bluntly that he knew nothing about it and had never discussed confidential matters with Kagan at any time. Kagan himself later admitted meeting Vaygaukas for chess games, but strenuously denied that any espionage was involved.

Wilson interpreted MI5's interest as a crude attempt to smear the Labor Party and him. But once the Conservative Government came into power they began to take a great interest in the material as well. Victor often used to complain to me about the quality of the intelligence reports No. 10 received from F Branch.

"They pull their punches all the time," he would say, "can't you give us something better?"

In 1972 he told me that Heath had been appalled at a recent Cabinet meeting, which was addressed by Jack Jones and Hugh Scanlon, the two powerful trade union bosses of the early 1970s.

"Ted thought they talked like Communists," he said. "I asked F Branch if they had anything, but of course they've got nothing substantial."

He knew from gossip that the recent Czech defectors were providing material about trade union and Labor Party subversion, and began pumping me for the details. I told him to minute me formally with a request and I would see what I could do. Later that day I got Victor's minute.

"The Prime Minister is anxious to see . . ." he began, in typical Victor style.

I sent Victor's note to F.J. for guidance. He returned it to me with a handwritten message in the margin: "Tell him what he wants to know!"

I drew the files, and began patiently to compose a lengthy brief on the intelligence provided by Frolik and August. I drew no conclusions, but neither did I leave anything out.

The whole of Whitehall came thundering down on my head. I was summoned by Sir John Hunt, the Cabinet Secretary, who asked what on earth I thought I was doing passing material about an opposition party into the government party's hands at such a delicate time.

I defended myself as vigorously as I could. It was not a question of politics. The head of the Central Policy Review Staff had requested a briefing, and I had given it to him and it had been approved by DGSS. It was not my fault if the material was unpalatable or embarrassing.

"If we refused to circulate intelligence because it was embarrassing, there would be little purpose in our sending anything at all!"

Both F.J. and Victor supported me loyally throughout. Victor relished the row and composed a series of elegant memorandums which winged their way through Whitehall defending the Security Service's right to provide intelligence requested of it by No. 10 Downing Street. Philip Allen was outraged by his flagrant flouting of Home Office prerogative, and refused to speak to me for years. To Victor he sent a terse note which he showed me gleefully. "Keep off the grass," thundered Allen ominously.

One afternoon, at the height of the row, I was in Victor's room in the Cabinet Office when Ted Heath put his head around the door.

"Prime Minister," said Victor, "I think you should meet Peter Wright, he is one of the stranger phenomena in Whitehall . . ."

Heath looked humorlessly over in my direction, and asked me where I worked.

"The Security Service , sir," I replied.

He grunted.

"Peter is responsible for the briefing on subversion which is currently causing the problem," said Victor cheerfully.

Heath immediately fixed me with a steely glare.

"You should not be indulging in politics," he glowered, "there are mechanisms for this sort of material."

He turned on his heel and stalked out.

"Christ, Victor," I said.

"Don't worry," replied Victor, "Ted's always like that. I'll talk to him later."

The following day Victor rang up. He told me Heath had devoured the briefing that night.

"Is this true, Victor?" he asked in amazement, and when told it was, redoubled his crusade to remain in power.

But not all the requests for information were legitimate. One evening Victor invited me around for drinks at St. James's Place.

"There's a businessman I think you should meet," he told me. "He is a wealthy industrialist."

I had been discussing retirement with Victor at the time. In 1972 I finally learned that the promise MI5 had made to me in 1955 about my pension was not to be honored. In order to join the Service I had been forced to give up fifteen years of pension rights with the Admiralty. At the time Cumming had talked smoothly of ex-gratia payments, and ways the Service could iron out these problems. But in the new, gray MI5 a gentleman's agreement was a thing of the past. According to the rules, I had no case for a pension, even though every scientist who joined the Intelligence Services after me (some fifty in number) was able to transfer his pension, largely through my pressure to rectify the inequity.

It was a bitter blow, and did much to sour my last few years in the Service. Inevitably I thought about the possibility of security work. It did not greatly appeal to me, but it seemed a stable way of propping up my savagely depleted pension. At first Victor and I discussed my joining N.M. Rothschild, but Hanley was unhappy about the proposal, so when Victor heard that this businessman was looking for someone to do security work, he suggested a meeting.

I took an instant dislike to the man. It was clear to me that he was on the make. Over drinks he talked loosely about needing advice and guidance from someone "in the know" without quite spelling out what he meant, or how much he was prepared to pay for it. Eventually he suggested I lunch with him and some colleagues at a London hotel to discuss his proposition in more detail.

His colleagues were a ramshackle bunch. They were retired people from various branches of intelligence and security organizations whose best years were well behind them. There were others, too, mainly businessmen who seemed thrilled to be in the same room as spies, and did not seem to care how out of date they were.

This time my would-be employer came straight to the point.

"We represent a group of people who are worried about the future of the country," he intoned.

He had something of the look of Angleton on a bad night about him. He said they were interested in working to prevent the return of a Labor government to power.

"It could spell the end of all the freedoms we know and cherish," he said.

The others nodded.

"And how do you suppose I can help?" I asked.

"Information," he replied, "we want information, and I am assured you have it."

"What precisely are you after?" I inquired.

"Anything on Wilson would be helpful. There are many people who would pay handsomely for material of that sort."

"But I am a serving member of the Security Service . . ." I began.

He waved his hand imperiously.

"Retire early. We can arrange something . . ."

I played along for the rest of the evening, but gave nothing away. The following day I went to see Hanley and told him what had happened. I suggested that I continue to monitor the group's activities as an agent, but Hanley thought discretion was a better policy.

"Leave it alone, Peter," he said, "it's a dirty game, and you're well out of it."

Hanley knew little about the material which had been gathered on Wilson and the Labor Party during the 1960s, so I encouraged him to study it. Elections were in the offing, and it could become relevant again, I told him.

"It's like FLUENCY," he said when he had read the files, "there's lots of smoke, but not a lot of fire."

Nevertheless, he agreed that it was prudent to reexamine the material. Angleton, in particular, was beginning to badger us constantly about Wilson, and I told Hanley it would be politic to be seen to be doing something.

As events moved to their political climax in early 1974, with the election of the minority Labor Government, MI5 was sitting on information which, if leaked, would undoubtedly have caused a political scandal of incalculable consequences. The news that the Prime Minister himself was being investigated would at the least have led to his resignation. The point was not lost on some MI5 officers.

One afternoon I was in my office when two colleagues came in. They were with three or four other officers. I closed the file I was working on and asked them how I could help.

"We understand you've reopened the Wilson case," said the senior one.

"You know I can't talk about that," I told him.

I felt a bit lame, but then I did not much enjoyed being cornered in my own office.

"Wilson's a bloody menace," said one of the younger officers, "and it's about time the public knew the truth."

It was not the first time I had heard that particular sentiment. Feelings had run high inside MI5 during 1968. There had been an effort to try to stir up trouble for Wilson then, largely because the *Daily Mirror* tycoon, Cecil King, who was a longtime agent of ours, made it clear that he would publish anything MI5 might care to leak in his direction. It was all part of Cecil King's "coup," which he was convinced would bring down the Labor Government and replace it with a coalition led by Lord Mountbatten.

I told F.J. in 1968 that feelings were running high, but he responded in a low-key manner.

"You can tell anyone who has ideas about leaking classified material that there will be nothing I can do to save them!"

He knew the message would get back.

But the approach in 1974 was altogether more serious. The plan was simple. In the run-up to the election which, given the level of instability in Parliament, must be due within a matter of months, MI5 would arrange for selective details of the intelligence about leading Labor Party figures, but especially Wilson, to be leaked to sympathetic pressmen. Using our contacts in the press and among union officials, word of the material contained in MI5 files and the fact that Wilson was considered a security risk would be passed around.

Soundings in the office had already been taken, and up to thirty officers had given their approval to the scheme. Facsimile copies of some files were to be made and distributed to overseas newspapers, and the matter was to be raised in Parliament for maximum effect. It was a carbon copy of the Zinoviev letter, which had done so much to destroy the first Ramsay MacDonald Government in 1928.

"We'll have him out," said one of them, "this time we'll have him out."

"But why do you need me?" I asked.

"Well, you don't like Wilson any more than we do . . . besides, you've got access to the latest files—the Gaitskell business, and all the rest of it."

"But they're kept in the DG's safe!"

"Yes, but you could copy them."

"I need some time to think," I pleaded. "I've got a lot to think about before I take a step like this. You'll have to give me a couple of days."

At first I was tempted. The devil makes work for idle hands, and I was playing out my time before retirement. A mad scheme like this was bound to tempt me. I felt an irresistible urge to lash out. The country seemed on the brink of catastrophe. Why not give it a little push? In any case, I carried the burden of so many secrets that lightening the load a little could only make things easier for me.

It was Victor who talked me out of it.

"I don't like Wilson any more than you do," he told me, "but you'll end up getting chopped if you go in for this."

He was right. I had little more than a year to go. Why destroy everything in a moment of madness?

A few days later I told the leader of the group that I would not get the files.

"I'd like to help you," I told him, "but I can't risk it. I've only got half a pension as it is. I can't afford to lose it all."

Some of the operational people became quite aggressive. They kept saying it was the last chance to fix Wilson.

"Once you've retired," they said, "we'll never get the files!"

But my mind was made up, and even their taunts of cowardice could not shake me.

Throughout the rest of 1974 and early 1975 I kept out of the country as much as possible, chasing VENONA traffic throughout the world. Although the full Wilson story never emerged, it was obvious to me that the boys had been actively pushing their plan as much as they could. No wonder Wilson was later to claim that he was the victim of a plot!

In the summer of 1975 I dined with Maurice Oldfield at Locketts. We regularly met for dinner. He was a lonely man, and liked nothing better than a good gossip at the end of the day. He finally made it to the top of MI6 after two abortive attempts, and I was happy for him. Maurice was a good man, but inclined to meddle. That night I could tell something was on his mind.

He turned the conversation to Wilson. How high had feelings been running there? he asked. He kept hearing all sorts of rumors.

I was noncommittal.

"Most of us don't like him. They think he's wrecking the country."

Maurice was clearly preoccupied with the subject, because he returned to it again and again.

"You're not telling me the truth," he said finally.

"I'm not with you, Maurice . . ."

"I was called in by the Prime Minister yesterday," he said, his tone suddenly changing. "He was talking about a plot. Apparently he's heard that your boys have been going around town stirring things up about him and Marcia Falkender, and Communists at No.10."

He trailed away as if it were all too distasteful for him.

"It's serious, Peter," he began again, "I need to know everything. Look what's happening in Washington with Watergate. The same thing will happen here unless we're very careful."

I ordered another brandy and decided to tell him everything I knew. When I had finished describing the plans of the previous summer he asked me if Hanley knew.

"No," I replied, "I thought it best just to forget the whole thing."

"I want you to go back to the office tomorrow and tell him everything."

Maurice tottered up to bed.

"Don't worry," he called back over his shoulder.

"I won't," I said, "I've only got a few months to go!"

When I saw Hanley the next morning, we went white as a sheet. He might have suspected that feelings against Wilson ran high in the office, but now he was learning that half of his staff were up to their necks in a plot to get rid of the Prime Minister. It was at times like that I was glad I never climbed the executive ladder.

Ironically, his first reaction was anger with Maurice.

"Bloody Maurice!" he raged. "Poking his nose into our business!"

When he had calmed down he asked me for the names.

I gave them. Having come so far, I could not very well refuse. As I reeled them off, I knew suddenly what Blunt had felt like. It was never easy to put on the mask and point the finger.

"Look after them, won't you?" I asked Hanley.

"There will have to be an inquiry, of course," he replied.

I left before the Wilson story ended, and Hanley and I never discussed it again. I heard that a member of the Security Commission was called in to make a private inquiry for the Cabinet Office, and it has since been reported that Hanley made a number of changes, mainly in the field of recruitment, with a view to introducing new blood into MI5. This presumably explains the cryptic letter I received from Michael Hanley shortly after I retired to Australia.

"You'll be pleased to note," he wrote, "that the firm has passed its recent examinations, and is doing rather well!"

Shortly afterward Wilson resigned. As we always used to say in the office: "Politicians may come and go, but the Security Service goes on forever."

The shambles surrounding Harold Wilson blew up just as the Hollis affair flickered briefly back into life in 1974. The case had remained buried since his interrogation in 1969. Originally I was hopeful that Hanley might revive things when he took over, but I could soon see that he took the view that sleeping dogs should lie. He had a deep desire to put the traumas of the past behind him, and was anxious to separate me as far as possible from current investigations and K Branch cases.

"I've got an open mind," he used to tell me whenever I raised the question.

Fear of scandal became the most important consideration affecting everyone with responsibility for the turmoil of the 1960s, now that there was a growing certainty that whatever the problem had been, it was at an end. I discussed with Victor whether there were any ways of reopening the case.

"Now is not the time," he would say. "We should bide our time, and I will look for a way of raising the matter with Ted. But not now. We'll just end up jeopardizing Hanley's job. The whole thing is too potent. We must let some time go by."

Fear of scandal reached fever pitch when, in 1975, Blunt was thought to be suffering from cancer, and likely to die. Victor approached me again, and asked me whether I thought it likely that Blunt would leave a last will and testament to be published on his death, blowing the lid off the whole affair. I had often asked Blunt about this, and he had always denied making any preparations, but there was a streak of vindictiveness in him which I never quite trusted.

Victor knew better than any outsider just what damage Blunt could do. Both he and Heath were obsessed with the damage the Profumo scandal had done to the last Conservative Government, and were terrified that Blunt could bring them down in the same way. It was not just the problem of the immunity; there was the horrendous possibility that he might name fellow conspirators, both living and dead, as well as the chance that he might choose to leave a more intimate record of the halcyon days of the 1930s. More than a handful of reputations stood to suffer if their sexual peccadilloes from that time were circulated on Fleet Street, not least the former Prime Minister, Anthony Eden.

Victor eventually pressed me to provide him with a full brief on the damage Blunt could do if he chose to tell all. When I was in D3 I had written a variety of papers for the Home Office on the Ring of Five, but they were mostly unsatisfactory. MI5 Legal Department insisted on removing names like Proctor and Watson on the grounds that we had no proof.

"That's not the point," I argued. "We should be providing the Home Office with intelligence. That's our job. If we filter out things we believe to be true just because we can't prove them, we're failing in our duty."

Victor agreed with my approach totally, and stressed that my briefing had to be as full as possible. I drew together the full history of the Ring of Five, and painstakingly showed how all the connections were made. Forty names were on the list in all. A few weeks later I saw Robert Armstrong about Agent 19. He thanked me for the document.

"Splendid piece of work," he beamed, "real intelligence. Not like the civil servant drafts we normally get from the Security Service."

Around this time word got back that Arthur and Stephen de Mowbray were themselves lobbying for the case against Hollis to be reopened. Arthur had retired, and Stephen de Mowbray's career was in steep decline. He had made himself deeply unpopular inside MI6 during the late 1960s by his unswerving support for Golitsin and all his theories. His mentor was Christopher Phillpotts, under whom he had served in Washington. Phillpotts brought him back to serve in Counterintelligence, but after Phillpotts retired in 1970, de Mowbray was left exposed. Dick White was determined to get rid of him if at all possible, but Maurice Oldfield suggested that a spell in Malta was the best compromise.

When de Mowbray returned in 1972 to find that the Hollis case was shelved, he began to agitate for action. Both Oldfield and Hanley were terrified in case de Mowbray took it into his head to take his fears about Soviet penetration to an MP. Arthur, too, was developing contacts in Parliament. After retirement he went off to work there as a clerk as a way of making up his pension. There were worries in case he decided to brief one of his newfound friends on the traumas of the past twenty years.

Hollis was not de Mowbray's only concern. He also believed that the whole system for appointing heads of the Secret Services was nepotic and potentially disastrous. He had a point, in that once a spy insinuated himself to the summit of an organization, he was in a perfect position to appoint fellow traitors to follow him.

Oldfield raised the question of de Mowbray at one of our quiet dinners.

"Can't you rein him in?" he asked. He made it clear that Hanley would view it favorably as well. Oldfield, too, had personal reasons for wishing to keep the Hollis affair buried. He had been passed over for the top job in MI6 when Dick White returned but was desperately hoping that he would yet get his chance as C.

I told him that I doubted whether in the end I could have much influence over him or Arthur.

"Yes, but they don't know what you know; they don't know how delicate things are. Any hint of scandal now could deal us all a grievous blow."

Poor Maurice was so transparent, you could read ambition in him like a book. Before the evening was out he began to talk about the future.

"Of course," he said, "if Rennie left, and I got the chance, I wouldn't want to stay long . . ."

His voice trailed away. I knew he wanted me to pass the message along.

A few weeks later I lunched with Stephen and tried to persuade him that now was not the time to push.

"There are things going on," I said, "I know it looks as if it's stalled. But there are many ways of skinning a cat. We just need to give it time."

He was not convinced. He thought I was in Hanley's pocket, and made no secret of it. In fact, I was still hopeful that the VENONA search authorized by Hanley might yet yield vital clues to the case. Perhaps some more traffic would be found hidden away in a dusty cupboard which would give us the matches to unlock the missing cryptonyms.

There had recently been a small breakthrough in the existing traffic which had given cause for hope. Geoffrey Sudbury was working on part of the HASP material which had never been broken out. Advanced computer analysis revealed that this particular traffic was not genuine VENONA. It did not appear to have been enciphered using a one-time pad, and from the nonrandom distribution of the groups, Sudbury hazarded a guess that it had been enciphered using some kind of directory.

We began the search in the British Library, and eventually

found a book of trade statistics from the 1930s which fitted. Overnight a huge chunk of HASP traffic was broken. The GRU traffic was similar to much that we had already broken. But there was one series of messages which was invaluable. The messages were sent from the GRU resident Simon Kremer to Moscow Center, and described his meetings with the GRU spy runner Sonia, alias Ruth Kuzchinski.

The Sonia connection had been dismissed throughout the 1960s as too tenuous to be relied upon. MI5 tended to believe the story that she came to Britain to escape Nazism and the war, and that she did not become active for Russian Intelligence until Klaus Fuchs volunteered his services in 1944. In particular GCHQ denied vehemently that Sonia could ever have been broadcasting her only radio messages from her home near Oxford during the period between 1941 and 1943.

But Kremer's messages utterly destroyed the established beliefs. They showed that Sonia had indeed been sent to the Oxford area by Russian Intelligence, and that during 1941 she was already running a string of agents. The traffic even contained the details of the payments she was making to these agents, as well as the times and durations of her own radio broadcasts. I thought bitterly of the way this new information might have influenced Hollis' interrogation had we had the material in 1969.

Once this was known I felt more sure than ever that Elli did exist, and that he was run by Sonia from Oxford, and that the secret of his identity lay in her transmission, which inexplicably had been lost all those years before. The only hope was to travel the world and search for any sign that her traffic had been taken elsewhere.

Over the four years from 1972 to 1976 I traveled 370,000 kilometers searching for new VENONA and Sonia's transmissions. In France, SDECE told me they had no material, even though Marcel told me he was sure they had taken it. Presumably one of the SAPPHIRE agents had long since destroyed it. In Germany they professed total ignorance. It was the same in Italy. Spain refused to entertain the request until we handed back Gibraltar. I spent months toiling around telegraph offices in Canada searching for traces of the telex links out there. But there was nothing. In Washington, extensive searches also drew a blank. It was heartbreaking to know that what I wanted had once existed, had once been filed and stored, but somehow had slipped through our fingers.

In 1974 Hanley and I began making preparations for the next CAZAB conference, which was due to take place in London in May. I told him he would likely face pressure from the Americans and the Canadians for some kind of statement about the Hollis case. We had successfully stalled any comment since the interrogation, but Angleton for one was determined to have something on the record.

"What shall I say?" asked Hanley.

I told him to play things low-key.

"Tell them the facts. There was a series of old allegations, and a number of candidates were possible starters. Hollis was one, and probably the best, but in the end, although we interrogated him, we were not able to form a firm conclusion."

The 1974 CAZAB conference was a far cry from the high-spirited gatherings of the 1960s. Too many faces around the table had disappeared. Spry had gone; Jim Bennett from the RCMP had gone, himself a suspect in a paralyzing mole hunt inside the RCMP with which I was peripherally involved (I believe that, despite Bennett's peculiar behavior under interrogation, he was not a spy); Helms had gone; and Angleton was clearly living on borrowed time. In Washington the Watergate scandal was at its height, and already the cupboard full of CIA skeletons was inching open.

Hanley made his short statement about the Hollis case. It was greeted silently. Most people had suffered the same traumas themselves, and knew just what pain and damage a case like that would have done. Hanley ended diplomatically by inviting the services represented to make whatever damage assessments they felt necessary in the light of his statement. It was a classic White-hall ploy. Lay out the difficult ground, but always let the other man draw the decisive conclusion!

I saw Angleton only once more after the CAZAB conference —in Washington at the end of the year. He knew he was being forced out. A new Director, William Colby, was determined to unseat him. Angleton and Colby had quarreled about the conduct of counterintelligence in Southeast Asia for several years. When Colby became Director the opportunity to get rid of Angleton came when *The New York Times* published a story naming Angleton as the mastermind behind a massive domestic mail surveillance program. Within a few days Angleton and all his senior men had resigned.

When I saw Angleton he was raging.

"Two hundred years of counterintelligence thrown away," he cursed, when he realized that the whole of his senior staff was departing. It was obvious that *The New York Times* story was only the first shot in the war. Within six months the CIA was submerged in a welter of Senate hearings, exposés, and mire. The year when the reckoning began was 1974. In Canada and Australia inquiries began into the past iniquities, alleged or real, of their intelligence services. We were the modern pariahs—hated, distrusted, hunted.

Oldfield and Hanley were terrified by the pace of events abroad, fearful above all that some of the revelations would spill over onto their own services. They realized, too, that the newly elected Labor Government might just be prepared to encourage such developments. It was in this context that Stephen de Mowbray finally decided that he had to act. In mid-1974 he approached a friend of his, Philip de Zulueta, a former private secretary to Alec Douglas-Home when he was Prime Minister, and outlined his fears about the penetration of MI5, and the method of appointing service chiefs. Zuluetta suggested he approach Sir John Hunt, the new Cabinet Secretary. After telling Maurice that he could restrain himself no longer, de Mowbray made his appointment with No. 10 Downing Street.

"What's that bloody de Mowbray doing now?" roared Hanley one morning.

It was the first I heard of the news.

"Bloody Maurice interfering again. How can he let one of his officers prance around to Downing Street and wash all our linen without asking me . . . it's intolerable!"

I told Hanley that I felt it was inevitable. In the end de Mowbray was always determined to make an approach over the heads of MI5 and MI6, and we ought to be thankful it was to No. 10 Downing Street, rather than through a parliamentary question.

The outcome was a review—a classic maneuver. At the time they always seem so hopeful; it is only afterward you realize they are designed to achieve the answer desired by those who set the inquiry up. This one was to be conducted by Lord Trend, the former Cabinet Secretary. He was to have all the papers, and as much time as he needed, to decide which of the two faiths was believable.

Trend first appeared in Leconfield House in late 1974. He was given an office, a safe, and a secretary, and left alone on the fifth floor. After a few weeks he telephoned me and asked me to come to his room.

He appeared a typical Oxford don, an aesthetic-looking man with a wide forehead and fairish gray hair.

"I don't want to talk about the case," he began, "I simply want to get a picture of how it was all done. Then I am going to go off and study and see people, and I will see you again at the end."

All ten volumes of the FLUENCY Working Party were stacked neatly on the desk in front of him, and for the rest of the morning we went through them.

"How did it all begin?" he wanted to know.

It was a question I had often asked myself as I sat in the evening poring over those same files. How did it all begin? Did it start in 1945, when Blunt left? Or did it start when Volkov and Gouzenko made their approaches? Perhaps it was much earlier, when a frail man with TB stepped off the boat from China and tried to get a job in British Intelligence. Or later, much later, when Tisler told us about the spy in MI5, or when Golitsin talked of spies, hundreds of them, thousands of them, everywhere. Or was the Mitchell case the first decisive moment, the first time we looked, and could not find the spy in our midst? How do you define the moment when a fear becomes a tangible presence? It is just there. It was always there. It was always there, from the beginning to the end.

The FLUENCY files looked curiously distant. They bulged with unseen hours of work. Minutes from every secret department were carefully recorded, tracing the distribution of this document and that document. Each allegation was carefully broken down; each suspect allotted a code name. At the end of the last file was the famous minute signed in my own hand, giving the names of those who needed urgent investigation.

On more than one occasion Trend asked about the delays in dealing with cases.

"It's very difficult," I explained, "to be told that the man you've worked with for years, who gave you your job, or whom you gave his job, is a spy. That was what Dick White and F.J. found so difficult to come to terms with . . . and that's why we adopted code names from the beginning, to depersonalize everything."

"Quite so . . ." said Trend.

"You do understand that all the FLUENCY decisions were unanimous. This was not just me on my own. There were six of us, and we all thought exactly the same."

"Ah yes," muttered Trend, pausing over an apparently innocuous exchange of documents in the file.

Trend seemed especially interested in the middling-grade agent. He asked me to explain how we had broken the allegation down, and the system we had used to allot marks to each of the thirty-four candidates.

I spent several hours explaining the VENONA He was fascinated by that infernal incomplete jigsaw which promised so much and revealed so little.

I described how we arrived at our identifications. Stanley, Hicks, and Johnson were almost certainly Philby, Burgess, and Blunt, though there was still room for doubt. Stanley was Philby because of the reference to Mexican affairs being the responsibility of his Department. Hicks was Burgess because in one message Moscow Center instructs Krotov to limit Hicks' reports to hard facts, and omit the theories.

"That's Guy to a tee," I said with a laugh, surprised by the intimacy with which I referred to a man I had met only on paper.

"And Johnson?" asked Trend.

"That is where the doubt is . . . There is a reference here"— I handed him a sheet of the VENONA with paper message ribbons embossed on it— "and you can see that Johnson is traveling abroad. That tallies with Blunt's movements. He went to Italy at the end of the week this message was received. But it is slightly odd that Krotov appears not to know of Johnson's plans. I asked Blunt about this, and he was positive that he told Krotov about his impending trip at least six weeks before."

"Could it have been anyone else?"

"The only officer who made a sudden trip abroad at the end of this week was Drat . . . I'm sorry, I mean Hollis, when he went to Canada to see Gouzenko."

"And . . . ?"

"I doubt it," I said quietly, "I somehow doubt it. I think Johnson was Blunt, and he was leading us astray on the six weeks business. Johnson is just too closely tied to Hicks and Stanley to be anyone else but Blunt. Anyway, there are three other cryptonyms still unidentified. Any of those could be Hollis."

I was impressed by Trend. He had a quick mind, and a very thorough one too. There was no skating across points. I came away from our first meeting feeling I had been grilled in a rather quiet, patient way. But what worried me was that he had a civil servant's training, not an intelligence officer's background. Would he be able to make the kinds of judgments required to make sense of a mass of contradictory intelligence material? He had no frame of reference, no way of judging the strength of the case against Hollis as against the strength of the case against other spies, like Philby, or Blunt, or Blake. Only years of experience in the secret world could give a man that kind of intuition.

Trend had a high reputation inside MI5. Most people preferred him to Norman Brooke, the previous Cabinet Secretary, who was renowned for getting bees in his bonnet. Norman Brooke and I shared the same club, and after he retired I occasionally used to talk to him. He was careful never to criticize his successor, but always gave the impression things were being handled much more badly now than in his day. Trend was a far more relaxed figure, and he fought the Treasury doughtily on behalf of the Secret Services throughout the 1960s.

Trend continued to work away in Leconfield House for another year. Occasionally we would meet in the corridor. He never said much, and it was late 1975 before I was called in to see him again. By that time we had finally left Leconfield House and moved to the dismal Grower Street offices.

He wanted to talk about the allegations. He thought they were all very old, when you stripped them down to the bone.

"Of course, but what is impressive is the coincidences of the dates of the allegations. They all come from exactly the same time. It's quite uncanny."

Golitsin, Trend said, did not seem to lead anywhere—"not

helpful" was the expression he used. I agreed that for the purposes of the case for high-level penetration Golitsin had given us nothing we could investigate. He was, at best, I conceded, an indicator that penetration had occurred.

Trend also discarded the middling-grade agent story.

"Very difficult case that," he agreed, "impossible not to look at, but I think right to discard today."

"Now Volkov," he began again, after turning to a relevant file and adjusting his spectacles.

Wasn't I being finicky in altering the thrust of the allegation after having the document retranslated? he asked.

"I don't see why," I replied. "There are really only two ways to proceed in cases like these. One way is to make guesses about what an allegation means, and where it leads, and how seriously to take it. The other way is to adopt a scholastic approach, and analyze everything very carefully and precisely and build scientifically on that bedrock."

"And then there's Elli," said Trend. "I see you checked the story with Akhmedov. But you've got no follow-up, have you? There's no Elli in the traffic."

"But I didn't expect that there would be," I replied. "Elli is an illegal, and if that's the case, his communications would be illegal, not through the Embassy. If we found Sonia's traffic I am sure we would find Elli. But we can't."

"And you still think Elli was Hollis?"

"Most certainly."

"And nothing since has caused you to doubt that?"

"No, if anything my conviction has become stronger."

Trend sighed patiently.

"But there's no ideological background . . ." he began.

"There's China."

"Ah, yes," he murmured, "China . . ." His voice trailed away. Trend was professional to the end. I never could detect just

what his feelings were. He certainly gave me the impression that
he thought the case for penetration was strong, but apart from a
fleeting reference to the fact that he doubted we had the right
candidate in Hollis, he gave nothing away.

Neither did I ever learn from Hanley what Trend's conclusions
were. The subject was never discussed, and I assume that Trend's
report was completed after I left the Service in January 1976. It
was only in 1981 that Mrs. Thatcher filled in that final gap. Lord
Trend, she told the House of Commons, had concluded that
Hollis was not an agent of the Russian Intelligence Service. He
had faith in a man's innocence, as I had faith in his treachery; as
another man might have faith in God, or Mammon. One man's
view, as I now realize, is in the end worthless. Only facts will ever
clear up the eternal mystery.

As I approached my final months in the office I felt a wave of
tiredness. I did not know whether to stay in England and fight, or
cut my losses and run. My health was bad, my pension derisory.
But I had my memories.

One afternoon toward Christmas I drove up to Cambridge
with Victor to his country house for the last time. Conversation
was difficult. So much needed to be said. So much was inside me,
bottled up and waiting to spill out.

"What are you going to do?" he asked.

"Oh, I don't know—maybe Australia," I replied.

The wet fenland fields flashed past the car. In the distance I
could feel the draw of the Cambridge spires.

"You want to be persuaded to go, don't you?" said Victor after
a while.

"I suppose so."

I was morose. I was on the losing side. The Reformation had
taken place in British Intelligence. Catholicism had given way to
Protestantism. My wars were wars of the past.

"You should go, Peter, get out there to the sun, get better, get fit, let someone else take the strain. You've done the work of three men," said Victor.

The car engine droned.

"Your problem, Peter," he said, "is that you know too many secrets."

Glossary

Abwehr	German Intelligence Service
ARL	Admiralty Research Laboratory (UK)
ASIO	Australian Security and Intelligence Organization
ASSA	Armed Services Security Agency (USA)
AWRE	Atomic Weapons Research Establishment (UK)
BSC	British Security Coordination
CIA	Central Intelligence Agency (USA). Its main function is foreign intelligence and espionage. Known internally as "the Company."
CPGB	Communist Party of Great Britain
D Branch	Counterespionage Branch of MI5 (UK)
D1	Head of Russian Counterespionage (D Branch) (UK)
DRPC	Defense Research Policy Committee (UK)
DSI	Defense Scientific Intelligence (UK)
DST	French Counterespionage Service (equivalent to MI5)
en clair	uncoded
FBI	Federal Bureau of Investigation (USA). Its main function is domestic counterintelligence.
GC&CS	Government Code and Cipher School (UK)
GCHQ	Government Communications Headquarters (UK)
GKNIIR	Joint organization between the KGB and GRU on scientific and technical intelligence (USSR)
GPU	See OGPU.
GRU	Soviet Military Intelligence

ISOS	Abwehr hand ciphers broken by British cryptanalysts.
JIC	Joint Intelligence Committee (UK)
KGB	Komitet Gosuderstvennoy Bezopasnosti (Committee of State Security) (USSR)
MGB	Ministry of State Security (USSR). The forerunner of the KGB.
MI5	British Security Service. (Formerly Section 5 of Military Intelligence, hence the name still commonly used.) Roughly equivalent to the American FBI (internal security) but it does perform certain counterintelligence functions overseas. Its main charge is to protect British secrets at home from foreign spies and to prevent domestic sabotage, subversion, and the theft of state secrets.
MI6	British Secret Intelligence Service. (Formerly Section 6 of Military Intelligence.) A civilian organization with functions resembling those of the American CIA. It is charged with gathering information overseas and other strategic services. Both MI5 and MI6 are controlled by the Joint Intelligence Committee.
NKVD	A forerunner of the KGB (USSR)
NSA	National Security Agency (USA)
OGPU	A forerunner of the KGB (USSR)
OSS	Office of Strategic Services (USA). The wartime forerunner of the CIA.
PF	Personal File (in the MI5 Registry)
RCMP	Royal Canadian Mounted Police
RNSS	Royal Naval Scientific Service (UK)
ROC	Radiations Operations Committee (UK)
RSS	Radio Security Service (UK)
SDECE	French Secret Intelligence Service (equivalent to MI6)
SERL	Services Electronics Research Laboratory (UK)
SF	Special Facility. A phone-tapping device.
SIME	Security Intelligence Middle East (UK)
SIS	MI6

traffic	Morse, telegraph, or radio communications signals containing genuine messages
UB	Polish Intelligence Service
Watchers	Officers of MI5's A Branch charged with visual surveillance and identification of persons presenting a security risk
Whitehall	A street in London where the principal government offices are situated. Used to signify the civil service or the bureaucracy.

Index

A1, 30
A2, 30, 38, 40, 50, 55, 68, 69, 72, 73, 84, 89, 90, 94, 240, 252, 259, 286, 423
A3, 30
A4, 30, 61, 116, 166
  see also Watchers
A Branch, 30, 32, 41, 50, 89, 116, 258, 452
A Branch Resources Index, 75, 155
Abwehr, 11, 99, 150, 311, 410, 411, 414, 415, 482
Admiralty, the, 19–20, 27, 28, 33, 34, 92, 93, 163, 170, 210, 212, 236, 318–21, 462
Admiralty Research Laboratory (ARL), 5, 6, 19–21, 33, 34, 186, 318, 323, 482
Agayants, I. I., 260
Agent 19, 442–44, 469
Air Bubble, see Soupert, Dr. Jean Paul
Akhmedov, Ismail, 354
Alexander, Hugh, 101–105, 136, 138, 184, 187
Allen, John, 434
Allen, Lord Philip, 438–39, 445, 461
All Russia Co-operative Society Limited (ARCOS), 43, 45, 287
American Intelligence, 45, 123, 124, 184, 185, 206, 230, 235, 340, 344, 345, 383, 385

Angleton, James, 129–31, 186, 188–94, 201, 203–205, 275, 302, 303, 339–40, 344–48, 381–89, 395, 396–97, 400, 416, 435–37, 456, 458, 463–64, 474
antisubmarine research program, 21, 33, 54, 212, 324
Apostles Society, 280, 306–307, 317–19, 329, 330, 334
Archer, Jane Sissmore, 363–64
ARCOS raid, 43, 45, 287
Armed Services Security Agency (ASSA), 228, 229, 234, 482
Armstrong, Robert, 442–44, 469–70
ARNIKA, 264–65
Atomic Weapons Research Establishment (AWRE), 148, 149, 164, 174, 211, 248, 482
Attlee, Clement, 6, 42, 70
August, 401, 454, 458–59, 460
Australian Security Intelligence Organization (ASIO), 82–83, 154, 234, 411, 447, 482

Bagot, Millicent, 48
Bailey, Don, 24
Baron, 301
Bay of Pigs invasion, 194, 201, 257
B Branch, 41, 44, 99, 423
B Branch, RCMP, 77
Beith, Freddie, 100–101
Belgian Sécurité d'Etat, 303
Belmont, Al, 114, 126–28, 175, 184, 340

Bennett, James, 77, 111, 338, 473
Berlin, Isaiah, 291, 305–306
Berlin Tunnel Operation, 59, 90, 162, 185, 197, 214, 340
Bissell, Richard, 194
Blake, George (Lambda 1), 59, 162, 214, 262, 266, 299, 323–24, 340, 369–70, 377, 424, 478
Blue Streak project, 28, 33
Blunt, Sir Anthony (Johnson), 3, 40, 71, 153, 208, 221, 233, 246, 270–80, 283–91, 293, 297–99, 302, 305–307, 314–21, 324–34, 336, 340, 350, 351, 353, 358–59, 362, 373, 378, 408, 417, 422, 428, 433, 438, 467, 469, 476, 477–78
Bossard, Frank, 342–44, 384, 385
Bowra, Maurice, 306
BRIDE, Operation, 229
Bridges, Edward, 94, 332
British Counterintelligence Directorate, 353
British Establishment, 148, 152, 290, 298, 307, 318, 347
British Intelligence, 2, 10, 24, 28, 44, 56, 83–85, 94–95, 123, 124, 131, 142–44, 206, 211, 217, 230, 235, 259, 294, 302, 309, 338, 340, 345–55, 359, 360, 381–86, 408–415, 437, 438, 448, 476, 480
British Military Intelligence, 83, 146, 265, 277, 280, 308
see also MI5; MI6
British Secret Intelligence Service (SIS), *see* MI6
British Security Coordination (BSC), 124, 412, 482
British Security Service, *see* MI5
Brooke, Norman, 478
Brookes, Tony, 430–32
Brookner, Anita, 333–34
Brundrett, Sir Frederick, 5–8, 18, 19, 22, 23, 28, 29, 53, 102, 145–47
Brundrett committee, 7, 23, 53, 102, 147–49

Building Research Station, 71, 75, 368
Burgess, Guy (Hicks), 3, 27, 40–44, 54, 56, 123, 124, 128–30, 153, 154, 185, 192, 208, 221, 233, 239, 245, 262, 272–73, 281, 286–90, 297, 298, 305–33, 350, 359, 409, 422, 426, 446, 477
Burk, Joe, 189

Cabinet Office, 122, 271, 438, 439, 461, 468
CABMAN, 59
Cairncross, John, 277–82, 288, 291, 292, 293, 297, 299, 305, 315, 325, 340, 359, 433
Cambridge University, 270–74, 280, 282, 285, 298, 300, 306, 317–319, 324, 326–29, 333–35, 376, 399, 480
Canadian Intelligence, 77, 191
Castro, Fidel, 194, 201–202, 205, 266
CAZAB, 348, 386–87, 398, 436, 447, 473–74
C Branch, 41, 46, 98, 163, 238, 282, 367, 371, 375, 377, 439–40, 471
Central Policy Review Staff (CPRS), *see* Think Tank
Chalet, Marcel, 303–305, 396, 472
Chisholm, Rory, 266
Chisholm, Mrs. Rory, 265–66
CHOIR, Operation, 73–77, 80–81, 84, 221
Churchill, Clarissa (Lady Avon), 306–307
Churchill, Mary, 443
Churchill, Winston, 20, 32*n*, 43, 56, 86, 87, 231, 302, 306, 442–43
CIA (The Company), 59, 123, 129, 161, 170, 179, 183–90, 194, 200–201, 203, 207–10, 231, 245, 249, 257–64, 275, 276, 302, 338–40, 344–48, 360, 369–70, 381–88, 397, 400, 435–36, 458, 473, 474, 482

ciphers, 100–108, 112, 131–32, 136–43, 168–69, 173, 175, 184, 186, 191, 227–34, 354, 471–73

Civil Service, 21, 33, 37, 70, 148, 153, 212, 282, 299, 305, 329–32, 335, 416–17, 439, 442, 444, 448, 449, 454, 478

Clan, 174, 211–12

Clyde Polaris submarine base, 209–10

Cockburn, Claud, 363, 425, 427

Cohen, Morris and Lona, *see* Kroger, Peter and Helen

Cohen, Sir Andrew, 334, 335

Colby, William, 474

Cold War, 7, 68, 76, 100, 105, 129, 184, 185, 206, 235, 237, 290, 388, 395

Colemore Committee, 144–45, 213

Collins, Bill, 100, 101, 169, 171, 172

Colonial Affairs, *see* E Branch

Colonial Office, 73, 195–200

Comintern, 287, 289, 300, 329, 330, 363, 427

Communism, 39, 201, 321, 324, 467

Communist Affairs Research Section (MI6), 363–64

Communist Party of Great Britain (CPGB), 41, 49, 50, 58, 69–71, 72, 73, 133, 221, 236, 250, 289, 305, 405, 409, 434, 482

computers, 102–104, 144, 193, 211, 234, 236, 247–48, 275, 450, 453–54, 471

Computer Working Party, 2, 450, 453

Conway, Godfrey, 303

Cook, Sir William, 28, 148, 211, 212, 248, 442

Cooper, Josh, 136–38

Cot, Pierre, 302–304

Counterclan, 174, 193, 211, 216, 258, 312

Counterespionage Department (MI5), 1, 2, 249, 250, 308, 346, 349, 356, 418, 458

see also D Branch

Counterespionage Department, RCMP, 77, 109, 338

Counterintelligence Section (MI6), 41, 294, 301, 348, 350, 352, 354–55, 359, 408, 411, 470

Courtauld Institute, 284, 285, 326, 333

COVERPOINT, Operation, 114, 121

Coyne, Gerald, 345–48, 381

CPGB, *see* Communist Party of Great Britain

Crabbe affair, 91–94, 143, 203, 218, 262, 293, 351, 408

Cram, Cleve, 170, 345–46, 347

cryptography, 227–34, 247–48, 289

Cuckney, Sir John, 40–42, 45

Cumming, Malcolm, 6, 7, 23, 26–39, 51, 53–56, 85, 87, 93–95, 97, 100, 114, 125, 222–23, 237, 242, 260, 274–76, 292–93, 295, 320, 346, 348, 441, 462

Cumming, Mansfield, 13, 31

Cyprus campaign, 142, 194–201, 450–51

D1, 47, 133, 155, 158, 160, 167, 207, 209, 236, 256, 275, 294–96, 482

D1 (Investigations), 294–96, 320, 375, 417, 420

D1 (Operations), 294, 379, 390, 392

D2, 155, 163, 167, 178, 370, 377, 403, 419

D3, 207, 258, 277, 283, 294, 297, 299, 301, 305, 308, 320, 327, 333, 338, 349, 352, 363–64, 366, 377, 405, 408, 412, 416–21, 423, 431, 433, 445, 450, 469

D4, 389, 390, 392

David, 232, 399

Day, John, 421–22, 424–29

D Branch, 38, 41, 46, 50, 56, 61, 100, 119, 133, 150–51, 158, 162, 171, 174, 180, 207, 237, 242, 250, 251, 258, 274, 275, 282, 294, 305, 320, 348, 370, 389,

D Branch *(cont.)*
406, 407, 419, 421, 432, 454,
482
Defense, Ministry of (MOD), 5, 7,
24, 118, 122, 195, 213, 305, 321,
456
Defense Research Policy
Committee (DRPC), 7, 147–49,
482
Defense Scientific Intelligence Unit
(DSI), 145, 482
de Gaulle, Charles, 140, 301, 302
de Mowbray, Stephen, 256, 396,
414, 470, 471, 474–75
Denham, Hugh, 101–105, 136, 184
Denman, Major, 57–58
Deutsch, Arnold, 287, 288
DEW WORM, Operation, 78–84, 90,
109, 222, 338, 339
de Zulueta, Philip, 474
Directorate of Science, 213–214,
221, 244, 248, 258
Dixon, Peter, 7, 144, 202, 205
Dollis Hill Laboratory, 58–59, 73,
91, 164, 166
Domeisen, Peter, 146
Double Cross System, 38, 43, 99,
100, 150, 151, 152, 262, 311,
384
Douglas-Home, Alec, 434, 474
Downing Street (No. 10), 442–44,
459, 461, 467, 475
Doyne Ditmass, Hal, 275, 276, 433
dragging, 229–30, 247
Dragon Returnees, 145–46
Driberg, Tom, 454–55
DRUG, Operation, 229
DST, 303–304, 482
Dunlap, Jack, 262
Dwyer, Peter, 355, 357
Dzerzhinsky, Feliks, 200, 261, 263

E Branch, 41, 50, 194, 195, 348,
377
Eden, Anthony, 92, 93, 95, 99,
107, 202, 203, 307, 469
Elli, 239, 351–59, 365, 369, 428,
472, 479

Elliott, Nicholas, 92, 93, 220, 246,
288, 361, 409
Ellis, Charles (Dickie), 410–16
Elwell, Charles, 170–71, 216, 217,
239
émigré communities, 151, 152, 156,
261, 409, 410, 413, 415, 458,
459
en clair, 66, 169, 482
ENGULF, 106, 109, 131, 136–38,
142–43, 174, 184–86, 192, 193
ENIGMA code, 99, 102, 277
EOKA, 195–97, 199, 201

F4, 68–69, 71, 72
Falber, Reuben, 221–22
Falkender, Marcia, 467
FBI, 77, 113, 114, 124–30, 175,
184–91, 209, 257, 270, 288, 338–
45, 383, 384, 385, 400, 435, 482
F Branch, 41, 48–50, 98, 250, 359,
361, 362, 452–53, 459–60
Fedora, 209, 267–68, 340, 343,
384–85
Fibonacci system (Chinese
arithmetic), 227
five of MI, 354–59
Floud, Bernard, 334–36
Floud, Peter, 334, 335
FLUENCY, 294, 338–39, 348–51,
353, 356, 359–72, 380, 403, 409,
411, 416–22, 463, 475–76
Foot, Sir Hugh, 195, 199
Foote, Alexander, 354
Foreign Office, 6, 24, 27, 88, 103,
138–40, 152, 156–57, 265, 281,
300, 311, 352, 359, 367, 368,
373, 390, 393–95, 413, 431, 434,
451
Foreign Office Northern
Department, 157, 394
Frawley, Ray, 105, 136, 143–44,
184
Friedman, Litzi, *see* Philby, Litzi
Frolik, 401, 454, 458–59, 460
Fuchs, Klaus, 63, 153, 231, 236,
299, 378, 472
Furnival Jones, Martin (F.J.), 154–

Furnival Jones, Martin *(cont.)*
55, 159, 163, 167–74, 180, 237–
38, 241–45, 257, 271, 293–94,
320, 336, 339, 347, 366–81, 390,
394, 397–99, 405, 406–407, 417–
41, 444–49, 458, 459, 460–61,
464, 476

Gaitskell, Hugh, 455–58, 465
Gardner, Meredith, 228–29, 234–
35
GCHQ, 67, 95, 98–116, 124, 132,
136–44, 168–69, 171, 174–77,
183, 185, 187, 193, 214, 215,
230–33, 235–36, 247–48, 250,
258, 265, 281–83, 312–13, 342–
44, 348, 352, 357, 367, 384, 433,
472, 482
Gee, Ethel, 163, 174
German Armed Forces ciphers
(ENIGMA), 99, 102
German Intelligence Service, *see*
Abwehr
Gestapo, 86, 299, 304, 415
Gibson, Harold, 279
Gideon, 109–11
Gilbert, Martin, 443–44
Glading, Percy, 43
Goleniewski, Michael (Sniper), 179,
300, 349, 351, 369–71, 377, 380–
85, 403–407
Golitsin, Anatoli, 207–10, 215–23,
233, 245, 260–61, 293, 300, 302,
323, 324, 325, 341, 349, 351,
361, 362, 369, 376, 383, 389,
395–403, 436, 437, 456, 470,
476, 478–79
Good, I. J., 433
Gossage, Ray, 20
Gouzenko, Igor, 78, 81, 232, 239,
351, 353–59, 365, 369, 389, 404,
428, 476, 477
Government Code and Cipher
School (GC & CS), 277, 482
Grant, Sokolov, 215–17
Gray, Gordon, 345–48, 381
Gray, Joan (Miss X), 289
great illegals, 287–90, 412, 413

Greenglass, Harry, 63
Greenhill, Dennis, 431
Gribanov, General, 208, 209
Grigovin, Sergei, 389–92
Grist, Evelyn, 56, 61
Grivas, George, 142, 194–201, 451
Gromov, Anatoli (Henry), 289
GRU (Soviet Military Intelligence),
78, 80–81, 175–76, 209, 228,
230, 232, 236–37, 247, 249, 259,
260–61, 263–65, 300, 301, 342,
343, 354–56, 358–59, 384, 410,
412, 472, 482
GRUFF signal, 132–35, 158
Guernsey, Terry, 77–79, 83, 109–
11, 155

Hagelin cipher machines, 103–106,
136–37
Hall, Reggie, 10–13
HALT, Operation, 100–102
Hamburger, Rudi, 310–11
Hammer, Armand, 130–31
Hampshire, Sir Stuart, 308, 311–15
Hanke, 370
Hanley, Sir Michael, 4, 300, 371–
82, 403–405, 418–21, 424, 439–
54, 462, 463, 468–74, 480
Hanslope Communications Center,
212
Harker, Brigadier, 47
HARP, 357
HARRIET case, 371, 375–76, 381–83,
419, 440
see also Hanley, Sir Michael
Harriman, Averill, 231
Harris, Tomas, 219, 329
Harrison, Francis Graham, 446
Hart, Herbert, 334
Hart, Jennifer Fisher Williams,
334–35, 446
Harvey, Bill, 185–94, 201–205, 388
HASP, 236, 301, 472
Hawkes, Johnny, 213
H Division, 101, 106, 136
Healey, Dennis, 305
Heath, Edward (Ted), 432–34,

Heath, Edward *(cont.)*
  437–38, 440–46, 452, 460–61,
  468
Helms, Richard, 186, 194, 200–201,
  275, 347, 381, 388, 473
Henry, 289
Henry, John, 6, 92–94, 202, 203,
  205
Herbert, Christopher, 430
Hicks, 232, 233, 477
Hinton, Geoffrey, 348
Hiss, Alger, 231, 262, 320
Hitler, Adolf, 85, 410, 411, 415
Hollis, Sir Roger, 3, 29, 37, 95–98,
  107, 112–16, 121–26, 147, 154,
  159–60, 163, 167, 170, 174, 181,
  182, 188, 195, 200, 201, 213,
  219, 222–26, 234, 237, 239–60,
  270–72, 275–77, 283, 291–99,
  305, 312, 314, 320, 329, 338–42,
  345–59, 361–85, 397, 403, 408,
  421–31, 440, 441, 445, 452, 458,
  468–80
Home Office, 58, 271, 334, 434,
  438, 445, 448, 461, 469
Hoover, J. Edgar, 113, 114, 122,
  124–30, 183, 185, 257, 381, 436
Houghton, Harry, 162–64, 167–74,
  176–80, 208, 299, 340, 341, 421,
  434
Houghton, Mrs. Harry, 162, 299,
  421
Hunt, Jim, 437
Hunt, Sir John, 460, 475

Intelligence Services, British, 27–
  28, 54, 95, 98, 212, 478
Intercontinental Ballistic Missiles
  (ICBMs), 266–68, 385
Intermediate Range Ballistic
  Missiles (IRBMs), 267
IRA, 2, 451
ISOS Abwehr codes, 311, 483

Jagger, Leslie, 50–52, 75–76, 89,
  101, 103, 104, 131, 150, 391
Johnson, 232, 233, 477
  see also Blunt, Sir Anthony

Joint Allied Intelligence
  Committee, 377
Joint Intelligence Committee (JIC),
  103, 107, 265, 348, 483
Joint Services Language School,
  376, 399, 409
Jones, Jack, 460
Jones, Sir John, 452, 453
Jones, R. V., 19, 32, 32n

K4, 421
K7, 421–23
Kagan, Joseph, 459
Kapitza, Peter, 327–28
Karamasines, Tom, 436
Karpekov, Nikolai, 178, 323, 341
K Branch, 421, 422, 450–53, 468
Keeler, Christine, 340
Kell, Vernon, 13, 31, 42, 43, 50,
  56, 60, 364
Kemp, R. J., 26, 28, 34–35, 118
Kennedy, John F., 194, 206, 266,
  302, 340, 383, 385, 388
KEYSTONE case, 109–10, 117, 132
KGB, 44, 60–62, 78, 81, 83, 91,
  92, 109–110, 111, 146–57, 165,
  167, 169, 175–76, 178, 185, 191,
  200, 207–209, 215–18, 228–39,
  245, 247, 249, 259–66, 279, 284,
  289, 303, 310, 322–24, 340, 351,
  355–61, 370, 376–77, 382–85,
  389–96, 399–404, 412, 430–35,
  447, 454–59, 483
Khrushchev, Nikita, 91–94, 129,
  260, 267
King, Cecil, 464
King, John Herbert, 413
Kirby, Henry, 85
Kirby Green, Philip, 196, 198
Kissinger, Henry, 435–36
Klimov, Major, 206–207
Klugman, James, 281, 313, 315,
  333, 337
Knight, Maxwell, 43, 174, 239, 289
Kompfner, Rudi, 313
Kondrashev, Sergei, 323–24
Korovin, 178, 324
Kosygin, Alexei, 434

Kremer, Simon, 472
Krivitsky, Walter, 287, 288, 349, 359, 389, 409, 412
Kroger, Peter and Helen, 168, 170, 173–77, 180, 259
Krotov, Boris, 232, 233, 237, 249, 289, 356, 433, 477
Kuzchinski, Ruth, 472
    see also Sonia
KX, 421
KY, 42, 430

Labarthe, André, 301
Labor Government, 312, 335, 345
Labor Party, 39, 70, 236, 271, 292, 305, 454, 455, 457–59, 462–65
Ladell, Dr., 204, 432, 456, 457
Lambda 1, 161, 162, 370
    see also Blake, George
Lambda 2, 161, 162
Last, Anne, 239, 240, 353
LAVINIA case, *see* Sniper; Goleniewski, Michael
Lecky, Terence, 348, 349
Leconfield House, 3, 23, 28–38, 47, 53, 55, 63, 69, 72, 74, 76, 114, 119, 125, 135, 143, 155, 166, 167, 169, 171, 188, 201, 214, 218, 221, 240, 245, 273, 276, 305, 346, 347, 349, 379, 398, 407, 426, 449, 475, 478
Lenin, Vladimir Ilyich, 86, 200, 263
Levinson, Art, 185
Liddell, Guy, 42, 43–44, 87, 254, 281, 285, 299, 308, 309, 314, 356, 422
Linney, 113, 114, 118–19, 121
LIONSBEARD, 166, 178, 180
List File, 49–50
Long, Leo, 277–82, 291, 292, 293, 297, 299, 305, 316, 325, 340, 359, 438
Lonsdale, Gordon Arnold, 163–83, 188, 190–93, 211, 220, 222, 224, 237, 242, 243–44, 249, 259, 341, 342, 421
LOVEBIRD, Operation, 118

Lucy Ring, 301
Luibimov, 239, 354
Lulakov, Lieutenant Commander, 120–21, 222
Lyalin, Oleg, 430–37, 459
Lyall, Archie, 426

McBarnet, Evelyn, 153, 178–79, 219, 237–40, 246, 273, 277, 281, 300, 349, 371, 378
McCarthyism, 235, 290, 307, 320, 416
McCaul, Michael (Macauley), 155–59, 339, 381, 392, 395, 398, 452
McCone, John, 257
MacDonald, Alec, 320, 348, 349, 366
Maclean, Donald, 3, 27, 40, 42, 44, 54, 123, 124, 128, 130, 153, 185, 192, 207, 221, 231, 233, 236, 239, 245, 262, 272, 273, 290, 297, 298, 300, 305, 308, 325, 327, 359, 367, 409, 446
Macmillan, Harold, 56, 73, 271, 441
Magan, Bill, 194–99, 295
Maly, Theodore (Theo), 287
Marriott, John, 38–39
Marshall, Arthur, 317
Martelli, Giuseppe, 340–43, 384, 385
Martin, Arthur, 153–56, 167–74, 178, 188, 192, 206–207, 215, 217–21, 223–26, 236–39, 241–47, 255–61, 270–71, 274–81, 291–97, 301, 308, 328, 339, 345, 348–50, 363, 372, 378, 396, 407–409, 420, 428, 433, 455–56, 470–71
Marxists, 313–14, 318, 319, 323
Marychurch, Peter, 193
Marshall, Arthur, 305–306
May, Alan Nunn, 153, 232
Mayer, Tess, *see* Rothschild, Tess
Mayhew, Christopher, 305
M Division (GCHQ), 136, 216
MI5, 1–4, 6, 8, 13, 16, 22–23, 27–109, 112–33, 138–64, 170–83,

MI5*(cont.)*
  190, 194–204, 210–14, 220–23,
  230, 233–43, 247, 249, 250–72,
  274, 276, 277, 281–314, 321,
  328–71, 375–87, 391, 396, 398,
  403–11, 416–22, 426–80, 483
MI6, 6, 7, 8, 11–13, 23, 27, 41, 43,
  45–46, 51, 53–56, 58, 59, 66, 78,
  79, 89–95, 98, 99, 107, 129,
  137–52, 157, 161–65, 176, 183–
  86, 191, 197–204, 211, 213, 219,
  220, 238, 243–47, 249, 250, 256–
  71, 277, 279–82, 290, 294, 295,
  301–303, 309, 310, 313, 324,
  340, 346–86, 383, 387, 392–96,
  407–15, 426, 438–41, 451, 466,
  470, 471, 475, 483
microdots, 149–50, 173
Millen, Dick, 125, 184
Mills, Cyril, 131–32
Mitchell, Graham, 56, 151, 180–81,
  222–26, 222–25, 237, 239, 241,
  242, 245–62, 270, 275, 291–93,
  338–45, 341–53, 359, 364, 365,
  375, 381, 385, 397, 422, 428,
  440, 476
Mitchell, H. T., 138
Modin, Yuri (Peter), 245, 247, 290
MOLE, Operation, 82–84, 222
MOP, 59
Morgan, Dr. Frank, 149, 150, 164–
  65, 210, 211, 248
Morrow, 120–22, 222
Moscow Center, 109, 110, 232,
  237, 356, 472, 477
Mossad, 436
Movements Analysis program, 155,
  275, 276, 433, 434
Mr. Reporter, 437–38
Mueselier, Admiral, 302
Murphy, Dave, 397

Nadiensky, 392–95
Nadiensky, Mrs., 392, 394
Nasser, Gamal Abdel, 103, 107,
  202–203
National Security Agency (NSA),
  U.S., 107, 124, 183–87, 192,

  193, 228, 230, 248, 262, 303,
  312, 348, 483
National Security Council, 340, 348
NATO, 208–10, 318, 320, 340
Naval Intelligence Department
  (NID), 10, 92, 162, 208, 360
Navy, British, 11, 21, 28, 33, 54,
  93, 101, 161, 214, 318, 323, 324
Nazism, 38, 39, 85, 313, 472
"neighbors," 356–58
Nicholson, Ben, 313
Nixon, Richard M., 436
NKVD, 62, 300, 353, 483
Nossenko, Yuri, 209, 210, 263,
  383–84, 436
Nutkin, "Squirrel," 74, 76

Oatsheaf, 458
OGPU, 260, 261, 483
O'Hanlon, Pat, 136, 143
Oldfield, Sir Maurice, 12, 269, 277,
  284, 411–12, 416, 435, 440, 466–
  67, 470–71, 474–75
Ordzhonikidze, 91–93, 143, 218
Orr-Ewing, Anne, 61, 246, 349,
  371, 423, 426
Otto, 287–88, 321–22, 326, 334,
  337
Overseas Security Service (OSS),
  129, 231, 483
Oxbridge intellectuals, 298, 314
Oxford Ring, 333–34
Oxford University, 298, 300, 306,
  308, 309, 329, 335, 359, 362,
  376, 423, 425–27, 446, 472

Pancheff, Bunny, 411, 414, 416
Paques, Georges, 303, 396
PARTY PIECE, Operation, 68–70,
  221
Patrick, Jim, 405, 406
Penkovsky, Oleg, 259–69, 383–85,
  409
Personal Files (PFs), 49, 483
Petrie, Sir David, 43, 47, 364
Petrov, Mr. and Mrs., 83
Philby, Eleanor, 245
Philby, Kim (Stanley), 3, 40, 53–59,

Philby, Kim (Stanley)*(cont.)*
 91, 99, 123, 129, 130, 153, 154,
 185, 192, 208, 218–24, 233–35,
 245–47, 249, 257, 262, 273, 287,
 288, 290, 291, 297–99, 301, 305,
 318, 323, 325, 328, 329, 336,
 340, 350–59, 361, 362, 365, 373,
 379, 389, 401, 408–11, 413, 427,
 428, 441, 478
Philby, Litzi, 288, 328, 409
Phillpotts, Christopher, 184, 349,
 408, 409, 411, 416, 470
Pieck, Mr. and Mrs. Henri, 287,
 413
Piggott, Lester, 387
PIG ROOT, Operation, 222
Playfair, Sir Edward, 306
Polish Intelligence Service, *see* UB
Politburo, 208, 260, 279, 358, 392
Pool, Phoebe, 333, 336
Pope-Hennessy, James, 306, 307
Popov, Colonel, 261, 264
Poretsky, Elizabeth, 287, 412–13
Poretsky, Ludwik, 287, 412
Porton Down Laboratory, 456, 457
Post Office Special Investigations
 Unit, 23, 56–57, 58, 105
Post Office Technical Department,
 8, 23, 58, 166, 218
Potter, Harold, 47–49
President's Foreign Intelligence
 Advisory Board (PFIAB), 345
Pribyl, Colonel, 112–13, 118, 121
Proctor, Dennis, 329–32, 337, 367,
 419, 469
Proctor, Varda, 332
Profumo affair, 271, 340, 429, 469

Radiations Operations Committee
 (ROC), 132, 133, 135, 142–43,
 144, 165, 174, 183, 184, 193,
 211, 213, 483
Radio Security Service (RSS), 99,
 109, 212, 308, 311, 312, 483
Rado, Alexander, 287
RAF, 113, 135, 165, 215, 312, 360
RAFTER, 117–22, 127, 131–33, 135,

 143, 149, 155, 159, 165–69, 174,
 178, 188, 190–92, 205, 216, 312
Ransome, David, 452
Rastvorov, Yuri, 351, 359–60, 361
Rees, Goronwy, 308–12
Registry, 2, 48–50, 57, 62, 125,
 162, 215, 222, 238, 278, 297–99,
 328, 350, 360, 401, 450
Reiss, Ignace, 412
Rennie, Sir John, 439, 471
Richardson, Maurice, 363, 425
Ring of Five, 207, 221, 245, 280,
 287–89, 300, 307, 315, 321, 325–
 28, 336–37, 378, 469
Roberts, Alfred, 303
Roberts, Tom, 406, 407
Robertson, James, 251
Robinson, Henry, 300
Rodin, General, 456
Rogov, Colonel, 113, 115
Roman, Harry, 161
Roosevelt, Franklin D., 20, 231,
 443
Rosa, 232, 399
Rosenberg, Ethel and Julius, 175,
 231, 235
Rote Drei, 287
Rote Kapelle (Red Orchestra), 287,
 300, 337, 377
Rothschild, Emma, 284
Rothschild, N. M., 462–63
Rothschild, Tess, 272–74, 285, 317,
 327, 399
Rothschild, Victor, 147–48, 213,
 218, 219, 271–74, 284, 318–19,
 327–29, 399, 437–46, 460–62,
 465, 468–69, 480–81
Royal Canadian Mounted Police
 (RCMP), 77–82, 109–11, 114,
 155, 191, 249, 264, 338, 354–55,
 473, 483
Royal Navy Scientific Service
 (RNSS), 5, 6, 18, 28, 212, 213,
 483
RUPEE, 264
Russell Jones, Barry, 388
Russian Counterespionage Section,

Russian Counterespionage Section (*cont.*)
46, 114, 120, 133, 150, 154, 155, 250, 275, 455
see also D1

Russian Intelligence Service, 44, 109, 121, 150, 153, 200, 209, 231–32, 287, 299, 316, 343, 344, 352, 416, 480
see also Soviet Intelligence

Sale, Tony, 116–17, 134–35, 158, 159, 166
SALT I arms control negotiations, 268
Sapphire Ring, 302, 472
Satellite intelligence, 2, 211, 312
SATYR, 28–29, 78, 82, 83, 104
Scanlon, Hugh, 460
SDECE, 302, 472, 483
Secret Intelligence Service (SIS), *see* MI6
Section V (MI6), 352–55, 358–62
Security Intelligence Middle East (SIME), 38–39, 483
Security Service, *see* MI5
Sedlecek, 301
Serial 3, 208, 209
Serial 8, 208
Serov, General, 260, 370
Services Electronics Research Laboratory (SERL), 7–8, 18–19, 22, 24, 483
SF (Special Facilities), 59, 71, 91, 105, 106, 108–109, 218, 221, 285, 322, 483
Shelepin, Alexander, 260, 396
Shergold, Harry, 266
Shipp, Cecil, 321–23
SIFE (Security Intelligence Far East), 360–62
SIGINT, 19, 115, 143, 184, 187, 188, 277, 280, 282, 342
Signals Intelligence, 3, 262
Sillitoe, Sir Percy, 7, 42, 98, 364, 381
Simkins, Anthony, 367–69, 371–74, 438

Sinclair, Sir John, 91, 99, 263
SK (KGB security division), 389
Skardon, Jim, 63, 64–66, 168, 378–79
Skripkin, Lieutenant, 351, 359, 360, 399, 427
Smedley, Agnes, 363, 425
Sniper (LAVINIA), 161, 162, 170, 179, 180, 188, 191, 299
see also Goleniewski, Michael
Socialist Workers' Party (SWP), 453, 454
Solie, Bruce, 436–37
Solomon, Flora, 218–19, 245, 328–29
Sonia, 287, 310, 472, 479
Sorge, Christiane, 413–14
Sorge, Richard, 287, 413–14
Sorpell, Michael, 299
Soupert, Dr. Jean Paul (Air Bubble), 303
Soviet Division (CIA), 386–88, 397, 458
Soviet Intelligence, 261–62, 265, 281, 287–88, 299, 315
Soviet Military Intelligence, *see* GRU
Special Branch, London, 30, 41, 42, 118–19, 120, 133, 171, 341, 392, 406, 432
Spell/Endspell sequence, 228–30
Spencer, Arthur, 168–69
SPETERS, 397
see also Mitchell, Graham
Spry, Sir Charles, 82–83, 473
Stables, Tony, 363
Staff D, 184, 185, 187, 191
Stalin, Joseph V., 129, 237, 239, 288, 345, 354, 400, 404
Stalin's Englishmen, 152–53, 345
Stanley, 207, 232, 233, 249, 358, 477
see also Philby, Kim
Steinbrecher, Herbert, 303
Stephenson, Sir William, 124, 204, 412
Stevens, Gregory, 403–408, 415
Stewart, Bob, 289, 315

Stewart, Patrick, 207–209, 252, 293, 320–21, 326, 349, 371, 380, 385, 409
STOCKADE, 138–42, 174, 184, 186, 192, 304–305, 431
Stone, Harry, 126, 128, 190, 339
Stonehouse, John, 455
Storer, John, 136, 216–17
Straight, Michael Whitney, 270, 271, 325
Sudbury, Geoffrey, 247, 352, 353, 357–58, 471
Suez Crisis, 103, 106–108, 123, 130, 198, 202, 203, 262, 408
Sullivan, Bill, 126, 128, 344
Sunningdale Agreement, 451
SUNSHINE, Operation, 196–99
Supply, Ministry of, 28, 342
Swedish Signals Intelligence Service, 143, 235
Symonds, Ronnie, 209, 256–58, 270, 291–95, 338

Taylor, John, 8, 23–25, 58–59, 73, 91, 138
Technics Document, 147, 293, 351
Templar, Sir Gerald, 195
Thatcher, Margaret, 480
Theo, 287
Thing, The, 25, 146, 367
Think Tank, 437–38, 442, 461
Thomson, J. J., 13
TIEPIN, Operation, 72
Tisler, Frantisek, 112–14, 129
Tisler affair, 115, 121, 122, 126, 127, 158, 182, 222, 224, 243, 365, 476
Top Hat, 209, 268, 342–45, 383–85
Tordella, Louis, 183–85, 188, 192–93, 303
Tory Party, 249, 292
Trade Delegation, Soviet, 43, 431, 459
trade unions, 454, 459, 460, 465
Transcription Department, 55, 59–60, 423
Treasury, 27, 46, 131, 145, 277, 281, 332, 432, 446, 478

Trend, Lord, 311–12, 475–80
Trepper, Leopold, 287
Trident Talks, 442–43
true bills, 350, 356, 369
Trust, the, 260, 261
Tudor Hart, Edith, 289, 315, 328
Turing, Alan, 101–102, 319

U2 surveillance, 267, 383
UB (Polish Intelligence Service), 82, 161, 179, 191, 383, 484
UKUSA agreement, 124, 187, 435
Ustinov, Klop, 85–88, 325
Ustinov, Mrs. Klop, 86
Ustinov, Peter, 85, 87

Vansittart, Robert, 85, 86
Van Vleet, 264
Vassall, John, 209–11, 323, 340, 396, 434
Vaygaukas, 459
VENONA, 227–39, 247–50, 289, 298, 301–304, 349, 352–53, 355–59, 399, 422, 433, 442, 450, 466, 471, 477
Vera, 354
VHF (Very High Frequency) signals, 132
Volkov, Konstantin, 300–301, 309–10, 349, 351–53, 355, 359, 365, 367, 369, 389, 400, 428, 476, 479
Von Petrov, Vladimir, 83, 389, 409–12, 414, 415
von Ribbentrop, Joachim, 308, 410, 411, 415

Waddell, Sir James, 438–39, 444
Wagh, Duncum, 163, 421–22
War Office, 6, 42, 317, 377, 414
Watchers (A4), 30, 61–67, 69, 76, 100, 112–22, 132, 151, 157–59, 163, 164, 167–68, 178–80, 222, 245, 250, 255, 259, 392, 393, 484
Watson, Alister, 317–27, 329, 337, 367, 419, 469
Weisband, William, 234

Western intelligence services, 130–31, 396–98, 400, 401, 434–35

West European Division (CIA), 190

Wharton, Harry, 430, 431, 459

White, Sir Dick Goldsmith, 31, 37–38, 44–45, 87, 93–99, 122, 123, 144–50, 154, 213, 219, 224, 243–44, 247, 250, 256, 262–63, 274, 281, 285, 294, 295, 308, 312, 314, 364, 378, 381, 408, 411, 416, 419, 422, 431, 437–41, 446, 448, 470, 471, 476

Whitehall, 6, 8, 32–46, 32n, 92, 97, 115, 253, 271, 367, 375, 381, 395, 408, 438, 439, 445–59, 460, 461, 474, 484

Whitman, Lish, 185

Wigg, George, 347

Willis, Hector, 213–14, 225, 248, 258–59

Wilson, Harold, 292, 312, 335, 345–47, 437, 441, 455, 457–59, 463–68

Winterborn, Hugh, 6, 26–28, 30, 32, 34, 45, 50, 53–56, 64, 66, 68–76, 88–90, 94, 105, 108, 114, 116, 119, 164, 169, 171, 172, 221, 222, 245, 252, 257, 259, 363

Woolwich Arsenal case, 43, 174, 289

Workers' Revolutionary Party (WRP), 453, 454

World War I, 10, 12, 13, 43, 60, 349

World War II, 6, 18–21, 43, 47, 70, 98, 100, 185, 259, 272, 287, 391, 413, 472

Wright, Lois, 17, 445

Wright, Maurice (G. M.), 5–19, 22, 26, 34, 114

Wright, Mrs. Maurice, 12, 16, 18

Wyke, John, 197

Wylie, Tom, 317

Wynn, Arthur, 335, 336, 446

Wynne, Greville, 259, 264, 395

X-Craft midget submarines, 21, 92

Y-Boxes, 49, 70

Y intercepts, 18

Young, Sir Arthur, 459

Young, Courtney, 47, 114, 116, 120, 133, 157, 272, 302

Zaehner, Robin, 308–11

Zilenski, 414

zu Putlitz, Baron Wolfgang, 85–86, 325